Shakespearean Tragedy

Shakespearean Tragedy

Lectures on
Hamlet, Othello, King Lear, Macbeth

A. C. BRADLEY, LL.D., LITT.D.
Sometime Professor of Poetry
in the University of Oxford

Introduction to the Fourth Edition by
Robert Shaughnessy

First edition 1904
Second edition 1905
First issued in St. Martin's Library 1957
Reprinted six times
Reprinted in Pocket Papermac four times
Reprinted in Macmillan Student Editions twelve times
Third edition 1992
Fourth edition 2007

Published by
PALGRAVE MACMILLAN
Houndmills, Basingstoke, Hampshire RG21 6XS and
175 Fifth Avenue, New York, N.Y. 10010
Companies and representatives throughout the world

PALGRAVE MACMILLAN is the global academic imprint of the
Palgrave Macmillan division of St. Martin's Press, LLC and of Palgrave Macmillan Ltd.
Macmillan® is a registered trademark in the United States, United Kingdom and
other countries. Palgrave is a registered trademark in the European Union and other
countries.

ISBN-13: 978-0-230-00188-6 hardback
ISBN-10: 0–230–00188-2 hardback
ISBN-13: 978-0-230-00189-3 paperback
ISBN-10: 0-230-00189-0 paperback

This book is printed on paper suitable for recycling and
made from fully managed and sustained forest sources.

A catalogue record for this book is available from the British Library.

Library of Congress Cataloging-in-Publication Data
Bradley, A. C. (Andrew Cecil), 1851–1935,
    Shakespearean tragedy: lectures on Hamlet, Othello, King Lear, Macbeth /
    A.C. Bradley; introduction to the fourth edition by Robert Shaughnessy.—4th ed.
        p. cm.
    Includes index.
    ISBN-13: 978-0-230-00188-6 (cloth)
    ISBN-10: 0–230–00188-2 (cloth)
    ISBN-13: 978-0-230-00189-3 (pbk.)
    ISBN-10: 0-230-00189-0 (pbk.)
    1. Shakespeare, William, 1564–1616–Tragedies. 2. Tragedy. I. Title.

PR2983.B7 2006
822.3´3—dc22

                                                                    2006043226

10   9   8   7   6   5   4   3   2   1
16   15   14   13   12   11   10   09   08   07
Printed in China

To my students

Preface

These lectures are based on a selection from materials used in teaching at Liverpool, Glasgow, and Oxford; and I have for the most part preserved the lecture form. The point of view taken in them is explained in the Introduction. I should, of course, wish them to be read in their order, and a knowledge of the first two is assumed in the remainder; but readers who may prefer to enter at once on the discussion of the several plays can do so by beginning at page 64.

Any one who writes on Shakespeare must owe much to his predecessors. Where I was conscious of a particular obligation, I have acknowledged it; but most of my reading of Shakespearean criticism was done many years ago, and I can only hope that I have not often reproduced as my own what belongs to another.

Many of the Notes will be of interest only to scholars, who may find, I hope, something new in them.

I have quoted, as a rule, from the Globe edition, and have referred always to its numeration of acts, scenes, and lines.

November, 1904

Note to Second and Subsequent Impressions

In these impressions I have confined myself to making some formal improvements, correcting indubitable mistakes, and indicating here and there my desire to modify or develop at some future time statements which seem to me doubtful or open to misunderstanding. The changes, where it seemed desirable, are shown by the inclusion of sentences in square brackets.

Contents

Introduction to the Fourth Edition

by ROBERT SHAUGHNESSY

I

It is just over a hundred years since Andrew Cecil Bradley, newly incumbent in the Chair of Poetry at Oxford University, composed the series of lectures that would form the basis of the work with which he rapidly became (and remains) synonymous: *Shakespearean Tragedy*, which was first published in 1904. He could hardly have anticipated that his book would still be in print a century later, still less would he have imagined the extent to which it would be circulated, appropriated, argued over and argued with, nor the various and sometimes surprising ways in which his own name would be identified with a critical method, and an approach to Shakespeare's tragic drama, that would be, by stages, admired, imitated, hotly contested, ignored, and rehabilitated. Describing the overall project of the book as an attempt to 'consider the four principal tragedies of Shakespeare from a single point of view', Bradley declared that his aim was to enhance 'dramatic appreciation', that is, 'to increase our understanding and enjoyment of these works as dramas; to learn to apprehend the action and some of the personages of each with a somewhat greater truth and intensity, so that they may assume in our imaginations a shape a little less unlike the shape they wore in the imagination of their creator'. Although later generations of critics would take particular exception to the emphasis on character, to the suggestion that reading and criticism should set themselves in pursuit of the artist's own conception of the work, and to the implication that the play will ideally live in the reader's imagination rather than on the stage, Bradley's determination to treat the plays of Shakespeare as drama (though not necessarily or straightforwardly as *theatre*) has remained a core principle of modern criticism. Bradley's Shakespeare is 'dramatic to the tips of his fingers'; throughout *Shakespearean Tragedy*, Bradley is concerned with the designs the plays have on their readers and audiences, with their mechanisms of construction, and with the intensity of the experiences they offer, with the clues they offer to actors as well as readers, and with the dynamics of audience response. The 'right way' to read Shakespeare is that of those who engage with the plays 'as if they were actors who had to study all the parts', hoping to 'realize fully and exactly the inner movements which produced these words and no other, these deeds and no other, at each particular moment'. But he would also discover in Shakespeare's tragic vision something akin to a humane, questioning and non-dogmatic philosophy of life that was more in tune with twentieth-century sentiment than the pious moralizing and strident nationalism of many of his critical contemporaries.

In its own time, *Shakespearean Tragedy* established itself firmly and quickly as a landmark work of criticism because it was a careful synthesis of conservatism and innovation, a summation of Victorian Shakespearean scholarship and a blueprint for the twentieth-century criticism that followed in its wake. Published at the moment when English Literature was gaining momentum as a university subject, Bradley's work appealed to an expanding constituency of lay readers as well as professional specialists; here was a book which set out to explicate, plainly, logically and systematically, how Shakespeare's plays work. Behind Bradley's criticism lay an immense body of nineteenth-century scholarship, both amateur and professional, including the industry of the American scholar Horace Howard Furness, who in 1871 initiated the New Variorum Shakespeare, an edition which assembled textual variants alongside excerpts of important critical commentary, and the work of the New Shakspere (*sic*) Society, founded in London two years later. The quasi-scientific labour of collation, collection and cataloguing was motivated by an underlying concern with the 'growth' of Shakespeare's 'mind and art',[1] a project which demanded a synthesis that would transcend antiquarianism; in 1875 this was provided by the Society's vice-president, and Professor of English at Trinity College, Dublin, Edward Dowden. The widely read *Shakspere: A Critical Study of His Mind and Art*, which was an important prototype for *Shakespearean Tragedy*, combined an appeal to the nineteenth-century interest in evolutionary development with an idealized biographical view of the national poet which connected 'the study of Shakspere's works with an enquiry after the personality of the writer', and proposed that 'the growth of his intellect and character from youth to full maturity, distinguishes the work from the greater number of preceding criticisms of Shakspere'. Dowden's 'Shakspere' is a manly, patriotic and inspirational figure, who, while 'prudent, industrious, and economical', was also given to 'brood . . . with a passionate intensity over that which cannot be known', and whose life and art both encompassed 'the infinite of meditation, the infinite of passion'. Dowden's Bard is both Hamlet and Henry V, achieving in his composition of the former 'a thorough comprehension of Hamlet's malady' that enabled him to create the latter, who 'through his union with the vital strength of the world . . . becomes one of the world's most glorious and beneficent forces'. And if Shakspeare's growth to maturity as a man and an artist provides a role model for all Victorian gentlemen, his work similarly offers spiritual sustenance: 'courage, and energy, and strength, to dedicate himself and his work to that – whatever it may be – which life has revealed to him as best, and highest, and most real'.[2]

Bradley generously acknowledged Dowden's work as a formative influence, recommended *Shakspere* as essential reading, and displayed little visible ambition to challenge or displace his renowned predecessor. Bradley shared Dowden's concern for '*a rich feeling for positive, concrete fact*', and for 'human character in its living play', and engaged with what has been called the 'Victorian problematic of faith and doubt'[3] that operates in Dowden's work. But the mood of optimism, qualified yet ultimately secure religious faith, and imperial self-confidence that informs *Shakspere* is replaced, in *Shakespearean Tragedy*, by a more anxious spirit of self-questioning, in a work which is tentative and provisional rather than definitive and dogmatic. Whereas Dowden read the entire canon through the lens of Shakspeare's imagined life history, Bradley largely excluded the author from the remit of his investigations, and narrowed the focus to the four 'great' tragedies.[4] This was not simply reflective of the intellectual preferences, temperament and tastes of the author; in its style and method, *Shakespearean Tragedy* was also a forerunner of a new kind of professionalism in literary criticism (despite Bradley's disingenuous claim that 'many an unscholarly lover of Shakespeare' was 'a far better critic than many a Shakespeare scholar'). It defined an approach and a method which became institutionalized, but it was, like many subsequent innovations in the field, the product of interdisciplinary dialogue.

A. C. Bradley began his academic career in 1874 in philosophy, as a Fellow, then a Lecturer, at Balliol College, Oxford. He identified with Idealism, a school of thought led by the charismatic Liberal don

T. H. Green, which rejected the conservative evangelism then dominant at Oxford, and which, as Bradley put it at the time, was
informed by an 'earnest effort to bring speculation into relation with
modern life . . . and to deal with branches of science, physical, social,
political, metaphysical, theological, aesthetic, as parts of a whole'.[5]
Though theologically inflected, the idealism of Green and his disciples rejected scriptural literalism and the conventional rituals of
religious observance; pluralist and internationalist in outlook, it advo-
cated self-sacrifice and social and cultural philanthropy (Bradley was
a supporter of the Workers' Educational Association and the
Association for Promoting the Education of Women, and at one time
associated with Fabianism); it was also closely allied with Liberal politics. Bradley's first publications were in the field of Classics, and,
although never prolific, he continued to write and lecture on philosophical and political topics throughout his career.[6] Green's movement came into conflict with the University authorities, and in 1882,
under circumstances which remain obscure, Bradley left, or was
compelled to leave, Oxford for the new post of Chair of Modern
Literature and History at the University College of Liverpool. From
there he went in 1889 to the Chair of English Literature at the
University of Glasgow, and it was here that he began to build a reputation as a literary academic, although he still published little. In 1900
he moved to London with the intention of retiring from professional
academic life, but found himself (rather against his initial inclinations) proposed for the Chair of Poetry at Oxford, to which, at the age
of fifty, he was duly elected in 1901. During his tenure at Liverpool
and Glasgow (which he regarded as a period of forced exile), Bradley
had been uncertain about his own role as a scholar and intellectual,
but the appointment instilled in him a new sense of his disciplinary
mission. In effect, it offered him the opportunity to formulate a new
rationale for literary study itself, to correct the popular misconception
that this was a frivolous or feminine subject, composed, as he put it,
of 'mere chatter about Shelley', or worse, 'mere idle voluptuousness'.[7]
Informed by his classical and philosophical training, literary criticism
would in Bradley's hands assume a properly ethical function, in that
it offered a way of thinking about poetry and philosophy as reciprocal activities, as reflected in his conviction 'that what imagination
loved as poetry reason might love as philosophy, and that in the end
these are two ways of saying the same thing'.[8]

Shakespearean Tragedy was a book whose time had come. One of its first reviewers declared that 'the Oxford Chair of Poetry has never produced a finer fruit . . . we have no hesitation in putting Professor Bradley's book far above any modern Shakespearean criticism that we know, worthy to rank very near the immortal work of Lamb and Coleridge', and took pains to note its 'freshness of method and distinction of form'; another, that 'One may well doubt whether in the whole field of English Literary Criticism anything has been written in the last twenty years more luminous, more masterly, more penetrating to the very centre of its subject.'[9] Others were more stinting in their praise: while 'popular in aim', Bradley's book was too preoccupied with matters 'which would never occupy the attention of anyone except a professional academic critic'; more damningly, 'every lecture teems with . . . irritating superfluities, aggravated it may be added by the unnecessary diffuseness with which they are discussed'.[10] More seriously, a *Times Literary Supplement* (*TLS*) reviewer took Bradley to task for his answer to the question, 'What is outside the text?': 'He says (by implication) a set of real lives.'[11] This anticipated the more trenchant criticisms of Bradley that would emerge some three decades later; in the meantime, it appeared that the guardedly favourable reaction that greeted *Shakespearean Tragedy* on its first publication accurately reflected the mood of its readership. The first print run of 1500 copies was published in December 1904; even at ten shillings a copy, it sold sufficiently well to warrant an equivalent run of the second edition three months later, and a further run in August of the same year; thereafter it was reprinted at annual or biannual intervals, achieving sales of more than 40,000 by 1937 (reissued after the war, the second edition was reprinted twenty-four times between 1957 and 1992).[12] Significantly, over two-thirds of this total were sold after 1921; it is no coincidence that this was the year in which Sir Henry Newbolt published his report on the findings of the Board of Education on the teaching of English in England, which, amongst other things, recommended the study of English literature, and of Shakespeare in particular, as 'the only basis possible for national education. . . . It is itself the English mind.'[13] Judicious without being judgemental, authoritative but accessible, Bradley's urbane scholarship was ideally positioned to respond to the new priority afforded to national literary education. Indeed, by the mid-1920s, Guy Boas satirically suggested that Bradley had acquired an authority to rival or even eclipse that of Shakespeare himself:

I dreamt last night that Shakespeare's ghost
Sat for a Civil Service post;
The English paper for the year
Had several questions on *King Lear*
Which Shakespeare answered very badly
Because he hadn't read his Bradley![14]

II

What, then, is it about Bradley's method and style of writing that has afforded *Shakespearean Tragedy* an enduring appeal? It is partly due to the book's careful balance of abstraction and particularity, or, to put it another way, of theoretical reflection and practical analysis. Bradley's method is, for the most part, based on pragmatic and sensitive close reading of the text, often in the form of a step-by-step journey through the play; and it is this, rather than his more theoretical pronouncements on tragedy, that accounts for his critical longevity and makes him still worth reading. But *Shakespearean Tragedy* prefaces its discussion of *Hamlet, King Lear, Othello* and *Macbeth* with two lectures addressing more general and theoretical concerns, and although Bradley advises readers 'who may prefer to enter at once on the discussion of the several plays' to skip them if they wish, it is worth identifying some of the critical suppositions upon which this detailed work rests. In the opening lecture, Bradley sets out to define 'Shakespeare's tragic conception' in the abstract. His starting point is the relationship between the private and the public spheres in tragic drama; he stipulates that the protagonist, according to the classical and medieval view, should be a man of 'high degree' whose fall 'affects the welfare of a whole nation or empire'. More than this, though, Shakespearean tragic heroes are 'exceptional beings':

> the hero, with Shakespeare, is a person of high degree or of public impor-
> tance, and . . . his actions or sufferings are of an unusual kind. But this is
> not all. His nature also is exceptional, and generally raises him in some
> respect much above the average level of humanity . . . by an intensifica-
> tion of the life which they share with others, they are raised above them.
> . . . Some, like Hamlet and Cleopatra, have genius. Others . . . are built
> on the grand scale; and desire, passion, or will attains in them a terrible
> force.

Bradley's preoccupation with the 'greatness' of his tragic heroes and
(less often) heroines, figured throughout the lectures in terms such as
'sublime' (applied to Macbeth and Lady Macbeth), 'genius' (Hamlet),
and 'colossal' (Othello), reflects a more patrician and high-minded
view of tragic drama than most of us would now be comfortable with,
but it is central to his understanding of the emotional impact of
tragedy that the predisposition of the protagonist to 'identify the
whole being with one interest, object, passion, or habit of mind'
produces a conflict 'which stirs not only sympathy and pity, but admiration, terror, and awe'. By characterizing the tragic conflict in terms
of the struggle between contradictory drives or forces, Bradley signals
both his debt to Hegel, whose theory of tragedy much influenced
Bradley and his Victorian predecessors, and his desire to move beyond
it. The tragic action, Hegel stated, derives its content from 'the world
of those forces which carry in themselves their own justification, and
are realized substantively in the volitional activity of mankind'; by
which he means 'the love of husband and wife, or parents, children
and kinsfolk . . . the life of communities, the patriotism of citizens,
the will of those in supreme power'.[15] Bradley offered his own
account of Hegel in a lecture written a few years before, summarizing
his view of 'the essential tragic fact' as 'the self-division and intestinal
warfare of the ethical substance, not so much the war of good with
evil as the war of good with good', a view which, Bradley points out,
works well in relation to classical Greek tragedy but seems too
schematic to apply either to Shakespeare or to 'modern tragedy' in
general, in which 'public or universal interests either do not appear at
all, or, if they appear, are scarcely more than a background for the real
subject'.[16] The 'real subject' is not the clash of abstract principles but
'personal – these particular characters with their struggle and their
fate';[17] in *Shakespearean Tragedy* Hegel's 'vague' formulation is
reworked as a straightforward question: 'Who are the combatants in
this conflict?'

Bradley's humanist account of Shakespearean tragedy is under-
pinned by the conviction that the catastrophe that occurs to the hero
is not merely circumstantial, the product of fate or accident; the
protagonist is, to a greater or lesser extent, responsible (though not
solely so) for his own demise, and his agency is both psychologically
and ethically significant. The 'human actions' which comprise
Shakespeare's plots are 'acts or omissions thoroughly expressive of the

doer', and thus 'the centre of the tragedy' lies, in a key formulation, 'in action issuing from character, or in character issuing in action'. The cornerstone of method, 'character', is taken as a given; later critics would argue that this is a conception foisted anachronistically upon a dramaturgy whose culture understood the term 'character' to refer to a person's handwriting or signature, rather than to their personality or their capacity for moral choice, and which, while engaging periodically with what we would now recognize as an emergent realism, constructed *dramatis personae* from a range of emblematic, stereotypical and allegorical resources and vocabularies. The concentration upon individuals, upon inner conflicts and the complexities of motive, also tends to minimize the political and social dimensions of the plays' action: there is, for example, little sense in Bradley's discussion of either *Macbeth* or *Hamlet* that these plays deal with the historical contradictions of feudalism,[18] or even that they are engaged in a serious reflection upon the merits of deposition and political assassination, or in his account of *King Lear* that it depicts an entire society in upheaval (Bradley's political insouciance is indicated by his remark that the division of the kingdom 'would probably have led quickly to war, but not to the agony which culminated in the storm on the heath', as if the former were a relatively minor concern).

For Bradley, character is Shakespeare's 'main interest', and as such it is amenable to systematic analysis and reasoned investigation; it is also the primary focus of his investigation of the relationship between the ethical and the psychological. Since deeds are expressive of the doer, Bradley initially plays down the significance of aspects of the plays which seem to interfere with characters' autonomy: the workings of chance or accident, 'abnormal conditions of mind' such as insanity, somnambulism and hallucinations, and supernatural elements: even where these do figure prominently in the action (as in *Macbeth*), they are 'always placed in the closest relation with character', giving 'confirmation and distinct form to inward movements already present and exerting an influence'. Bradley's Shakespeare (who 'confined his view to the world of non-theological observation and thought') is rational and secular; his tragic universe cannot be comprehended in religious terms, nor can the 'ultimate power' in that universe be 'adequately described as a law or order which we can see to be just and benevolent'. The predominant emotion that we feel at the end of tragic drama is a desolating sense of waste;

human existence, it seems, is nothing more than a relentless and inescapable cycle of futile self-destruction:

> Everywhere, from the crushed rocks beneath our feet to the soul of man, we see power, intelligence, life and glory, which astound us and seem to call for worship. And everywhere we see them perishing, devouring one another and destroying themselves, often with dreadful pain, as though they came into being for no other end.

Men and women 'fight blindly in the dark, and the power that works through them makes them the instrument of a design which is not theirs', a design which annihilates the distinctions between good and bad intent, as 'man's thought, translated into act, is transformed into the opposite of itself . . . whatsoever he dreams of doing, he achieves that which he least dreamed of, his own destruction'. If there is an 'ultimate power' in the world of Shakespearean tragedy, according to Bradley, it has to be characterized not in terms of 'justice and merit', whereby tragic heroes, villains and victims are allocated the rewards and punishments they and their actions deserve, but simply as a conflict between good and evil. These qualities are defined as 'everything . . . in human beings which we take to be excellent or the reverse'; the 'moral power' which confronts evil is 'akin to all that we admire and revere in the characters themselves'. If the plays show us that the good may temporarily – and at huge cost – triumph over evil, they none the less reiterate the fact that the conflict between them is perpetual, 'the inexplicable fact . . . of a world travailing for perfection, but bringing to birth, together with glorious good, an evil which it is able to overcome only by self-torture and self-waste'.

Bradley's thinking is not altogether consistent: although the world of Shakespearean tragedy is avowedly secular, the 'moral order' seems none the less to possess almost metaphysical powers of its own, capable of taking positive action through the human agents that both are, and are not, its instruments. However keenly he wishes to relinquish the idea that the ruling power in the world can be ascribed to a god or gods, his need to affirm that there still is a principle of tragic justice, that there is an 'ultimate power' at work, leads him back to an anthropomorphic view of good and evil. Bradley also, perhaps rather too insistently, reiterates the point that tragedy 'does not leave us crushed, rebellious or desperate', a statement that seems oddly quiescent and politically conservative when considered alongside his more liberal and progressive tendencies. In the event, Bradley's readings of individual plays are at variance with the secular principles established here. If *King Lear* seems, in the 'bitter contrast between . . . faith and the events we witness', to 'indicate an intention to show things at their worst, and to return the sternest of replies to that question of the ultimate power and . . . appeals for retribution', in *Macbeth* and *Hamlet*, by contrast, 'the feeling of a supreme power or destiny is particularly marked' and it 'has also at times a peculiar tone, which may be called, in a sense, religious', conveying 'a reminder that the apparent failure of Hamlet's life is not the ultimate truth concerning him'.

If the first lecture represents Bradley at his most abstract and philosophical, the second shows him primarily concerned with the practicalities of plot construction and narrative exposition, and with the ways in which these shape and manipulate audience sympathies and responses. Bradley's sharp awareness of the medium for which the plays were originally composed, the theatre, is to the fore here: stating that 'the play is meant primarily for the theatre', he admits that the complex, multi-layered attentiveness to all aspects of the tragic conflict that emerges from reading, study, reflection and analysis is not necessarily within the remit of the theatrical event: 'that struggle in the hero's soul which sometimes accompanies the outward struggle is of the highest importance for the total effect of a tragedy', but in performance 'the outward conflict, with its influence on the fortunes of the hero, is the aspect which first catches, if it does not engross, attention'. Throughout *Shakespearean Tragedy*, Bradley sometimes differentiates between, and sometimes conflates, the experiences of reading and theatrical viewing, whilst registering that the relationship between these two ways of experiencing the drama is not easily complementary or necessarily mutually supportive. On the one hand, Bradley seems in little doubt that the sensitive and thoughtful reader is capable of accommodating a wider, subtler and more nuanced range of responses than the theatregoer: thus, 'When we are immersed in a tragedy, we feel towards dispositions, actions, and persons such emotions as attraction and repulsion, pity, wonder, fear, horror, perhaps hatred'; the spectator, conversely, reacts in a more raw and immediate fashion to the 'excitement' of the street-fights, battles and crowd scenes, and may even find the experience almost physically disturbing, particularly in 'certain places where the tension in the minds of the audience becomes extreme', as in the mid-point in

Othello, where 'the audience is not what it was at the beginning', having 'been attending for some time', and having 'been through a certain amount of agitation', 'the extreme tension which now arises may therefore easily tire and displease it'. This may seem overly fastidious, and seems to imagine the spectator as a swooning Victorian heroine, in need of a good dose of the smelling salts, but it none the less signals an attitude towards the theatre that is, at the very least, ambivalent. On the other hand, Bradley also appeals on a few occasions to theatregoing experience as a kind of check against untrammelled speculation, referring to 'minutiae which we notice only because we study him, but which nobody ever notices in a stage performance'; and prefacing thirty pages of close discussion of the possible motives for Hamlet's delay by observing that 'the majority of the spectators . . . certainly do not question themselves about his character or the cause of his delay'. Having speculated at length, likewise, on Hamlet's silence about Ophelia (of which more in a moment), Bradley concedes that 'scarcely any spectators or readers of *Hamlet* notice this silence at all', and that since Shakespeare 'wrote primarily for the theatre and not for students' it might be better not to concern oneself with the problem.

Bradley's Shakespeare, though 'dramatic to his fingertips', seems to have shared Bradley's uncertainty over the worth of the medium for which he was writing, in that 'he knew that the immense majority of his audience were incapable of distinguishing between rough and finished work. He often felt the degradation having to live by pleasing them,' and clearly 'did not regard his plays as mere stage-dramas of the moment'. To a large extent, Bradley's view is attributable to what we can assume to be his experience of Shakespearean production in his own time, and his clear sense of how alien it was to Shakespeare's own theatre. Shakespeare, Bradley was well aware, wrote for a theatre in which 'there was no scenery, scene followed scene with scarcely any pause' (accounting for 'peculiarities of construction which would injure a play written for our stage but were perfectly well-fitted for that very different stage'), but his patience as an Edwardian theatregoer would have been sorely tested by productions reliant upon 'a great deal of scenery, which takes a long time to set and change'. During the period in which Bradley gave his lectures, the signature style for Shakespeare was defined on the London stage by the abundantly detailed and magnificently cumbersome productions mounted by Sir Herbert Beerbohm Tree at His Majesty's Theatre, notoriously typified by the live rabbits that inhabited the forests of his 1900 *A Midsummer Night's Dream*. Had Bradley travelled forty miles in the other direction, to Stratford-upon-Avon's recently built Shakespeare Memorial Theatre, he might have found work more to his taste in the shape of the work mounted under the direction of Sir Frank Benson during its annual summer festival seasons. Benson, who in the course of thirty years at Stratford staged all but two of Shakespeare's plays, as well as tirelessly touring nationally and internationally, was known for an athletic style of production that had both its admirers and its detractors. Max Beerbohm wrote of his *Henry V* that 'the fielding was excellent, and so was the batting. Speech after speech was sent spinning across the boundary, and one was constantly inclined to shout "Well *played*, sir! Well played *indeed*!" As a branch of university cricket, the whole performance was, indeed, beyond praise.'[19]   Bradley, like many a fine English Shakespearean scholar after him, was an avid cricket fan, and it is pleasant, though probably idle, to speculate that a touch of the Bensonian sporting sublime might have held an appeal for the man who, when once invited to a match between current and former Balliol College students, is reported to have asked if he might umpire, 'Because there is nothing in life like the bowler's face at the moment he delivers the ball.'[20]

Away from the pitch, the commitment to reading the plays sequentially forms one of the basic principles of the lectures, which address each of the four 'great' tragedies in turn. As the play which had, even by Bradley's time, attracted more interest in its protagonist than any other, *Hamlet* provides a point of departure, initially framed by Bradley in terms of the discrepancy between what the play appears to be about, and what, on closer inspection, it actually is:

> Suppose you were to describe the plot of *Hamlet* to a person quite ignorant of the play, and suppose you were careful to tell your hearer nothing about Hamlet's character, what impression would your sketch make on him? Would he not exclaim: 'What a sensational story! Why, here are some eight violent deaths, not to speak of adultery, a ghost, a mad woman, and a fight in a grave! If I did not know that the play was Shakespeare's, I should have thought it must have been one of those early tragedies of blood and horror from which he is said to have redeemed the stage'?

It is, as Bradley intends, a perfectly fair and understandable response, as is the further question that the play, considered solely for its plot, also prompts: 'But why in the world did not Hamlet obey the Ghost at once, and so save seven of those eight lives?' If the answer is that 'the whole story turns upon the peculiar character of the hero', and the aim of the discussion is to elaborate the dynamics and the detail of that characterization, the way that Bradley poses the question establishes the Socratic method of debate and exposition that is particularly evident in the *Hamlet* lectures, in which (sometimes at what seems like inordinate length) he rehearses arguments and counter-arguments (and Bradley is generally fairer and more generous to his predecessors, even when he disagrees with them, than his crit- ics have been to him) before – tentatively – proposing his own solu- tions to the problems he has encountered in the play (chiefly, in the first instance, the question of why Hamlet delays the killing of Claudius). Seemingly naïve, Bradley's imagined auditor, apparently unschooled in Shakespeare, grasps the essential truth: that the rela- tionship between action, character and ideas in the play is at the very least anomalous, and at most, paradoxical, troubling, and vexingly contradictory.

This becomes particularly evident in the penultimate section of his second lecture, where, significantly, the assurance of performance is contrasted with the indeterminacy of critical interpretation:

> The actor who plays Hamlet must make up his mind as to the interpre-
> tation of every word and deed of the character. Even if at some point he
> feels no certainty as to which of the two interpretations is right, he must
> still choose one or the other. The mere critic is not obliged to do this.
> Where he remains in doubt he may say so, and, if the matter is of impor-
> tance, he ought to say so.

The specific problem at hand is the issue of 'Hamlet's love for Ophelia' (or rather, how to interpret Hamlet's silence about his feel- ings for her), with regard to which, Bradley concedes, 'I am unable to arrive at a conviction as to the meaning of some of his words and deeds, and I question whether from the mere text of the play a sure interpretation of them can be drawn.' This is a candid and, in relation to his otherwise confident exposition of why Hamlet thinks, speaks and acts as he does, dangerous admission, and for safety's sake Bradley reserves the topic for 'separate treatment', quarantining it from 'the general discussion of Hamlet's character'. For one contemporary reviewer, at least, the whole discussion was symptomatic of Bradley's doggedly perverse habit of pursuing the wrong questions, in that it was typical of how 'The real points of interest and importance in the drama are not so much as touched on and the particularity with which what is touched on is dealt with is almost invariably in an inverse ratio to its importance.'[21] To modern readers, however, Bradley may seem unusually prescient, anticipating contemporary critical preoccupations with the openness, iterability and indeterminacy of the text, and with its penchant for reflecting upon and interrogating its own methods of interpretation. First, we might register Bradley's oddly diminishing reference to the 'mere' text, a seemingly innocuous phrase which has the potential to generate a certain amount of mischief for Bradley's critical principles. Most of the time, he assumes that the text will yield the answers to the problems it poses, if pressed hard enough; that it is, in a scientific sense, knowable; that within the court of enquiry that stages acts of critical judgement, it provides both an authoritative, stable body of evidence and reliable, relatively transparent guidelines for its own interpretation. Here he seems to suggest that, at least in this instance but possibly in others, there might be some other means of arbitration, outside of and quite possibly independent of the text itself. For Bradley, there are three ways of reading Hamlet's behaviour towards Ophelia: that his love for her remained constant, but duty obliged him to behave as if it were otherwise; that his love, 'though never lost, was, after Ophelia's apparent rejection of him, mingled with suspicion and resentment'; and that 'like all his healthy feelings', it was 'weakened and deadened by melancholy' to the point where it became practically insignificant.

Although 'the facts', as he puts it, seem almost to force this idea on us', Bradley is none the less aware that the three interpretations remain equally plausible, equally capable of being supported by the textual evidence, and, crucially, equally playable: in effect, what Bradley confronts here is the exhilarating, but also profoundly disconcerting, openness of a text whose enigmas might only be solved – temporarily and provisionally, never definitively – through choices made in performance. Moreover, as Bradley recognizes, an equally disorientating aspect of Hamlet's actions towards Ophelia (and, although he doesn't say so, by extension elsewhere) is the impossibility of definitively distinguishing the 'real' from the feigned: 'what is pretence, and what sincerity, appears to me an insoluble problem'. If as modern theatregoers we have less difficulty acknowledging multiple, even mutually contradictory treatments of Shakespearean character (sometimes within the same production), we might still remember that transferring to the stage the conundrums of a text which is obsessively preoccupied with the paradoxical interplay of acting and action, playing and pretence, theatre and life, far from settling the question, only adds further layers of deception, role-playing and masquerade.

In the first edition of *Shakespearean Tragedy*, this discussion concluded with a confession: 'I am driven to suspend judgment, and also to suspect that the text admits of no sure interpretation.' But even this could not be his last word on the subject. It is in keeping with the agnostic, relentlessly self-interrogating quality of Bradley's method that this parting shot was supplemented, in subsequent editions, with a further caveat: 'This paragraph states my view imperfectly.' This interpolation, which intriguingly introduces yet further layers of hermeneutic insecurity to an already labyrinthine analysis, was one of the second-edition revisions intended to indicate Bradley's 'desire to modify or develop at some future time statements which seem . . . doubtful or open to misunderstanding'; but it also encourages us to be aware that Bradley's text is formed from an accretion of views added as it was successively reissued. More than most critical texts, its seemingly monolithic status is undermined from within by its deter-mination to trace thought in process. Some of the same spirit of ongo-ing investigative enquiry informs Bradley's endnotes, which at one level explore subsidiary issues, and expand upon topics too recondite, convoluted or incidental to be comfortably accommodated in the main text: thus he speculates upon (without supplying definitive solu-tions to) ambiguities or inconsistencies in the plays' time schemes and patterning of events, as well as textual variants and questions of possi-ble interpolation, abbreviations and revision, especially where these have an impact upon characterization or narrative. At another level, the thirty-two notes enable Bradley to document his own marginalia, to register revisions and qualifications to his own initial formulations, and to record his second and third thoughts (he later added to Note O, 'Othello on Desdemona's Last Words', 'I wish to withdraw the whole note'), as well as counter-arguments (closing Note T, on *King Lear*, he wrote that 'I do not mean to imply, by writing this note, that I believe in the hypotheses suggested in it').

Bradley's engagement with *Othello* is a much less tortuous and equivocal affair: this is 'the most painfully exciting and the most terrible' of the tragedies, and the characterization of its hero is 'comparatively simple'. The most substantial component of his discussion of this play is his discussion of the character of Iago, in which he attempts to counter both the Coleridgean view that the figure is driven by an explicable 'motiveless malignity', and the theatrical stereotype of 'the melodramatic villain . . . a person whom everyone knows for a scoundrel at the first glance', by closely dissecting a psychology dominated by his 'longing to satisfy the sense of power'. For most readers and theatregoers today, the play's tragic nexus lies in its conjunction of race and sexuality, and the arguments continue as to whether the play depicts Othello in an anti-discriminatory fashion, as a sympathetic figure, or exploits the racism and misogyny of its own time. It is almost unheard of now for Othello to be played by a white actor in blackface (although this practice survived, in the British theatre at least, until the early 1980s), and the universally accepted principle that the part should be played by an actor of colour has generally encouraged a liberal view of the play's handling of race and sexuality. As a product of the late Victorian era (and, perhaps, as an Oxford don addressing a cohort of female undergraduates), who would only have seen Othello played by a white actor, Bradley found himself in a more difficult position with regard to both: 'the subject of sexual jealousy', he writes, is for many of his contemporaries 'not merely painful but so repulsive that not even the intense tragic emotions which the story generates can overcome this repulsion', and, lest his listeners should be in any doubt about the nature of this jealousy, he offers a graphic account of what it entails:

> Such jealousy as Othello's converts human nature into chaos, and liberates the beast in man . . . the animal in man forcing itself into his consciousness in naked grossness, and he writhing before it but powerless to deny it entrance, gasping inarticulate images of pollution, and finding relief only in a bestial thirst for blood . . .

We post-Freudians may wish to linger over the implications of what sounds like a rape fantasy, as 'man', naked and defiled, is subjected to forced entry, reduced to inarticulate gasping; Bradley's first readers might have registered here familiar associations between the breakdown of order, loss of dignity and self-control, unbridled sexuality, and animal instincts; in the cultural context of an imperial nation, these replayed darker anxieties about the struggle between its own allegedly civilizing mission and the forces of barbarism. Although Bradley claims to be dealing with jealousy here, the lurid prose can barely suppress the fear of miscegenation which had so troubled earlier critics, and which continues to haunt the critical and cultural reception of the play.

To give him his due, Bradley is relatively liberal-minded about the question of Othello's race: asserting that Othello is 'a black man, and not . . . a light-brown one', he criticizes the theatrical convention, initiated by Edmund Kean in the early nineteenth century, of toning down his skin colour so as not to offend white audiences, and he directly confronts the racism of Coleridge's judgement that 'it would be something monstrous to conceive this beautiful Venetian girl falling in love with a veritable negro'[22] by pointing out that this is precisely the view taken by Brabantio ('a filthy-minded cynic'). Bradley also registers with amusement the 'horror of most American critics . . . at the idea of a black Othello'. That Othello, 'the noblest soul on earth', is a black (African) man is also crucial to Bradley's view of Desdemona, whose tragedy is to have 'met in life with the reward of those who rise too far above our common level'; in effect, he suggests, we collude with the prejudices that destroy her if 'we consent to forgive her for loving a brown man, but find it monstrous that she should love a black one'. Bradley might have been content to leave it at that; unfortunately (but entirely characteristically) he caps the discussion with a qualifying footnote which seems to revert to a position which the preceding pages had worked hard to overturn. Once again, it is Bradley's distrust of the theatre that generates the difficulty: prompted to speculate as to whether Othello 'should be represented as a black in our theatres now', Bradley recoils in horror: 'if we saw Othello coal-black with the bodily eye, the aversion of our blood, an aversion which comes as near to being merely physical as anything human can, would overpower our imagination and sink us below not Shakespeare only but the audiences of the seventeenth and eighteenth centuries'. It is not easy to determine here what it is that Bradley is most appalled by: the image of a 'coal-black' Othello, to which 'we' have an instinctive aversion, or the degradation of admitting to such a sentiment.

Bradley's treatment of Desdemona gives rein to another tendency which modern readers will find embarrassingly cloying or offensive: that is, his habit of idealizing and sentimentalizing Shakespeare's heroines. Desdemona is 'a child of nature', the 'sweetest and most pathetic of Shakespeare's women, as innocent as Miranda and as loving as Viola', who 'can oppose to wrong nothing but the infinite endurance and forgiveness of a love that knows not how to resist or repent', who discovers in her marriage 'the sweet and submissive being of her girlhood' and whose death leaves us 'penetrated by the sense of her heavenly sweetness and self-surrender'. Bradley's Ophelia is, similarly, a figure of 'pathetic beauty, which makes analysis of her character seem almost a desecration'; she is 'sweet and lovable', and 'her whole character is that of simple unselfish affection'. The heavy hand of late Victorian patriarchy, and its preference for pure, meek women who remain loyal to their destroyers even as they suffer in silence, is all too evident here.

Even more mawkish is Bradley's rapturous evocation of the apotheosis of this type in Cordelia, 'a thing enskyed and sainted', about whom 'to use many words . . . seems to be a kind of impiety'. It is, in part, Bradley's idolization of Cordelia, and what seems to be an unwillingness to face the unspeakable meanness of her arbitrary and undeserved death, that leads him to a reading of *King Lear* that some subsequent critics have rejected as hopelessly, and dishonestly, sentimental. Proposing that the play (or, as he significantly terms it on this occasion, 'poem') should be retitled *The Redemption of King Lear*, and that Lear dies under the illusory impression that Cordelia is alive ('any actor is false to the text who does not attempt to express, in Lear's last accents and gestures and look, an unbearable *joy*'), he offers the play's ultimate moral, revealed as Lear and Cordelia exit to prison: 'Let us renounce the world, hate it, and lose it gladly. The only real thing in it is the soul, with its courage, patience, devotion. And nothing outward can touch that.' If this optimistic belief in the integrity and inviolability of the self seems strained even in the light of what happens in the play (as Edgar grimly reminds us, 'The worst is not / As long as we can say "This is the worst"' [IV.i.27–8]), and would appear to have been even more thoroughly discredited by both the political and intellectual history of the twentieth century, it none the less reflects a genuine effort, on Bradley's part, to reconcile the play's devastating impact with the relatively benign philosophy of tragedy that he outlines elsewhere. He arrives at this position by frankly acknowledging, and perhaps exaggerating, the play's weaknesses and defects as a stage-play. *King Lear* is, for Bradley, a problem, a work in which Shakespeare's artistry, his vision, and the medium in which he is working, are in conflict: 'Shakespeare's greatest achievement, but . . . *not* his best play.' Observing that it is 'too huge for the stage', he presents a vivid, impressionistic account of the world of the play, characterized by

> the vastness of the convulsion both of nature and of human passion; the vagueness of the scene where the action takes place, and of the movements of the figures which cross this scene; the strange atmosphere, cold and dark, which strikes on us as we enter this scene, enfolding these figures and magnifying their dim outlines like a winter mist; the half-realized suggestions of vast universal powers working in the world of individual fates and passions . . .

The theatre, or at least Bradley's own theatre, is plainly inadequate to the task of accommodating a work composed on this epic, even cosmic, scale; at another level, the play trades in theatrical effects that are at war with the higher imaginative faculties: the blinding of Gloster, for example, produces a 'physical horror' which in performance would produce 'a sensation so violent as to overpower the purely tragic emotions', and are thus merely 'revolting or shocking'. The blinding 'belongs rightly to *King Lear* in its proper world of imagination; it is a blot upon *King Lear* as a stage-play'. Here, and throughout the discussion of *King Lear*, Bradley is at his most antitheatrical (and he has been much criticized for it), and if again he seems overly fastidious, the distinction that he makes between the visceral reaction of the theatregoer and the more finely-honed response of the reader is as much an ethical as an aesthetic one: 'the physical horror, though not lost, is so far deadened that it can do its duty as a stimulus to pity, and to that appalled dismay at the extremity of human cruelty which it is of the essence of the tragedy to excite'. Although this reaction seems inconsistent with the Shakespeare who, 'dramatic to his fingertips', wrote 'primarily for the theatre and not for students', what Bradley recognizes, in both of these examples, is the reductive literalism of the theatre with which he was most familiar. He is in more contentious territory when he writes that 'the number of essential characters is so large, their actions and movements are so complicated . . . that the reader's attention, rapidly transferred from one centre of interest to another, is overstrained', and that the play is plagued with 'improbabilities, inconsistencies, sayings and doings which suggest questions only to be answered by conjecture'. Bradley, who seems to consider the prospect of military conflict in Lear's divided kingdom to be 'but a trifle here' (V.iii.271) compared with 'the agony which culminated in the storm upon the heath', is not insensitive to the inevitable narrative complexity, and the shifting and divided allocation of sympathies, that the play, considered as a political tragedy as well as a tale of titanic individual suffering, inevitably entails; but these are not the things that interest him about it. He also provides a long list of mysteries and lapses in terms of motivation, explanation and incident, ranging from Gloster's inexplicable pilgrimage to Dover to commit suicide to Edgar's apparently crazy decision (in II.iii) to 'return from his hollow tree . . . to his father's castle in order to soliloquize'. Some of these objections are (and have been) readily answered: as a non-naturalistic, partly emblematic drama conceived for an open platform stage, *King Lear* is not bound by the strictures of plausible characterization and precise location that apply to realist fictions, and, as Bradley happily concedes elsewhere, spectators and readers tend to excuse or ignore inconsistencies which become nigglingly evident in sustained study, although, as Maynard Mack has put it, 'no one has succeeded in arguing away' the 'gross improbabilities' he enumerates.[23]

The situation is rather different from Bradley's difficulties over Hamlet's silence about Ophelia: in this instance, the lacunae in the text prompt him not to suspend judgement but to define the play as a 'defective drama'. But, far from rendering the work a failure, its many deficiencies as a stage-play actually work in quite the opposite way: it is as if Bradley needs to loosen its allegiances to the theatre in order to reveal 'purely dramatic qualities which far outweigh its defects', and a 'greatness' which 'consists partly in imaginative effects of a wider kind'. Particularly in his first lecture on *Lear*, Bradley is responsive to the play as a symbolic or semi-allegorical drama, and is much less interested in the psychological investigation of 'character in action' than in evoking a sense of poetic and philosophical immensity, a world 'filled with gloom' in which 'shapes approach and recede, whose half-seen faces and motions touch us with dread, horror, or the most painful pity – sympathies and antipathies which we seem to be feeling not only for them but for the whole race'; in this, 'the most terrible picture that Shakespeare ever painted of the world', humanity could not appear 'more pitiably infirm or more hopelessly bad'. Bradley is in tune with the predominant mood of twentieth-century criticism here (much more so, for example, than his eminent critical contemporary Sir Walter Raleigh, who reassuringly wrote that in this play Shakespeare 'found in the splendours of courage and love a remedy for despair'[24]), but it is not a position with which he felt comfortable. Hence his reservations and qualifications, partly expressed in what he himself defines as a 'heresy' which 'all the best authority is against': his conviction that, although just about tolerable 'so long as we regard *King Lear* simply as a work of poetic imagination', Cordelia's undeserved and unexpected death and Lear's consequent anguish are contrived and cruelly arbitrary, reflecting a design which is 'not strictly dramatic or tragic'. 'The sudden blow out of the darkness', he writes, 'seems now only what we might have expected in a world so wild and monstrous,' and the philosophy of tragedy that underpins this truth is irreconcilable with 'mere' stage drama. But it is also not the only truth, and Bradley's reading of the play differs from the more determinedly nihilistic and apocalyptic accounts that have followed in his wake in its recognition that it is – perhaps only – in the depths of utter abjection that redemption becomes possible:

> power and prosperity . . . are worthless, or worse; it is not on them, but on the renunciation of them, that the gods throw incense. They breed lust, pride, hardness of heart, the insolence of office, cruelty, scorn, hypocrisy, contention, war, murder, self-destruction. The whole story beats this indictment of prosperity into the brain. . . . The judgment of this world is a lie; its goods, which we covet, corrupt us; its ills, which break our bodies, set our souls free . . .

This is the context, at least with regard to this play, in which Bradley's dangerously vulnerable essentialist vision of a core of inviolable selfhood needs to be seen: a volatile combination of Fabian righteousness and a radically levelling, residual Christian ethic of renunciation. And it is this perspective which makes Cordelia's death (almost) worthwhile, and which allows Bradley's account of *King Lear* to close, via an evocation of *The Tempest*, on a note of stoic optimism: 'Bear free and patient thoughts.'

  Shakespearean Tragedy is a book which is very attentive to the rhythm, tonal variety, shape and architecture of its argument, not only within individual lectures but in the architecture of the whole, and the final chapters on *Macbeth* provide a suitably Wagnerian climax to the cycle. It is, Bradley contends, 'the most vehement, the most concentrated, perhaps we might say the most tremendous, of the tragedies', and his prose is vividly responsive to this, evoking a dramatic landscape which, though it occasionally seems to dip to the level of Gothic melodrama ('an unearthly light flickers about the head of the doomed man'), is suffused with a Romantic majesty and grandeur (the tragedy, he declares, is 'sublime', a term which he elsewhere defines in terms of 'the expression of the absolute power of the spirit . . . overwhelming greatness of power'[25]). Abandoning the cooler analytic style of the earlier lectures, Bradley plunges the reader into a hellish world of gloom and violent disorder; in what is the most impressionistic, as well as the most powerfully visualized, of his accounts of the tragedies, he imagines *Macbeth* enacted amidst 'a black night broken by flashes of light and colour':

> the lights and colours of the thunderstorm in the first scene; of the dagger hanging before Macbeth's eyes and glittering alone in the midnight air; of the torch borne by the servant when he and his lord come upon Banquo crossing the castle-court to his room; of the torch, again, which Fleance carried to light his father to death . . . of the torches that flared in the hall on the face of the Ghost and the blanched cheeks of Macbeth; of the flames beneath the boiling caldron from which the apparitions in the cavern rose; of the taper which showed to the Doctor and Gentlewoman the wasted face and blank eyes of Lady Macbeth.

This is a creative as well as a critical response to the play: no longer fettered by the constraints of the text, Bradley combines here moments which are explicitly staged, images that are inferred or suggested, and almost novelistic details which variously derive from imaginative reading, memories of stage performance, and the visions of eighteenth- and nineteenth-century artists and illustrators – most strikingly, those of William Blake, Johan Zoffany and Henry Fuseli. The effects of compression that Bradley employs in his exposition of the play's action similarly produce an almost cinematic re-ordering of structure and chronology as montage ('Banquo rides homeward to meet his assassins . . . Macbeth bids the stars to hide their fires . . . Lady Macbeth calls on thick night to come'), reinforcing the sense of events relentlessly unfolding within a nightmarish perpetual present.

Bradley's *Macbeth*, it seems, occupies the theatre of the mind, unbounded by the practical limits either of the Edwardian stage or of Shakespeare's, and as such provides ready ammunition for those who consider that he was indifferent, or hostile, to the plays' status as performance texts, or, even less legitimately, that he approached the dramas as if they were novels (he did not). Yet in some ways this way of envisaging the relationship between the text, the imagination and performance renders him curiously prescient; although he could hardly have known it, it is in tune with some of the most adventurous *avant-garde* theatrical thinking of his own time, as represented in the work of symbolist writers and practitioners like Maurice Maeterlinck, August Strindberg and Edward Gordon Craig. Writing in 1911 of the ghosts in *Macbeth*, Craig presents a visionary account of Shakespearean *mise en scène* that is oddly reminiscent of Bradley: 'it is by the necromancy of . . . "partial tones", by the introduction of influences felt even when unseen, at times impalpable as the "shadow of a shadow", yet realized even then as dominant forces, sometimes malefic, sometimes beneficent', that Shakespeare works his magic; the 'momentary visualization of the unseen forces which dominate the action' is 'a clear command from Shakespeare that the men of the theatre shall rouse their imagination and let their reasonable logic slumber'.[26]

Bradley's attentiveness to the particular style of *Macbeth* is informed by the recognition that here, as perhaps in no other of the great tragedies, Shakespeare's preoccupations are less secular than metaphysical, and that the play focuses on 'the obscurer regions of man's being, on phenomena which make it seem that he is in the power of secret forces lurking below, and independent of his consciousness and will'. In previous lectures, the interest in unconscious motivation had been explored psychologically, and Bradley's method was in this respect broadly in tune both with the emerging discourse of psychoanalysis (Freud's *The Psychopathology of Everyday Life* also appeared in 1904) and with the priority given by theatre practitioners such as Stanislavsky to subtext ('a web of innumerable, varied inner patterns inside a play and a part, woven from "magic ifs", given circumstances, all sorts of figments of the imagination, inner movements, objects of attention, smaller and greater truths'[27]). In his reading of *Macbeth*, the 'secret forces' are of a different magnitude; they are the mechanisms of an irrational, arbitrarily violent universe in a constant state of convulsion. A little philosophical juggling is needed here if this is not to reduce the action either to a straightforwardly theological conflict between good and evil or to a tragedy of predestination: faced with the metaphysical claims of a play calculated 'to excite supernatural alarm and, even more, a dread of the presence of evil', Bradley once again reformulates the earlier assertion that 'the Elizabethan drama was almost wholly secular', by offering a definition of that 'evil' as 'not only the evil slumbering in the hero's soul, but all those obscurer influences of the evil around him and in the world'. Thus 'the inward powers of the soul answer in their essence to vaster powers without, which support them and assure the effect of their exertion'.

Although the *Macbeth* lectures pay due attention, in Bradley's systematic way, to the secondary characters, the chief focus of attention is upon the title figures. 'Think of sublime figures', Bradley declared in the *Oxford Lectures on Poetry*, 'and you find that, whether they are radiant or gloomy, violent or peaceful, terrible or adorable, they all impress the imagination by their immense or even irresistible might.'[28] Describing *Macbeth*, and the Macbeths, repeatedly, as 'sublime', Bradley seems not just impressed but awed and even overwhelmed by their immensity and power. They are the titanic embodiment of the turbulent landscape that Bradley has already evoked so vividly: 'within them is all that we felt without – the darkness of night, lit with the flame of tempest and the hues of blood, and haunted by wild and direful shapes, "murdering ministers", spirits of remorse, and maddening visions of peace lost and judgment to come'. Bradley's journey through the dark night of the Macbeths' souls is momentous and compelling, not just for the almost Stanislavskian attention to psychological detail and character progression (particularly in the case of Macbeth), but also because it is in these lectures, finally, that he addresses the implications of the fetishistic attachment to 'greatness' that has, to a greater or lesser extent, haunted the book. If Macbeth is the closest to the model of the Nietzschean *übermensch* that provides one template for the Bradleian tragic hero, he is a figure less of admiration, wonder and awe than of utter terror: a relentless, sadistic, amoral and ultimately self-annihilating mechanism of destruction, the incarnation of greatness and its horrifying nemesis. Yet, for Bradley, this is evil of a crucially different order from that practised by Iago, Goneril and Edmund. What keeps Macbeth, however precariously,

within the bounds of the human is his capacity for ethical reflection
and moral choice, a capacity which is realized, importantly, through
the exercise of the imagination. Rather than operating in relation to
'the overt language of moral ideas, commands, and prohibitions',
Macbeth's 'better nature' is 'expressed through images which alarm
and horrify. His imagination is thus the best of him, something
usually deeper and higher than his conscious thoughts . . . the terrifying images . . . are really the protest of his deepest self.' Here, perhaps,
Bradley offers a solution to the unresolved problem, outlined in the
introductory lecture, of where and how to locate goodness, in a post-
theological universe. The exercise of the imagination does not only
enable the tragic hero to envisage the distinction between good and
evil; it is the only ground on which morality is viable.

This is one of the ways that Bradley differentiates Lady Macbeth
from her husband; for though, like him, she displays the 'greatness' of
'courage and force of will', she has 'little imagination', and hence,
implicitly more limited scope for moral choice. Lady Macbeth's imagination, for Bradley, has a prosaic quality quite unlike that of her
husband, her spoken utterances indicating that 'things remain at the
most terrible moment precisely what they were at the calmest, plain
facts which stand in a given relation to a certain deed, not visions
which tremble and flicker in the light of other worlds'. None the less,
it is the 'ghastly realism' of her final speeches, and her 'self-restraint in
suffering' that define the closing mood of *Shakespearean Tragedy*,
counterpointing the *Sturm und Drang* of the penultimate lecture with
a quieter, more reflective tone. Despite his earlier caution about
'abnormal conditions' such as somnambulism being of secondary
dramatic significance (because they are not 'what we would call deeds
in the fullest sense, deeds expressive of character'), it is Lady Macbeth's
sleepwalking scene, under the pretext of an examination of the play's
style, that shapes his closing remarks. Exploring the seemingly
random play of images in her speech, we find in Bradley's summation
a hushed, minor-key reprise of the action of the play, as well as of his
own associative reading of it; more than this, though, we register, with
a quiet sense of surprise, that the heartrendingly stark simplicity of
utterance conveys 'a far more desolating misery' than even that of
Macbeth himself. Seen alongside this deeply personalized, un-
settlingly human, expression of loneliness, mortality and regret, 'all
the language of poetry . . . seems to be touched with unreality, and

these brief toneless sentences seem the only voice of truth'. The effect may be 'for the moment' only, but Bradley's use of the phrase 'extraordinarily impressive' to describe it is doubly felicitous: it brilliantly captures the impact and resonance of this scene, and its positioning as (save for the endnotes) his book's final word provides a startling, and moving, coda to everything that has preceded it.

III

There is, implicitly, a subtler allegory in play here in Bradley's exposition of the relationship between imagination and morality. By positioning the imagination as the basis of a secular ethics, Bradley made what would prove to be a decisive and enduring contribution to the historical mission of English literary studies, a project which would subsequently articulate itself in much more explicit terms, as the rise of literature within the academy not only compensated for the parallel decline in theology and philosophy, but absorbed many of those disciplines' former functions with regard to the cultivation of hearts and minds. There is neither the space nor the need here to give an account of Bradley's critical afterlife during the century that followed the first publication of *Shakespearean Tragedy*, but I will indicate here some of the ways in which Bradley continued to exert an influence, and to provoke disagreement and debate. We have already seen that Bradley had acquired a canonical status by the 1920s, and as such tended to be eulogized by his admirers, but there were a number of more considered attempts to assess Bradley's place in critical history. C. H. Herford, writing in 1923, acknowledged the significance of his 'purely critical interpretation', while also suggesting that the 'literary and aesthetic way of approaching Shakespeare' was at odds with 'the beginning of the more intensive study of the Elizabethan stage'.[29] The theatre-director-turned-scholar Harley Granville-Barker disagreed, praising Bradley's lectures on *Hamlet* and *Othello* as 'like a very great actor's conception of the parts', and endorsing the view that for Bradley 'the plays are plays and never cease to be plays'.[30]

The first sign that the critical tide was turning against not only Bradley but the whole school of character-centred interpretation he is alleged to have fostered came in 1932, in a paper delivered by the young L. C. Knights to the Shakespeare Association. Its provocative title, 'How Many Children had Lady Macbeth?', was a conscious parody of Bradley's discursive, notoriously speculative endnotes, and since the essay never gets round to considering, let alone answering, this question, we take it for granted that this is a preposterous line of enquiry. For Knights, the preoccupation with character interferes – disastrously – with the appreciation of Shakespearean drama as 'a dramatic poem', which we should read 'as we should read any other poem'.[31] Inspired by the practical criticism of his Cambridge colleague I. A. Richards, Knights targeted Bradley in order to define the agenda for what would subsequently come to define itself as the New Criticism, an enterprise which sought to exclude elements it considered extrinsic to the text, which it treated as an integrated and self-contained verbal artefact; during the period of New Criticism's dominance, from the 1930s through to the 1950s, Bradley seemed, to many, deeply unfashionable. Knights's title was given to him by his colleague, the father of the critical movement which came to be known as Cambridge English, F. R. Leavis, and Knights's skirmish was succeeded in 1937 by a furious frontal assault by Leavis himself. In 1932, in the first issue of the house journal of Cambridge English, *Scrutiny*, Leavis launched an *ad hominem* attack on Bradley ('His method is not intelligent enough . . . the defect of intelligence is a default on the part of sensibility') and on his 'detective, psychological, moral, philosophical or acrostical approaches'.[32] Five years on, in the essay 'Diabolic Intellect and the Noble Hero' (subtitled 'The Sentimentalist's *Othello*'), Leavis's ferocity was undiminished: denouncing Bradley as 'still a very potent and mischievous influence', and, insisting that '*Othello* . . . is poetic drama, a dramatic poem, and not a psychological novel written in dramatic form and draped in poetry,' he proceeds, as he sees it, to demolish the 'sustained and sanctioned perversity' of Bradley's reading of the play, replacing his 'noble' view of Othello with a figure given over to 'self-pride . . . ferocious stupidity, an insane and self-deceiving passion'.[33]

The hostility to Bradley that was voiced by both Knights and Leavis was fuelled by polemic and based on a selective, and misrepresentative, reading of *Shakespearean Tragedy* itself, which is by no means as fixated on 'character' as the critical caricatures of it have suggested, and during the 1950s and 1960s Bradley enjoyed something of a critical rehabilitation. In 1968, G. K. Hunter observed that views of Bradley had tended to polarize, in that 'most references to Bradley's book since the time of its publication have been either resentful of its influence or (alternatively) defensive about its virtues'.[34] Attempting to arbitrate between these positions, Hunter proposed that it was time to re-situate Bradley's work in the philosophical and critical context of its own time; a few years later, this task was taken up at greater length by Katharine Cooke in her full-length study of Bradley's work and its influence, which somewhat optimistically concluded that 'it is doubtful now whether a critic could produce a work on a subject which Bradley had handled without paying some attention to Bradley's conclusions on that subject', and that 'it is to what Bradley said that attention is now being paid'.[35] Bradley retained his imitators and disciples during the 1970s, and in 1981 John Bayley (who happened to be married to another philosopher who turned to literature, the novelist Iris Murdoch) published *Shakespeare and Tragedy*, a work proudly heralded by its publisher as a 'long overdue' successor to 'such classic works as A. C. Bradley's *Shakespearean Tragedy*'. Bayley shared Bradley's interest in interiority, but subordinated 'both action and idea' to 'the mere fact and story of consciousness': 'It is the imminence of action which brings that consciousness into prominence, but it remains independent of action. The tragedy itself may be bounded in a nutshell, but the minds of Hamlet, of Macbeth and Othello, make them kings of infinite space.'[36] As a scholar whose previous output had been chiefly in the area of prose fiction, Bayley demonstrates a strongly, apparently Bradleian, taste for character, and as a consequence the main effect of his study is to domesticate even the most public and political of the tragedies. In his introduction to the new edition of *Shakespearean Tragedy* which appeared in 1984, the performance critic John Russell Brown suggested another emphasis, finding in Bradley an affinity with the politically committed perspective of the playwright Edward Bond, who wrote of Shakespeare that 'Had [he] not spent his creative life desperately struggling to reconcile problems that obsessed him he could not have written with such intellectual strength and passionate beauty'; revisiting this 'necessary masterpiece' a decade on, Brown affirmed that 'Few books of criticism give us the sensation of being close to a creative mind, but *Shakespearean Tragedy* . . . does just that.'[37] Most recently of all, in a book intended for a mass readership, *Shakespeare: The Invention of the Human*, Harold Bloom has positioned himself as a worthy inheritor of the character-centred tradition of interpretation 'that includes Samuel Johnson, William Hazlitt,

A. C. Bradley and Harold Goddard', claiming that 'Personality, in our
sense, is a Shakespearean invention, and is not only Shakespeare's
greatest originality but also the authentic cause of his perpetual per-
vasiveness,' and 'Our ideas as to what makes the self authentically
human owe more to Shakespeare than ought to be possible, but then
he has become a Scripture.'[38]

Reviewing Bloom's book, Terence Hawkes was not alone in detect-
ing the ghost of the 'dread' Bradley 'stalking its seven hundred and
more pages'; however, as another respondent observed, 'although written in the critical tradition of A. C. Bradley, Bloom's book could not
have been written in the age of Bradley, simply because Bloom is
seldom inspired by his friends; it is his enemies, rather, who motivate
his choices'.[39] The 'enemies' Bloom has in his sights – broadly speaking, the politically and theoretically inclined criticisms that first
emerged during the 1980s – have not been particularly kindly
disposed towards Bradley either. Jonathan Dollimore's *Radical Tragedy*
(1984; revised editions 1989, 2003) pointed out that the arguments
over 'character' had 'tended to obscure the extent to which Bradley's
metaphysic of tragedy has remained dominant'.[40] Similarly, in his
introduction to the ground-breaking collection of essays *Alternative
Shakespeares* (1985), John Drakakis devoted a substantial component
of his critical survey of nineteenth- and twentieth-century scholarship
to a discussion of *Shakespearean Tragedy*, tracing Bradley's indebted-
ness to Hegel and cogently arguing that he succeeds in uniting 'the
principle of universality with that of the specific individual traits of
character' by placing 'the demands of family and state' in 'an anterior
relation to the autonomous consciousness of the protagonist'. The
idea that these institutions 'might conceivably *determine* character, or
that the notion of character so produced may be anything but unified'
is beyond the grasp of Bradley's analysis.[41] Elsewhere in the volume,
in an essay which sets out to summarize and exemplify the post-
structuralist approach to Shakespeare, Christopher Norris takes as a
case study Leavis's attack on Bradley's reading of *Othello*: it is an indication of how far the targets had changed that it is not Bradley, who
is neither defended nor denigrated but taken as a given, but Leavis,
whom Norris subjects to the most detailed examination.[42] Terence
Hawkes reiterated the critique in his introduction to the second
volume of *Alternative Shakespeares* (1996): 'Bradley's commitment to
the almost palpable existence of single, unitary individuals . . . still

seems the "natural" and "obvious" one'; for Hawkes, this concern 'may ultimately reflect deep-lying dimensions of Western ideology', rendering Bradley's Shakespeare 'one of our century's most representative myths'.[43]

Hawkes has conducted a more extended, and entertaining, examination of Bradley in an essay which formed part of a larger investigation of the institutionalization of English studies during the first half of the twentieth century, *That Shakespeherian Rag* (1986). Combining biographical and cultural history, post-structuralist theory, and ideological critique, *Shakespearean Tragedy* is identified by Hawkes as a work that 'exercises the kind of invisible or subliminal influence on our view of the world that proves deeply and lastingly persuasive', and which advances a theory of reading that rests 'on the notion that the words on the page transparently express character, and that a vital consistency exists between these elements'. Focusing upon the discussion of Hamlet's love for Ophelia, Hawkes explores the ways in which, in spite of itself, Bradley's argument undermines and contradicts this theory, revealing a vertiginous uncertainty in Bradley's attempts to interpret the Prince's, and the text's, unreadable silences, and gesturing towards 'his entrapment in textuality' and 'the condition that haunts all the lectures on Shakespearian tragedy; there is – as Derrida puts it – no *hors-texte*: no firm, no perfect ground from which to mount an objective survey of its imperfections'.[44]

'We who, since Freud, since Saussure, since Marx, Barthes, or Derrida, have felt compelled to listen to the sounds silence makes in a text, to respond to what is *not* said as if it were as significant as what is said,' Hawkes wryly remarks, 'can hardly feel superior to Bradley as he wrestles with this matter.'[45] However ironically intended, the remark none the less suggests why, even – perhaps especially – after theory, Bradley is still well worth reading. Bradley is indisputably a key figure in the history of Shakespearean criticism, and anyone interested in how we got to where we are now cannot afford to ignore him; those of us who would think ourselves extremely fortunate were our own scholarly efforts to remain in circulation for a tenth of the time that Bradley's have might have much to learn from him in terms of how to address an audience, construct an argument, and communicate excitement about a play. Bradley's criticism may strike us as reactionary, misguided or plain wrong on occasions, but it is informed by intimate knowledge of and love for Shakespeare's plays, and as often as not prompts those who read him to turn back to them, even if it is to find grounds for disagreement with him. It is also characterized by its honesty, integrity and fairness, by its willingness to weigh alternatives and give due consideration to points of view with which Bradley disagrees, and by its refusal to ignore or suppress evidence which complicates or contravenes his own view. Whatever institutional forces shaped *Shakespearean Tragedy*'s subsequent fortunes in the English-speaking world, it is motivated by a strong sense of the value of criticism itself, not just as a tool for passing exams, but as a component of a lifetime of engagement with the plays. And, regardless of the dismay of professional literary theorists, its method stubbornly retains its appeal to readers and theatregoers, who continue to show an interest in character, not because they naively mistake art for life, but because it offers a viable means of testing the ethical implications of actions, motives and beliefs. In a recent retrospective on Bradley, Adrian Poole has suggested his efforts to reach a 'fair understanding' of Shakespeare's characters provide a 'good fiction' that 'governs most of our dealings in everyday life and constitutes one of the bases of a good society'; Michael Bristol, similarly, has spoken up for what he calls a lay tradition of 'vernacular criticism', which is 'based on epistemic realism with respect to such unobservable phenomena as motives, intentions, attitudes, ethical disposition, and the like', and which thus enables its practitioners to 'reflect about ethical choices and ethical consequences' and to 'look for the reasons literary figures might have for the actions they perform'.[46]

In Shakespeare's tragedies, these choices and consequences concern us, often very deeply, because they are matters of life and death; particularly in the current cultural climate, spending a few snatched hours in the theatre, alone with the book, or before a DVD, enables us not only to come face to face with what is both best and worst about ourselves, but also, in the very transience of the experience, to remind ourselves of the incomparable preciousness, as well as the fragility, of human life itself. For me, the real heart of *Shakespearean Tragedy* lies here, in its recognition of a basic humanity that can only truly be understood when one has lost everything, like Bradley's Lear, who only then 'learns to feel and to pray for the miserable and houseless poor, to discern the falseness of flattery and the brutality of authority, and to pierce below the differences of rank and authority to the common humanity beneath'. There is much to separate Bradley from Terry Eagleton, the Marxist theoretician who has latterly attempted to combine dialectical materialism with a radical Christian eschatology, and who has written brilliantly and movingly of Western culture's urgent need to recover and redefine its sense of the tragic, but there is still valuable common ground between the Edwardian scholar and the Eagleton who writes that 'the deathly emptiness of the dispossessed is the only source from which a more jubilant, self-delighting existence can ultimately spring'; and, indeed, that unless we are prepared to make this identification, 'in the sense of tackling the injustice which gives birth to a monstrous terror . . . the consequence can only be tragedy in a more horrific, everyday meaning of the term'.[47] At a time when the 'combatants in the conflict' on the global stage are all too readily cast as, on the one hand, a theocratic fundamentalism that exploits the miseries of poverty, injustice and dispossession in order to murder those whom it regards as infidels, and on the other, a system sustained by the combination of economic exploitation and military force, a rediscovery of the tragic dialectic is both timely and deeply necessary. *Shakespearean Tragedy*, read in the light of the century of history that has passed since its first publication, is an excellent place to start.

Notes

1. F. J. Furnivall, 'The New Shakspere Society (Founder's Prospectus Revised', *Transactions of the New Shakspere Society*, 1st series, no. 1 (1874), p. 6; quoted in Hugh Grady, *The Modernist Shakespeare: Critical Texts in a Material World* (Oxford: Clarendon Press, 1991), p. 43.

2. Edward Dowden, *Shakspere: A Critical Study of His Mind and Art* (London: Henry S. King, 1875), pp. v, pp. 33–4, 160, 430.

3. Dowden, *Shakspere*, p. 23; Simon Shepherd and Peter Womack, *English Drama: A Cultural History* (Oxford: Blackwell, 1996), p. 106.

4. Bradley's essays on *Coriolanus*, *The Two Noble Kinsmen*, and Feste are published in *A Miscellany* (London: Macmillan, 1929); *Oxford Lectures on Poetry* (1909; repr. London: Macmillan, 1965) includes 'The Rejection of Falstaff', 'Shakespeare's *Antony and Cleopatra*', 'Shakespeare the Man', and 'Shakespeare's Theatre and Audience'.

5. Cited in Melvin Richter, *The Politics of Conscience: T. H. Green and his Age* (London: Weidenfeld and Nicolson, 1964), p. 161.

6. These publications included 'International Morality: the United States of Europe', a lecture delivered in London in 1915, and *The Ideals of Religion*, the Gifford Lectures delivered at the University of Glasgow, 1907, published posthumously (London: Macmillan, 1940).

7. A. C. Bradley, letter to Gilbert Murray, 3 February 1901, quoted in G. K. Hunter, 'A. C. Bradley', *Oxford Dictionary of National Biography*, ed. H. C. G. Matthew and Brian Harrison (Oxford: Oxford University Press, 2004).

8. Bradley, *Oxford Lectures on Poetry*, p. 394.

9. *The Spectator*, 28 January 1905; *Times Literary Supplement* (*TLS*), 10 February 1905, quoted in Katherine Cooke, *A. C. Bradley and his Influence in Twentieth-Century Criticism* (Oxford: Clarendon Press, 1972), p. 190.

10. R. Y. Tyrell, 'Tragedy', *Academy*, 11 March 1905; *Westminster Gazette*, 28 January 1905; quoted in Cooke, *A. C. Bradley*, pp. 184–5.

11. A. B. Walkley, *TLS*, 7 April 1905, quoted in Cooke, *A. C. Bradley*, p. 192.

12. I am indebted to Alysoun Sanders, Archivist for Palgrave Macmillan, for these figures.

13. Sir Henry Newbolt et al., *The Teaching of English in England* (London: HMSO, 1921), p. 21.

14. *Punch*, 17 February 1926; quoted in Cooke, *A. C. Bradley*, pp. 191–2.

15. G. W. F. Hegel, 'Tragedy as a Dramatic Art', in *Hegel on Tragedy*, ed. Anne and Henry Paolucci (New York: Harper and Row, 1962), pp. 46–7. For a discussion of Bradley's debts to Hegel, see Graham Holderness, 'Are Shakespeare's Tragic Heroes "Fatally Flawed"? Discuss', *Critical Survey*, 1:1 (1989), 56–7.

16. Bradley, *Oxford Lectures on Poetry*, pp. 71, 77.

17. Ibid., p. 77.

18. See Graham Holderness, *Shakespeare Recycled: The Making of Historical Drama* (London: Harvester Wheatsheaf, 1992).

19. Max Beerbohm, *Around Theatres* (1924; repr. London: Rupert Hart-Davis, 1953), p. 143; quoted in Stanley Wells, *Shakespeare for all Time* (Basingstoke: Palgrave Macmillan, 2002), p. 321.

20. Reported in J. W. Mackail, 'Andrew Cecil Bradley', *Proceedings of the British Academy*, 21 (1935), 385–92 (p. 391).

21. *Westminster Gazette*, 28 January 1905; quoted in Cooke, *A. C. Bradley*, p. 3.

22. *Coleridge on Shakspeare*, ed. Terence Hawkes (Harmondsworth: Penguin, 1959), p. 188.

23. Maynard Mack, *King Lear in Our Time* (1965; repr. London: Routledge, 2005), p. 3.

24. Walter Raleigh, *Shakespeare* (London: Macmillan, 1907), p. 13.
25. Bradley, *Oxford Lectures on Poetry*, p. 47.
26. Edward Gordon Craig, *On the Art of the Theatre* (London: William Heinemann, 1911), pp. 265–6.
27. Constantin Stanislavsky, *Building a Character*, trans. Elizabeth Hapgood Reynolds (London: Max Reinhardt, 1950), p. 113.
28. Bradley, *Oxford Lectures on Poetry*, p. 46.
29. C. H. Herford, *A Sketch of Recent Shakespearean Investigation, 1893–1923* (London: Blackie, 1923), pp. 32–7.
30. Harley Granville-Barker, 'Some Tasks for Dramatic Scholarship', in *Essays by Divers Hands*, ed. F. S. Boas (London, 1923), p. 20.
31. L. C. Knights, 'How Many Children had Lady Macbeth?', in *Explorations: Essays in Criticism Mainly on the Literature of the Seventeenth Century* (Harmondsworth: Penguin, 1964), pp. 16, 28.
32. F. R. Leavis, 'The Literary Mind', *Scrutiny*, 1:1 (1932), 20–32 (p. 25).
33. F. R. Leavis, 'Diabolic Intellect and the Noble Hero: the Sentimentalist's *Othello*', in *The Common Pursuit* (Harmondsworth: Penguin, 1962), pp. 136, 146–7.
34. G. K. Hunter, 'A. C. Bradley's *Shakespearean Tragedy*', *Essays and Studies*, 21 (1968), 101–17 (p. 101).
35. Cooke, *A. C. Bradley*, p. 233.
36. John Bayley, *Shakespeare and Tragedy* (London: Routledge & Kegan Paul, 1981), p. 6.
37. John Russell Brown, 'A New Introduction', *Shakespearean Tragedy*, 2nd edition (Basingstoke: Macmillan, 1985), p. xxiii; 'Introduction to the Third Edition', *Shakespearean Tragedy*, 3rd edition (Basingstoke: Macmillan, 1992), p. xxxiii.
38. Harold Bloom, *Shakespeare: The Invention of the Human* (London: Fourth Estate, 1999), pp. 4, 17.
39. Terence Hawkes, 'Bloom with a View'; Mustapha Fahmi, 'Shakespeare: the Orientation of the Human', both in *Harold Bloom's Shakespeare*, ed. Christy Desment and Robert Sawyer (Basingstoke: Palgrave Macmillan, 2001), pp. 27, 107.
40. Jonathan Dollimore, *Radical Tragedy: Religion, Ideology and Power in the Drama of Shakespeare and his Contemporaries*, 2nd edition (Brighton: Harvester Wheatsheaf, 1989), p. 53.
41. John Drakakis, 'Introduction', *Alternative Shakespeares* (London: Methuen, 1985), pp. 6–7.
42. Christopher Norris, 'Post-structuralist Shakespeare: Text and Ideology', in *Alternative Shakespeares*, pp. 47–66.
43. Terence Hawkes, 'Introduction', *Alternative Shakespeares*, vol. 2 (London: Routledge, 1996), p. 5.

44. Terence Hawkes, 'A Sea Shell', in *That Shakespeherian Rag: Essays on a Critical Process* (London: Methuen, 1986), pp. 31, 36, 40.

45. Ibid., pp. 38-9.

46. Adrian Poole, 'New Impressions IX: A. C. Bradley's *Shakespearean Tragedy*', *Essays in Criticism*, 55 (2005), 58–70 (p. 70); Michael D. Bristol, 'Vernacular Criticism and the Scenes Shakespeare Never Wrote', *Shakespeare Survey*, 53 (2000), 89–102 (p. 95). From a different but related perspective, Carol Chillington Rutter responds to Knight's parodically Bradleian question about Lady Macbeth's children by pointing out that 'in the theatre, it cannot be ducked . . . Lady Macbeths have made it a matter of considerable urgency to account for her missing children' ('Remind Me: How Many Children had Lady Macbeth?', *Shakespeare Survey*, 57 (2004), 38–53, at p. 40).

47. Terry Eagleton, *Sweet Violence: The Idea of the Tragic* (Oxford: Blackwell, 2003), p. 296; 'A Response', *Literature and Theology*, 19:2 (2005), 132–8 (p. 138).

Original Introduction

In these lectures I propose to consider the four principal tragedies of Shakespeare from a single point of view. Nothing will be said of Shakespeare's place in the history either of English literature or of the drama in general. No attempt will be made to compare him with other writers. I shall leave untouched, or merely glanced at, questions regarding his life and character, the development of his genius and art, the genuineness, sources, texts, inter-relations of his various works. Even what may be called, in a restricted sense, the 'poetry' of the four tragedies – the beauties of style, diction, versification – I shall pass by in silence. Our one object will be what, again in a restricted sense, may be called dramatic appreciation; to increase our understanding and enjoyment of these works as dramas; to learn to apprehend the action and some of the personages of each with a somewhat greater truth and intensity, so that they may assume in our imaginations a shape a little less unlike the shape they wore in the imagination of their creator. For this end all those studies that were mentioned just now, of literary history and the like, are useful and even in various degrees necessary. But an overt pursuit of them is not necessary here, nor is any one of them so indispensable to our object as that close familiarity with the plays, that native strength and justice of perception, and that habit of reading with an eager mind, which make many an unscholarly lover of Shakespeare a far better critic than many a Shakespeare scholar.

Such lovers read a play more or less as if they were actors who had to study all the parts. They do not need, of course, to imagine whereabouts the persons are to stand, or what gestures they ought to use; but they want to realize fully and exactly the inner movements which produced these words and no other, these deeds and no other, at each particular moment. This, carried through a drama, is the right way to read the dramatist Shakespeare; and the prime requisite here is therefore a vivid and intent imagination. But this alone will hardly suffice. It is necessary also, especially to a true conception of the whole, to compare, to analyse, to dissect. And such readers often shrink from this task, which seems to them prosaic or even a desecration. They misunderstand, I believe. They would not shrink if they remembered two things. In the first place, in this process of comparison and analysis, it is not requisite, it is on the contrary ruinous, to set imagination aside and to substitute some supposed 'cold reason'; and it is only want of practice that makes the concurrent use of analysis and of poetic perception difficult or irksome. And, in the second place, these dissecting processes, though they are also imaginative, are still, and are meant to be, nothing but means to an end. When they have finished their work (it can only be finished for the time) they give place to the end, which is that same imaginative reading or re-creation of the drama from which they set out, but a reading now enriched by the products of analysis, and therefore far more adequate and enjoyable.

This, at any rate, is the faith in the strength of which I venture, with merely personal misgivings, on the path of analytic interpretation. And so, before coming to the first of the four tragedies, I propose to discuss some preliminary matters which concern them all. Though each is individual through and through, they have, in a sense, one and the same substance; for in all of them Shakespeare represents the tragic aspect of life, the tragic fact. They have, again, up to a certain point, a common form or structure. This substance and this structure, which would be found to distinguish them, for example, from Greek tragedies, may, to diminish repetition, be considered once for all; and in considering them we shall also be able to observe characteristic differences among the four plays. And to this may be added the little that it seems necessary to premise on the position of these dramas in Shakespeare's literary career.

Much that is said on our main preliminary subjects will naturally hold good, within certain limits, of other dramas of Shakespeare beside *Hamlet*, *Othello*, *King Lear*, and *Macbeth*. But it will often apply to these other works only in part, and to some of them more fully than to others. *Romeo and Juliet*, for instance, is a pure tragedy, but it is an early work, and in some respects an immature one. *Richard III* and *Richard II*, *Julius Caesar*, *Antony and Cleopatra*, and *Coriolanus* are tragic histories or historical tragedies, in which Shakespeare acknowledged in practice a certain obligation to follow his authority, even when that authority offered him an undramatic material. Probably he himself would have met some criticisms to which these plays are open by appealing to their historical character, and by denying that such works are to be judged by the standard of pure tragedy.

In any case, most of these plays, perhaps all, do show, as a matter of fact, considerable deviations from that standard; and, therefore, what is said of the pure tragedies must be applied to them with qualifications which I shall often take for granted without mention. There remain *Titus Andronicus* and *Timon of Athens.* The former I shall leave out of account, because, even if Shakespeare wrote the whole of it, he did so before he had either a style of his own or any characteristic tragic conception. *Timon* stands on a different footing. Parts of it are unquestionably Shakespeare's, and they will be referred to in one of the later lectures. But much of the writing is evidently not his, and as it seems probable that the conception and construction of the whole tragedy should also be attributed to some other writer, I shall omit this work too from our preliminary discussions.

THE SUBSTANCE OF
SHAKESPEAREAN TRAGEDY

The question we are to consider in this lecture may be stated in a variety of ways. We may put it thus: What is the substance of a Shakespearean tragedy, taken in abstraction both from its form and from the differences in point of substance between one tragedy and another? Or thus: What is the nature of the tragic aspect of life as represented by Shakespeare? What is the general fact shown now in this tragedy and now in that? And we are putting the same question when we ask: What is Shakespeare's tragic conception, or conception of tragedy?

These expressions, it should be observed, do not imply that Shakespeare himself ever asked or answered such a question; that he set himself to reflect on the tragic aspects of life, that he framed a tragic conception, and still less that, like Aristotle* or Corneille,* he had a theory of the kind of poetry called tragedy. These things are all possible; how far any one of them is probable we need not discuss; but none of them is presupposed by the question we are going to consider. This question implies only that, as a matter of fact, Shakespeare in writing tragedy did represent a certain aspect of life in a certain way, and that through examination of his writings we ought to be able, to some extent, to describe this aspect and way in terms addressed to the understanding. Such a description, so far as it is true and adequate, may, after these explanations, be called indifferently an account of the substance of Shakespearean tragedy, or an account of Shakespeare's conception of tragedy or view of the tragic fact.

Two further warnings may be required. In the first place, we must remember that the tragic aspect of life is only one aspect. We cannot arrive at Shakespeare's whole dramatic way of looking at the world from his tragedies alone, as we can arrive at Milton's way of regarding things, or at Wordsworth's or at Shelley's, by examining almost any one of their important works. Speaking very broadly, one can say that these poets at their best always look at things in one light; but *Hamlet* and *Henry IV* and *Cymbeline* reflect things from quite distinct positions, and Shakespeare's whole dramatic view is not to be identified with any one of these reflections. And, in the second place, I may repeat that in these lectures, at any rate for the most part, we are to be content with his *dramatic* view, and are not to ask whether it corresponded exactly with his opinions or creed outside his poetry – the opinions or creed of the being whom we sometimes oddly call 'Shakespeare the man'.* It does not seem likely that outside his poetry he was a very simple-minded Catholic or Protestant or Atheist, as some have maintained; but we cannot be sure, as with those other poets we can, that in his works he expressed his deepest and most cherished convictions on ultimate questions, or even that he had any. And in his dramatic conceptions there is enough to occupy us.

1

In approaching our subject it will be best, without attempting to shorten the path by referring to famous theories of the drama, to start directly from the facts, and to collect from them gradually an idea of Shakespearean Tragedy. And first, to begin from the outside, such a tragedy brings before us a considerable number of persons (many more than the persons in a Greek play, unless the members of the Chorus are reckoned among them); but it is pre-eminently the story of one person, the 'hero',[1] or at most of two, the 'hero' and 'heroine'. Moreover, it is only in the love-tragedies, *Romeo and Juliet* and *Antony and Cleopatra*, that the heroine is as much the centre of the action as the hero. The rest, including *Macbeth*, are single stars. So that, having noticed the peculiarity of these two dramas, we may henceforth, for the sake of brevity, ignore it, and may speak of the tragic story as being concerned primarily with one person.

The story, next, leads up to, and includes, the *death* of the hero. On the one hand (whatever may be true of tragedy elsewhere) no play at the end of which the hero remains alive is, in the full Shakespearean sense, a tragedy; and we no longer class *Troilus and Cressida* or *Cymbeline* as such, as did the editors of the Folio. On the other hand,

---

[1] *Julius Caesar* is not an exception to this rule. Caesar, whose murder comes in the Third Act, is in a sense the dominating figure in the story, but Brutus is the 'hero'.

the story depicts also the troubled part of the hero's life which precedes and leads up to his death; and an instantaneous death occurring by 'accident' in the midst of prosperity would not suffice for it. It is, in fact, essentially a tale of suffering and calamity conducting to death.

The suffering and calamity are, moreover, exceptional. They befall a conspicuous person. They are themselves of some striking kind. They are also, as a rule, unexpected, and contrasted with previous happiness or glory. A tale, for example, of a man slowly worn to death by disease, poverty, little cares, sordid vices, petty persecutions, however piteous or dreadful it might be, would not be tragic in the Shakespearean sense.

Such exceptional suffering and calamity, then, affecting the hero, and – we must now add – generally extending far and wide beyond him, so as to make the whole scene a scene of woe, are an essential ingredient in tragedy, and a chief source of the tragic emotions, and especially of pity. But the proportions of this ingredient, and the direction taken by tragic pity, will naturally vary greatly. Pity, for example, has a much larger part in *King Lear* than in *Macbeth*, and is directed in the one case chiefly to the hero, in the other chiefly to minor characters.

Let us now pause for a moment on the ideas we have so far reached. They would more than suffice to describe the whole tragic fact as it presented itself to the mediaeval mind. To the mediaeval mind a tragedy meant a narrative rather than a play, and its notion of the matter of this narrative may readily be gathered from Dante* or, still better, from Chaucer.* Chaucer's *Monk's Tale* is a series of what he calls 'tragedies'; and this means in fact a series of tales *de Casibus Illustrium Virorum* – stories of the Falls of Illustrious Men, such as Lucifer, Adam, Hercules and Nebuchadnezzar. And the Monk ends the tale of Croesus thus:

> Anhanged was Cresus, the proudè kyng;
> His roial tronè myghte hym nat availle.
> Tragédie is noon oother maner thyng,
> Ne kan in syngyng criè ne biwaille
> But for that Fortune alwey wole assaile
> With unwar strook the regnès that been proude;
> For whan men trusteth hire, thanne wol she faille,
> And covere hire brightè facè with a clowde.*

A total reverse of fortune, coming unawares upon a man who 'stood in high degree', happy and apparently secure – such was the tragic fact to the mediaeval mind. It appealed strongly to common human sympathy and pity; it startled also another feeling, that of fear. It frightened men and awed them. It made them feel that man is blind and helpless, the plaything of an inscrutable power, called by the name of Fortune or some other name – a power which appears to smile on him for a little, and then on a sudden strikes him down in his pride.

Shakespeare's idea of the tragic fact is larger than this idea and goes beyond it; but it includes it, and it is worth while to observe the identity of the two in a certain point which is often ignored. Tragedy with Shakespeare is concerned always with persons of 'high degree'; often with kings or princes; if not, with leaders in the state like Coriolanus, Brutus, Antony; at the least, as in *Romeo and Juliet*, with members of great houses, whose quarrels are of public moment. There is a decided difference here between *Othello* and our three other tragedies, but it is not a difference of kind. Othello himself is no mere private person; he is the General of the Republic. At the beginning we see him in the Council-Chamber of the Senate. The consciousness of his high position never leaves him. At the end, when he is determined to live no longer, he is as anxious as Hamlet not to be misjudged by the great world, and his last speech begins,

> Soft you; a word or two before you go.
> I have done the state some service, and they know it.[2]

And this characteristic of Shakespeare's tragedies, though not the most vital, is neither external nor unimportant. The saying that every death-bed is the scene of the fifth act of a tragedy has its meaning, but it would not be true if the word 'tragedy' bore its dramatic sense. The pangs of despised love and the anguish of remorse, we say, are the same in a peasant and a prince; but, not to insist that they cannot be so when the prince is really a prince, the story of the prince, the

---

[2] *Timon of Athens*, we have seen, was probably not designed by Shakespeare, but even *Timon* is no exception to the rule. The sub-plot is concerned with Alcibiades and his army, and Timon himself is treated by the Senate as a man of great importance. *Arden of Feversham** and *A Yorkshire Tragedy** would certainly be exceptions to the rule; but I assume that neither of them is Shakespeare's; and if either is, it belongs to a different species from his admitted tragedies. See, on this species, Symonds,* *Shakespere's Predecessors*, ch. xi.

triumvir, or the general, has a greatness and dignity of its own. His fate affects the welfare of a whole nation or empire; and when he falls suddenly from the height of earthly greatness to the dust, his fall produces a sense of contrast, of the powerlessness of man, and of the omnipotence – perhaps the caprice – of Fortune or Fate, which no tale of private life can possibly rival.

Such feelings are constantly evoked by Shakespeare's tragedies – again in varying degrees. Perhaps they are the very strongest of the emotions awakened by the early tragedy of *Richard II*, where they receive a concentrated expression in Richard's famous speech about the antic Death, who sits in the hollow crown

> That rounds the mortal temples of a king,

grinning at his pomp, watching till his vanity and his fancied security have wholly encased him round, and then coming and boring with a little pin through his castle wall. And these feelings, though their predominance is subdued in the mightiest tragedies, remain powerful there. In the figure of the maddened Lear we see

> A sight most pitiful in the meanest wretch,
> Past speaking of in a king;

and if we would realize the truth in this matter we cannot do better than compare with the effect of *King Lear* the effect of Tourgénief's* parallel and remarkable tale of peasant life, *A King Lear of the Steppes*.

2

A Shakespearean tragedy as so far considered may be called a story of exceptional calamity leading to the death of a man in high estate. But it is clearly much more than this, and we have now to regard it from another side. No amount of calamity which merely befell a man, descending from the clouds like lightning, or stealing from the darkness like pestilence, could alone provide the substance of its story. Job was the greatest of all the children of the east, and his afflictions were well-nigh more than he could bear; but even if we imagined them wearing him to death, that would not make his story tragic. Nor yet would it become so, in the Shakespearean sense, if the fire, and the great wind from the wilderness, and the torments of his flesh were conceived as sent by a supernatural power, whether just or malignant.

The calamities of tragedy do not simply happen, nor are they sent; they proceed mainly from actions, and those the actions of men.

We see a number of human beings placed in certain circumstances; and we see, arising from the co-operation of their characters in these circumstances, certain actions. These actions beget others, and these others beget others again, until this series of inter-connected deeds leads by an apparently inevitable sequence to a catastrophe. The effect of such a series on imagination is to make us regard the sufferings which accompany it, and the catastrophe in which it ends, not only or chiefly as something which happens to the persons concerned, but equally as something which is caused by them. This at least may be said of the principal persons, and, among them, of the hero, who always contributes in some measure to the disaster in which he perishes.

This second aspect of tragedy evidently differs greatly from the first. Men, from this point of view, appear to us primarily as agents, 'themselves the authors of their proper woe'; and our fear and pity, though they will not cease or diminish, will be modified accordingly. We are now to consider this second aspect, remembering that it too is only one aspect, and additional to the first, not a substitute for it.

The 'story' or 'action' of a Shakespearean tragedy does not consist, of course, solely of human actions or deeds; but the deeds are the predominant factor. And these deeds are, for the most part, actions in the full sense of the word; not things done ''tween asleep and wake', but acts or omissions thoroughly expressive of the doer – characteristic deeds. The centre of the tragedy, therefore, may be said with equal truth to lie in action issuing from character, or in character issuing in action.

Shakespeare's main interest lay here. To say that it lay in *mere* character, or was a psychological interest, would be a great mistake, for he was dramatic to the tips of his fingers. It is possible to find places where he has given a certain indulgence to his love of poetry, and even to his turn for general reflections; but it would be very difficult, and in his later tragedies perhaps impossible, to detect passages where he has allowed such freedom to the interest in character apart from action. But for the opposite extreme, for the abstraction of mere 'plot' (which is a very different thing from the tragic 'action'), for the kind of interest which predominates in a novel like *The Woman in White*,* it is clear that he cared even less. I do not mean that this interest is absent from his dramas; but it is subordinate to others, and is so inter-woven with them that we are rarely conscious of it apart, and rarely feel in any great strength the half-intellectual, half-nervous excitement of following an ingenious complication. What we do feel strongly, as a tragedy advances to its close, is that the calamities and catastrophe follow inevitably from the deeds of men, and that the main source of these deeds is character. The dictum that, with Shakespeare, 'charac-ter is destiny' is no doubt an exaggeration, and one that may mislead (for many of his tragic personages, if they had not met with peculiar circumstances, would have escaped a tragic end, and might even have lived fairly untroubled lives); but it is the exaggeration of a vital truth.

This truth, with some of its qualifications, will appear more clearly if we now go on to ask what elements are to be found in the 'story' or 'action', occasionally or frequently, beside the characteristic deeds, and the sufferings and circumstances, of the persons. I will refer to three of these additional factors.

(*a*) Shakespeare, occasionally and for reasons which need not be discussed here, represents abnormal conditions of mind; insanity, for example, somnambulism, hallucinations. And deeds issuing from these are certainly not what we called deeds in the fullest sense, deeds expressive of character. No; but these abnormal conditions are never introduced as the origin of deeds of any dramatic moment. Lady Macbeth's sleep-walking has no influence whatever on the events that follow it. Macbeth did not murder Duncan because he saw a dagger in the air: he saw the dagger because he was about to murder Duncan. Lear's insanity is not the cause of a tragic conflict any more than Ophelia's; it is, like Ophelia's, the result of a conflict; and in both cases the effect is mainly pathetic. If Lear were really mad when he divided his kingdom, if Hamlet were really mad at any time in the story, they would cease to be tragic characters.

(*b*) Shakespeare also introduces the supernatural into some of his tragedies; he introduces ghosts, and witches who have supernatural knowledge. This supernatural element certainly cannot in most cases, if in any, be explained away as an illusion in the mind of one of the characters. And further, it does contribute to the action, and is in more than one instance an indispensable part of it: so that to describe human character, with circumstances, as always the *sole* motive force in this action would be a serious error. But the supernatural is always placed in the closest relation with character. It gives a confirmation and a distinct form to inward movements already present and exerting an influence; to the sense of failure in Brutus, to the stifled workings of conscience in Richard, to the half-formed thought or the horrified memory of guilt in Macbeth, to suspicion in Hamlet. Moreover, its influence is never of a compulsive kind. It forms no more than an element, however important, in the problem which the hero has to face; and we are never allowed to feel that it has removed his capacity or responsibility for dealing with this problem. So far indeed are we from feeling this, that many readers run to the opposite extreme, and openly or privately regard the supernatural as having nothing to do with the real interest of the play.

(*c*) Shakespeare, lastly, in most of his tragedies allows to 'chance' or 'accident' an appreciable influence at some point in the action. Chance or accident here will be found, I think, to mean any occurrence (not supernatural, of course) which enters the dramatic sequence neither from the agency of a character, nor from the obvious surrounding circumstances.[3] It may be called an accident, in this sense, that Romeo never got the Friar's message about the potion, and that Juliet did not awake from her long sleep a minute sooner; an accident that Edgar arrived at the prison just too late to save Cordelia's life; an accident that Desdemona dropped her handkerchief at the most fatal of moments; an accident that the pirate ship attacked Hamlet's ship, so that he was able to return forthwith to Denmark. Now this operation of accident is a fact, and a prominent fact, of human life. To exclude it *wholly* from tragedy, therefore, would be, we may say, to fail in truth. And, besides, it is not merely a fact. That men may start a course of events but can neither calculate nor control it, is a *tragic* fact. The dramatist may use accident so as to make us feel this; and there are also other dramatic uses to which it may be put. Shakespeare accordingly admits it. On the other hand, any *large* admission of chance into the tragic sequence[4] would certainly weaken, and might destroy, the sense of the causal connection of character, deed, and catastrophe. And Shakespeare really uses it very sparingly. We seldom find ourselves exclaiming, 'What an unlucky

---

[3] Even a deed would, I think, be counted an 'accident', if it were the deed of a very minor person whose character had not been indicated; because such a deed would not issue from the little world to which the dramatist had confined our attention.

[4] Comedy stands in a different position. The tricks played by chance often form a principal part of the comic action.

accident!' I believe most readers would have to search painfully for instances. It is, further, frequently easy to see the dramatic intention of an accident; and some things which look like accidents have really a connection with character, and are therefore not in the full sense accidents. Finally, I believe it will be found that almost all the prominent accidents occur when the action is well advanced and the impression of the causal sequence is too firmly fixed to be impaired.

Thus it appears that these three elements in the 'action' are subordinate, while the dominant factor consists in deeds which issue from character. So that, by way of summary, we may now alter our first statement, 'A tragedy is a story of exceptional calamity leading to the death of a man in high estate', and we may say instead (what in its turn is one-sided, though less so), that the story is one of human actions producing exceptional calamity and ending in the death of such a man.[5]

Before we leave the 'action', however, there is another question that may usefully be asked. Can we define this 'action' further by describing it as a conflict?

The frequent use of this idea in discussions on tragedy is ultimately due, I suppose, to the influence of Hegel's* theory on the subject, certainly the most important theory since Aristotle's. But Hegel's view of the tragic conflict is not only unfamiliar to English readers and difficult to expound shortly, but it had its origin in reflections on Greek tragedy and, as Hegel was well aware, applies only imperfectly to the works of Shakespeare.[6] I shall, therefore, confine myself to the idea of conflict in its more general form. In this form it is obviously suitable to Shakespearean tragedy; but it is vague, and I will try to make it more precise by putting the question, Who are the combatants in this conflict?

Not seldom the conflict may quite naturally be conceived as lying between two persons, of whom the hero is one; or, more fully, as lying between two parties or groups, in one of which the hero is the leading figure. Or if we prefer to speak (as we may quite well do if we

---

[5] It may be observed that the influence of the three elements just considered is to strengthen the tendency, produced by the sufferings considered first, to regard the tragic persons as passive rather than as agents.

[6] An account of Hegel's view may be found in *Oxford Lectures on Poetry*.

know what we are about) of the passions, tendencies, ideas, principles, forces, which animate these persons or groups, we may say that two of such passions or ideas, regarded as animating two persons or groups, are the combatants. The love of Romeo and Juliet is in conflict with the hatred of their houses, represented by various other characters. The cause of Brutus and Cassius struggles with that of Julius, Octavius and Antony. In *Richard II* the King stands on one side, Bolingbroke and his party on the other. In *Macbeth* the hero and heroine are opposed to the representatives of Duncan. In all these cases the great majority of the *dramatis personæ* fall without difficulty into antagonistic groups, and the conflict between these groups ends with the defeat of the hero.

Yet one cannot help feeling that in at least one of these cases, *Macbeth*, there is something a little external in this way of looking at the action. And when we come to some other plays this feeling increases. No doubt most of the characters in *Hamlet, King Lear, Othello*, or *Antony and Cleopatra* can be arranged in opposed groups;[7] and no doubt there is a conflict; and yet it seems misleading to describe this conflict as one *between these groups*. It cannot be simply this. For though Hamlet and the King are mortal foes, yet that which engrosses our interest and dwells in our memory at least as much as the conflict between them, is the conflict *within* one of them. And so it is, though not in the same degree, with *Antony and Cleopatra* and even with *Othello*; and, in fact, in a certain measure, it is so with nearly all the tragedies. There is an outward conflict of persons and groups, there is also a conflict of forces in the hero's soul; and even in *Julius Caesar* and *Macbeth* the interest of the former can hardly be said to exceed that of the latter.

The truth is, that the type of tragedy in which the hero opposes to a hostile force an undivided soul, is not the Shakespearean type. The souls of those who contend with the hero may be thus undivided; they generally are; but, as a rule, the hero, though he pursues his fated way,

---

7 The reader, however, will find considerable difficulty in placing some very important characters in these and other plays. I will give only two or three illustrations. Edgar is clearly not on the same side as Edmund, and yet it seems awkward to range him on Gloster's side when Gloster wishes to put him to death. Ophelia is in love with Hamlet, but how can she be said to be of Hamlet's party against the King and Polonius, or of their party against Hamlet? Desdemona worships Othello, yet it sounds odd to say that Othello is on the same side with a person whom he insults, strikes and murders.

is, at least at some point in the action, and sometimes at many, torn by an inward struggle; and it is frequently at such points that Shakespeare shows his most extraordinary power. If further we compare the earlier tragedies with the later, we find that it is in the latter, the maturest works, that this inward struggle is most emphasized. In the last of them, *Coriolanus*, its interest completely eclipses towards the close of the play that of the outward conflict. *Romeo and Juliet, Richard III, Richard II*, where the hero contends with an outward force, but comparatively little with himself, are all early plays.

If we are to include the outer and the inner struggle in a conception more definite than that of conflict in general, we must employ some such phrase as 'spiritual force'. This will mean whatever forces act in the human spirit, whether good or evil, whether personal passion or impersonal principle; doubts, desires, scruples, ideas – whatever can animate, shake, possess, and drive a man's soul. In a Shakespearean tragedy some such forces are shown in conflict. They are shown acting in men and generating strife between them. They are also shown, less universally, but quite as characteristically, generating disturbance and even conflict in the soul of the hero. Treasonous ambition in Macbeth collides with loyalty and patriotism in Macduff and Malcolm: here is the outward conflict. But these powers or principles equally collide in the soul of Macbeth himself: here is the inner. And neither by itself could make the tragedy.[8]

We shall see later the importance of this idea. Here we need only observe that the notion of tragedy as a conflict emphasizes the fact that action is the centre of the story, while the concentration of interest, in the greater plays, on the inward struggle emphasizes the fact that this action is essentially the expression of character.

3

Let us now turn from the 'action' to the central figure in it; and, ignoring the characteristics which distinguish the heroes from one another,

---

[8] I have given names to the 'spiritual forces' in *Macbeth* merely to illustrate the idea, and without any pretension to adequacy. Perhaps, in view of some interpretation of Shakespeare's plays, it will be as well to add that I do not dream of suggesting that in any of his dramas Shakespeare imagined two abstract principles or passions conflicting, and incorporated them in persons; or that there is any necessity for a reader to define for himself the particular forces which conflict in a given case.

let us ask whether they have any common qualities which appear to be essential to the tragic effect.

One they certainly have. They are exceptional beings. We have seen already that the hero, with Shakespeare, is a person of high degree or of public importance, and that his actions or sufferings are of an unusual kind. But this is not all. His nature also is exceptional, and generally raises him in some respect much above the average level of humanity. This does not mean that he is an eccentric or a paragon. Shakespeare never drew monstrosities of virtue; some of his heroes are far from being 'good'; and if he drew eccentrics he gave them a subordinate position in the plot. His tragic characters are made of the stuff we find within ourselves and within the persons who surround them. But, by an intensification of the life which they share with others, they are raised above them; and the greatest are raised so far that, if we fully realize all that is implied in their words and actions, we become conscious that in real life we have known scarcely any one resembling them. Some, like Hamlet and Cleopatra, have genius. Others, like Othello, Lear, Macbeth, Coriolanus, are built on the grand scale; and desire, passion, or will attains in them a terrible force. In almost all we observe a marked one-sidedness, a predisposition in some particular direction; a total incapacity, in certain circumstances, of resisting the force which draws in this direction; a fatal tendency to identify the whole being with one interest, object, passion, or habit of mind. This, it would seem, is, for Shakespeare, the fundamental tragic trait. It is present in his early heroes, Romeo and Richard II, infatuated men, who otherwise rise comparatively little above the ordinary level. It is a fatal gift, but it carries with it a touch of greatness; and when there is joined to it nobility of mind, or genius, or immense force, we realize the full power and reach of the soul, and the conflict in which it engages acquires that magnitude which stirs not only sympathy and pity, but admiration, terror, and awe.

The easiest way to bring home to oneself the nature of the tragic character is to compare it with a character of another kind. Dramas like *Cymbeline* and the *Winter's Tale*, which might seem destined to end tragically, but actually end otherwise, owe their happy ending largely to the fact that the principal characters fail to reach tragic dimensions. And, conversely, if these persons were put in the place of the tragic heroes, the dramas in which they appeared would cease to be tragedies. Posthumus would never have acted as Othello did;

Othello, on his side, would have met Iachimo's challenge with something more than words. If, like Posthumus, he had remained convinced of his wife's infidelity, he would not have repented her execution; if, like Leontes, he had come to believe that by an unjust accusation he had caused her death, he would never have lived on, like Leontes. In the same way the villain Iachimo has no touch of tragic greatness. But Iago comes nearer to it, and if Iago had slandered Imogen and had supposed his slanders to have led to her death, he certainly would not have turned melancholy and wished to die. One reason why the end of the *Merchant of Venice* fails to satisfy us is that Shylock is a tragic character, and that we cannot believe in his accepting his defeat and the conditions imposed on him. This was a case where Shakespeare's imagination ran away with him, so that he drew a figure with which the destined pleasant ending would not harmonize.

In the circumstances where we see the hero placed, his tragic trait, which is also his greatness, is fatal to him. To meet these circumstances something is required which a smaller man might have given, but which the hero cannot give. He errs, by action or omission; and his error, joining with other causes, brings on him ruin. This is always so with Shakespeare. As we have seen, the idea of the tragic hero as a being destroyed simply and solely by external forces is quite alien to him; and not less so is the idea of the hero as contributing to his destruction only by acts in which we see no flaw. But the fatal imperfection or error, which is never absent, is of different kinds and degrees. At one extreme stands the excess and precipitancy of Romeo, which scarcely, if at all, diminish our regard for him; at the other the murderous ambition of Richard III. In most cases the tragic error involves no conscious breach of right; in some (*e.g.* that of Brutus or Othello) it is accompanied by a full conviction of right. In Hamlet there is a painful consciousness that duty is being neglected; in Antony a clear knowledge that the worse of two courses is being pursued; but Richard and Macbeth are the only heroes who do what they themselves recognize to be villainous. It is important to observe that Shakespeare does admit such heroes,[9] and also that he appears to feel, and exerts himself to meet, the difficulty that arises from their

---

[9] Aristotle apparently would exclude them.

admission. The difficulty is that the spectator must desire their defeat and even their destruction; and yet this desire, and the satisfaction of it, are not tragic feelings. Shakespeare gives to Richard therefore a power which excites astonishment, and a courage which extorts admiration. He gives to Macbeth a similar, though less extraordinary, greatness, and adds to it a conscience so terrifying in its warnings and so maddening in its reproaches that the spectacle of inward torment compels a horrified sympathy and awe which balance, at the least, the desire for the hero's ruin.

The tragic hero with Shakespeare, then, need not be 'good', though generally he is 'good' and therefore at once wins sympathy in his error. But it is necessary that he should have so much of greatness that in his error and fall we may be vividly conscious of the possibilities of human nature.[10] Hence, in the first place, a Shakespearean tragedy is never, like some miscalled tragedies, depressing. No one ever closes the book with the feeling that man is a poor mean creature. He may be wretched and he may be awful, but he is not small. His lot may be heart-rending and mysterious, but it is not contemptible. The most confirmed of cynics ceases to be a cynic while he reads these plays. And with this greatness of the tragic hero (which is not always confined to him) is connected, secondly, what I venture to describe as the centre of the tragic impression. This central feeling is the impression of waste. With Shakespeare, at any rate, the pity and fear which are stirred by the tragic story seem to unite with, and even to merge in, a profound sense of sadness and mystery, which is due to this impression of waste. 'What a piece of work is man', we cry; 'so much more beautiful and so much more terrible than we knew! Why should he be so if this beauty and greatness only tortures itself and throws itself away?' We seem to have before us a type of the mystery of the whole world, the tragic fact which extends far beyond the limits of tragedy. Everywhere, from the crushed rocks beneath our feet to the soul of man, we see power, intelligence, life and glory, which astound us and seem to call for our worship. And everywhere we see them perishing, devouring one another and destroying themselves, often with dreadful pain, as though they came into being for no other end.

---

[10] Richard II is perhaps an exception, and I must confess that to me he is scarcely a tragic character, and that, if he is nevertheless a tragic figure, he is so only because his fall from prosperity to adversity is so great.

Tragedy is the typical form of this mystery, because that greatness of soul which it exhibits oppressed, conflicting and destroyed, is the highest existence in our view. It forces the mystery upon us, and it makes us realize so vividly the worth of that which is wasted that we cannot possibly seek comfort in the reflection that all is vanity.

4

In this tragic world, then, where individuals, however great they may be and however decisive their actions may appear, are so evidently not the ultimate power, what is this power? What account can we give of it which will correspond with the imaginative impressions we receive? This will be our final question.

The variety of the answers given to this question shows how difficult it is. And the difficulty has many sources. Most people, even among those who know Shakespeare well and come into real contact with his mind, are inclined to isolate and exaggerate some one aspect of the tragic fact. Some are so much influenced by their own habitual beliefs that they import them more or less into their interpretation of every author who is 'sympathetic' to them. And even where neither of these causes of error appears to operate, another is present from which it is probably impossible wholly to escape. What I mean is this. Any answer we give to the question proposed ought to correspond with, or to represent in terms of the understanding, our imaginative and emotional experience in reading the tragedies. We have, of course, to do our best by study and effort to make this experience true to Shakespeare; but, that done to the best of our ability, the experience is the matter to be interpreted, and the test by which the interpretation must be tried. But it is extremely hard to make out exactly what this experience is, because, in the very effort to make it out, our reflecting mind, full of everyday ideas, is always tending to transform it by the application of these ideas, and so to elicit a result which, instead of representing the fact, conventionalizes it. And the consequence is not only mistaken theories; it is that many a man will declare that he feels in reading a tragedy what he never really felt, while he fails to recognize what he actually did feel. It is not likely that we shall escape all these dangers in our effort to find an answer to the question regarding the tragic world and the ultimate power in it.

It will be agreed, however, first, that this question must not be answered in 'religious' language. For although this or that *dramatis persona* may speak of gods or of God, of evil spirits or of Satan, of heaven and of hell, and although the poet may show us ghosts from another world, these ideas do not materially influence his representation of life, nor are they used to throw light on the mystery of its tragedy. The Elizabethan drama was almost wholly secular; and while Shakespeare was writing he practically confined his view to the world of non-theological observation and thought, so that he represents it substantially in one and the same way whether the period of the story is pre-Christian or Christian.[11] He looked at this 'secular' world most intently and seriously; and he painted it, we cannot but conclude, with entire fidelity, without the wish to enforce an opinion of his own, and, in essentials, without regard to anyone's hopes, fears, or beliefs. His greatness is largely due to this fidelity in a mind of extraordinary power; and if, as a private person, he had a religious faith, his tragic view can hardly have been in contradiction with this faith, but must have been included in it, and supplemented, not abolished, by additional ideas.

Two statements, next, may at once be made regarding the tragic fact as he represents it: one, that it is and remains to us something piteous, fearful and mysterious; the other, that the representation of it does not leave us crushed, rebellious or desperate. These statements will be accepted, I believe, by any reader who is in touch with Shakespeare's mind and can observe his own. Indeed such a reader is rather likely to complain that they are painfully obvious. But if they are true as well as obvious, something follows from them in regard to our present question.

From the first it follows that the ultimate power in the tragic world is not adequately described as a law or order which we can see to be just and benevolent – as, in that sense, a 'moral order': for in that case the spectacle of suffering and waste could not seem to us so fearful and mysterious as it does. And from the second it follows that this ultimate power is not adequately described as a fate, whether malicious and cruel, or blind and indifferent to human happiness and goodness: for in that case the spectacle would leave us desperate or rebellious. Yet one or other of these two ideas will be found to govern

---

[11] I say substantially; but the concluding remarks on *Hamlet* will modify a little the statements above.

most accounts of Shakespeare's tragic view or world. These accounts isolate and exaggerate single aspects, either the aspect of action or that of suffering; either the close and unbroken connection of character, will, deed and catastrophe, which, taken alone, shows the individual simply as sinning against, or failing to conform to, the moral order and drawing his just doom on his own head; or else that pressure of outward forces, that sway of accident, and those blind and agonized struggles, which, taken alone, show him as the mere victim of some power which cares neither for his sins nor for his pain. Such views contradict one another, and no third view can unite them; but the several aspects from whose isolation and exaggeration they spring are both present in the fact, and a view which would be true to the fact and to the whole of our imaginative experience must in some way combine these aspects.

Let us begin, then, with the idea of fatality and glance at some of the impressions which give rise to it, without asking at present whether this idea is their natural or fitting expression. There can be no doubt that they do arise and that they ought to arise. If we do not feel at times that the hero is, in some sense, a doomed man; that he and others drift struggling to destruction like helpless creatures borne on an irresistible flood towards a cataract; that, faulty as they may be, their fault is far from being the sole or sufficient cause of all they suffer; and that the power from which they cannot escape is relentless and immovable, we have failed to receive an essential part of the full tragic effect.

The sources of these impressions are various, and I will refer only to a few. One of them is put into words by Shakespeare himself when he makes the player-king in *Hamlet* say:

Our thoughts are ours, their ends none of our own;

'their ends' are the issues or outcomes of our thoughts, and these, says the speaker, are not our own. The tragic world is a world of action, and action is the translation of thought into reality. We see men and women confidently attempting it. They strike into the existing order of things in pursuance of their ideas. But what they achieve is not what they intended; it is terribly unlike it. They understand nothing, we say to ourselves, of the world on which they operate. They fight blindly in the dark, and the power that works through them makes them the instrument of a design which is not theirs. They act freely, and yet their action binds them hand and foot. And it makes no difference whether they meant well or ill. No one could mean better than Brutus, but he contrives misery for his country and death for himself. No one could mean worse than Iago, and he too is caught in the web he spins for others. Hamlet, recoiling from the rough duty of revenge, is pushed into blood-guiltiness he never dreamed of, and forced at last on the revenge he could not will. His adversary's murders, and no less his adversary's remorse, bring about the opposite of what they sought. Lear follows an old man's whim, half generous, half selfish; and in a moment it looses all the powers of darkness upon him. Othello agonizes over an empty fiction, and, meaning to execute solemn justice, butchers innocence and strangles love. They understand themselves no better than the world about them. Coriolanus thinks that his heart is iron, and it melts like snow before a fire. Lady Macbeth, who thought she could dash out her own child's brains, finds herself hounded to death by the smell of a stranger's blood. Her husband thinks that to gain a crown he would jump the life to come, and finds that the crown has brought him all the horrors of that life. Everywhere, in this tragic world, man's thought, translated into act, is transformed into the opposite of itself. His act, the movement of a few ounces of matter in a moment of time, becomes a monstrous flood which spreads over a kingdom. And whatsoever he dreams of doing, he achieves that which he least dreamed of, his own destruction.

All this makes us feel the blindness and helplessness of man. Yet by itself it would hardly suggest the idea of fate, because it shows man as in some degree, however slight, the cause of his own undoing. But other impressions come to aid it. It is aided by everything which makes us feel that a man is, as we say, terribly unlucky; and of this there is, even in Shakespeare, not a little. Here come in some of the accidents already considered, Juliet's waking from her trance a minute too late. Desdemona's loss of her handkerchief at the only moment when the loss would have mattered, that insignificant delay which cost Cordelia's life. Again, men act, no doubt, in accordance with their characters; but what is it that brings them just the one problem which is fatal to them and would be easy to another, and sometimes brings it to them just when they are least fitted to face it? How is it that Othello comes to be the companion of the one man in the world who is at once able enough, brave enough, and vile enough to ensnare him? By what strange fatality does it happen that Lear has such daughters and Cordelia such sisters? Even character itself contributes to these feelings of fatality. How could men escape, we cry, such vehement propensities as drive Romeo, Antony, Coriolanus, to their doom? And why is it that a man's virtues help to destroy him, and that his weakness or defect is so intertwined with everything that is admirable in him that we can hardly separate them even in imagination?

If we find in Shakespeare's tragedies the source of impressions like these, it is important, on the other hand, to notice what we do *not* find there. We find practically no trace of fatalism in its more primitive, crude and obvious forms. Nothing, again, makes us think of the actions and sufferings of the persons as somehow arbitrarily fixed beforehand without regard to their feelings, thoughts and resolutions. Nor, I believe, are the facts ever so presented that it seems to us as if the supreme power, whatever it may be, had a special spite against a family or an individual. Neither, lastly, do we receive the impression (which, it must be observed, is not purely fatalistic) that a family, owing to some hideous crime or impiety in early days, is doomed in later days to continue a career of portentous calamities and sins. Shakespeare, indeed, does not appear to have taken much interest in heredity, or to have attached much importance to it. (See, however, 'heredity' in the Index.)

What, then, is this 'fate' which the impressions already considered lead us to describe as the ultimate power in the tragic world? It appears to be a mythological expression for the whole system or order, of which the individual characters form an inconsiderable and feeble part; which seems to determine, far more than they, their native dispositions and their circumstances, and, through these, their action; which is so vast and complex that they can scarcely at all understand it or control its workings; and which has a nature so definite and fixed that whatever changes take place in it produce other changes inevitably and without regard to men's desires and regrets. And whether this system or order is best called by the name of fate or no,[12]

---

[12] I have raised no objection to the use of the idea of fate, because it occurs so often both in conversation and in books about Shakespeare's tragedies that I must suppose it to be natural to many readers. Yet I doubt whether it would be so if Greek tragedy had never been written; and I must in candour confess that to me it does not often occur while I am reading, or when I have just read, a tragedy of Shakespeare. Wordsworth's lines,* for example, about

  poor humanity's afflicted will
  Struggling in vain with ruthless destiny

it can hardly be denied that it does appear as the ultimate power in the tragic world, and that it has such characteristics as these. But the name 'fate' may be intended to imply something more – to imply that this order is a blank necessity, totally regardless alike of human weal and of the difference between good and evil or right and wrong. And such an implication many readers would at once reject. They would maintain, on the contrary, that this order shows characteristics of quite another kind from those which made us give it the name of fate, characteristics which certainly should not induce us to forget those others, but which would lead us to describe it as a moral order and its necessity as a moral necessity.

5

Let us turn, then, to this idea. It brings into the light those aspects of the tragic fact which the idea of fate throws into the shade. And the argument which leads to it in its simplest form may be stated briefly thus: 'Whatever may be said of accidents, circumstances and the like, human action is, after all, presented to us as the central fact in tragedy, and also as the main cause of the catastrophe. That necessity which so much impresses us is, after all, chiefly the necessary connection of actions and consequences. For these actions we, without even raising a question on the subject, hold the agents responsible; and the tragedy would disappear for us if we did not. The critical action is, in greater or less degree, wrong or bad. The catastrophe is, in the main, the return of this action on the head of the agent. It is an example of justice; and that order which, present alike within the agents and outside them, infallibly brings it about, is therefore just. The rigour of its justice is terrible, no doubt, for a tragedy is a terrible story; but, in spite of fear and pity, we acquiesce, because our sense of justice is satisfied.'

Now, if this view is to hold good, the 'justice' of which it speaks must be at once distinguished from what is called 'poetic justice'. 'Poetic justice' means that prosperity and adversity are distributed in proportion to the merits of the agents. Such 'poetic justice' is in

---

do not represent the impression I receive; much less do images which compare man to a puny creature helpless in the claws of a bird of prey. The reader should examine himself closely on this matter.

flagrant contradiction with the facts of life, and it is absent from Shakespeare's tragic picture of life; indeed, this very absence is a ground of constant complaint on the part of Dr. Johnson.* Δράσαντι παθεῖν,* 'the doer must suffer' – this we find in Shakespeare. We also find that villainy never remains victorious and prosperous at the last. But an assignment of amounts of happiness and misery, an assignment even of life and death, in proportion to merit, we do not find. No one who thinks of Desdemona and Cordelia; or who remembers that one end awaits Richard III and Brutus, Macbeth and Hamlet; or who asks himself which suffered most, Othello or Iago; will ever accuse Shakespeare of representing the ultimate power as 'poetically' just.

And we must go further. I venture to say that it is a mistake to use at all these terms of justice and merit or desert. And this for two reasons. In the first place, essential as it is to recognize the connection between act and consequence, and natural as it may seem in some cases (*e.g.* Macbeth's) to say that the doer only gets what he deserves, yet in very many cases to say this would be quite unnatural. We might not object to the statement that Lear deserved to suffer for his folly, selfishness and tyranny; but to assert that he deserved to suffer what he did suffer is to do violence not merely to language but to any healthy moral sense. It is, moreover, to obscure the tragic fact that the consequences of action cannot be limited to that which would appear to us to follow 'justly' from them. And, this being so, when we call the order of the tragic world just, we are either using the word in some vague and unexplained sense, or we are going beyond what is shown us of this order, and are appealing to faith.

But, in the second place, the ideas of justice and desert are, it seems to me, in *all* cases – even those of Richard III and of Macbeth and Lady Macbeth – untrue to our imaginative experience. When we are immersed in a tragedy, we feel towards dispositions, actions, and persons such emotions as attraction and repulsion, pity, wonder, fear, horror, perhaps hatred; but we do not *judge*. This is a point of view which emerges only when, in reading a play, we slip, by our own fault or the dramatist's, from the tragic position, or when, in thinking about the play afterwards, we fall back on our everyday legal and moral notions. But tragedy does not belong, any more than religion belongs, to the sphere of these notions; neither does the imaginative attitude in presence of it. While we are in its world we watch what is, seeing that so it happened and must have happened, feeling that it is piteous, dreadful, awful, mysterious, but neither passing sentence on the agents, nor asking whether the behaviour of the ultimate power towards them is just. And, therefore, the use of such language in attempts to render our imaginative experience in terms of the understanding is, to say the least, full of danger.[13]

Let us attempt then to re-state the idea that the ultimate power in the tragic world is a moral order. Let us put aside the ideas of justice and merit, and speak simply of good and evil. Let us understand by these words, primarily, moral good and evil, but also everything else in human beings which we take to be excellent or the reverse. Let us understand the statement that the ultimate power or order is 'moral' to mean that it does not show itself indifferent to good and evil, or equally favourable or unfavourable to both, but shows itself akin to good and alien from evil. And, understanding the statement thus, let us ask what grounds it has in the tragic fact as presented by Shakespeare.

Here, as in dealing with the grounds on which the idea of fate rests, I choose only two or three out of many. And the most important is this. In Shakespearean tragedy the main source of the convulsion which produces suffering and death is never good: good contributes to this convulsion only from its tragic implication with its opposite in one and the same character. The main source, on the contrary, is in every case evil; and, what is more (though this seems to have been little noticed), it is in almost every case evil in the fullest sense, not mere imperfection but plain moral evil. The love of Romeo and Juliet conducts them to death only because of the senseless hatred of their houses. Guilty ambition, seconded by diabolic malice and issuing in murder, opens the action in *Macbeth*. Iago is the main source of the convulsion in *Othello*; Goneril, Regan and Edmund in *King Lear*. Even when this plain moral evil is not the obviously prime source within the play, it lies behind it: the situation with which Hamlet has

---

[13] It is dangerous, I think, in reference to all really good tragedies, but I am dealing here only with Shakespeare's. In not a few Greek tragedies it is almost inevitable that we should think of justice and retribution, not only because the *dramatis personæ* often speak of them, but also because there is something casuistical about the tragic problem itself. The poet treats the story in such a way that the question, Is the hero doing right or wrong? is almost forced upon us. But this is not so with Shakespeare. *Julius Caesar* is probably the only one of his tragedies in which the question suggests itself to us, and this is one of the reasons why that play has something of a classic air. Even here, if we ask the question, we have no doubt at all about the answer.

to deal has been formed by adultery and murder. *Julius Caesar* is the only tragedy in which one is even tempted to find an exception to this rule. And the inference is obvious. If it is chiefly evil that violently disturbs the order of the world, this order cannot be friendly to evil or indifferent between evil and good, any more than a body which is convulsed by poison is friendly to it or indifferent to the distinction between poison and food.

Again, if we confine our attention to the hero, and to those cases where the gross and palpable evil is not in him but elsewhere, we find that the comparatively innocent hero still shows some marked imperfection or defect – irresolution, precipitancy, pride, credulousness, excessive simplicity, excessive susceptibility to sexual emotions, and the like. These defects or imperfections are certainly, in the wide sense of the word, evil, and they contribute decisively to the conflict and catastrophe. And the inference is again obvious. The ultimate power which shows itself disturbed by this evil and reacts against it, must have a nature alien to it. Indeed its reaction is so vehement and 'relentless' that it would seem to be bent on nothing short of good in perfection, and to be ruthless in its demand for it.

To this must be added another fact, or another aspect of the same fact. Evil exhibits itself everywhere as something negative, barren, weakening, destructive, a principle of death. It isolates, disunites, and tends to annihilate not only its opposite but itself. That which keeps the evil man[14] prosperous, makes him succeed, even permits him to exist, is the good in him (I do not mean only the obviously 'moral' good). When the evil in him masters the good and has its way, it destroys other people through him, but it also destroys *him*. At the close of the struggle he has vanished, and has left behind him nothing that can stand. What remains is a family, a city, a country, exhausted, pale and feeble, but alive through the principle of good which animates it; and, within it, individuals who, if they have not the brilliance or greatness of the tragic character, still have won our respect and confidence. And the inference would seem clear. If existence in an order depends on good, and if the presence of evil is hostile to such existence, the inner being or soul of this order must be akin to good.

---

[14] It is most essential to remember that an evil man is much more than the evil in him. I may add that in this paragraph I have, for the sake of clearness, considered evil in its most pronounced form; but what is said would apply, *mutatis mutandis*, to evil as imperfection, etc.

These are aspects of the tragic world at least as clearly marked as those which, taken alone, suggest the idea of fate. And the idea which they in their turn, when taken alone, may suggest, is that of an order which does not indeed award 'poetic justice', but which reacts through the necessity of its own 'moral' nature both against attacks made upon it and against failure to conform to it. Tragedy, on this view, is the exhibition of that convulsive reaction; and the fact that the spectacle does not leave us rebellious or desperate is due to a more or less distinct perception that the tragic suffering and death arise from collision, not with a fate or blank power, but with a moral power, a power akin to all that we admire and revere in the characters themselves. This perception produces something like a feeling of acquiescence in the catastrophe, though it neither leads us to pass judgment on the characters nor diminishes the pity, the fear, and the sense of waste, which their struggle, suffering and fall evoke. And, finally, this view seems quite able to do justice to those aspects of the tragic fact which give rise to the idea of fate. They would appear as various expressions of the fact that the moral order acts not capriciously or like a human being, but from the necessity of its nature, or, if we prefer the phrase, by general laws – a necessity or law which of course knows no exceptions and is as 'ruthless' as fate.

It is impossible to deny to this view a large measure of truth. And yet without some amendment it can hardly satisfy. For it does not include the whole of the facts, and therefore does not wholly correspond with the impressions they produce. Let it be granted that the system or order which shows itself omnipotent against individuals is, in the sense explained, moral. Still – at any rate for the eye of sight – the evil against which it asserts itself, and the persons whom this evil inhabits, are not really something outside the order, so that they can attack it or fail to conform to it; they are within it and a part of it. It itself produces them – produces Iago as well as Desdemona, Iago's cruelty as well as Iago's courage. It is not poisoned, it poisons itself. Doubtless it shows by its violent reaction that the poison *is* poison, and that its health lies in good. But one significant fact cannot remove another, and the spectacle we witness scarcely warrants the assertion that the order is responsible for the good in Desdemona, but Iago for the evil in Iago. If we make this assertion we make it on grounds other than the facts as presented in Shakespeare's tragedies.

Nor does the idea of a moral order asserting itself against attack or want of conformity answer in full to our feelings regarding the tragic character. We do not think of Hamlet merely as failing to meet its demand, of Antony as merely sinning against it, or even of Macbeth as simply attacking it. What we feel corresponds quite as much to the idea that they are *its* parts, expressions, products; that in their defect or evil *it* is untrue to its soul of goodness, and falls into conflict and collision with itself; that, in making them suffer and waste themselves, *it* suffers and wastes itself; and that when, to save its life and regain peace from this intestinal struggle, it casts them out, it has lost a part of its own substance – a part more dangerous and unquiet, but far more valuable and nearer to its heart, than that which remains – a Fortinbras, a Malcolm, an Octavius. There is no tragedy in its expulsion of evil: the tragedy is that this involves the waste of good.

Thus we are left at last with an idea showing two sides or aspects which we can neither separate nor reconcile. The whole or order against which the individual part shows itself powerless seems to be animated by a passion for perfection: we cannot otherwise explain its behaviour towards evil. Yet it appears to engender this evil within itself, and in its effort to overcome and expel it it is agonized with pain, and driven to mutilate its own substance and to lose not only evil but priceless good. That this idea, though very different from the idea of a blank fate, is no solution of the riddle of life is obvious; but why should we expect it to be such a solution? Shakespeare was not attempting to justify the ways of God to men, or to show the universe as a Divine Comedy. He was writing tragedy, and tragedy would not be tragedy if it were not a painful mystery. Nor can he be said even to point distinctly, like some writers of tragedy, in any direction where a solution might lie. We find a few references to gods or God, to the influence of the stars, to another life: some of them certainly, all of them perhaps, merely dramatic – appropriate to the person from whose lips they fall. A ghost comes from Purgatory to impart a secret out of the reach of its hearer – who presently meditates on the question whether the sleep of death is dreamless. Accidents once or twice remind us strangely of the words, 'There's a divinity that shapes our ends.' More important are other impressions. Sometimes from the very furnace of affliction a conviction seems borne to us that somehow, if we could see it, this agony counts as nothing against the heroism and love which appear in it and thrill our hearts. Sometimes we are driven to cry out that these mighty or heavenly spirits who perish are too great for the little space in which they move, and that they vanish not into nothingness but into freedom. Sometimes from these sources and from others comes a presentiment, formless but haunting and even profound, that all the fury of conflict, with its waste and woe, is less than half the truth, even an illusion, 'such stuff as dreams are made on'. But these faint and scattered intimations that the tragic world, being but a fragment of a whole beyond our vision, must needs be a contradiction and no ultimate truth, avail nothing to interpret the mystery. We remain confronted with the inexplicable fact, or the no less inexplicable appearance, of a world travailing for perfection, but bringing to birth, together with glorious good, an evil which it is able to overcome only by self-torture and self-waste. And this fact or appearance is tragedy.[15]

---

[15] [Partly in order not to anticipate later passages, I abstained from treating fully here the question why we feel, at the death of the tragic hero, not only pain but also reconciliation and sometimes even exultation. As I cannot at present make good this defect, I would ask the reader to refer to the word *Reconciliation* in the Index. See also, in *Oxford Lectures on Poetry, Hegel's Theory of Tragedy*, especially pp. 90, 91.]

LECTURE II

CONSTRUCTION IN SHAKESPEARE'S TRAGEDIES

Having discussed the substance of a Shakespearean tragedy, we should naturally go on to examine the form. And under this head many things might be included; for example, Shakespeare's methods of characterization, his language, his versification, the construction of his plots. I intend, however, to speak only of the last of these subjects, which has been somewhat neglected;[1] and, as construction is a more or less technical matter, I shall add some general remarks on Shakespeare as an artist.

1

As a Shakespearean tragedy represents a conflict which terminates in a catastrophe, any such tragedy may roughly be divided into three parts. The first of these sets forth or expounds the situation,[2] or state of affairs, out of which the conflict arises; and it may, therefore, be called the Exposition. The second deals with the definite beginning, the growth and the vicissitudes of the conflict. It forms accordingly the bulk of the play, comprising the Second, Third and Fourth Acts, and usually a part of the First and a part of the Fifth. The final section of the tragedy shows the issue of the conflict in a catastrophe.[3]

---

[1] The famous critics of the Romantic Revival seem to have paid very little attention to this subject. Mr. R. G. Moulton* has written an interesting book on *Shakespeare as a Dramatic Artist* (1885). In parts of my analysis I am much indebted to Gustav Freytag's* *Technik des Dramas*, a book which deserves to be much better known than it appears to be to Englishmen interested in the drama. I may add, for the benefit of classical scholars, that Freytag has a chapter on Sophocles. The reader of his book will easily distinguish, if he cares to, the places where I follow Freytag, those where I differ from him, and those where I write in independence of him. I may add that in speaking of construction I have thought it best to assume in my hearers no previous knowledge of the subject; that I have not attempted to discuss how much of what is said of Shakespeare would apply also to other dramatists; and that I have illustrated from the tragedies generally, not only from the chosen four.

[2] This word throughout the lecture bears the sense it has here, which, of course, is not its usual dramatic sense.

[3] In the same way a comedy will consist of three parts, showing the 'situation', the 'complication' or 'entanglement', and the *dénouement* or 'solution'.

27

The application of this scheme of division is naturally more or less arbitrary. The first part glides into the second, and the second into the third, and there may often be difficulty in drawing the lines between them. But it is still harder to divide spring from summer, and summer from autumn; and yet spring is spring, and summer summer.

The main business of the Exposition, which we will consider first, is to introduce us into a little world of persons; to show us their positions in life, their circumstances, their relations to one another, and perhaps something of their characters; and to leave us keenly interested in the question what will come out of this condition of things. We are left thus expectant, not merely because some of the persons interest us at once, but also because their situation in regard to one another points to difficulties in the future. This situation is not one of conflict,[4] but it threatens conflict. For example, we see first the hatred of the Montagues and Capulets; and then we see Romeo ready to fall violently in love; and then we hear talk of a marriage between Juliet and Paris; but the exposition is not complete, and the conflict has not definitely begun to arise, till, in the last scene of the First Act, Romeo the Montague sees Juliet the Capulet and becomes her slave.

The dramatist's chief difficulty in the exposition is obvious, and it is illustrated clearly enough in the plays of unpractised writers; for example, in *Remorse*,* and even in *The Cenci*.* He has to impart to the audience a quantity of information about matters of which they generally know nothing and never know all that is necessary for his purpose.[5] But the process of merely acquiring information is unpleasant, and the direct imparting of it is undramatic. Unless he uses a prologue, therefore, he must conceal from his auditors the fact that they are being informed, and must tell them what he wants them to know by means which are interesting on their own account. These means, with Shakespeare, are not only speeches but actions and events. From the very beginning of the play, though the conflict has not arisen, things are happening and being done which in some

---

[4] It is possible, of course, to open the tragedy with the conflict already begun, but Shakespeare never does so.

[5] When the subject comes from English history, and especially when the play forms one of a series, some knowledge may be assumed. So in *Richard III*. Even in *Richard II* not a little knowledge seems to be assumed, and this fact points to the existence of a popular play on the earlier part of Richard's reign. Such a play exists,* though it is not clear that it is a genuine Elizabethan work. See the *Jahrbuch d. deutschen Sh.-Gesellschaft* for 1899.

degree arrest, startle and excite; and in a few scenes we have mastered the situation of affairs without perceiving the dramatist's designs upon us. Not that this is always so with Shakespeare. In the opening scene of his early *Comedy of Errors*, and in the opening speech of *Richard III*, we feel that the speakers are addressing us; and in the second scene of the *Tempest* (for Shakespeare grew at last rather negligent of technique) the purpose of Prospero's long explanation to Miranda is palpable. But in general Shakespeare's expositions are masterpieces.[6]

His usual plan in tragedy is to begin with a short scene, or part of a scene, either full of life and stir, or in some other way arresting. Then, having secured a hearing, he proceeds to conversations at a lower pitch, accompanied by little action but conveying much information. For example, *Romeo and Juliet* opens with a street-fight, *Julius Caesar* and *Coriolanus* with a crowd in commotion; and when this excitement has had its effect on the audience, there follow quiet speeches, in which the cause of the excitement, and so a great part of the situation, are disclosed. In *Hamlet* and *Macbeth* this scheme is employed with great boldness. In *Hamlet* the first appearance of the Ghost occurs at the fortieth line, and with such effect that Shakespeare can afford to introduce at once a conversation which explains part of the state of affairs at Elsinore; and the second appearance, having again increased the tension, is followed by a long scene, which contains no action but introduces almost all the *dramatis personæ* and adds the information left wanting. The opening of *Macbeth* is even more remarkable, for there is probably no parallel to its first scene, where the senses and imagination are assaulted by a storm of thunder and supernatural alarm. This scene is only eleven lines long, but its influence is so great that the next can safely be occupied with a mere report of Macbeth's battles – a narrative which would have won much less attention if it had opened the play.

When Shakespeare begins his exposition thus he generally at first makes people talk about the hero, but keeps the hero himself for some time out of sight, so that we await his entrance with curiosity, and sometimes with anxiety. On the other hand, if the plays open with a

---

[6] This is one of several reasons why many people enjoy reading him, who, on the whole, dislike reading plays. A main cause of this very general dislike is that the reader has not a lively enough imagination to carry him with pleasure through the exposition, though in the theatre, where his imagination is helped, he would experience little difficulty.

quiet conversation, this is usually brief, and then at once the hero enters and takes action of some decided kind. Nothing, for example, can be less like the beginning of *Macbeth* than that of *King Lear*. The tone is pitched so low that the conversation between Kent, Gloster, and Edmund is written in prose. But at the thirty-fourth line it is broken off by the entrance of Lear and his court, and without delay the King proceeds to his fatal division of the kingdom.

This tragedy illustrates another practice of Shakespeare's. *King Lear* has a secondary plot, that which concerns Gloster and his two sons. To make the beginning of this plot quite clear, and to mark it off from the main action, Shakespeare gives it a separate exposition. The great scene of the division of Britain and the rejection of Cordelia and Kent is followed by the second scene, in which Gloster and his two sons appear alone, and the beginning of Edmund's design is disclosed. In *Hamlet*, though the plot is single, there is a little group of characters possessing a certain independent interest – Polonius, his son, and his daughter; and so the third scene is devoted wholly to them. And again, in *Othello*, since Roderigo is to occupy a peculiar position almost throughout the action, he is introduced at once, alone with Iago, and his position is explained before the other characters are allowed to appear.

But why should Iago open the play? Or, if this seems too presumptuous a question, let us put it in the form, What is the effect of his opening the play? Is it that we receive at the very outset a strong impression of the force which is to prove fatal to the hero's happiness, so that, when we see the hero himself, the shadow of fate already rests upon him? And an effect of this kind is to be noticed in other tragedies. We are made conscious at once of some power which is to influence the whole action to the hero's undoing. In *Macbeth* we see and hear the Witches, in *Hamlet* the Ghost. In the first scene of *Julius Caesar* and of *Coriolanus* those qualities of the crowd are vividly shown which render hopeless the enterprise of the one hero and wreck the ambition of the other. It is the same with the hatred between the rival houses in *Romeo and Juliet*, and with Antony's infatuated passion. We realize them at the end of the first page, and are almost ready to regard the hero as doomed. Often, again, at one or more points during the exposition this feeling is reinforced by some expression that has an ominous effect. The first words we hear from Macbeth, 'So foul and fair a day I have not seen', echo, though he knows it not, the last words we heard from the Witches, 'Fair is foul, and foul is fair'. Romeo, on his way with his friends to the banquet, where he is to see Juliet for the first time, tells Mercutio that he has had a dream. What the dream was we never learn, for Mercutio does not care to know, and breaks into his speech about Queen Mab; but we can guess its nature from Romeo's last speech in the scene:

> My mind misgives
> Some consequence yet hanging in the stars
> Shall bitterly begin his fearful date
> With this night's revels.

When Brabantio, forced to acquiesce in his daughter's stolen marriage, turns, as he leaves the council-chamber, to Othello, with the warning,

> Look to her, Moor, if thou hast eyes to see;
> She has deceived her father, and may thee,

this warning, and no less Othello's answer, 'My life upon her faith', make our hearts sink. The whole of the coming story seems to be prefigured in Antony's muttered words (I.ii.120):

> These strong Egyptian fetters I must break,
> Or lose myself in dotage;

and, again, in Hamlet's weary sigh, following so soon on the passion-ate resolution stirred by the message of the Ghost:

> The time is out of joint. Oh cursed spite,
> That ever I was born to set it right.

These words occur at a point (the end of the First Act) which may be held to fall either within the exposition or beyond it. I should take the former view, though such questions, as we saw at starting, can hardly be decided with certainty. The dimensions of this first section of a tragedy depend on a variety of causes, of which the chief seems to be the comparative simplicity or complexity of the situation from which the conflict arises. Where this is simple the exposition is short, as in *Julius Caesar* and *Macbeth*. Where it is complicated the exposition requires more space, as in *Romeo and Juliet*, *Hamlet* and *King Lear*. Its completion is generally marked in the mind of the reader by a feeling that the action it contains is for the moment complete but has left a problem. The lovers have met, but their families are at deadly enmity; the hero seems at the height of success, but has admitted the thought of murdering his sovereign; the old king has divided his kingdom between two hypocritical daughters, and has rejected his true child; the hero has acknowledged a sacred duty of revenge, but is weary of life: and we ask, What will come of this? Sometimes, I may add, a certain time is supposed to elapse before the events which answer our question make their appearance and the conflict begins; in *King Lear*, for instance, about a fortnight; in *Hamlet* about two months.

2

We come now to the conflict itself. And here one or two preliminary remarks are necessary. In the first place, it must be remembered that our point of view in examining the construction of a play will not always coincide with that which we occupy in thinking of its whole dramatic effect. For example, that struggle in the hero's soul which sometimes accompanies the outward struggle is of the highest importance for the total effect of a tragedy; but it is not always necessary or desirable to consider it when the question is merely one of construction. And this is natural. The play is meant primarily for the theatre; and theatrically the outward conflict, with its influence on the fortunes of the hero, is the aspect which first catches, if it does not engross, attention. For the average playgoer of every period the main interest of *Hamlet* has probably lain in the vicissitudes of his long duel with the King; and the question, one may almost say, has been which will first kill the other. And so, from the point of view of construction, the fact that Hamlet spares the King when he finds him praying, is, from its effect on the hero's fortunes, of great moment; but the cause of the fact, which lies within Hamlet's character, is not so.

In the second place we must be prepared to find that, as the plays vary so much, no single way of regarding the conflict will answer precisely to the construction of all; that it sometimes appears possible to look at the construction of a tragedy in two quite different ways, and that it is material to find the best of the two; and that thus, in any given instance, it is necessary first to define the opposing sides in the conflict. I will give one or two examples. In some tragedies, as we saw in our first lecture, the opposing forces can, for practical purposes, be identified with opposing persons or groups. So it is in *Romeo and*

Juliet and *Macbeth*. But it is not always so. The love of Othello may be said to contend with another force, as the love of Romeo does; but Othello cannot be said to contend with Iago as Romeo contends with the representatives of the hatred of the houses, or as Macbeth contends with Malcolm and Macduff. Again, in *Macbeth* the hero, however much influenced by others, supplies the main driving power of the action; but in *King Lear* he does not. Possibly, therefore, the conflict, and with it the construction, may best be regarded from different points of view in these two plays, in spite of the fact that the hero is the central figure in each. But if we do not observe this we shall attempt to find the same scheme in both, and shall either be driven to some unnatural view or to a sceptical despair of perceiving any principle of construction at all.

With these warnings, I turn to the question whether we can trace any distinct method or methods by which Shakespeare represents the rise and development of the conflict.

(1) One at least is obvious, and indeed it is followed not merely during the conflict but from beginning to end of the play. There are, of course, in the action certain places where the tension in the minds of the audience becomes extreme. We shall consider these presently. But, in addition, there is, all through the tragedy, a constant alternation of rises and falls in this tension or in the emotional pitch of the work, a regular sequence of more exciting and less exciting sections. Some kind of variation of pitch is to be found, of course, in all drama, for it rests on the elementary facts that relief must be given after emotional strain, and that contrast is required to bring out the full force of an effect. But a good drama of our own time shows nothing approaching to the *regularity* with which in the plays of Shakespeare and of his contemporaries the principle is applied. And the main cause of this difference lies simply in a change of theatrical arrangements. In Shakespeare's theatre, as there was no scenery, scene followed scene with scarcely any pause; and so the readiest, though not the only, way to vary the emotional pitch was to interpose a whole scene where the tension was low between scenes where it was high. In our theatres there is a great deal of scenery, which takes a long time to set and change; and therefore the number of scenes is small, and the variations of tension have to be provided within the scenes, and still more by the pauses between them. With Shakespeare there are, of course, in any long scene variations of tension, but the scenes are

numerous and, compared with ours, usually short, and variety is given principally by their difference in pitch.

It may further be observed that, in a portion of the play which is relatively unexciting, the scenes of lower tension may be as long as those of higher; while in a portion of the play which is specially exciting the scenes of low tension are shorter, often much shorter, than the others. The reader may verify this statement by comparing the First or the Fourth Act in most of the tragedies with the Third; for, speaking very roughly, we may say that the First and Fourth are relatively quiet acts, the Third highly critical. A good example is the Third Act of *King Lear*, where the scenes of high tension (II., iv., vi.) are respectively 95, 186 and 122 lines in length, while those of low tension (I., iii., v.) are respectively 55, 26 and 26 lines long. Scene vii., the last of the Act, is, I may add, a very exciting scene, though it follows scene vi., and therefore the tone of scene vi. is greatly lowered during its final thirty lines.

(2) If we turn now from the differences of tension to the sequence of events within the conflict, we shall find the principle of alteration at work again in another and a quite independent way. Let us for the sake of brevity call the two sides in the conflict A and B. Now, usually, as we shall see presently, through a considerable part of the play, perhaps the first half, the cause of A is, on the whole, advancing; and through the remaining part it is retiring, while that of B advances in turn. But, underlying this broad movement, all through the conflict we shall find a regular alternation of smaller advances and retirals; first A seeming to win some ground, and then the counter-action of B being shown. And since we always more or less decidedly prefer A to B or B to A, the result of this oscillating movement is a constant alternation of hope and fear, or rather of a mixed state predominantly hopeful and a mixed state predominantly apprehensive. An example will make the point clear. In *Hamlet* the conflict begins with the hero's feigning to be insane from disappointment in love, and we are shown his immediate success in convincing Polonius. Let us call this an advance of A. The next scene shows the King's great uneasiness about Hamlet's melancholy, and his scepticism as to Polonius's explanation of its cause: advance of B. Hamlet completely baffles Rosencrantz and Guildenstern, who have been sent to discover his secret, and he arranges for the test of the play-scene: advance of A. But immediately before the play-scene his soliloquy on suicide fills us with misgiving;

and his words to Ophelia, overheard, so convince the King that love is *not* the cause of his nephew's strange behaviour, that he determines to get rid of him by sending him to England: advance of B. The play-scene proves a complete success: decided advance of A. Directly after it Hamlet spares the King at prayer, and in an interview with his mother unwittingly kills Polonius, and so gives his enemy a perfect excuse for sending him away (to be executed): decided advance of B. I need not pursue the illustration further. This oscillating movement can be traced without difficulty in any of the tragedies, though less distinctly in one or two of the earliest.

(3) Though this movement continues right up to the catastrophe, its effect does not disguise that much broader effect to which I have already alluded, and which we have now to study. In all the tragedies, though more clearly in some than in others, one side is distinctly felt to be on the whole advancing up to a certain point in the conflict, and then to be on the whole declining before the reaction of the other. There is therefore felt to be a critical point in the action, which proves also to be a turning point. It is critical sometimes in the sense that, until it is reached, the conflict is not, so to speak, clenched; one of the two sets of forces might subside, or a reconciliation might somehow be effected; while, as soon as it is reached, we feel this can no longer be. It is critical also because the advancing force has apparently asserted itself victoriously, gaining, if not all it could wish, still a very substantial advantage; whereas really it is on the point of turning downward towards its fall. This Crisis, as a rule, comes somewhere near the middle of the play; and where it is well marked it has the effect, as to construction, of dividing the play into five parts instead of three; these parts showing (1) a situation not yet one of conflict, (2) the rise and development of the conflict, in which A or B advances on the whole till it reaches (3) the Crisis, on which follows (4) the decline of A or B towards (5) the Catastrophe. And it will be seen that the fourth and fifth parts repeat, though with a reversal of direction as regards A or B, the movement of the second and third, working towards the catastrophe as the second and third worked towards the crisis.

In developing, illustrating and qualifying this statement, it will be best to begin with the tragedies in which the movement is most clear and simple. These are *Julius Caesar* and *Macbeth*. In the former the fortunes of the conspiracy rise with vicissitudes up to the crisis of the assassination (III.i.); they then sink with vicissitudes to the catastrophe, where Brutus and Cassius perish. In the latter, Macbeth, hurrying, in spite of much inward resistance, to the murder of Duncan, attains the crown, the upward movement being extraordinarily rapid, and the crisis arriving early: his cause then turns slowly downward, and soon hastens to ruin. In both these tragedies the simplicity of the constructional effect, it should be noticed, depends in part on the fact that the contending forces may quite naturally be identified with certain persons, and partly again on the fact that the defeat of one side is the victory of the other. Octavius and Antony, Malcolm and Macduff, are left standing over the bodies of their foes.

This is not so in *Romeo and Juliet* and *Hamlet*, because here, although the hero perishes, the side opposed to him, being the more faulty or evil, cannot be allowed to triumph when he falls. Otherwise the type of construction is the same. The fortunes of Romeo and Juliet rise and culminate in their marriage (II.vi), and then begin to decline before the opposition of their houses, which, aided by accidents, produces a catastrophe, but is thereupon converted into a remorseful reconciliation. Hamlet's cause reaches its zenith in the success of the play-scene (III.ii). Thereafter the reaction makes way, and he perishes through the plot of the King and Laertes. But they are not allowed to survive their success.

The construction in the remaining Roman plays follows the same plan, but in both plays (as in *Richard II* and *Richard III*) it suffers from the intractable nature of the historical material, and is also influenced by other causes. In *Coriolanus* the hero reaches the topmost point of success when he is named consul (II.iii), and the rest of the play shows his decline and fall; but in this decline he attains again for a time extraordinary power, and triumphs, in a sense, over his original adversary, though he succumbs to another. In *Antony and Cleopatra* the advance of the hero's cause depends on his freeing himself from the heroine, and he appears to have succeeded when he becomes reconciled to Octavius and marries Octavia (III.ii); but he returns to Egypt and is gradually driven to his death which involves that of the heroine.

There remain two of the greatest of the tragedies, and in both of them a certain difficulty will be felt. *King Lear* alone among these plays has a distinct double action. Besides this, it is impossible, I think, from the point of view of construction, to regard the hero as the leading figure. If we attempt to do so, we must either find the crisis in the First Act (for after it Lear's course is downward), and this is absurd, or else we must say that the usual movement is present but its direction is reversed, the hero's cause first sinking to the lowest point (in the Storm-scenes) and then rising again. But this also will not do; for though his fortunes may be said to rise again for a time, they rise only to fall once more to a catastrophe. The truth is, that after the First Act, which is really filled by the exposition, Lear suffers but hardly initiates action at all; and the right way to look at the matter, *from the point of view of construction*, is to regard Goneril, Regan and Edmund as the leading characters. It is they who, in the conflict, initiate action. Their fortune mounts to the crisis, where the old King is driven out into the storm and loses his reason, and where Gloster is blinded and expelled from his home (III.vi. and vii.). Then the counter-action begins to gather force, and their cause to decline; and, although they win the battle, they are involved in the catastrophe which they bring on Cordelia and Lear. Thus, we may still find in *King Lear* the usual scheme of an ascending and a descending movement of one side in the conflict.

The case of *Othello* is more peculiar. In its whole constructional effect *Othello* differs from the other tragedies, and the cause of this difference is not hard to find, and will be mentioned presently. But how, after it is found, are we to define the principle of the construction? On the one hand the usual method seems to show itself. Othello's fortune certainly advances in the early part of the play, and it may be considered to reach its topmost point in the exquisite joy of his reunion with Desdemona in Cyprus; while soon afterwards it begins to turn, and then falls to the catastrophe. But the topmost point thus comes very early (II.i.), and, moreover, is but faintly marked; indeed, it is scarcely felt as a crisis at all. And, what is still more significant, though reached by conflict, it is not reached by conflict with the force which afterwards destroys it. Iago, in the early scenes, is indeed shown to cherish a design against Othello, but it is not Iago against whom he has at first to assert himself, but Brabantio; and Iago does not even begin to poison his mind until the third scene of the Third Act.

Can we then, on the other hand, following the precedent of *King Lear*, and remembering the probable chronological juxtaposition of the two plays, regard Iago as the leading figure from the point of view of construction? This might at first seem the right view; for it is the case that *Othello* resembles *King Lear* in having a hero more acted upon than acting, or rather a hero driven to act by being acted upon. But then, if Iago is taken as the leading figure, the usual mode of construction is plainly abandoned, for there will nowhere be a crisis followed by a descending movement. Iago's cause advances, at first slowly and quietly, then rapidly, but it does nothing but advance until the catastrophe swallows his dupe and him together. And this way of regarding the action does positive violence, I think, to our natural impressions of the earlier part of the play.

I think, therefore, that the usual scheme is so far followed that the drama represents first the rise of the hero, and then his fall. But, however this question may be decided, one striking peculiarity remains, and is the cause of the unique effect of *Othello*. In the first half of the play the main conflict is merely incubating; then it bursts into life, and goes storming, without intermission or change of direction, to its close. Now, in this peculiarity *Othello* is quite unlike the other tragedies; and in the consequent effect, which is that the second half of the drama is immeasurably more exciting than the first, it is approached only by *Antony and Cleopatra*. I shall therefore reserve it for separate consideration, though in proceeding to speak further of Shakespeare's treatment of the tragic conflict I shall have to mention some devices which are used in *Othello* as well as in the other tragedies.

3

Shakespeare's general plan, we have seen, is to show one set of forces advancing, in secret or open opposition to the other, to some decisive success, and then driven downward to defeat by the reaction it provokes. And the advantages of this plan, as seen in such a typical instance as *Julius Caesar*, are manifest. It conveys the movement of the conflict to the mind with great clearness and force. It helps to produce the impression that in his decline and fall the doer's act is returning on his own head. And, finally, as used by Shakespeare, it makes the first half of the play intensely interesting and dramatic. Action which effects a striking change in an existing situation is naturally watched with keen interest; and this we find in some of these tragedies. And the spectacle, which others exhibit, of a purpose forming itself and, in spite of outward obstacles and often of inward resistance, forcing its way onward to a happy consummation or a terrible deed, not only gives scope to that psychological subtlety in which Shakespeare is scarcely rivalled, but is also dramatic in the highest degree.

But when the crisis has been reached there come difficulties and dangers, which, if we put Shakespeare for the moment out of mind, are easily seen. An immediate and crushing counter-action would, no doubt, sustain the interest, but it would precipitate the catastrophe, and leave a feeling that there has been too long a preparation for a final effect so brief. What seems necessary is a momentary pause, followed by a counter-action which mounts at first slowly, and afterwards, as it gathers force, with quickening speed. And yet the result of this arrangement, it would seem, must be, for a time, a decided slackening of tension. Nor is this the only difficulty. The persons who represent the counter-action and now take the lead, are likely to be comparatively unfamiliar, and therefore unwelcome, to the audience; and, even if familiar, they are almost sure to be at first, if not permanently, less interesting than those who figured in the ascending movement, and on whom attention has been fixed. Possibly, too, their necessary prominence may crowd the hero into the background. Hence the point of danger in this method of construction seems to lie in that section of the play which follows the crisis and has not yet approached the catastrophe. And this section will usually comprise the Fourth Act, together, in some cases, with a part of the Third and a part of the Fifth.

Shakespeare was so masterly a playwright, and had so wonderful a power of giving life to unpromising subjects, that to a large extent he was able to surmount this difficulty. But illustrations of it are easily to be found in his tragedies, and it is not always surmounted. In almost all of them we are conscious of that momentary pause in the action, though, as we shall see, it does not generally occur *immediately* after the crisis. Sometimes he allows himself to be driven to keep the hero off the stage for a long time while the counter-action is rising; Macbeth, Hamlet and Coriolanus during about 450 lines, Lear for nearly 500, Romeo for about 550 (it matters less here, because Juliet is quite as important as Romeo). How can a drama in which this happens compete, in its latter part, with *Othello*? And again, how can deliberations between Octavius, Antony and Lepidus, between Malcolm and Macduff, between the Capulets, between Laertes and the King, keep us at the pitch, I do not say of the crisis, but even of the action which led up to it? Good critics – writers who have criticized Shakespeare's dramas from within, instead of applying to them some standard ready-made by themselves or derived from dramas and a theatre of quite other kinds than his – have held that some of his greatest tragedies fall off in the Fourth Act, and that one or two never wholly recover themselves. And I believe most readers would find, if they examined their impressions, that to their minds *Julius Caesar, Hamlet, King Lear* and *Macbeth* have all a tendency to 'drag' in this section of the play, and that the first and perhaps also the last of these four fail even in the catastrophe to reach the height of the greatest scenes that have preceded the Fourth Act. I will not ask how far these impressions are justified. The difficulties in question will become clearer and will gain in interest if we look rather at the means which have been employed to meet them, and which certainly have in part, at least, overcome them.

(*a*) The first of these is always strikingly effective, sometimes marvellously so. The crisis in which the ascending force reaches its zenith is followed quickly, or even without the slightest pause, by a reverse or counter-blow not less emphatic and in some cases even more exciting. And the effect is to make us feel a sudden and tragic change in the direction of the movement, which, after ascending more or less gradually, now turns sharply downward. To the assassination of Caesar (III.i.) succeeds the scene in the Forum (III.ii.), where Antony carries the people away in a storm of sympathy with the dead man and of fury against the conspirators. We have hardly realized their victory before we are forced to anticipate their ultimate defeat and to take the liveliest interest in their chief antagonist. In *Hamlet* the thrilling success of the play-scene (III.ii.) is met and undone at once by the counter-stroke of Hamlet's failure to take vengeance (III.iii.) and his misfortune in killing Polonius (III.iv.). Coriolanus has no sooner gained the consulship than he is excited to frenzy by the tribunes and driven into exile. On the marriage of Romeo follows immediately the brawl which leads to Mercutio's death and the banishment of the hero (II.vi. and III.i.). In all of these instances excepting that of *Hamlet* the scene of the counter-stroke is at least as exciting as that of the crisis, perhaps more so. Most people, if asked to mention the scene that occupies the *centre* of the action in *Julius Caesar* and in *Coriolanus*, would mention the scenes of Antony's speech and Coriolanus' banishment. Thus that apparently necessary pause in the action does not, in any of these dramas, come directly after the crisis. It is deferred; and in several cases it is by various devices deferred for some little time; *e.g.* in *Romeo and Juliet* till the hero has left Verona, and Juliet is told that her marriage with Paris is to take place 'next Thursday morn' (end of Act III.); in *Macbeth* till the murder of Duncan has been followed by that of Banquo, and this by the banquet-scene. Hence the point where this pause occurs is very rarely reached before the end of the Third Act.

(*b*) Either at this point, or in the scene of the counter-stroke which precedes it, we sometimes find a peculiar effect. We are reminded of the state of affairs in which the conflict began. The opening of *Julius Caesar* warned us that, among a people so unstable and so easily led this way or that, the enterprise of Brutus is hopeless; the days of the Republic are done. In the scene of Antony's speech we see this same people again. At the beginning of *Antony and Cleopatra* the hero is about to leave Cleopatra for Rome. Where the play takes, as it were, a fresh start after the crisis, he leaves Octavia for Egypt. In *Hamlet*, when the counter-stroke succeeds to the crisis, the Ghost, who had appeared in the opening scenes, reappears. Macbeth's action in the first part of the tragedy followed on the prediction of the Witches who promised him the throne. When the action moves forward again after the banquet-scene the Witches appear once more, and make those fresh promises which again drive him forward. This repetition of a first effect produces a fateful feeling. It generally also stimulates expectation as to the new movement about to begin. In *Macbeth* the scene is, in addition, of the greatest consequence from the purely theatrical point of view.

(*c*) It has yet another function. It shows, in Macbeth's furious irritability and purposeless savagery, the internal reaction which accompanies the outward decline of his fortunes. And in other plays also the exhibition of such inner changes forms a means by which interest is sustained in this difficult section of a tragedy. There is no point in *Hamlet* where we feel more hopeless than that where the hero, having missed his chance, moralizes over his irresolution and determines to cherish now only thoughts of blood, and then departs without an effort for England. One purpose, again, of the quarrel-scene between Brutus and Cassius (IV.iii.), as also of the appearance of Caesar's ghost just afterwards, is to indicate the inward changes. Otherwise the introduction of this famous and wonderful scene can hardly be defended on strictly dramatic grounds. No one would consent to part with it, and it is invaluable in sustaining interest during the progress of the reaction, but it is an episode, the removal of which would not affect the actual sequence of events (unless we may hold that, but for the emotion caused by the quarrel and reconciliation, Cassius would not have allowed Brutus to overcome his objection to the fatal policy of offering battle at Philippi).

(*d*) The quarrel-scene illustrates yet another favourite expedient. In this section of a tragedy Shakespeare often appeals to an emotion different from any of those excited in the first half of the play, and so provides novelty and generally also relief. As a rule this new emotion is pathetic; and the pathos is not terrible or lacerating, but, even if painful, is accompanied by the sense of beauty and by an outflow of admiration or affection, which come with an inexpressible sweetness after the tension of the crisis and the first counter-stroke. So it is with the reconciliation of Brutus and Cassius, and the arrival of the news of Portia's death. The most famous instance of this effect is the scene (IV.vii.) where Lear wakes up from sleep and finds Cordelia bending over him, perhaps the most tear-compelling passage in literature. Another is the short scene (IV.ii.) in which the talk of Lady Macduff and her little boy is interrupted by the entrance of the murderers, a passage of touching beauty and heroism. Another is the introduction of Ophelia in her madness (twice in different parts of IV.v.), where the effect, though intensely pathetic, is beautiful and moving rather than harrowing; and this effect is repeated in a softer tone in the description of Ophelia's death (end of Act IV.). And in *Othello* the passage where pathos of *this* kind reaches its height is certainly that where Desdemona and Emilia converse, and the willow-song is sung, on the eve of the catastrophe (IV.iii.).

(*e*) Sometimes, again, in this section of a tragedy we find humorous or semi-humorous passages. On the whole such passages occur most frequently in the early or middle part of the play, which naturally grows more sombre as it nears the close; but their occasional introduction in the Fourth Act, and even later, affords variety and relief, and also heightens by contrast the tragic feelings. For example, there is a touch of comedy in the conversation of Lady Macduff with her little boy. Purely and delightfully humorous are the talk and behaviour of the servants in that admirable scene where Coriolanus comes disguised in mean apparel to the house of Aufidius (IV.v.); of a more mingled kind is the effect of the discussion between Menenius and the sentinels in V.ii.; and in the very middle of the supreme scene between the hero, Volumnia, and Virgilia, little Marcus makes us burst out laughing (V.iii.). A little before the catastrophe in *Hamlet* comes the grave-digger passage, a passage ever welcome, but of a length which could hardly be defended on purely dramatic grounds; and still later, occupying some hundred and twenty lines of the very last scene, we have the chatter of Osric with Hamlet's mockery of it. But the acme of audacity is reached in *Antony and Cleopatra*, where, quite close to the end, the old countryman who brings the asps to Cleopatra discourses on the virtues and vices of the worm, and where his last words, 'Yes, forsooth: I wish you joy o' the worm', are followed, without the intervention of a line, by the glorious speech,

> Give me my robe; put on my crown;
> I have Immortal longings in me. . . .

In some of the instances of pathos or humour just mentioned we have been brought to that part of the play which immediately precedes, or even contains, the catastrophe. And I will add at once three remarks which refer specially to this final section of a tragedy.

(*f*) In several plays Shakespeare makes here an appeal which in his own time was evidently powerful: he introduces scenes of battle. This is the case in *Richard III, Julius Caesar, King Lear, Macbeth* and *Antony and Cleopatra*. Richard, Brutus and Cassius, and Macbeth die on the battlefield. Even if his use of this expedient were not enough to show that battle-scenes were extremely popular in the Elizabethan theatre, we know it from other sources. It is a curious comment on the futility of our spectacular effects that in our theatre these scenes, in which we strive after an 'illusion' of which the Elizabethans never dreamt, produce comparatively little excitement, and to many spectators are even somewhat distasteful.[7] And although some of them thrill the imagination of the reader, they rarely, I think, quite satisfy the *dramatic* sense. Perhaps this is partly because a battle is not the most favourable place for the exhibition of tragic character; and it is worth notice that Brutus, Cassius and Antony do not die fighting, but commit suicide after defeat. The actual battle, however, does make us

---

[7] The end of *Richard III* is perhaps an exception.

feel the greatness of Antony, and still more does it help us to regard Richard and Macbeth in their day of doom as heroes, and to mingle sympathy and enthusiastic admiration with desire for their defeat.

(*g*) In some of the tragedies, again, an expedient is used, which Freytag has pointed out (though he sometimes finds it, I think, where it is not really employed). Shakespeare very rarely makes the least attempt to surprise by his catastrophes. They are felt to be inevitable, though the precise way in which they will be brought about is not, of course, foreseen. Occasionally, however, where we dread the catastrophe because we love the hero, a moment occurs, just before it, in which a gleam of false hope lights up the darkening scene; and, though we know it is false, it affects us. Far the most remarkable example is to be found in the final Act of *King Lear*. Here the victory of Edgar and the deaths of Edmund and the two sisters have almost made us forget the design on the lives of Lear and Cordelia. Even when we are reminded of it there is still room for hope that Edgar, who rushes away to the prison, will be in time to save them; and, however familiar we are with the play, the sudden entrance of Lear, with Cordelia dead in his arms, comes on us with a shock. Much slighter, but quite perceptible, is the effect of Antony's victory on land, and of the last outburst of pride and joy as he and Cleopatra meet (IV.viii.). The frank apology of Hamlet to Laertes, their reconciliation, and a delusive appearance of quiet and even confident firmness in the tone of the hero's conversation with Horatio, almost blind us to our better knowledge, and give to the catastrophe an added pain. Those in the audience who are ignorant of *Macbeth*, and who take more simply than most readers now can do the mysterious prophecies concerning Birnam Wood and the man not born of woman, feel, I imagine, just before the catastrophe, a false fear that the hero may yet escape.

(*h*) I will mention only one point more. In some cases Shakespeare spreads the catastrophe out, so to speak, over a considerable space, and thus shortens that difficult section which has to show the development of the counter-action. This is possible only where there is, besides the hero, some character who engages our interest in the highest degree, and with whose fate his own is bound up. Thus the murder of Desdemona is separated by some distance from the death of Othello. The most impressive scene in *Macbeth*, after that of Duncan's murder, is the sleep-walking scene; and it may truly, if not literally, be said to show the catastrophe of Lady Macbeth. Yet it is the opening scene of the Fifth Act, and a number of scenes in which Macbeth's fate is still approaching intervene before the close. Finally, in *Antony and Cleopatra* the heroine equals the hero in importance, and here the death of Antony actually occurs in the Fourth Act, and the whole of the Fifth is devoted to Cleopatra.

Let us now turn to *Othello* and consider briefly its exceptional scheme of construction. The advantage of this scheme is obvious. In the second half of the tragedy there is no danger of 'dragging', of any awkward pause, any undue lowering of pitch, any need of scenes which, however fine, are more or less episodic. The tension is extreme, and it is relaxed only for brief intervals to permit of some slight relief. From the moment when Iago begins to poison Othello's mind we hold our breath. *Othello* from this point onwards is certainly the most exciting of Shakespeare's plays, unless possibly *Macbeth* in its first part may be held to rival it. And *Othello* is such a masterpiece that we are scarcely conscious of any disadvantage attending its method of construction, and may even wonder why Shakespeare employed this method – at any rate in its purity – in this tragedy alone. Nor is it any answer to say that it would not elsewhere have suited his material. Even if this be granted, how was it that he only once chose a story to which this method was appropriate? To his eyes, or for his instinct, there must have been some disadvantage in it. And dangers in it are in fact not hard to see.

In the first place, where the conflict develops very slowly, or, as in *Othello*, remains in a state of incubation during the first part of a tragedy, that part cannot produce the tension proper to the corresponding part of a tragedy like *Macbeth*, and may even run the risk of being somewhat flat. This seems obvious, and it is none the less true because in *Othello* the difficulty is overcome. We may even see that in *Othello* a difficulty was felt. The First Act is full of stir, but it is so because Shakespeare has filled it with a kind of preliminary conflict between the hero and Brabantio – a personage who then vanishes from the stage. The long first scene of the Second Act is largely occupied with mere conversations, artfully drawn out to dimensions which can scarcely be considered essential to the plot. These expedients are fully justified by their success, and nothing more consummate in their way is to be found in Shakespeare than Othello's speech to the Senate and Iago's two talks with Rodrigo. But the fact that Shakespeare can make a plan succeed does not show that the plan is, abstractedly considered, a good plan; and if the scheme of construction in *Othello* were placed, in the shape of a mere outline, before a play-wright ignorant of the actual drama, he would certainly, I believe, feel grave misgivings about the first half of the play.

There is a second difficulty in the scheme. When the middle of the tragedy is reached, the audience is not what it was at the beginning. It has been attending for some time, and has been through a certain amount of agitation. The extreme tension which now arises may therefore easily tire and displease it, all the more if the matter which produces the tension is very painful, if the catastrophe is not less so, and if the limits of the remainder of the play (not to speak of any other consideration) permit of very little relief. It is one thing to watch the scene of Duncan's assassination at the beginning of the Second Act, and another thing to watch the murder of Desdemona at the beginning of the Fifth. If Shakespeare has wholly avoided this difficulty in *Othello*, it is by treating the first part of the play in such a manner that the sympathies excited are predominantly pleasant and therefore not exhausting. The scene in the Council Chamber, and the scene of the reunion at Cyprus, give almost unmixed happiness to the audience; however repulsive Iago may be, the humour of his gulling of Rodrigo is agreeable; even the scene of Cassio's intoxication is not, on the whole, painful. Here we come to the great temptation-scene, where the conflict emerges into life (III.iii.), with nerves unshaken and feelings much fresher than those with which we greet the banquet-scene in *Macbeth* (III.iv.), or the first of the storm-scenes in *King Lear* (III.i.). The same skill may be observed in *Antony and Cleopatra*, where, as we saw, the second half of the tragedy is the more exciting. But, again, the success due to Shakespeare's skill does not show that the scheme of construction is free from a characteristic danger; and on the whole it would appear to be best fitted for a plot which, though it may cause painful agitation as it nears the end, actually ends with a solution instead of a catastrophe.

But for Shakespeare's scanty use of this method there may have been a deeper, though probably an unconscious, reason. The method suits a plot based on intrigue. It may produce intense suspense. It may stir most powerfully the tragic feelings of pity and fear. And it throws into relief that aspect of tragedy in which great or beautiful lives seem caught in the net of fate. But it is apt to be less favourable to the exhibition of character, to show less clearly how an act returns upon the agent, and to produce less strongly the impression of an inexorable order working in the passions and actions of men, and labouring through their agony and waste towards good. Now, it seems clear from his tragedies that what appealed most to Shakespeare was this latter class of effects. I do not ask here whether *Othello* fails to produce, in the same degree as the other tragedies, these impressions; but Shakespeare's preference for them may have been one reason why he habitually chose a scheme of construction which produces in the final Acts but little of strained suspense, and presents the catastrophe as a thing foreseen and following with a psychological and moral necessity on the action exhibited in the first part of the tragedy.

4

The more minute details of construction cannot well be examined here, and I will not pursue the subject further. But its discussion suggests a question which will have occurred to some of my hearers. They may have asked themselves whether I have not used the words 'art' and 'device' and 'expedient' and 'method' too boldly, as though Shakespeare were a conscious artist, and not rather a writer who constructed in obedience to an extraordinary dramatic instinct, as he composed mainly by inspiration. And a brief explanation on this head will enable me to allude to a few more points, chiefly of construction, which are not too technical for a lecture.

In speaking, for convenience, of devices and expedients, I did not intend to imply that Shakespeare always deliberately aimed at the effects which he produced. But *no* artist always does this, and I see no reason to doubt that Shakespeare often did it, or to suppose that his method of constructing and composing differed, except in degree, from that of the most 'conscious' of artists. The antithesis of art and inspiration, though not meaningless, is often most misleading. Inspiration is surely not incompatible with considerate workmanship. The two may be severed, but they need not be so, and where a genuinely poetic result is being produced they cannot be so. The glow of a first conception must in some measure survive or rekindle itself in the work of planning and executing; and what is called a technical expedient may 'come' to a man with as sudden a glory as a splendid image. Verse may be easy and unpremeditated, as Milton says his was, and yet many a word in it may be changed many a time, and the last change be more 'inspired' than the original. The difference between poets in these matters is no doubt considerable, and sometimes important, but it can only be a difference of less and more. It is probable that Shakespeare often wrote fluently, for Jonson* (a better authority than Heminge and Condell*) says so; and for anything we can tell he may also have constructed with unusual readiness. But we know that he revised and re-wrote (for instance in *Love's Labour's Lost* and *Romeo and Juliet* and *Hamlet*); it is almost impossible that he can have worked out the plots of his best plays without much reflection and many experiments; and it appears to me scarcely more possible to mistake the signs of deliberate care in some of his famous speeches. If a 'conscious artist' means one who holds his work away from him, scrutinizes and judges it, and, if need be, alters it and alters it till it comes as near satisfying him as he can make it, I am sure that Shakespeare frequently employed such conscious art. If it means, again, an artist who consciously aims at the effects he produces, what ground have we for doubting that he frequently employed such art, though probably less frequently than a good many other poets?

But perhaps the notion of a 'conscious artist' in drama is that of one who studies the theory of the art, and even writes with an eye to its 'rules'. And we know it was long a favourite idea that Shakespeare was totally ignorant of the 'rules'. Yet this is quite incredible. The rules referred to, such as they were, were not buried in Aristotle's Greek nor even hidden away in Italian treatises. He could find pretty well all of them in a book so current and famous as Sidney's* *Defence of Poetry*. Even if we suppose that he refused to open this book (which is most unlikely) how could he possibly remain ignorant of the rules in a society of actors and dramatists and amateurs who must have been incessantly talking about plays and playwriting, and some of whom were ardent champions of the rules and full of contempt for the lawlessness of the popular drama? Who can doubt that at the Mermaid* Shakespeare heard from Jonson's lips much more censure of his offences against 'art' than Jonson ever confided to Drummond* or to paper? And is it not most probable that those battles between the two which Fuller* imagines, were waged often on the field of dramatic criticism? If Shakespeare, then, broke some of the 'rules', it was not from ignorance. Probably he refused, on grounds of art itself, to trouble himself with rules derived from forms of drama long extinct. And it is not unlikely that he was little interested in theory as such, and more than likely that he was impatient of pedantic distinctions between 'pastoral-comical, historical-pastoral, tragical-historical, tragical-comical-historical-pastoral, scene individual or poem unlimited'. But that would not prove that he never reflected on his art, or could not explain, if he cared to, what *he* thought would be good general rules for the drama of his own time. He could give advice about play-acting. Why should we suppose that he could not give advice about play-making?

Still Shakespeare, though in some considerable degree a 'conscious' artist, frequently sins against art; and if his sins were not due to ignorance or inspiration, they must be accounted for otherwise. Neither can there be much doubt about their causes (for they have more than one cause), as we shall see if we take some illustrations of the defects themselves.

Among these are not to be reckoned certain things which in dramas written at the present time would rightly be counted defects. There are, for example, in most Elizabethan plays peculiarities of construction which would injure a play written for our stage but were perfectly well-fitted for that very different stage – a stage on which again some of the best-constructed plays of our time would appear absurdly faulty. Or take the charge of improbability. Shakespeare certainly has improbabilities which are defects. They are most frequent in the winding up of his comedies (and how many comedies are there in the world which end satisfactorily?). But his improbabilities are rarely psychological, and in some of his plays there occurs one kind of improbability, which is no defect, but simply a characteristic which has lost in our day much of its former attraction. I mean that the story, in most of the comedies and many of the tragedies of the Elizabethans, was *intended* to be strange and wonderful. These plays were tales of romance dramatized, and they were meant in part to satisfy the same love of wonder to which the romances appealed. It is no defect in the Arthurian legends, or the old French romances, or many of the stories in the *Decameron*,* that they are improbable: it is a virtue. To criticize them as though they were of the same species as a realistic novel, is, we should all say, merely stupid. Is it anything else to criticize in the same way *Twelfth Night* or *As You Like It*? And so, even when the difference between comedy and tragedy is allowed for, the improbability of the opening of *King Lear*, so often censured, is no defect. It is not out of character, it is only extremely unusual and strange. But it was meant to be so; like the marriage of the black Othello with Desdemona, the Venetian senator's daughter.

To come then to real defects, (*a*) one may be found in places where Shakespeare strings together a number of scenes, some very short, in which the *dramatis personæ* are frequently changed; as though a novelist were to tell his story in a succession of short chapters, in which he flitted from one group of his characters to another. This method shows itself here and there in the pure tragedies (*e.g.* in the last Act of *Macbeth*), but it appears most decidedly where the historical material was undramatic, as in the middle part of *Antony and Cleopatra*. It was made possible by the absence of scenery, and doubtless Shakespeare used it because it was the easiest way out of a difficulty. But, considered abstractedly, it is a defective method, and, even as used by Shakespeare, it sometimes reminds us of the merely narrative arrangement common in plays before his time.

(*b*) We may take next the introduction or excessive development of matter neither required by the plot nor essential to the exhibition of character: *e.g.* the references in *Hamlet* to theatre-quarrels of the day, and the length of the player's speech and also of Hamlet's directions to him respecting the delivery of the lines to be inserted in the 'Murder of Gonzago'. All this was probably of great interest at the time when *Hamlet* was first presented; most of it we should be very sorry to miss; some of it seems to bring us close to Shakespeare himself; but who can defend it from the point of view of constructive art?

(*c*) Again, we may look at Shakespeare's soliloquies. It will be agreed that in listening to a soliloquy we ought never to feel that we are being addressed. And in this respect, as in others, many of the soliloquies are master-pieces. But certainly in some the purpose of giving information lies bare, and in one or two the actor openly speaks to the audience. Such faults are found chiefly in the early plays, though there is a glaring instance at the end of Belarius's speech in *Cymbeline* (III.iii.99 ff.), and even in the mature tragedies something of this kind may be traced. Let anyone compare, for example, Edmund's soliloquy in *King Lear*, I.ii., 'This is the excellent foppery of the world' with Edgar's in II.iii., and he will be conscious that in the latter the purpose of giving information is imperfectly disguised.[8]

(*d*) It cannot be denied, further, that in many of Shakespeare's plays, if not in all, there are inconsistencies and contradictions, and also that questions are suggested to the reader which it is impossible for him to answer with certainty. For instance, some of the indications of the lapse of time between Othello's marriage and the events of the later Acts flatly contradict one another; and it is impossible to make out whether Hamlet was at Court or at the University when his father was murdered. But it should be noticed that often what seems a defect of this latter kind is not really a defect. For instance, the difficulty about Hamlet's age (even if it cannot be resolved by the text alone) did not exist for Shakespeare's audience. The moment Burbage* entered it must have been clear whether the hero was twenty or thirty. And in like manner many questions of dramatic interpretation which trouble us could never have arisen when the plays were first produced, for the actor would be instructed by the author how to render any critical and possibly ambiguous passage. (I have heard it remarked, and the remark I believe is just, that Shakespeare seems to have relied on such instructions less than most of his contemporaries; one fact out of several which might be adduced to prove that he did not regard his plays as mere stage-dramas of the moment.)

(*e*) To turn to another field, the early critics were no doubt often provokingly wrong when they censured the language of particular passages in Shakespeare as obscure, inflated, tasteless, or 'pestered with metaphors'; but they were surely right in the general statement that his language often shows these faults. And this is a subject which later criticism has never fairly faced and examined.

(*f*) Once more, to say that Shakespeare makes all his serious characters talk alike,[9] and that he constantly speaks through the mouths

---

[8] I do not discuss the general question of the justification of soliloquy, for it concerns not Shakespeare only, but practically all dramatists down to quite recent times. I will only remark that neither soliloquy nor the use of verse can be condemned on the mere ground that they are 'unnatural.' *No* dramatic language is 'natural'; *all* dramatic language is idealized. So that the question as to soliloquy must be one as to the degree of idealization and the balance of advantages and disadvantages. (Since this lecture was written I have read some remarks on Shakespeare's soliloquies to much the same effect by E. Kilian* in the *Jahrbuch d. deutschen Shakespeare-Gesellschaft* for 1903.)

[9] If by this we mean that these characters all speak what is recognizably Shakespeare's style, of course it is true; but it is no accusation. Nor does it follow that they all speak alike; and in fact they are far from doing so.

of his *dramatis personæ* without regard to their individual natures, would be to exaggerate absurdly; but it is true that in his earlier plays these faults are traceable in some degree, and even in *Hamlet* there are striking passages where dramatic appropriateness is sacrificed to some other object. When Laertes speaks the lines beginning,

> For nature, crescent, does not grow alone
> In thews and bulk,

who can help feeling that Shakespeare is speaking rather than Laertes? Or when the player-king discourses for more than twenty lines on the instability of human purpose, and when King Claudius afterwards insists to Laertes on the same subject at almost equal length, who does not see that Shakespeare, thinking but little of dramatic fitness, wishes in part simply to write poetry, and partly to impress on the audience thoughts which will help them to understand, not the player-king nor yet King Claudius, but Hamlet himself, who, on his side – and here quite in character – has already enlarged on the same topic in the most famous of his soliloquies?

(g) Lastly, like nearly all the dramatists of his day and of times much earlier, Shakespeare was fond of 'gnomic' passages, and introduces them probably not more freely than his readers like, but more freely than, I suppose, a good play-wright now would care to do. These passages, it may be observed, are frequently rhymed (*e.g. Othello*, I.iii.201 ff., II.i.149 ff.). Sometimes they were printed in early editions with inverted commas round them, as are in the First Quarto Polonius's 'few precepts' to Laertes.

If now we ask whence defects like these arose, we shall observe that some of them are shared by the majority of Shakespeare's contemporaries, and abound in the dramas immediately preceding his time. They are characteristics of an art still undeveloped, and, no doubt, were not perceived to be defects. But though it is quite probable that in regard to one or two kinds of imperfection (such as the superabundance of 'gnomic' passages) Shakespeare himself erred thus ignorantly, it is very unlikely that in most cases he did so, unless in the first years of his career of authorship. And certainly he never can have thought it artistic to leave inconsistencies, obscurities, or passages of bombast in his work. Most of the defects in his writings must be due to indifference or want of care.

I do not say that all were so. In regard, for example, to his occasional bombast and other errors of diction, it seems hardly doubtful that his perception was sometimes at fault, and that, though he used the English language like no one else, he had not that *sureness* of taste in words which has been shown by some much smaller writers. And it seems not unlikely that here he suffered from his comparative want of 'learning' – that is, of familiarity with the great writers of antiquity. But nine-tenths of his defects are not, I believe, the errors of an inspired genius, ignorant of art, but the sins of a great but negligent artist. He was often, no doubt, overworked and pressed for time. He knew that the immense majority of his audience were incapable of distinguishing between rough and finished work. He often felt the degradation of having to live by pleasing them. Probably in hours of depression he was quite indifferent to fame, and perhaps in another mood the whole business of play writing seemed to him a little thing. None of these thoughts and feelings influenced him when his subject had caught hold of him. To imagine that *then* he 'winged his roving flight' for 'gain' or 'glory', or wrote from any cause on earth but the necessity of expression, with all its pains and raptures, is mere folly. He was possessed: his mind must have been in a white heat: he worked, no doubt, with the *furia* of Michael Angelo.* And if he did not succeed at once – and how can even he have always done so? – he returned to the matter again and again. Such things as the scenes of Duncan's murder or Othello's temptation, such speeches as those of the Duke to Claudio and of Claudio to his sister about death, were not composed in an hour and tossed aside; and if they have defects, they have not what Shakespeare thought defects. Nor is it possible that his astonishingly individual conceptions of character can have been struck out at a heat: prolonged and repeated thought must have gone to them. But of small inconsistencies in the plot he was often quite careless. He seems to have finished off some of his comedies with a hasty and even contemptuous indifference, as if it mattered nothing how the people got married, or even who married whom, so long as enough were married somehow. And often, when he came to parts of his scheme that were necessary but not interesting to him, he wrote with a slack hand, like a craftsman of genius who knows that his natural gift and acquired skill will turn out something more than good enough for his audience: wrote probably fluently but certainly negligently, sometimes only half saying what he meant, and some-times saying the opposite, and now and then, when passion was required, lapsing into bombast because he knew he must heighten his style but would not take the trouble to inflame his imagination. It may truly be said that what injures such passages is not inspiration, but the want of it. But, as they are mostly passages where no poet could expect to be inspired, it is even more true to say that here Shakespeare lacked the conscience of the artist who is determined to make everything as good as he can. Such poets as Milton,* Pope,* Tennyson,* habitually show this conscience. They left probably scarcely anything that they felt they could improve. No one could dream of saying that of Shakespeare.

Hence comes what is perhaps the chief difficulty in interpreting his works. Where his power or art is fully exerted it really does resemble that of nature. It organizes and vitalizes its product from the centre outward to the minutest markings on the surface, so that when you turn upon it the most searching light you can command, when you dissect it and apply to it the test of a microscope, still you find in it nothing formless, general or vague, but everywhere structure, character, individuality. In this his great things, which seem to come whenever they are wanted, have no companions in literature except the few greatest things in Dante; and it is a fatal error to allow his carelessness elsewhere to make one doubt whether here one is not seeking more than can be found. It is very possible to look for subtlety in the wrong place in Shakespeare, but in the right places it is not possible to find too much. But then this characteristic, which is one source of his endless attraction, is also a source of perplexity. For in these parts of his plays which show him neither in his most intense nor in his most negligent mood, we are often unable to decide whether something that seems inconsistent, indistinct, feeble, exaggerated, is really so, or whether it was definitely meant to be as it is, and has an intention which we ought to be able to divine; whether, for example, we have before us some unusual trait in character, some abnormal movement of mind, only surprising to us because we understand so very much less of human nature than Shakespeare did, or whether he wanted to get his work done and made a slip, or in using an old play adopted hastily something that would not square with his own conception, or even refused to trouble himself with minutiae which we notice only because we study him, but which nobody ever notices in a stage performance. We know well enough what Shakespeare is doing when at the end of

Measure for Measure he marries Isabella to the Duke – and a scandalous proceeding it is; but who can ever feel sure that the doubts which vex him as to some not unimportant points in *Hamlet* are due to his own want of eyesight or to Shakespeare's want of care?

SHAKESPEARE'S TRAGIC PERIOD – *HAMLET*

1

Before we come to-day to *Hamlet*, the first of our four tragedies, a few remarks must be made on their probable place in Shakespeare's literary career. But I shall say no more than seems necessary for our restricted purpose, and, therefore, for the most part shall merely be stating widely accepted results of investigation, without going into the evidence on which they rest.[1]

Shakespeare's tragedies fall into two distinct groups, and these groups are separated by a considerable interval. He wrote tragedy – pure, like *Romeo and Juliet*, historical, like *Richard III* – in the early years of his career of authorship, when he was also writing such comedies as *Love's Labour's Lost* and the *Midsummer Night's Dream*. Then came a time, lasting some half-dozen years, during which he composed the most mature and humorous of his English History plays (the plays with Falstaff in them), and the best of his romantic comedies (the plays with Beatrice and Jaques and Viola in them).

---

[1] It may be convenient to some readers for the purposes of this book to have by them a list of Shakespeare's plays, arranged in periods. No such list, of course, can command general assent, but the following (which does not throughout represent my own views) would perhaps meet with as little objection from scholars as any other. For some purposes the Third and Fourth Periods are better considered to be one. Within each period the so-called Comedies, Histories and Tragedies are respectively grouped together; and for this reason, as well as others, the order within each period does not profess to be chronological (*e.g.* it is not implied that the *Comedy of Errors* preceded *1 Henry VI* or *Titus Andronicus*). Where Shakespeare's authorship of any considerable part of a play is questioned, widely or by specially good authority, the name of the play is printed in italics.

First Period (to 1595?): Comedy of Errors, Love's Labour's Lost, Two Gentlemen of Verona, Midsummer-Night's Dream; *1 Henry VI*, *2 Henry VI*, *3 Henry VI*, Richard III, Richard II; *Titus Andronicus*, Romeo and Juliet.

Second Period (to 1602?): Merchant of Venice, All's Well (better in Third Period?), *Taming of the Shrew*, Much Ado, As You Like It, Merry Wives, Twelfth Night; King John, 1 Henry IV, 2 Henry IV, Henry V; Julius Caesar, Hamlet.

Third Period (to 1608?): Troilus and Cressida, Measure for Measure; Othello, King Lear, *Timon of Athens*, Macbeth, Antony and Cleopatra, Coriolanus.

Fourth Period: Pericles, Cymbeline, Winter's Tale, Tempest, *Two Noble Kinsmen*, *Henry VIII*.

There are no tragedies belonging to these half-dozen years, nor any dramas approaching tragedy. But now, from about 1601 to about 1608, comes tragedy after tragedy – *Julius Caesar, Hamlet, Othello, King Lear, Timon of Athens, Macbeth, Antony and Cleopatra* and *Coriolanus*; and their companions are plays which cannot indeed be called tragedies, but certainly are not comedies in the same sense as *As You Like It* or the *Tempest*. These seven years, accordingly, might, without much risk of misunderstanding, be called Shakespeare's tragic period.[2] And after it he wrote no more tragedies, but chiefly romances more serious and less sunny than *As You Like It*, but not much less serene.

The existence of this distinct tragic period, of a time when the dramatist seems to have been occupied almost exclusively with deep and painful problems, has naturally helped to suggest the idea that the 'man' also, in these years of middle age, from thirty-seven to forty-four, was heavily burdened in spirit; that Shakespeare turned to tragedy not merely for change, or because he felt it to be the greatest form of drama and felt himself equal to it, but also because the world had come to look dark and terrible to him; and even that the railings of Thersites and the maledictions of Timon express his own contempt and hatred for mankind. Discussion of this large and difficult subject, however, is not necessary to the dramatic appreciation of any of his works, and I shall say nothing of it here, but shall pass on at once to draw attention to certain stages and changes which may be observed within the tragic period. For this purpose too it is needless to raise any question as to the respective chronological positions of *Othello, King Lear* and *Macbeth*. What is important is also generally admitted: that *Julius Caesar* and *Hamlet* precede these plays, and that *Antony and Cleopatra* and *Coriolanus* follow them.[3]

---

[2] The reader will observe that this 'tragic period' would not exactly coincide with the 'Third Period' of the division given in the last note. For *Julius Caesar* and *Hamlet* fall in the Second Period, not the Third; and I may add that, as *Pericles* was entered at Stationers' Hall in 1608 and published in 1609, it ought strictly to be put in the Third Period – not the Fourth. The truth is that *Julius Caesar* and *Hamlet* are given to the Second Period mainly on the ground of style; while a Fourth Period is admitted, not mainly on that ground (for there is no great difference here between *Antony* and *Coriolanus* on the one side and *Cymbeline* and the *Tempest* on the other), but because of a difference in substance and spirit. If a Fourth Period were admitted on grounds of form, it ought to begin with *Antony and Cleopatra*.

[3] I should go perhaps too far if I said that it is generally admitted that *Timon of Athens* also precedes the two Roman tragedies; but its precedence seems to me so nearly certain that I assume it in what follows.

If we consider the tragedies first on the side of their substance, we find at once an obvious difference between the first two and the remainder. Both Brutus and Hamlet are highly intellectual by nature and reflective by habit. Both may even be called, in a popular sense, philosophic; Brutus may be called so in a stricter sense. Each, being also a 'good' man, shows accordingly, when placed in critical circumstances, a sensitive and almost painful anxiety to do right. And though they fail – of course in quite different ways – to deal successively with these circumstances, the failure in each case is connected rather with their intellectual nature and reflective habit than with any yielding to passion. Hence the name 'tragedy of thought', which Schlegel gave to *Hamlet*, may be given also, as in effect it has been by Professor Dowden, to *Julius Caesar*. The later heroes, on the other hand, Othello, Lear, Timon, Macbeth, Antony, Coriolanus, have, one and all, passionate natures, and, speaking roughly, we may attribute the tragic failure in each of these cases to passion. Partly for this reason, the later plays are wilder and stormier than the first two. We see a greater mass of human nature in commotion, and we see Shakespeare's own powers exhibited on a larger scale. Finally, examination would show that, in all these respects, the first tragedy, *Julius Caesar*, is further removed from the later type than is the second, *Hamlet*.

These two earlier works are both distinguished from most of the succeeding tragedies in another though a kindred respect. Moral evil is not so intently scrutinized or so fully displayed in them. In *Julius Caesar*, we may almost say, everybody means well. In *Hamlet*, though we have a villain, he is a small one. The murder which gives rise to the action lies outside the play, and the centre of attention within the play lies in the hero's efforts to do his duty. It seems clear that Shakespeare's interest, since the early days when under Marlowe's influence he wrote *Richard III*, has not been directed to the more extreme or terrible forms of evil. But in the tragedies that follow *Hamlet* the presence of this interest is equally clear. In Iago, in the 'bad' people of *King Lear*, even in Macbeth and Lady Macbeth, human nature assumes shapes which inspire not mere sadness or repulsion but horror and dismay. If in *Timon* no monstrous cruelty is done, we still watch ingratitude and selfishness so blank that they provoke a loathing we never felt for Claudius; and in this play and *King Lear* we can fancy that we hear at times the *saeva indignatio*, if not the despair, of Swift.* This prevalence of abnormal or appalling forms of evil, side by side with vehement passion, is another reason why the convulsion depicted in these tragedies seems to come from a deeper source, and to be vaster in extent, than the conflict in the two earlier plays. And here again *Julius Caesar* is further removed than *Hamlet* from *Othello, King Lear,* and *Macbeth.*

But in regard to this second point of difference a reservation must be made, on which I will speak a little more fully, because, unlike the matter hitherto touched on, its necessity seems hardly to have been recognized. *All* of the later tragedies may be called tragedies of passion, but not all of them display these extreme forms of evil. Neither of the last two does so. Antony and Coriolanus are, from one point of view, victims of passion; but the passion that ruins Antony also exalts him, he touches the infinite in it; and the pride and self-will of Coriolanus, though terrible in bulk, are scarcely so in quality; there is nothing base in them, and the huge creature whom they destroy is a noble, even a lovable, being. Nor does either of these dramas, though the earlier depicts a corrupt civilization, include even among the minor characters anyone who can be called villainous or horrible. Consider, finally, the impression left on us at the close of each. It is remarkable that this impression, though very strong, can scarcely be called purely tragic; or, if we call it so, at least the feeling of reconciliation which mingles with the obviously tragic emotions is here exceptionally well-marked. The death of Antony, it will be remembered, comes before the opening of the Fifth Act. The death of Cleopatra, which closes the play, is greeted by the reader with sympathy and admiration, even with exultation at the thought that she has foiled Octavius; and these feelings are heightened by the deaths of Charmian and Iras, heroically faithful to their mistress, as Emilia was to hers. In *Coriolanus* the feeling of reconciliation is even stronger. The whole interest towards the close has been concentrated on the question whether the hero will persist in his revengeful design of storming and burning his native city, or whether better feelings will at last overpower his resentment and pride. He stands on the edge of a crime beside which, at least in outward dreadfulness, the slaughter of an individual looks insignificant. And when, at the sound of his mother's voice and the sight of his wife and child, nature asserts itself and he gives way, although we know he will lose his life, we care little for that: he has saved his soul. Our relief, and our exultation in the power of goodness, are so great that the actual catastrophe which follows and mingles sadness with these feelings leaves them but little diminished, and as we close the book we feel, it seems to me, more as we do at the close of *Cymbeline* than as we do at the close of *Othello*. In saying this I do not in the least mean to criticize *Coriolanus*. It is a much nobler play as it stands than it would have been if Shakespeare had made the hero persist, and we had seen him amid the flaming ruins of Rome, awaking suddenly to the enormity of his deed and taking vengeance on himself; but that would surely have been an ending more strictly tragic than the close of Shakespeare's play. Whether this close was simply due to his unwillingness to contradict his historical authority on a point of such magnitude we need not ask. In any case *Coriolanus* is, in more than an outward sense, the end of his tragic period. It marks the transition to his latest works, in which the powers of repentance and forgiveness charm to rest the tempest raised by error and guilt.

If we turn now from the substance of the tragedies to their style and versification, we find on the whole a corresponding difference between the earlier and the later. The usual assignment of *Julius Caesar*, and even of *Hamlet*, to the end of Shakespeare's Second Period – the period of *Henry V* – is based mainly, we saw, on considerations of form. The general style of the serious parts of the last plays from English history is one of full, noble, and comparatively equable eloquence. The 'honey-tongued' sweetness and beauty of Shakespeare's early writing, as seen in *Romeo and Juliet* or the *Midsummer Night's Dream*, remain; the ease and lucidity remain; but there is an accession of force and weight. We find no great change from this style when we come to *Julius Caesar*,[4] which may be taken to mark its culmination. At this point in Shakespeare's literary development he reaches, if the phrase may be pardoned, a limited perfection. Neither thought on the one side, nor expression on the other, seems to have any tendency to outrun or contend with its fellow. We receive an impression of easy mastery and complete harmony, but not so strong an impression of inner power bursting into outer life. Shakespeare's style is perhaps nowhere else so free from defects, and yet almost every one of his subsequent plays contains writing which is

---

[4] That play, however, is distinguished, I think, by a deliberate endeavour after a dignified and unadorned simplicity – a Roman simplicity perhaps.

greater. To speak familiarly, we feel in *Julius Caesar* that, although not even Shakespeare could better the style he has chosen, he has not let himself go.

In reading *Hamlet* we have no such feeling, and in many parts (for there is in the writing of *Hamlet* an unusual variety)[5] we are conscious of a decided change. The style in these parts is more rapid and vehement, less equable and less simple; and there is a change of the same kind in the versification. But on the whole the *type* is the same as in *Julius Caesar*, and the resemblance of the two plays is decidedly more marked than the difference. If Hamlet's soliloquies, considered simply as compositions, show a great change from Jaques's speech, 'All the world's a stage', and even from the soliloquies of Brutus, yet *Hamlet* (for instance in the hero's interview with his mother) is like *Julius Caesar*, and unlike the later tragedies, in the fullness of its eloquence, and passages like the following belong quite definitely to the style of the Second Period:

> *Mar.*   It faded on the crowing of the cock.
> Some say that ever 'gainst that season comes
> Wherein our Saviour's birth is celebrated,
> The bird of dawning singeth all night long;
> And then, they say, no spirit dare stir abroad;
> The nights are wholesome; then no planets strike,
> No fairy takes, nor witch hath power to charm,
> So hallow'd and so gracious is the time.
> *Hor.*   So have I heard and do in part believe it.
> But, look, the morn, in russet mantle clad,
> Walks o'er the dew of yon high eastward hill.

This bewitching music is heard again in Hamlet's farewell to Horatio:

> If thou didst ever hold me in thy heart,
> Absent thee from felicity awhile,
> And in this harsh world draw thy breath in pain,
> To tell my story.

But after *Hamlet* this music is heard no more. It is followed by a music vaster and deeper, but not the same.

The changes observable in *Hamlet* are afterwards, and gradually, so

---

[5] It is quite probable that this may arise in part from the fact, which seems hardly doubtful, that the tragedy was revised, and in places rewritten, some little time after its first composition.

greatly developed that Shakespeare's style and versification at last become almost new things. It is extremely difficult to illustrate this briefly in a manner to which no just exception can be taken, for it is almost impossible to find in two plays passages bearing a sufficiently close resemblance to one another in occasion and sentiment. But I will venture to put by the first of those quotations from *Hamlet* this from *Macbeth*:

> *Dun.*   This castle hath a pleasant seat; the air
> Nimbly and sweetly recommends itself
> Unto our gentle senses.
> *Ban.*   This guest of summer,
> The temple-haunting martlet, does approve,
> By his loved mansionry, that the heaven's breath
> Smells wooingly here: no jutty, frieze,
> Buttress, nor coign of vantage, but this bird
> Hath made his pendent bed and procreant cradle;
> Where they most breed and haunt,
> I have observed, The air is delicate;

and by the second quotation from *Hamlet* this from *Antony and Cleopatra*:

> The miserable change now at my end
> Lament nor sorrow at; but please your thoughts
> In feeding them with those my former fortunes
> Wherein I lived, the greatest prince o' the world,
> The noblest; and do now not basely die,
> Not cowardly put off my helmet to
> My countryman, – a Roman by a Roman
> Valiantly vanquish'd. Now my spirit is going;
> I can no more.

It would be almost an impertinence to point out in detail how greatly these two passages, and especially the second, differ in effect from those in *Hamlet*, written perhaps five or six years earlier. The versification, by the time we reach *Antony and Cleopatra*, has assumed a new type; and although this change would appear comparatively slight in a typical passage from *Othello* or even from *King Lear*, its approach through these plays to *Timon* and *Macbeth* can easily be traced. It is accompanied by a similar change in diction and construction. After *Hamlet* the style, in the more emotional passages, is heightened. It becomes grander, sometimes wilder, sometimes more swelling, even tumid. It is also more concentrated, rapid, varied, and, in construction, less regular, not seldom twisted or elliptical. It is, therefore, not so easy and lucid and in the more ordinary dialogue it is sometimes involved and obscure, and from these and other causes deficient in charm.[6] On the other hand, it is always full of life and movement, and in great passages produces sudden, strange, electrifying effects which are rarely found in earlier plays, and not so often even in *Hamlet*. The more pervading effect of beauty gives place to what may almost be called explosions of sublimity or pathos.

There is room for differences of taste and preference as regards the style and versification of the end of Shakespeare's Second Period, and those of the later tragedies and last romances. But readers who miss in the latter the peculiar enchantment of the earlier will not deny that the changes in form are in entire harmony with the inward changes. If they object to passages where, to exaggerate a little, the sense has rather to be discerned beyond the words than found in them, and if they do not wholly enjoy the movement of so typical a speech as this,

> Yes, like enough, high-battled Caesar will
> Unstate his happiness, and be staged to the show,
> Against a sworder! I see men's judgments are
> A parcel of their fortunes; and things outward
> Do draw the inward quality after them,
> To suffer all alike. That he should dream,
> Knowing all measures, the full Caesar will
> Answer his emptiness! Caesar, thou hast subdued
> His judgment too,

they will admit that, in traversing the impatient throng of thoughts not always completely embodied, their minds move through an astonishing variety of ideas and experiences, and that a style less generally poetic than that of *Hamlet* is also a style more invariably dramatic. It may be that, for the purposes of tragedy, the highest point was reached during the progress of these changes, in the most critical passages of *Othello, King Lear* and *Macbeth*.[7]

---

[6] This, if we confine ourselves to the tragedies, is, I think, especially the case in *King Lear* and *Timon*.

[7] The first, at any rate, of these three plays is, of course, much nearer to *Hamlet*, especially in versification, than to *Antony and Cleopatra*, in which Shakespeare's final style first shows itself practically complete. It has been impossible, in the brief treatment of this subject, to say what is required of the individual plays.

2

Suppose you were to describe the plot of *Hamlet* to a person quite ignorant of the play, and suppose you were careful to tell your hearer nothing about Hamlet's character, what impression would your sketch make on him? Would he not exclaim: 'What a sensational story! Why, here are some eight violent deaths, not to speak of adultery, a ghost, a mad woman, and a fight in a grave! If I did not know that the play was Shakespeare's, I should have thought it must have been one of those early tragedies of blood and horror from which he is said to have redeemed the stage'? And would he not then go on to ask: 'But why in the world did not Hamlet obey the Ghost at once, and so save seven of those eight lives?'

The exclamation and this question both show the same thing, that the whole story turns upon the peculiar character of the hero. For without this character the story would appear sensational and horrible; and yet the actual *Hamlet* is very far from being so, and even has a less terrible effect than *Othello, King Lear* or *Macbeth*. And again, if we had no knowledge of this character, the story would hardly be intelligible; it would at any rate at once suggest that wondering question about the conduct of the hero; while the story of any of the other three tragedies would sound plain enough and would raise no such question. It is further very probable that the main change made by Shakespeare in the story as already represented on the stage, lay in a new conception of Hamlet's character and so of the cause of his delay. And, lastly, when we examine the tragedy, we observe two things which illustrate the same point. First, we find by the side of the hero no other figure of tragic proportions, no one like Lady Macbeth or Iago, no one even like Cordelia or Desdemona; so that, in Hamlet's absence, the remaining characters could not yield a Shakespearean tragedy at all. And, secondly, we find among them two, Laertes and Fortinbras, who are evidently designed to throw the character of the hero into relief. Even in the situations there is a curious parallelism; for Fortinbras, like Hamlet, is the son of a king, lately dead, and succeeded by his brother; and Laertes, like Hamlet, has a father slain, and feels bound to avenge him. And with this parallelism in situation there is a strong contrast in character; for both Fortinbras and Laertes possess in abundance the very quality which the hero seems to lack, so that, as we read, we are tempted to exclaim that either of them would have accomplished Hamlet's task in a day. Naturally, then, the tragedy of *Hamlet* with Hamlet left out has become the symbol of extreme absurdity; while the character itself has probably exerted a greater fascination, and certainly has been the subject of more discussion, than any other in the whole literature of the world.

Before, however, we approach the task of examining it, it is as well to remind ourselves that the virtue of the play by no means wholly depends on this most subtle creation. We are all aware of this, and if we were not so the history of *Hamlet*, as a stage-play, might bring the fact home to us. It is to-day the most popular of Shakespeare's tragedies on our stage; and yet a large number, perhaps even the majority of the spectators, though they may feel some mysterious attraction in the hero, certainly do not question themselves about his character or the cause of his delay, and would still find the play exceptionally effective, even if he were an ordinary brave young man and the obstacles in his path were purely external. And this has probably always been the case. *Hamlet* seems from the first to have been a favourite play; but until late in the eighteenth century, I believe, scarcely a critic showed that he perceived anything specially interesting in the character. Hanmer,* in 1730, to be sure, remarks that 'there appears no reason at all in nature why this young prince did not put the usurper to death as soon as possible'; but it does not even cross his mind that this apparent 'absurdity' is odd and might possibly be due to some design on the part of the poet. He simply explains the absurdity by observing that, if Shakespeare had made the young man go 'naturally to work', the play would have come to an end at once! Johnson, in like manner, notices that 'Hamlet is, through the whole piece, rather an instrument than an agent', but it does not occur to him that this peculiar circumstance can be anything but a defect in Shakespeare's management of the plot. Seeing, they saw not. Henry Mackenzie,* the author of *The Man of Feeling*, was, it would seem, the first of our critics to feel the 'indescribable charm' of Hamlet, and to divine something of Shakespeare's intention. 'We see a man', he writes, 'who in other circumstances would have exercised all the moral and social virtues, placed in a situation in which even the amiable qualities of his mind serve but to aggravate his distress and to perplex his conduct.'[8] How significant is

---

[8] *The Mirror*, 18th April, 1780, quoted by Furness,* *Variorum Hamlet*, ii.148. In the above remarks I have relied mainly on Furness's collection of extracts from early critics.

the fact (if it be the fact) that it was only when the slowly rising sun of Romance began to flush the sky that the wonder, beauty and pathos of this most marvellous of Shakespeare's creations began to be visible! We do not know that they were perceived even in his own day, and perhaps those are not wholly wrong who declare that this creation, so far from being a characteristic product of the time, was a vision of

> the prophetic soul
> Of the wide world dreaming on things to come.

But the dramatic splendour of the whole tragedy is another matter, and must have been manifest not only in Shakespeare's day but even in Hanmer's.

It is indeed so obvious that I pass it by, and proceed at once to the central question of Hamlet's character. And I believe time will be saved, and a good deal of positive interpretation may be introduced, if, without examining in detail any one theory, we first distinguish classes or types of theory which appear to be in various ways and degrees insufficient or mistaken. And we will confine our attention to sane theories; – for on this subject, as on all questions relating to Shakespeare, there are plenty of merely lunatic views: the view, for example, that Hamlet, being a disguised woman in love with Horatio, could hardly help seeming unkind to Ophelia; or the view that, being a very clever and wicked young man who wanted to oust his innocent uncle from the throne, he 'faked' the Ghost with this intent.

But, before we come to our types of theory, it is necessary to touch on an idea, not unfrequently met with, which would make it vain labour to discuss or propose any theory at all. It is sometimes said that Hamlet's character is not only intricate but unintelligible. Now this statement might mean something quite unobjectionable and even perhaps true and important. It might mean that the character cannot be *wholly* understood. As we saw, there may be questions which we cannot answer with certainty now, because we have nothing but the text to guide us, but which never arose for the spectators who saw *Hamlet* acted in Shakespeare's day; and we shall have to refer to such questions in these lectures. Again, it may be held without any improbability that, from carelessness or because he was engaged on this play for several years, Shakespeare left inconsistencies in his exhibition of the character which must prevent us from being certain of his ulti-

mate meaning. Or, possibly, we may be baffled because he has illustrated in it certain strange facts of human nature, which he had
noticed but of which we are ignorant. But then all this would apply
in some measure to other characters in Shakespeare, and it is not this
that is meant by the statement that Hamlet is unintelligible. What is
meant is that Shakespeare *intended* him to be so, because he himself
was feeling strongly, and wished his audience to feel strongly, what a
mystery life is, and how impossible it is for us to understand it. Now
here, surely, we have mere confusion of mind. The mysteriousness of
life is one thing, the psychological unintelligibility of a dramatic character is quite another; and the second does not show the first, it shows
only the incapacity or folly of the dramatist. If it did show the first, it
would be very easy to surpass Shakespeare in producing a sense of
mystery: we should simply have to portray an absolutely nonsensical
character. Of course *Hamlet* appeals powerfully to our sense of the
mystery of life, but so does *every* good tragedy; and it does so not
because the hero is an enigma to us, but because, having a fair understanding of him, we feel how strange it is that strength and weakness
should be so mingled in one soul, and that this soul should be
doomed to such misery and apparent failure.

(1) To come, then, to our typical views, we may lay it down, first,
that no theory will hold water which finds the cause of Hamlet's delay
merely, or mainly, or even to any considerable extent, in external difficulties. Nothing is easier than to spin a plausible theory of this kind.
What, it may be asked,[9] was Hamlet to do when the Ghost had left
him with its commission of vengeance? The King was surrounded not
merely by courtiers but by a Swiss body-guard: how was Hamlet to get
at him? Was he then to accuse him publicly of the murder? If he did,
what would happen? How would he prove the charge? All that he had
to offer in proof was – a ghost-story! Others, to be sure, had seen the
Ghost, but no one else had heard its revelations. Obviously, then, even
if the court had been honest, instead of subservient and corrupt, it
would have voted Hamlet mad, or worse, and would have shut him up
out of harm's way. He could not see what to do, therefore, and so he
waited. Then came the actors, and at once with admirable promptness

---

[9] I do not profess to reproduce any one theory, and, still less, to do justice to the ablest exponent of this kind of view, Werder* (*Vorlesungen über Hamlet*, 1875), who, by no means, regards
Hamlet's difficulties as *merely* external.

he arranged for the play-scene, hoping that the King would betray his guilt to the whole court. Unfortunately the King did not. It is true that immediately afterwards Hamlet got his chance; for he found the King defenceless on his knees. But what Hamlet wanted was not a private revenge, to be followed by his own imprisonment or execution; it was public justice. So he spared the King, and, as he unluckily killed Polonius just afterwards, he had to consent to be despatched to England. But, on the voyage there, he discovered the King's commission, ordering the King of England to put him immediately to death; and, with this in his pocket, he made his way back to Denmark. For now, he saw, the proof of the King's attempt to murder him would procure belief also for the story of the murder of his father. His enemy, however, was too quick for him, and his public arraignment of that enemy was prevented by his own death.

A theory like this sounds very plausible – so long as you do not remember the text. But no unsophisticated mind, fresh from the reading of *Hamlet*, will accept it; and, as soon as we begin to probe it, fatal objections arise in such numbers that I choose but a few, and indeed I think the first of them is enough.

(*a*) From beginning to end of the play, Hamlet never makes the slightest reference to any external difficulty. How is it possible to explain this fact in conformity with the theory? For what conceivable reason should Shakespeare conceal from us so carefully the key to the problem?

(*b*) Not only does Hamlet fail to allude to such difficulties, but he always assumes that he *can* obey the Ghost,[10] and he once asserts this in so many words ('Sith I have cause and will and strength and means To do't', IV.iv.45).

(*c*) Again, why does Shakespeare exhibit Laertes quite easily raising the people against the King? Why but to show how much more easily Hamlet, whom the people loved, could have done the same thing, if that was the plan he preferred?

(*d*) Again, Hamlet did *not* plan the play-scene in the hope that the King would betray his guilt to the court. He planned it, according to his own account, in order to convince *himself* by the King's agitation

---

[10] I give one instance. When he spares the King, he speaks of killing him when he is drunk asleep, when he is in his rage, when he is awake in bed, when he is gaming, as if there were in none of these cases the least obstacle (III.iii.89 ff.).

that the Ghost had spoken the truth. This is perfectly clear from II.ii. 625 ff. and from III.ii.80 ff. Some readers are misled by the words in the latter passage:

> if his occulted guilt
> Do not itself unkennel in one speech,
> It is a damned ghost that we have seen.

The meaning obviously is, as the context shows, 'if his hidden guilt do not betray itself *on occasion of* one speech', viz., the 'dozen or sixteen lines' with which Hamlet has furnished the player, and of which only six are delivered, because the King does not merely show his guilt in his face (which was all Hamlet had hoped, III.ii.90) but rushes from the room.

It may be as well to add that, although Hamlet's own account of his reason for arranging the play-scene may be questioned, it is impossible to suppose that, if his real design had been to provoke an open confession of guilt, he could have been unconscious of this design.

(*e*) Again, Hamlet never once talks, or shows a sign of thinking, of the plan of bringing the King to public justice; he always talks of using his 'sword' or his 'arm'. And this is so just as much after he has returned to Denmark with the commission in his pocket as it was before this event. When he has told Horatio the story of the voyage, he does not say, 'Now I can convict him'; he says, 'Now am I not justified in using this arm?'

This class of theory, then, we must simply reject. But it suggests two remarks. It is of course quite probable that, when Hamlet was 'thinking too precisely on the event', he was considering, among other things, the question how he could avenge his father without sacrificing his own life or freedom. And assuredly, also, he was anxious that his act of vengeance should not be misconstrued, and would never have been content to leave a 'wounded name' behind him. His dying words prove that.

(2) Assuming, now, that Hamlet's main difficulty — almost the whole of his difficulty — was internal, I pass to views which, acknowledging this, are still unsatisfactory because they isolate one element in his character and situation and treat it as the whole.

According to the first of these typical views, Hamlet was restrained by conscience or a moral scruple; he could not satisfy himself that it was right to avenge his father.

This idea, like the first, can easily be made to look very plausible, if we vaguely imagine the circumstances without attending to the text. But attention to the text is fatal to it. For, on the one hand, scarcely anything can be produced in support of it, and, on the other hand, a great deal can be produced in its disproof. To take the latter point first, Hamlet, it is impossible to deny, habitually assumes, without any questioning, that he *ought* to avenge his father. Even when he doubts, or thinks that he doubts, the honesty of the Ghost, he expresses no doubt as to what his duty will be if the Ghost turns out honest: 'If he but blench I know my course'. In the two soliloquies where he reviews his position (II.ii., 'O what a rogue and peasant slave am I,' and IV.iv., 'How all occasions do inform against me') he reproaches himself bitterly for the neglect of his duty. When he reflects on the possible causes of this neglect he never mentions among them a moral scruple. When the Ghost appears in the Queen's chamber, he confesses, conscience-stricken, that, lapsed in time and passion, he has let go by the acting of its command; but he does not plead that his conscience stood in his way. The Ghost itself says that it comes to whet his 'almost blunted purpose'; and conscience may unsettle a purpose but does not blunt it. What natural explanation of all this can be given on the conscience theory?

And now what can be set against this evidence? One solitary passage.[11] Quite late, after Hamlet has narrated to Horatio the events of his voyage, he asks him (V.ii.63)

> Does it not, think'st thee, stand me now upon –
> He that hath kill'd my king and whored my mother,
> Popp'd in between the election and my hopes,
> Thrown out his angle for my proper life,

---

[11] It is surprising to find quoted, in support of the conscience view, the line 'Thus conscience does make cowards of us all', and to observe the total misinterpretation of the soliloquy *To be or not to be*, from which the line comes. In this soliloquy Hamlet is not thinking of the duty laid upon him at all. He is debating the question of suicide. No one oppressed by the ills of life, he says, would continue to bear them if it were not for speculation about his possible fortune in another life. And then, generalizing, he says (what applies to himself, no doubt, though he shows no consciousness of the fact) that such speculation or reflection makes men hesitate and shrink like cowards from great actions and enterprises. 'Conscience' does not mean moral sense or scrupulosity, but this reflection on the *consequences* of action. It is the same thing as the 'craven scruple of thinking too precisely on the event' of the speech in IV. iv. As to the use of 'conscience', see Schmidt,* *s.v.* and the parallels there given. The *Oxford Dictionary* also gives many examples of similar uses of 'conscience', though it unfortunately lends its authority to the misinterpretation criticized.

> And with such cozenage – is't not perfect conscience
> To quit him with this arm? and is't not to be damn'd
> To let this canker of our nature come
> In further evil?

Here, certainly, is a question of conscience in the usual present sense of the word; and, it may be said, does not this show that all along Hamlet really has been deterred by moral scruples? But I ask first how, in that case, the facts just adduced are to be explained: for they must be explained, not ignored. Next, let the reader observe that even if this passage did show that *one* hindrance to Hamlet's action was his conscience, it by no means follows that this was the sole or the chief hindrance. And, thirdly, let him observe, and let him ask himself whether the coincidence is a mere accident, that Hamlet is here almost repeating the words he used in vain self-reproach some time before (IV.iv.56):

> How stand I then,
> That have a father kill'd, a mother stain'd,
> Excitements of my reason and my blood,
> And let all sleep?

Is it not clear that he is speculating just as vainly now, and that this question of conscience is but one of his many unconscious excuses for delay? And, lastly, is it not so that Horatio takes it? He declines to discuss that unreal question, and answers simply,

> It must be shortly known to him from England
> What is the issue of the business there.

In other words, 'Enough of this endless procrastination. What is wanted is not reasons for the deed, but the deed itself'. What can be more significant?

Perhaps, however, it may be answered: 'Your explanation of this passage may be correct, and the facts you have mentioned do seem to be fatal to the theory of conscience in its usual form. But there is another and subtler theory of conscience. According to it, Hamlet, so far as his explicit consciousness went, was sure that he ought to obey the Ghost; but in the depths of his nature, and unknown to himself, there was a moral repulsion to the deed. The conventional moral ideas of his time, which he shared with the Ghost, told him plainly that he ought to avenge his father; but a deeper conscience in him, which was in advance of his time, contended with these explicit conventional ideas. It is because this deeper conscience remains below the surface that he fails to recognize it, and fancies he is hindered by cowardice or sloth or passion or what not; but it emerges into light in that speech to Horatio. And it is just because he has this nobler moral nature in him that we admire and love him.'

Now I at once admit not only that this view is much more attractive and more truly tragic than the ordinary conscience theory, but that it has more verisimilitude. But I feel no doubt that it does not answer to Shakespeare's meaning, and I will simply mention, out of many objections to it, three which seem to be fatal. (*a*) If it answers to Shakespeare's meaning, why in the world did he conceal that meaning until the last Act? The facts adduced above seem to show beyond question that, on the hypothesis, he did so. That he did so is surely next door to incredible. In any case, it certainly requires an explanation, and certainly has not received one. (*b*) Let us test the theory by reference to a single important passage, that where Hamlet finds the King at prayer and spares him. The reason Hamlet gives himself for sparing the King is that, if he kills him now, he will send him to heaven, whereas he desires to send him to hell. Now, this reason may be an unconscious excuse, but is it believable that, if the real reason had been the stirrings of his deeper conscience, *that* could have masked itself in the form of a desire to send his enemy's soul to hell? Is not the idea quite ludicrous? (*c*) The theory requires us to suppose that, when the Ghost enjoins Hamlet to avenge the murder of his father, it is laying on him a duty which *we* are to understand to be no duty but the very reverse. And is not that supposition wholly contrary to the natural impression which we all receive in reading the play? Surely it is clear that, whatever we in the twentieth century may think about Hamlet's duty, we are meant in the play to assume that he *ought* to have obeyed the Ghost.

The conscience theory, then, in either of its forms we must reject. But it may remind us of points worth noting. In the first place, it is certainly true that Hamlet, in spite of some appearances to the contrary, was, as Goethe* said, of a most moral nature, and had a great anxiety to do right. In this anxiety he resembles Brutus, and it is stronger in him than in any of the later heroes. And, secondly, it is highly probable that in his interminable broodings the kind of paralysis with which he was stricken masked itself in the shape of conscientious scruples as well as in many other shapes. And, finally, in his shrinking from the deed there was probably, together with much else, something which may be called a moral, though not a conscientious, repulsion: I mean a repugnance to the idea of falling suddenly on a man who could not defend himself. This, so far as we can see, was the only plan that Hamlet ever contemplated. There is no positive evidence in the play that he regarded it with the aversion that any brave and honourable man, one must suppose, would feel for it; but, as Hamlet certainly was brave and honourable, we may presume that he did so.

(3) We come next to what may be called the sentimental view of Hamlet, a view common both among his worshippers and among his defamers. Its germ may perhaps be found in an unfortunate phrase of Goethe's (who of course is not responsible for the whole view): 'a lovely, pure and most moral nature, *without the strength of nerve which forms a hero*, sinks beneath a burden which it cannot bear and must not cast away'.* When this idea is isolated, developed and popular- ized, we get the picture of a graceful youth, sweet and sensitive, full of delicate sympathies and yearning aspirations, shrinking from the touch of everything gross and earthly; but frail and weak, a kind of Werther,* with a face like Shelley's and a voice like Mr. Tree's.* And then we ask in tender pity, how could such a man perform the ter- rible duty laid on him?

How, indeed! And what a foolish Ghost even to suggest such a duty! But this conception, though not without its basis in certain beautiful traits of Hamlet's nature, is utterly untrue. It is too kind to Hamlet on one side, and it is quite unjust to him on another. The 'conscience' theory at any rate leaves Hamlet a great nature which you can admire and even revere. But for the 'sentimental' Hamlet you can feel only pity not unmingled with contempt. Whatever else he is, he is no *hero*.

But consider the text. This shrinking, flower-like youth – how could he possibly have done what we *see* Hamlet do? What likeness to him is there in the Hamlet who, summoned by the Ghost, bursts from his terrified friends with the cry:

> Unhand me, gentlemen!
> By heaven, I'll make a ghost of him that lets me;

the Hamlet who scarcely once speaks to the King without an insult, or to Polonius without a gibe; the Hamlet who storms at Ophelia and speaks daggers to his mother; the Hamlet who, hearing a cry behind the arras, whips out his sword in an instant and runs the eavesdropper through; the Hamlet who sends his 'school-fellows' to their death and never troubles his head about them more; the Hamlet who is the first man to board a pirate ship, and who fights with Laertes in the grave; the Hamlet of the catastrophe, an omnipotent fate, before whom all the court stands helpless, who, as the truth breaks upon him, rushes on the King, drives his foil right through his body,[12] then seizes the poisoned cup and forces it violently between the wretched man's lips, and in the throes of death has force and fire enough to wrest the cup from Horatio's hand ('By heaven, I'll have it!') lest he should drink and die? This man, the Hamlet of the play, is a heroic, terrible figure. He would have been formidable to Othello or Macbeth. If the sentimental Hamlet had crossed him, he would have hurled him from his path with one sweep of his arm.

This view, then, or any view that approaches it, is grossly unjust to Hamlet, and turns tragedy into mere pathos. But, on the other side, it is too kind to him. It ignores the hardness and cynicism which were indeed no part of his nature, but yet, in this crisis of his life, are indubitably present and painfully marked. His sternness, itself left out of sight by this theory, is no defect; but he is much more than stern. Polonius possibly deserved nothing better than the words addressed to his corpse:

> Thou wretched, rash, intruding fool, farewell!
> I took thee for thy better: take thy fortune:
> Thou find'st to be too busy is some danger;

yet this was Ophelia's father, and, whatever he deserved, it pains us, for Hamlet's sake, to hear the words:

> This man shall set me packing:
> I'll lug the guts into the neighbour room.

There is the same insensibility in Hamlet's language about the fate of Rosencrantz and Guildenstern; and, observe, their deaths were not in the least required by his purpose. Grant, again, that his cruelty to

---

[12] The King does not die of the *poison* on the foil, like Laertes and Hamlet. They are wounded before he was, but they die after him.

Ophelia was partly due to misunderstanding, partly forced on him, partly feigned; still one surely cannot altogether so account for it, and still less can one so account for the disgusting and insulting grossness of his language to her in the play-scene. I know this is said to be merely an example of the custom of Shakespeare's time. But it is not so. It is such language as you will find addressed to a woman by no other hero of Shakespeare's, not even in that dreadful scene where Othello accuses Desdemona. It is a great mistake to ignore these things, or to try to soften the impression which they naturally make on one. That this embitterment, callousness, grossness, brutality, should be induced on a soul so pure and noble is profoundly tragic; and Shakespeare's business was to show this tragedy, not to paint an ideally beautiful soul unstained and undisturbed by the evil of the world and the anguish of conscious failure.[13]

(4) There remains, finally, that class of view which may be named after Schlegel* and Coleridge.* According to this, *Hamlet* is the tragedy of reflection. The cause of the hero's delay is irresolution; and the cause of this irresolution is excess of the reflective or speculative

---

[13] I may add here a word on one small matter. It is constantly asserted that Hamlet wept over the body of Polonius. Now, if he did, it would make no difference to my point in the paragraph above; but there is no warrant in the text for the assertion. It is based on some words of the Queen (IV.i.24), in answer to the King's question, 'Where is he gone?':

> To draw apart the body he hath killed:
> O'er whom his very madness, like some ore
> Among a mineral of metals base,
> Shows itself pure; he weeps for what is done

But the Queen, as was pointed out by Doering, is trying to screen her son. She has already made the false statement that when Hamlet, crying, 'A rat! a rat!', ran his rapier through the arras, it was because he heard *something stir* there, whereas we know that what he heard was a man's voice crying, 'What ho! help, help, help!' And in this scene she has come straight from the interview with her son, terribly agitated, shaken with 'sighs' and 'profound heaves', in the night (line 30). Now we know what Hamlet said to the body, and of the body, in that interview; and there is assuredly no sound of tears in the voice that said those things and others. The only sign of relenting is in the words (III.iv.171):

> For this same lord,
> I do repent: but heaven hath pleased it so,
> To punish me with this and this with me,
> That I must be their scourge and minister.

His mother's statement, therefore, is almost certainly untrue, though it may be to her credit. (It is just conceivable that Hamlet wept at III.iv.130, and that the Queen supposed he was weeping for Polonius.)

Perhaps, however, he may have wept over Polonius's body afterwards? Well, in the *next* scene (IV.ii.) we see him *alone* with the body, and are therefore likely to witness his genuine feelings. And his first words are, 'Safely stowed'!

habit of mind. He has a general intention to obey the Ghost, but 'the native hue of resolution is sicklied o'er with the pale cast of thought'. He is 'thought-sick'. 'The whole', says Schlegel, 'is intended to show how a calculating consideration which aims at exhausting, so far as human foresight can, all the relations and possible consequences of a deed, cripples[14] the power of acting. . . . Hamlet is a hypocrite towards himself; his far-fetched scruples are often mere pretexts to cover his want of determination. . . . He has no firm belief in himself or in anything else. . . . He loses himself in labyrinths of thought.' So Coleridge finds in Hamlet 'an almost enormous intellectual activity and a proportionate aversion to real action consequent upon it' (the aversion, that is to say, is consequent on the activity). Professor Dowden* objects to this view, very justly, that it neglects the emotional side of Hamlet's character, 'which is quite as important as the intellectual'; but, with this supplement, he appears on the whole to adopt it. Hamlet, he says, 'loses a sense of fact because with him each object and event transforms and expands itself into an idea. . . . He cannot steadily keep alive within himself a sense of the importance of any positive, limited thing, – a deed, for example'. And Professor Dowden explains this condition by reference to Hamlet's life. 'When the play opens he has reached the age of thirty years . . . and he has received culture of every kind except the culture of active life. During the reign of the strong-willed elder Hamlet there was no call to action for his meditative son. He has slipped on into years of full manhood still a haunter of the university, a student of philosophies, an amateur in art, a ponderer on the things of life and death, who has never formed a resolution or executed a deed' (*Shakespeare, his Mind and Art*, 4th ed., pp. 132, 133).

On the whole, the Schlegel–Coleridge theory (with or without Professor Dowden's modification and amplification) is the most widely received view of Hamlet's character. And with it we come at last into close contact with the text of the play. It not only answers, in some fundamental respects, to the general impression produced by the drama, but it can be supported by Hamlet's own words in his soliloquies – such words, for example, as those about the native hue of resolution, or those about the craven scruple of thinking too precisely

---

[14] Not 'must cripple', as the English translation has it.

on the event. It is confirmed, also, by the contrast between Hamlet on the one side, and Laertes and Fortinbras on the other; and, further, by the occurrence of those words of the King to Laertes (IV.vii.119 f.), which, if they are not in character, are all the more important as showing what was in Shakespeare's mind at the time:

> that we would do
> We should do when we would; for this 'would' changes,
> And hath abatements and delays as many
> As there are tongues, are hands, are accidents;
> And then this 'should' is like a spendthrift sigh
> That hurts by easing.

And, lastly, even if the view itself does not suffice, the *description* given by its adherents of Hamlet's state of mind, as we see him in the last four Acts, is, on the whole and so far as it goes, a true description. The energy of resolve is dissipated in an endless brooding on the deed required. When he acts, his action does not proceed from this deliberation and analysis, but is sudden and impulsive, evoked by an emergency in which he has no time to think. And most of the reasons he assigns for his procrastination are evidently not the true reasons, but unconscious excuses.

Nevertheless this theory fails to satisfy. And it fails not merely in this or that detail, but as a whole. We feel that its Hamlet does not fully answer to our imaginative impression. He is not nearly so inadequate to this impression as the sentimental Hamlet, but still we feel he is inferior to Shakespeare's man and does him wrong. And when we come to examine the theory we find that it is partial and leaves much unexplained. I pass that by for the present, for we shall see, I believe, that the theory is also positively misleading, and that in a most important way. And of this I proceed to speak.

Hamlet's irresolution, or his aversion to real action, is, according to the theory, the *direct* result of 'an almost enormous intellectual activity' in the way of 'a calculating consideration which attempts to exhaust all the relations and possible consequences of a deed'. And this again proceeds from an original one-sidedness of nature, strengthened by habit, and, perhaps, by years of speculative inaction. The theory describes, therefore, a man in certain respects like Coleridge himself, on one side a man of genius, on the other side, the side of will, deplorably weak, always procrastinating and avoiding unpleasant duties, and often reproaching himself in vain; a man, observe, who at *any* time and in *any* circumstances would be unequal to the task assigned to Hamlet. And thus, I must maintain, it degrades Hamlet and travesties the play. For Hamlet, according to all the indications in the text, was not naturally or normally such a man, but rather, I venture to affirm, a man who at any *other* time and in any *other* circumstances than those presented would have been perfectly equal to his task; and it is, in fact, the very cruelty of his fate that the crisis of his life comes on him at the one moment when he cannot meet it, and when his highest gifts, instead of helping him, conspire to para-lyse him. This aspect of the tragedy the theory quite misses; and it does so because it misconceives the cause of that irresolution which, on the whole, it truly describes. For the cause was not directly or mainly an habitual excess of reflectiveness. The direct cause was a state of mind quite abnormal and induced by special circumstances – a state of profound melancholy. Now, Hamlet's reflectiveness doubtless played a certain part in the *production* of that melancholy, and was thus one indirect contributory cause of his irresolution. And, again, the melan-choly, once established, displayed, as one of its *symptoms*, an excessive reflection on the required deed. But excess of reflection was not, as the theory makes it, the *direct* cause of the irresolution at all; nor was it the *only* indirect cause; and in the Hamlet of the last four Acts it is to be considered rather a symptom of his state than a cause of it.

These assertions may be too brief to be at once clear, but I hope they will presently become so.

3

Let us first ask ourselves what we can gather from the play, immedi-ately or by inference, concerning Hamlet as he was just before his father's death. And I begin by observing that the text does not bear out the idea that he was one-sidedly reflective and indisposed to action. Nobody who knew him seems to have noticed this weakness. Nobody regards him as a mere scholar who has 'never formed a reso-lution or executed a deed'. In a court which certainly would not much admire such a person he is the observed of all observers. Though he has been disappointed of the throne everyone shows him respect; and he is the favourite of the people, who are not given to worship philosophers. Fortinbras, a sufficiently practical man, considered that he was likely, had he been put on, to have proved most royally. He has Hamlet borne by four captains 'like a soldier' to his grave; and Ophelia says that Hamlet *was* a soldier. If he was fond of acting, an aesthetic pursuit, he was equally fond of fencing, an athletic one: he practised it assiduously even in his worst days.[15] So far as we can conjecture from what we see of him in those bad days, he must normally have been charmingly frank, courteous and kindly to everyone, of whatever rank, whom he liked or respected, but by no means timid or deferential to others; indeed, one would gather that he was rather the reverse, and also that he was apt to be decided and even imperious if thwarted or interfered with. He must always have been fearless – in the play he appears insensible to fear of any ordinary kind. And, finally, he must have been quick and impetuous in action; for it is downright impossible that the man we see rushing after the Ghost, killing Polonius, dealing with the King's commission on the ship, boarding the pirate, leaping into the grave, executing his final vengeance, could *ever* have been shrinking or slow in an emergency. Imagine Coleridge doing any of these things!

If we consider all this, how can we accept the notion that Hamlet's was a weak and one-sided character? 'Oh, but he spent ten or twelve years at a University!' Well, even if he did, it is possible to do that without becoming the victim of excessive thought. But the statement that he did rests upon a most insecure foundation.[16]

Where then are we to look for the seeds of danger?

(1) Trying to reconstruct from the Hamlet of the play, one would not judge that his temperament was melancholy in the present sense of the word; there seems nothing to show that; but one would judge that by temperament he was inclined to nervous instability, to rapid and perhaps extreme changes of feeling and mood, and that he was disposed to be, for the time, absorbed in the feeling or mood that possessed him, whether it were joyous or depressed. This temperament the Elizabethans would have called melancholic; and Hamlet seems to be an example of it, as Lear is of a temperament mixedly choleric and sanguine. And the doctrine of temperaments was so familiar in Shakespeare's time – as Burton,* and earlier prose-writers,

---

[15] He says so to Horatio, whom he has no motive for deceiving (V.ii.218). His contrary statement (II.ii.308) is made to Rosencrantz and Guildenstern.

[16] See Note B.

and many of the dramatists show – that Shakespeare may quite well have given this temperament to Hamlet consciously and deliberately. Of melancholy in its developed form, a habit, not a mere temperament, he often speaks. He more than once laughs at the passing and half-fictitious melancholy of youth and love; in Don John in *Much Ado* he had sketched the sour and surly melancholy of discontent; in Jaques a whimsical self-pleasing melancholy; in Antonio in the *Merchant of Venice* a quiet but deep melancholy, for which neither the victim nor his friends can assign any cause.[17] He gives to Hamlet a temperament which would not develop into melancholy unless under some exceptional strain, but which still involved a danger. In the play we see the danger realized, and find a melancholy quite unlike any that Shakespeare had as yet depicted, because the temperament of Hamlet is quite different.

(2) Next, we cannot be mistaken in attributing to the Hamlet of earlier days an exquisite sensibility, to which we may give the name 'moral', if that word is taken in the wide meaning it ought to bear. This, though it suffers cruelly in later days, as we saw in criticizing the sentimental view of Hamlet, never deserts him; it makes all his cynicism, grossness and hardness appear to us morbidities, and has an inexpressibly attractive and pathetic effect. He had the soul of the youthful poet as Shelley and Tennyson have described it, an unbounded delight and faith in everything good and beautiful. We know this from himself. The world for him was *herrlich wie am ersten Tag** – 'This goodly frame the earth, this most excellent canopy the air, this brave, o'erhanging firmament, this majestical roof fretted with golden fire'. And not nature only: 'What a piece of work is a man! how noble in reason! how infinite in faculty! in form and moving how express and admirable! in action how like an angel! in apprehension how like a god!' This is no commonplace to Hamlet; it is the language of a heart thrilled with wonder and swelling into ecstasy.

Doubtless it was with the same eager enthusiasm he turned to those around him. Where else in Shakespeare is there anything like Hamlet's adoration of his father? The words melt into music when-

---

[17] The critics have laboured to find a cause, but it seems to me Shakespeare simply meant to portray a pathological condition; and a very touching picture he draws. Antonio's sadness, which he describes in the opening lines of the play, would never drive him to suicide, but it makes him indifferent to the issue of the trial, as all his speeches in the trial-scene show.

ever he speaks of him. And, if there are no signs of any such feeling towards his mother, though many signs of love, it is characteristic that he evidently never entertained a suspicion of anything unworthy in her – characteristic, and significant of his tendency to see only what is good unless he is forced to see the reverse. For we find this tendency elsewhere, and find it going so far that we must call it a disposition to idealize, to see something better than what is there, or at least to ignore deficiencies. He says to Laertes, 'I loved you ever', and he describes Laertes as a 'very noble youth', which he was far from being. In his first greeting of Rosencrantz and Guildenstern, where his old self revives, we trace the same affectionateness and readiness to take men at their best. His love for Ophelia, too, which seems strange to some, is surely the most natural thing in the world. He saw her innocence, simplicity and sweetness, and it was like him to ask no more; and it is noticeable that Horatio, though entirely worthy of his friendship, is, like Ophelia, intellectually not remarkable. To the very end, however clouded, this generous disposition, this 'free and open nature', this unsuspiciousness survive. They cost him his life; for the King knew them, and was sure that he was too 'generous and free from all contriving' to 'peruse the foils'. To the very end, his soul, however sick and tortured it may be, answers instantaneously when good and evil are presented to it, loving the one and hating the other. He is called a sceptic who has no firm belief in anything, but he is never sceptical about *them.*

And the negative side of his idealism, the aversion to evil, is perhaps even more developed in the hero of the tragedy than in the Hamlet of earlier days. It is intensely characteristic. Nothing, I believe, is to be found elsewhere in Shakespeare (unless in the rage of the disillusioned idealist Timon) of quite the same kind as Hamlet's disgust at his uncle's drunkenness, his loathing of his mother's sensuality, his astonishment and horror at her shallowness, his contempt for everything pretentious or false, his indifference to everything merely external. This last characteristic appears in his choice of the friend of his heart, and in a certain impatience of distinctions of rank or wealth. When Horatio calls his father 'a goodly king', he answers, surely with an emphasis on 'man',

> He was a man, take him for all in all,
> I shall not look upon his like again.

He will not listen to talk of Horatio being his 'servant'. When the others speak of their 'duty' to him, he answers, 'Your love, as mine to you'. He speaks to the actor precisely as he does to an honest courtier. He is not in the least a revolutionary, but still, in effect, a king and a beggar are all one to him. He cares for nothing but human worth, and his pitilessness towards Polonius and Osric and his 'school-fellows' is not wholly due to morbidity, but belongs in part to his original character.

Now, in Hamlet's moral sensibility there undoubtedly lay a danger. Any great shock that life might inflict on it would be felt with extreme intensity. Such a shock might even produce tragic results. And, in fact, *Hamlet* deserves the title 'tragedy of moral idealism' quite as much as the title 'tragedy of reflection'.

(3) With this temperament and this sensibility we find, lastly, in the Hamlet of earlier days, as of later, intellectual genius. It is chiefly this that makes him so different from all those about him, good and bad alike, and hardly less different from most of Shakespeare's other heroes. And this, though on the whole the most important trait in his nature, is also so obvious and so famous that I need not dwell on it at length. But against one prevalent misconception I must say a word of warning. Hamlet's intellectual power is not a specific gift, like a genius for music or mathematics or philosophy. It shows itself, fitfully, in the affairs of life as unusual quickness of perception, great agility in shifting the mental attitude, a striking rapidity and fertility in resource; so that, when his natural belief in others does not make him unwary, Hamlet easily sees through them and masters them, and no one can be much less like the typical helpless dreamer. It shows itself in conversation chiefly in the form of wit or humour; and, alike in conversation and in soliloquy, it shows itself in the form of imagination quite as much as in that of thought in the stricter sense. Further, where it takes the latter shape, as it very often does, it is not philosophic in the technical meaning of the word. There is really nothing in the play to show that Hamlet ever was 'a student of philosophies', unless it be the famous lines which, comically enough, exhibit this supposed victim of philosophy as its critic:

> There are more things in heaven and earth, Horatio,
> Than are dreamt of in your philosophy.[18]

---

[18] Of course 'your' does not mean Horatio's philosophy in particular. 'Your' is used as the Gravedigger uses it when he says that 'your water is a sore decayer of your . . . dead body.'

His philosophy, if the word is to be used, was, like Shakespeare's own, the immediate product of the wondering and meditating mind; and such thoughts as that celebrated one, 'There is nothing either good or bad but thinking makes it so', surely needed no special training to produce them. Or does Portia's remark, 'Nothing is good without respect', *i.e.*, out of relation, prove that she had studied metaphysics?

Still Hamlet had speculative genius without being a philosopher, just as he had imaginative genius without being a poet. Doubtless in happier days he was a close and constant observer of men and manners, noting his results in those tables which he afterwards snatched from his breast to make in wild irony his last note of all, that one may smile and smile and be a villain. Again and again we remark that passion for generalization which so occupied him, for instance, in reflections suggested by the King's drunkenness that he quite forgot what it was he was waiting to meet upon the battlements. Doubtless, too, he was always considering things, as Horatio thought, too curiously. There was a necessity in his soul driving him to penetrate below the surface and to question what others took for granted. That fixed habitual look which the world wears for most men did not exist for him. He was for ever unmaking his world and rebuilding it in thought, dissolving what to others were solid facts, and discovering what to others were old truths. There were no old truths for Hamlet. It is for Horatio a thing of course that there's a divinity that shapes our ends, but for Hamlet it is a discovery hardly won. And throughout this kingdom of the mind, where he felt that man, who in action is only like an angel, is in apprehension like a god, he moved (we must imagine) more than content, so that even in his dark days he declares he could be bounded in a nutshell and yet count himself a king of infinite space, were it not that he had bad dreams.

If now we ask whether any special danger lurked *here*, how shall we answer? We must answer, it seems to me, 'Some danger, no doubt, but, granted the ordinary chances of life, not much.' For, in the first place, that idea which so many critics quietly take for granted – the idea that the gift and the habit of meditative and speculative thought tend to produce irresolution in the affairs of life – would be found by no means easy to verify. Can you verify it, for example, in the lives of the philosophers, or again the lives of men whom you have personally known to be addicted to such speculation? I cannot. Of course, individual peculiarities being set apart, absorption in *any* intellectual interest, together with withdrawal from affairs, may make a man slow and unskilful in affairs; and doubtless, individual peculiarities being again set apart, a mere student is likely to be more at a loss in a sudden and great practical emergency than a soldier or a lawyer. But in all this there is no difference between a physicist, a historian, and a philosopher; and again, slowness, want of skill, and even helplessness are something totally different from the peculiar kind of irresolution that Hamlet shows. The notion that speculative thinking specially tends to produce *this* is really a mere illusion.

In the second place, even if this notion were true, it has appeared that Hamlet did *not* live the life of a mere student, much less of a mere dreamer, and that his nature was by no means simply or even one-sidedly intellectual, but was healthily active. Hence, granted the ordinary chances of life, there would seem to be no great danger in his intellectual tendency and his habit of speculation; and I would go further and say that there was nothing in them, taken alone, to unfit him even for the extraordinary call that was made upon him. In fact, if the message of the Ghost had come to him within a week of his father's death, I see no reason to doubt that he would have acted on it as decisively as Othello himself, though probably after a longer and more anxious deliberation. And therefore the Schlegel–Coleridge view (apart from its descriptive value) seems to me fatally untrue, for it implies that Hamlet's procrastination was the normal response of an over-speculative nature confronted with a difficult practical problem.

On the other hand, under conditions of a peculiar kind, Hamlet's reflectiveness certainly might prove dangerous to him, and his genius might even (to exaggerate a little) become his doom. Suppose that violent shock to his moral being of which I spoke; and suppose that under this shock, any possible action being denied to him, he began to sink into melancholy; then, no doubt, his imaginative and generalizing habit of mind might extend the effects of this shock through his whole being and mental world. And if, the state of melancholy being thus deepened and fixed, a sudden demand for difficult and decisive action in a matter connected with the melancholy arose, this state might well have for one of its symptoms an endless and futile mental dissection of the required deed. And, finally, the futility of this process, and the shame of his delay, would further weaken him and enslave him to his melancholy still more. Thus the speculative habit would be *one* indirect cause of the morbid state which hindered action; and it would also reappear in a degenerate form as one of the *symptoms* of this morbid state.

Now this is what actually happens in the play. Turn to the first words Hamlet utters when he is alone; turn, that is to say, to the place where the author is likely to indicate his meaning most plainly. What do you hear?

> O, that this too too solid flesh would melt,
> Thaw and resolve itself into a dew!
> Or that the Everlasting had not fix'd
> His canon 'gainst self-slaughter! O God! God!
> How weary, stale, flat and unprofitable,
> Seem to me all the uses of this world!
> Fie on't! ah fie! 'tis an unweeded garden,
> That grows to seed; things rank and gross in nature
> Possess it merely.

Here are a sickness of life, and even a longing for death, so intense that nothing stands between Hamlet and suicide except religious awe. And what has caused them? The rest of the soliloquy so thrusts the answer upon us that it might seem impossible to miss it. It was not his father's death; that doubtless brought deep grief, but mere grief for some one loved and lost does not make a noble spirit loathe the world as a place full only of things rank and gross. It was not the vague suspicion that we know Hamlet felt. Still less was it the loss of the crown; for though the subserviency of the electors might well disgust him, there is not a reference to the subject in the soliloquy, nor any sign elsewhere that it greatly occupied his mind. It was the moral shock of the sudden ghastly disclosure of his mother's true nature, falling on him when his heart was aching with love, and his body doubtless was weakened by sorrow. And it is essential, however disagreeable, to realize the nature of this shock. It matters little here whether Hamlet's age was twenty or thirty: in either case his mother was a matron of mature years. All his life he had believed in her, we may be sure, as such a son would. He had seen her not merely devoted to his father, but hanging on him like a newly-wedded bride, hanging on him

> As if increase of appetite had grown
> By what it fed on.

He had seen her following his body 'like Niobe, all tears'. And then within a month – 'O God! a beast would have mourned longer' – she married again, and married Hamlet's uncle, a man utterly contemptible and loathsome in his eyes; married him in what to Hamlet was incestuous wedlock;[19] married him not for any reason of state, nor even out of old family affection, but in such a way that her son was forced to see in her action not only an astounding shallowness of feeling but an eruption of coarse sensuality, 'rank and gross',[20] speeding post-haste to its horrible delight. Is it possible to conceive an experience more desolating to a man such as we have seen Hamlet to be; and is its result anything but perfectly natural? It brings bewildered horror, then loathing, then despair of human nature. His whole mind is poisoned. He can never see Ophelia in the same light again: she is a woman, and his mother is a woman: if she mentions the word 'brief' to him, the answer drops from his lips like venom, 'as woman's love'. The last words of the soliloquy, which is *wholly* concerned with this subject, are,

But, break, my heart, for I must hold my tongue!

He can do nothing. He must lock in his heart, not any suspicion of his uncle that moves obscurely there, but that horror and loathing; and if his heart ever found relief, it was when those feelings, mingled with the love that never died out in him, poured themselves forth in a flood as he stood in his mother's chamber beside his father's marriage-bed.[21]

If we still wonder, and ask why the effect of this shock should be so tremendous, let us observe that *now* the conditions have arisen under which Hamlet's highest endowments, his moral sensibility and

---

[19] This aspect of the matter leaves us comparatively unaffected, but Shakespeare evidently means it to be of importance. The Ghost speaks of it twice, and Hamlet thrice (once in his last furious words to the King). If, as we must suppose, the marriage was universally admitted to be incestuous, the corrupt acquiescence of the court and the electors to the crown would naturally have a strong effect on Hamlet's mind.

[20] It is most significant that the metaphor of this soliloquy reappears in Hamlet's adjuration to his mother (III.iv.150):

Repent what's past; avoid what is to come;
And do not spread the compost on the weeds
To make them ranker.

[21] If the reader will now look at the only speech of Hamlet's that precedes the soliloquy, and is more than one line in length – the speech beginning 'Seems, madam! nay, it *is*' – he will understand what, surely, when first we come to it, sounds very strange and almost boastful. It is not, in effect, about Hamlet himself at all; it is about his mother (I do not mean that it is intentionally and consciously so; and still less that she understood it so).

his genius, become his enemies. A nature morally blunter would have felt even so dreadful a revelation less keenly. A slower and more limited and positive mind might not have extended so widely through its world the disgust and disbelief that have entered it. But Hamlet has the imagination which, for evil as well as good, feels and sees all things in one. Thought is the element of his life, and his thought is infected. He cannot prevent himself from probing and lacerating the wound in his soul. One idea, full of peril, holds him fast, and he cries out in agony at it, but is impotent to free himself ('Must I remember?' 'Let me not think on't'). And when, with the fading of his passion, the vividness of this idea abates, it does so only to leave behind a boundless weariness and a sick longing for death.

And this is the time which his fate chooses. In this hour of uttermost weakness, this sinking of his whole being towards annihilation, there comes on him, bursting the bounds of the natural world with a shock of astonishment and terror, the revelation of his mother's adultery and his father's murder, and, with this, the demand on him, in the name of everything dearest and most sacred, to arise and act. And for a moment, though his brain reels and totters,[22] his soul leaps up in passion to answer this demand. But it comes too late. It does but strike home the last rivet in the melancholy which holds him bound.

> The time is out of joint! O cursed spite
> That ever I was born to set it right –

so he mutters within an hour of the moment when he vowed to give his life to the duty of revenge; and the rest of the story exhibits his vain efforts to fulfil this duty, his unconscious self-excuses and unavailing self-reproaches, and the tragic results of his delay.

4

'Melancholy,' I said, not dejection, nor yet insanity. That Hamlet was not far from insanity is very probable. His adoption of the pretence of madness may well have been due in part to fear of the reality; to an instinct of self-preservation, a fore-feeling that the pretence would enable him to give some utterance to the load that pressed on his heart and brain, and a fear that he would be unable altogether to repress

---

[22] See Note D.

such utterance. And if the pathologist calls his state melancholia, and even proceeds to determine its species, I see nothing to object to in that; I am grateful to him for emphasizing the fact that Hamlet's melancholy was no mere common depression of spirits; and I have no doubt that many readers of the play would understand it better if they read an account of melancholia in a work on mental diseases. If we like to use the word 'disease' loosely, Hamlet's condition may truly be called diseased. No exertion of will could have dispelled it. Even if he had been able at once to do the bidding of the Ghost he would doubt-less have still remained for some time under the cloud. It would be absurdly unjust to call *Hamlet* a study of melancholy, but it contains such a study.

But this melancholy is something very different from insanity, in anything like the usual meaning of that word. No doubt it might develop into insanity. The longing for death might become an irre-sistible impulse to self-destruction; the disorder of feeling and will might extend to sense and intellect; delusions might arise; and the man might become, as we say, incapable and irresponsible. But Hamlet's melancholy is some way from this condition. It is a totally different thing from the madness which he feigns; and he never, when alone or in company with Horatio alone, exhibits the signs of that madness. Nor is the dramatic use of this melancholy, again, open to the objections which would justly be made to the portrayal of an insanity which brought the hero to a tragic end. The man who suffers as Hamlet suffers – and thousands go about their business suffering thus in greater or less degree – is considered irresponsible neither by other people nor by himself: he is only too keenly conscious of his responsibility. He is therefore, so far, quite capable of being a tragic agent, which an insane person, at any rate according to Shakespeare's practice, is not.[23] And, finally, Hamlet's state is not one which a healthy mind is unable sufficiently to imagine. It is probably not further from average experience, nor more difficult to realize, than the great tragic passions of Othello, Antony or Macbeth.

Let me try to show now, briefly, how much this melancholy accounts for.

It accounts for the main fact, Hamlet's inaction. For the *immediate* cause of that is simply that his habitual feeling is one of disgust at life

---

[23] See p. 8.

and everything in it, himself included – a disgust which varies in intensity, rising at times into a longing for death, sinking often into weary apathy, but is never dispelled for more than brief intervals. Such a state of feeling is inevitably adverse to *any* kind of decided action; the body is inert, the mind indifferent or worse; its response is, 'it does not matter', 'it is not worth while', 'it is no good'. And the action required of Hamlet is very exceptional. It is violent, dangerous, difficult to accomplish perfectly, on one side repulsive to a man of honour and sensitive feeling, on another side involved in a certain mystery (here come in thus, in their subordinate place, various causes of inaction assigned by various theories). These obstacles would not suffice to prevent Hamlet from acting, if his state were normal; and against them there operate, even in his morbid state, healthy and positive feelings, love of his father, loathing of his uncle, desire of revenge, desire to do duty. But the retarding motives acquire an unnatural strength because they have an ally in something far stronger than themselves, the melancholic disgust and apathy; while the healthy motives, emerging with difficulty from the central mass of diseased feeling, rapidly sink back into it and 'lose the name of action'. We *see* them doing so; and sometimes the process is quite simple, no analytical reflection on the deed intervening between the outburst of passion and the relapse into melancholy.[24] But this melancholy is perfectly consistent also with that incessant dissection of the task assigned, of which the Schlegel–Coleridge theory makes so much. For those endless questions (as we may imagine them), 'Was I deceived by the Ghost? How am I to do the deed? When? Where? What will be the consequence of attempting it – success, my death, utter misunderstanding, mere mischief to the State? Can it be right to do it, or noble to kill a defenceless man? What is the good of doing it in such a world as this?' – all this, and whatever else passed in a sickening round through Hamlet's mind, was not the healthy and right deliberation of a man with such a task, but otiose thinking hardly deserving the name of thought, an unconscious weaving of pretexts for inaction, aimless tossings on a sick bed, symptoms of melancholy which only increased it by deepening self-contempt.

---

[24] *E.g.* in the transition, referred to above, from desire for vengeance into the wish never to have been born; in the soliloquy, 'O what a rogue'; in the scene at Ophelia's grave. The Schlegel–Coleridge theory does not account for the psychological movement in those passages.

Again, (*a*) this state accounts for Hamlet's energy as well as for his lassitude, those quick decided actions of his being the outcome of a nature normally far from passive, now suddenly stimulated, and producing healthy impulses which work themselves out before they have time to subside. (*b*) It accounts for the evidently keen satisfaction which some of these actions give to him. He arranges the play-scene with lively interest, and exults in its success, not really because it brings him nearer to his goal, but partly because it has hurt his enemy and partly because it has demonstrated his own skill (III.ii.286–304). He looks forward almost with glee to countermining the King's designs in sending him away (III.iv.209), and looks back with obvious satisfaction, even with pride, to the address and vigour he displayed on the voyage (V.ii.1–55). These were not *the* action on which his morbid self-feeling had centred; he feels in them his old force, and escapes in them from his disgust. (*c*) It accounts for the pleasure with which he meets old acquaintances, like his 'school-fellows' or the actors. The former observed (and we can observe) in him a 'kind of joy' at first, though it is followed by 'much forcing of his disposition' as he attempts to keep his joy and his courtesy alive in spite of the misery which so soon returns upon him and the suspicion he is forced to feel. (*d*) It accounts no less for the painful features of his character as seen in the play, his almost savage irritability on the one hand, and on the other his self-absorption, his callousness, his insensibility to the fates of those whom he despises, and to the feelings even of those whom he loves. These are frequent symptoms of such melancholy, and (*e*) they sometimes alternate, as they do in Hamlet, with bursts of transitory, almost hysterical, and quite fruitless emotion. It is to these last (of which a part of the soliloquy, 'O what a rogue', gives a good example) that Hamlet alludes when, to the Ghost, he speaks of himself as 'lapsed in *passion*', and it is doubtless partly his conscious weakness in regard to them that inspires his praise of Horatio as a man who is not 'passion's slave'.[25]

---

[25] Hamlet's violence at Ophelia's grave, though probably intentionally exaggerated, is another example of this want of self-control. The Queen's description of him (V.i.307),

> This is mere madness;
> And thus awhile the fit will work on him;
> Anon, as patient as the female dove,
> When that her golden couplets are disclosed,
> His silence will sit drooping,

Finally, Hamlet's melancholy accounts for two things which seem to be explained by nothing else. The first of these is his apathy or 'lethargy'. We are bound to consider the evidence which the text supplies of this, though it is usual to ignore it. When Hamlet mentions, as one possible cause of his inaction, his 'thinking too precisely on the event', he mentions another, 'bestial oblivion'; and the thing against which he inveighs in the greater part of that soliloquy (IV.iv.) is not the excess or the misuse of reason (which for him here and always is god-like), but this *bestial* oblivion or '*dullness*', this 'letting all *sleep*', this allowing of heaven-sent reason to 'fust unused':

> What is a man,
> If his chief good and market of his time
> Be but to *sleep* and feed? a *beast*, no more.[26]

So, in the soliloquy in II.ii. he accuses himself of being 'a *dull* and muddy-mettled rascal', who 'peaks [mopes] like John-a-dreams, unpregnant of his cause', dully indifferent to his cause.[27] So, when the Ghost appears to him the second time, he accuses himself of being tardy and lapsed in *time*; and the Ghost speaks of his purpose being almost *blunted*, and bids him not to *forget* (cf. 'oblivion'). And so, what is emphasized in those undramatic but significant speeches of the player-king and of Claudius is the mere dying away of purpose or of love.[28] Surely what all this points to is not a condition of excessive but useless mental activity (indeed there is, in reality, curiously little about that in the text), but rather one of dull, apathetic, brooding gloom, in which Hamlet, so far from analysing his duty, is not thinking of it at all, but for the time literally *forgets* it. It seems to me we are driven to think of Hamlet *chiefly* thus during the long time which elapsed between the appearance of the Ghost and the events presented in the Second Act. The Ghost, in fact, had more reason than we suppose at first for leaving with Hamlet as his parting injunction the command, 'Remember me', and for greeting him, on re-appearing,

---

may be true to life, though it is evidently prompted by anxiety to excuse his violence on the ground of his insanity. On this passage see further Note G.

[26] Throughout, I italicize to show the connection of ideas.

[27] Cf. *Measure for Measure*, IV.iv.23, 'This deed . . . makes me unpregnant and dull to all proceedings.'

[28] III.ii.196 ff., IV.vii.111 ff.: *e.g.*,

> Purpose is but the slave to *memory*,
> Of violent birth but poor validity.

with the command, 'Do not forget'.[29] These little things in Shakespeare are not accidents.

The second trait which is fully explained only by Hamlet's melancholy is his own inability to understand why he delays. This emerges in a marked degree when an occasion like the player's emotion or the sight of Fortinbras's army stings Hamlet into shame at his inaction. '*Why*,' he asks himself in genuine bewilderment, 'do I linger? Can the cause be cowardice? Can it be sloth? Can it be thinking too precisely of the event? And does *that* again mean cowardice? What is it that makes me sit idle when I feel it is shameful to do so, and when I have *cause, and will, and strength, and means* to act?' A man irresolute merely because he was considering a proposed action too minutely would not feel this bewilderment. A man might feel it whose conscience secretly condemned the act which his explicit consciousness approved; but we have seen that there is no sufficient evidence to justify us in conceiving Hamlet thus. These are the questions of a man stimulated for the moment to shake off the weight of his melancholy, and, because for the moment he is free from it, unable to understand the paralysing pressure which it exerts at other times.

I have dwelt thus at length on Hamlet's melancholy because, from the psychological point of view, it is the centre of the tragedy, and to omit it from consideration or to underrate its intensity is to make Shakespeare's story unintelligible. But the psychological point of view is not equivalent to the tragic; and, having once given its due weight to the fact of Hamlet's melancholy, we may freely admit, or rather may be anxious to insist, that this pathological condition would excite but little, if any, tragic interest if it were not the condition of a nature distinguished by that speculative genius on which the Schlegel–Coleridge type of theory lays stress. Such theories misinterpret the connection between that genius and Hamlet's failure, but still it is this connection which gives to his story its peculiar fascination and makes it appear (if the phrase may be allowed) as the symbol of a tragic mystery inherent in human nature. Wherever this mystery touches us,

---

[29] So, before, he had said to him:

> And duller should'st thou be than the fat weed
> That roots itself in ease on Lethe wharf,
> Would'st thou not stir in this.

On Hamlet's soliloquy after the Ghost's disappearance see Note D.

wherever we are forced to feel the wonder and awe of man's godlike 'apprehension' and his 'thoughts that wander through eternity', and at the same time are forced to see him powerless in his petty sphere of action, and powerless (it would appear) from the very divinity of his thought, we remember Hamlet. And this is the reason why, in the great ideal movement which began towards the close of the eighteenth century, this tragedy acquired a position unique among Shakespeare's dramas, and shared only by Goethe's *Faust*. It was not that *Hamlet* is Shakespeare's greatest tragedy or most perfect work of art; it was that *Hamlet* most brings home to us at once the sense of the soul's infinity, and the sense of the doom which not only circumscribes that infinity but appears to be its offspring.

LECTURE IV

HAMLET

The only way, if there is any way, in which a conception of Hamlet's character could be proved true, would be to show that it, and it alone, explains all the relevant facts presented by the text of the drama. To attempt such a demonstration here would obviously be impossible, even if I felt certain of the interpretation of all the facts. But I propose now to follow rapidly the course of the action in so far as it specially illustrates the character, reserving for separate consideration one important but particularly doubtful point.

1

We left Hamlet, at the close of the First Act, when he had just received his charge from the spirit of his father; and his condition was vividly depicted in the fact that, within an hour of receiving this charge, he had relapsed into that weariness of life or longing for death which is the immediate cause of his later inaction. When next we meet him, at the opening of the Second Act, a considerable time has elapsed, apparently as much as two months.[1] The ambassadors sent to the King of Norway (I.ii.27) are just returning. Laertes, whom we saw leaving Elsinore (I.iii.), has been in Paris long enough to be in want of fresh supplies. Ophelia has obeyed her father's command (given in I.iii.), and has refused to receive Hamlet's visits or letters. What has Hamlet done? He has put on an 'antic disposition' and established a reputation for lunacy, with the result that his mother has become deeply anxious about him, and with the further result that the King, who was formerly so entirely at ease regarding him that he wished him to stay on at Court, is now extremely uneasy and very desirous to discover the cause of his 'transformation'. Hence Rosencrantz and Guildenstern have been sent for, to

---

[1] In the First Act (I.ii.138) Hamlet says that his father has been dead not quite two months. In the Third Act (III.ii.135) Ophelia says King Hamlet has been dead 'twice two months'. The events of the Third Act are separated from those of the Second by one night (II.ii.565).

cheer him by their company and to worm his secret out of him; and they are just about to arrive. Beyond exciting thus the apprehensions of his enemy Hamlet has done absolutely nothing; and, as we have seen, we must imagine him during this long period sunk for the most part in 'bestial oblivion' or fruitless broodings, and falling deeper and deeper into the slough of despond.

Now he takes a further step. He suddenly appears unannounced in Ophelia's chamber; and his appearance and behaviour are such as to suggest both to Ophelia and to her father that his brain is turned by disappointment in love. How far this step was due to the design of creating a false impression as to the origin of his lunacy, how far to other causes, is a difficult question; but such a design seems certainly present. It succeeds, however, only in part; for, although Polonius is fully convinced, the King is not so, and it is therefore arranged that the two shall secretly witness a meeting between Ophelia and Hamlet. Meanwhile Rosencrantz and Guildenstern arrive, and at the King's request begin their attempts, easily foiled by Hamlet, to pluck out the heart of his mystery. Then the players come to Court, and for a little while one of Hamlet's old interests revives, and he is almost happy. But only for a little while. The emotion shown by the player in reciting the speech which tells of Hecuba's grief for her slaughtered husband awakes into burning life the slumbering sense of duty and shame. He must act. With the extreme rapidity which always distinguishes him in his healthier moments, he conceives and arranges the plan of having the 'Murder of Gonzago' played before the King and Queen, with the addition of a speech written by himself for the occasion. Then, longing to be alone, he abruptly dismisses his guests, and pours out a passion of self-reproach for his delay, asks himself in bewilderment what can be its cause, lashes himself into a fury of hatred against his foe, checks himself in disgust at his futile emotion, and quiets his conscience for the moment by trying to convince himself that he has doubts about the Ghost, and by assuring himself that, if the King's behaviour at the play-scene shows but a sign of guilt, he 'knows his course'.

Nothing, surely, can be plainer than the meaning of this famous soliloquy. The doubt which appears at its close, instead of being the natural conclusion of the preceding thoughts, is totally inconsistent with them. For Hamlet's self-reproaches, his curses on his enemy, and his perplexity about his own inaction, one and all imply his faith in the identity and truthfulness of the Ghost. Evidently this sudden doubt, of which there has not been the slightest trace before, is no genuine doubt; it is an unconscious fiction, an excuse for his delay – and for its continuance.

A night passes, and the day that follows it brings the crisis. First takes place that interview from which the King is to learn whether disappointed love is really the cause of his nephew's lunacy. Hamlet is sent for; poor Ophelia is told to walk up and down, reading her prayer-book; Polonius and the King conceal themselves behind the arras. And Hamlet enters, so deeply absorbed in thought that for some time he supposes himself to be alone. What is he thinking of? 'The Murder of Gonzago', which is to be played in a few hours, and on which everything depends? Not at all. He is meditating on suicide; and he finds that what stands in the way of it, and counterbalances its infinite attraction, is not any thought of a sacred unaccomplished duty, but the doubt, quite irrelevant to that issue, whether it is not ignoble in the mind to end its misery, and, still more, whether death *would* end it. Hamlet, that is to say, is here, in effect, precisely where he was at the time of his first soliloquy ('O that this too too solid flesh would melt') two months ago, before ever he heard of his father's murder.[2] His reflections have no reference to this particular moment; they represent that habitual weariness of life with which his passing outbursts of emotion or energy are contrasted. What can be more significant than the fact that he is sunk in these reflections on the very day which is to determine for him the truthfulness of the Ghost? And how is it possible for us to hope that, if that truthfulness should be established, Hamlet will be any nearer to his revenge?[3]

His interview with Ophelia follows; and its result shows that his delay is becoming most dangerous to himself. The King is satisfied that, whatever else may be the hidden cause of Hamlet's madness, it is not love. He is by no means certain even that Hamlet is mad at all.

---

[2] The only difference is that in the 'To be or not to be' soliloquy there is no reference to the idea that suicide is forbidden by 'the Everlasting'. Even this, however, seems to have been present in the original form of the speech, for the version in the First Quarto has a line about our being 'borne before an everlasting Judge'.

[3] The present position of the 'To be or not to be' soliloquy, and of the interview with Ophelia, appears to have been due to an afterthought of Shakespeare's; for in the First Quarto they precede, instead of following, the arrival of the players, and consequently the arrangement for the play-scene. This is a notable instance of the truth that 'inspiration' is by no means confined to a poet's first conceptions.

He has heard that infuriated threat, 'I say, we will have no more marriages; those that are married, all but one, shall live; the rest shall keep as they are.' He is thoroughly alarmed. He at any rate will not delay. On the spot he determines to send Hamlet to England. But, as Polonius is present, we do not learn at once the meaning of this purpose.

Evening comes. The approach of the play-scene raises Hamlet's spirits. He is in his element. He feels that he is doing *something* towards his end, striking a stroke, but a stroke of intellect. In his instructions to the actor on the delivery of the inserted speech, and again in his conversation with Horatio just before the entry of the Court, we see the true Hamlet, the Hamlet of the days before his father's death. But how characteristic it is that he appears quite as anxious that his speech should not be ranted as that Horatio should observe its effect upon the King! This trait appears again even at that thrilling moment when the actor is just going to deliver the speech. Hamlet sees him beginning to frown and glare like the conventional stage-murderer, and calls to him impatiently, 'Leave thy damnable faces and begin!'[4]

Hamlet's device proves a triumph far more complete than he had dared to expect. He had thought the King might 'blench', but he does much more. When only six of the 'dozen or sixteen lines' have been spoken he starts to his feet and rushes from the hall, followed by the whole dismayed Court. In the elation of success – an elation at first almost hysterical – Hamlet treats Rosencrantz and Guildenstern, who are sent to him, with undisguised contempt. Left to himself, he declares that now he could

> drink hot blood,
> And do such bitter business as the day
> Would quake to look on.

He has been sent for by his mother, and is going to her chamber; and so vehement and revengeful is his mood that he actually fancies himself in danger of using daggers to her as well as speaking them.[5]

---

[4] Cf. again the scene at Ophelia's grave, where a strong strain of aesthetic disgust is traceable in Hamlet's 'towering passion' with Laertes: 'Nay, an thou'lt mouth, I'll rant as well as thou' (V.i.306).

[5] O heart, lose not thy nature; let not ever
The soul of Nero enter this firm bosom:

In this mood, on his way to his mother's chamber, he comes upon the King, alone, kneeling, conscience-stricken and attempting to pray. His enemy is delivered into his hands.

> Now might I do it pat, now he is praying:
> And now I'll do it: and so he goes to heaven:
> And so am I revenged.[6] That would be scanned.

He scans it; and the sword that he drew at the words, 'And now I'll do it', is thrust back into its sheath. If he killed the villain now he would send his soul to heaven; and he would fain kill soul as well as body.

That this again is an unconscious excuse for delay is now pretty generally agreed, and it is needless to describe again the state of mind which, on the view explained in our last lecture, is the real cause of Hamlet's failure here. The first five words he utters, 'Now might I do it', show that he has no effective *desire* to 'do it'; and in the little sentences that follow, and the long pauses between them, the endeavour at a resolution, and the sickening return of melancholic paralysis, however difficult a task they set to the actor, are plain enough to a reader. And any reader who may retain a doubt should observe the fact that, when the Ghost reappears, Hamlet does not think of justifying his delay by the plea that he was waiting for a more perfect vengeance. But in one point the great majority of critics, I think, go astray. The feeling of intense hatred which Hamlet expresses is not the cause of his sparing the King, and in his heart he knows this; but it does not at all follow that this feeling is unreal. All the evidence afforded by the play goes to show that it is perfectly genuine, and I see no reason whatever to doubt that Hamlet would have been very sorry to send his father's murderer to heaven, nor much to doubt that he would have been glad to send him to perdition. The reason for refusing to accept his own version

---

Nero, who put to death his mother who had poisoned her husband. This passage is surely remarkable. And so are the later words (III.iv.28):

> A bloody deed! almost as bad, good mother,
> As kill a king, and marry with his brother.

Are we to understand that at this time he really suspected her of complicity in the murder? We must remember that the Ghost had not told him she was innocent of that.

[6] I am inclined to think that the note of interrogation put after 'revenged' in a late Quarto is right.

of his motive in sparing Claudius is not that his sentiments are horrible, but that elsewhere, and also in the opening of his speech here, we can see that his reluctance to act is due to other causes.

The incident of the sparing of the King is contrived with extraordinary dramatic insight. On the one side we feel that the opportunity was perfect. Hamlet could not possibly any longer tell himself that he had no certainty as to his uncle's guilt. And the external conditions were most favourable; for the King's remarkable behaviour at the play-scene would have supplied a damning confirmation of the story Hamlet had to tell about the Ghost. Even now, probably, in a Court so corrupt as that of Elsinore, he could not with perfect security have begun by charging the King with the murder; but he could quite safely have killed him first and given his justification afterwards, especially as he would certainly have had on his side the people, who loved him and despised Claudius. On the other hand, Shakespeare has taken care to give this perfect opportunity so repulsive a character that we can hardly bring ourselves to wish that the hero should accept it. One of his minor difficulties, we have seen, probably was that he seemed to be required to attack a defenceless man: and here this difficulty is at its maximum.

This incident is, again, the turning-point of the tragedy. So far, Hamlet's delay, though it is endangering his freedom and his life, has done no irreparable harm; but his failure here is the cause of all the disasters that follow. In sparing the King, he sacrifices Polonius, Ophelia, Rosencrantz and Guildenstern, Laertes, the Queen and himself. This central significance of the passage is dramatically indicated in the following scene by the reappearance of the Ghost and the repetition of its charge.

Polonius is the first to fall. The old courtier, whose vanity would not allow him to confess that his diagnosis of Hamlet's lunacy was mistaken, had suggested that, after the theatricals, the Queen should endeavour in a private interview with her son to penetrate the mystery, while he himself would repeat his favourite part of eavesdropper (III.i.184 ff.). It has now become quite imperative that the Prince should be brought to disclose his secret; for his choice of the 'Murder of Gonzago', and perhaps his conduct during the performance, have shown a spirit of exaggerated hostility against the King which has excited general alarm. Rosencrantz and Guildenstern discourse to Claudius on the extreme importance of his preserving his invaluable life, as though Hamlet's insanity had now clearly shown itself to be homicidal.[7] When, then, at the opening of the interview between Hamlet and his mother, the son, instead of listening to her remonstrances, roughly assumes the offensive, she becomes alarmed; and when, on her attempting to leave the room, he takes her by the arm and forces her to sit down, she is terrified, cries out, 'Thou wilt not murder me?' and screams for help. Polonius, behind the arras, echoes her call; and in a moment Hamlet, hoping the concealed person is the King, runs the old man through the body.

Evidently this act is intended to stand in sharp contrast with Hamlet's sparing of his enemy. The King would have been just as defenceless behind the arras as he had been on his knees; but here Hamlet is already excited and in action, and the chance comes to him so suddenly that he has no time to 'scan' it. It is a minor consideration, but still for the dramatist not unimportant, that the audience would wholly sympathize with Hamlet's attempt here, as directed against an enemy who is lurking to entrap him, instead of being engaged in a business which perhaps to the bulk of the audience then, as now, seemed to have a 'relish of salvation in't'.

We notice in Hamlet, at the opening of this interview, something of the excited levity which followed the *dénouement* of the play-scene. The death of Polonius sobers him; and in the remainder of the interview he shows, together with some traces of his morbid state, the peculiar beauty and nobility of his nature. His chief desire is not by any means to ensure his mother's silent acquiescence in his design of revenge; it is to save her soul. And while the rough work of vengeance is repugnant to him, he is at home in this higher work. Here that fatal feeling, 'it is no matter', never shows itself. No father-confessor could be more selflessly set upon his end of redeeming a fellow-creature from degradation, more stern or pitiless in denouncing the sin, or

---

[7] III.iii.1–26. The state of affairs at Court at this time, though I have not seen it noticed by critics, seems to me puzzling. It is quite clear from III.ii.310 ff., from the passage just cited, and from IV.vii.1–5 and 30 ff., that everyone sees in the play-scene a gross and menacing insult to the King. Yet no one shows any sign of perceiving in it also an accusation of murder. Surely that is strange. Are we perhaps meant to understand that they do perceive this, but out of subservience choose to ignore the fact? If that were Shakespeare's meaning, the actors could easily indicate it by their looks. And if it were so, any sympathy we may feel for Rosencrantz and Guildenstern in their fate would be much diminished. But the mere text does not suffice to decide either this question or the question whether the two courtiers were aware of the contents of the commission they bore to England.

more eager to welcome the first token of repentance. There is something infinitely beautiful in that sudden sunshine of faith and love
which breaks out when, at the Queen's surrender,

> O Hamlet, thou has cleft my heart in twain,

he answers,

> O throw away the worser part of it,
> And live the purer with the other half.

The truth is that, though Hamlet hates his uncle and acknowledges
the duty of vengeance, his whole heart is never in this feeling or this
task; but his whole heart is in his horror at his mother's fall and in his
longing to raise her. The former of these feelings was the inspiration
of his first soliloquy; it combines with the second to form the inspiration of his eloquence here. And Shakespeare never wrote more
eloquently than here.

I have already alluded to the significance of the reappearance of the
Ghost in this scene; but why does Shakespeare choose for the particular moment of its reappearance the middle of a speech in which
Hamlet is raving against his uncle? There seems to be more than one
reason. In the first place, Hamlet has already attained his object of
stirring shame and contrition in his mother's breast, and is now yielding to the old temptation of unpacking his heart with words, and
exhausting in useless emotion the force which should be stored up in
his will. And, next, in doing this he is agonizing his mother to no
purpose, and in despite of her piteous and repeated appeals for mercy.
But the Ghost, when it gave him his charge, had expressly warned him
to spare her; and here again the dead husband shows the same tender
regard for his weak unfaithful wife. The object of his return is to
repeat his charge:

> Do not forget: this visitation
> Is but to whet thy almost blunted purpose;

but, having uttered the reminder, he immediately bids the son to help
the mother and 'step between her and her fighting soul'.

And, whether intentionally or not, another purpose is served by
Shakespeare's choice of this particular moment. It is a moment when
the state of Hamlet's mind is such that we cannot suppose the Ghost
to be meant for an hallucination; and it is of great importance here

that the spectator or reader should not suppose any such thing. He is further guarded by the fact that the Ghost proves, so to speak, his identity by showing the same traits as were visible on his first appearance – the same insistence on the duty of remembering, and the same concern for the Queen. And the result is that we construe the Ghost's interpretation of Hamlet's delay ('almost blunted purpose') as the truth, the dramatist's own interpretation. Let me add that probably no one in Shakespeare's audience had any doubt of his meaning here. The idea of later critics and readers that the Ghost is an hallucination is due partly to failure to follow the indications just noticed, but partly also to two mistakes, the substitution of our present intellectual atmosphere for the Elizabethan, and the notion that, because the Queen does not see and hear the Ghost, it is meant to be unreal. But a ghost, in Shakespeare's day, was able for any sufficient reason to confine its manifestation to a single person in a company; and here the sufficient reason, that of sparing the Queen, is obvious.[8]

At the close of this scene it appears that Hamlet has somehow learned of the King's design of sending him to England in charge of his two 'school-fellows'. He has no doubt that this design covers some villainous plot against himself, but neither does he doubt that he will succeed in defeating it; and, as we saw it, he looks forward with pleasure to this conflict of wits. The idea of refusing to go appears not to occur to him. Perhaps (for here we are left to conjecture) he feels that he could not refuse unless at the same time he openly accused the King of his father's murder (a course which he seems at no time to contemplate); for by the slaughter of Polonius he has supplied his enemy with the best possible excuse for getting him out of the country. Besides, he has so effectually warned this enemy, that after the death of Polonius is discovered, he is kept under guard (IV.iii.14). He consents, then, to go. But on his way to the shore he meets the army of Fortinbras on its march to Poland; and the sight of these men going cheerfully to risk death 'for an eggshell', and 'making mouths at the invisible event', strikes him with shame as he remembers how he, with

---

[8] This passage in *Hamlet* seems to have been in Heywood's* mind when, in *The Second Part of the Iron Age* (Pearson's reprint, vol. iii., p. 423), he makes the Ghost of Agamemnon appear in order to satisfy the doubts of Orestes as to his mother's guilt. No reader could possibly think that this Ghost was meant to be an hallucination; yet Clytemnestra cannot see it. The Ghost of King Hamlet, I may add, goes further than that of Agamemnon, for he is audible, as well as visible, to the privileged person.

so much greater cause for action, 'lets all sleep'; and he breaks out into the soliloquy, 'How all occasions do inform against me!'

This great speech, in itself not inferior to the famous 'To be or not to be', is absent not only from the First Quarto but from the Folio. It is therefore probable that, at any rate by the time when the Folio appeared (1623), it had become customary to omit it in theatrical representation; and this is still the custom. But, while no doubt it is dramatically the least indispensable of the soliloquies, it has a direct dramatic value, and a great value for the interpretation of Hamlet's character. It shows that Hamlet, though he is leaving Denmark, has not relinquished the idea of obeying the Ghost. It exhibits very strikingly his inability to understand why he has delayed so long. It contains that assertion which so many critics forget, that he has 'cause and will and strength and means to do it'. On the other hand – and this was perhaps the principal purpose of the speech – it convinces us that he has learnt little or nothing from his delay, or from his failure to seize the opportunity presented to him after the play-scene. For, we find, both the motive and the gist of the speech are precisely the same as those of the soliloquy at the end of the Second Act ('O what a rogue'). There too he was stirred to shame when he saw a passionate emotion awakened by a cause which, compared with his, was a mere eggshell. There too he stood bewildered at the sight of his own dullness, and was almost ready to believe – what was justly incredible to him – that it was the mask of mere cowardice. There too he determined to delay no longer: if the King should but blench, he knew his course. Yet this determination led to nothing then; and why, we ask ourselves in despair, should the bloody thoughts he now resolves to cherish ever pass beyond the realm of thought?

Between this scene (IV.iv.) and the remainder of the play we must again suppose an interval, though not a very long one. When the action recommences, the death of Polonius has led to the insanity of Ophelia and the secret return of Laertes from France. The young man comes back breathing slaughter. For the King, afraid to put Hamlet on his trial (a course likely to raise the question of his own behaviour at the play, and perhaps to provoke an open accusation),[9] has

---

[9] I think it is clear that it is this fear which stands in the way of the obvious plan of bringing Hamlet to trial and getting him shut up or executed. It is much safer to hurry him off to his doom in England before he can say anything about the murder which he has somehow discovered.

attempted to hush up the circumstances of Polonius's death, and has given him a hurried and inglorious burial. The fury of Laertes, there-fore, is directed in the first instance against the King: and the ease with which he raises the people, like the King's fear of a judicial enquiry, shows us how purely internal were the obstacles which the hero had to overcome. This impression is intensified by the broad contrast between Hamlet and Laertes, who rushes headlong to his revenge, and is determined to have it though allegiance, conscience, grace and damnation stand in his way (IV.v.130). But the King, though he has been hard put to it, is now in his element and feels safe. Knowing that he will very soon hear of Hamlet's execution in England, he tells Laertes that his father died by Hamlet's hand, and expresses his willingness to let the friends of Laertes judge whether he himself has any responsibility for the deed. And when, to his aston-ishment and dismay, news comes that Hamlet has returned to Denmark, he acts with admirable promptitude and address, turns Laertes round his finger, and arranges with him for the murder of their common enemy. If there were any risk of the young man's reso-lution faltering, it is removed by the death of Ophelia. And now the King has but one anxiety – to prevent the young men from meeting before the fencing-match. For who can tell what Hamlet might say in his defence, or how enchanting his tongue might prove?[10]

Hamlet's return to Denmark is due partly to his own action, partly to accident. On the voyage he secretly possesses himself of the royal commission, and substitutes for it another, which he himself writes and seals, and in which the King of England is ordered to put to death, not Hamlet, but Rosencrantz and Guildenstern. Then the ship is attacked by a pirate, which, apparently, finds its intended prize too strong for it, and makes off. But as Hamlet 'in the grapple', eager for fighting, has boarded the assailant, he is carried off in it, and by promises induces the pirates to put him ashore in Denmark.

In what spirit does he return? Unquestionably, I think, we can observe a certain change, though it is not great. First, we notice here and there what seems to be a consciousness of power, due probably to

---

Perhaps the Queen's resistance, and probably Hamlet's great popularity with the people, are additional reasons. (It should be observed that as early as III.i.194 we hear of the idea of 'confin-ing' Hamlet as an alternative to sending him to England.)

[10] I am inferring from IV.vii.,129, 130, and the last words of the scene.

his success in counter-mining Claudius and blowing the courtiers to the moon, and to his vigorous action in the sea-fight. But I doubt if this sense of power is more marked than it was in the scenes following the success of the 'Murder of Gonzago'. Secondly, we nowhere find any direct expression of that weariness of life and that longing for death which were so marked in the first soliloquy and in the speech 'To be or not to be'. This may be a mere accident, and it must be remembered that in the Fifth Act we have no soliloquy. But in the earlier Acts the feelings referred to do not appear *merely* in soliloquy, and I incline to think that Shakespeare means to show in the Hamlet of the Fifth Act a slight thinning of the dark cloud of melancholy, and means us to feel it tragic that this change comes too late. And, in the third place, there is a trait about which doubt is impossible – a sense in Hamlet that he is in the hands of Providence. This had, indeed, already shown itself at the death of Polonius[11] and perhaps at Hamlet's farewell to the King,[12] but the idea seems now to be constantly present in his mind. 'There's a divinity that shapes our ends,' he declares to Horatio in speaking of the fighting in his heart that would not let him sleep, and of his rashness in groping his way to the courtiers to find their commission. How was he able, Horatio asks, to seal the substituted commission?

Why, even in that was heaven ordinant,

Hamlet answers; he had his father's signet in his purse. And though he has a presentiment of evil about the fencing-match he refuses to yield to it: 'we defy augury: there is special providence in the fall of a sparrow . . . the readiness is all'.

---

[11] III.iv.172:

> For this same lord,
> I do repent: but heaven hath pleased it so,
> To punish me with this and this with me,
> That I must be their scourge and minister:

i.e. the scourge and minister of 'heaven', which has a plural sense elsewhere also in Shakespeare.

[12] IV.iii.48:

> *Ham.* For England!
> *King.*   Ay, Hamlet.
> *Ham.*   Good.
> *King.* So is it, if thou knew'st our purposes.
> *Ham.* I see a cherub that sees them.

Though these passages strike us more when put together thus than when they come upon us at intervals in reading the play, they have a marked effect on our feeling about Hamlet's character and still more about the events of the action. But I find it impossible to believe, with some critics, that they indicate any material change in his general condition, or the formation of any effective resolution to fulfil the appointed duty. On the contrary, they seem to express that kind of religious resignation which, however beautiful in one aspect, really deserves the name of fatalism rather than that of faith in Providence, because it is not united to any determination to do what is believed to be the will of Providence. In place of this determination, the Hamlet of the Fifth Act shows a kind of sad or indifferent self-abandonment, as if he secretly despaired of forcing himself to action, and were ready to leave his duty to some other power than his own. *This* is really the main change which appears in him after his return to Denmark, and which had begun to show itself before he went – this, and not a determination to act, nor even an anxiety to do so.

For when he returns he stands in a most perilous position. On one side of him is the King, whose safety depends on his death, and who has done his best to murder him; on the other, Laertes, whose father and sister he has sent to their graves, and of whose behaviour and probable attitude he must surely be informed by Horatio. What is required of him, therefore, if he is not to perish with his duty undone, is the utmost wariness and the swiftest resolution. Yet it is not too much to say that, except when Horatio forces the matter on his attention, he shows no consciousness of this position. He muses in the graveyard on the nothingness of life and fame, and the base uses to which our dust returns, whether it be a court jester's or a world-conqueror's. He learns that the open grave over which he muses has been dug for the woman he loved; and he suffers one terrible pang, from which he gains relief in frenzied words and frenzied action – action which must needs intensify, if that were possible, the fury of the man whom he has, however unwittingly, so cruelly injured. Yet he appears utterly unconscious that he has injured Laertes at all, and asks him:

What is the reason that you use me thus?

And as the sharpness of the first pang passes, the old weary misery returns, and he might almost say to Ophelia, as he does to her brother:

I loved you ever: but it is no matter.

'It is no matter': *nothing* matters.

The last scene opens. He narrates to Horatio the events of the voyage and his uncle's attempt to murder him. But the conclusion of the story is no plan of action, but the old fatal question, 'Ought I not to act?'[13] And, while he asks it, his enemies have acted. Osric enters with an invitation to him to take part in a fencing-match with Laertes. This match – he is expressly told so – has been arranged by his deadly enemy the King; and his antagonist is a man whose hands but a few hours ago were at his throat, and whose voice he had heard shouting 'The devil take thy soul!' But he does not think of that. To fence is to show a courtesy, and to himself it is a relief – action, and not the one hateful action. There is something noble in his carelessness, and also in his refusal to attend to the presentiment which he suddenly feels (and of which he says, not only 'the readiness is all', but also 'it is no matter'). Something noble; and yet, when a sacred duty is still undone, ought one to be so ready to die? With the same carelessness, and with that trustfulness which makes us love him, but which is here so fatally misplaced, he picks up the first foil that comes to his hand, asks indifferently, 'These foils have all a length?' and begins. And Fate descends upon his enemies, and his mother, and himself.

But he is not left in utter defeat. Not only is his task at last accomplished, but Shakespeare seems to have determined that his hero should exhibit in his latest hour all the glorious power and all the nobility and sweetness of his nature. Of the first, the power, I spoke before,[14] but there is a wonderful beauty in the revelation of the second. His body already labouring in the pangs of death, his mind soars above them. He forgives Laertes; he remembers his wretched mother and bids her adieu, ignorant that she has preceded him. We hear now no word of lamentation or self-reproach. He has will, and just time, to think, not of the past or of what might have been, but of the future; to forbid his friend's death in words more pathetic in their sadness than even his agony of spirit had been; and to take care, so far

---

[13] On this passage see pp. 70–1. Hamlet's reply to Horatio's warning sounds, no doubt, determined; but so did 'I know my course'. And is it not significant that, having given it, he abruptly changes the subject?

[14] Pp. 73–4.

as in him lies, for the welfare of the State which he himself should have guided. Then in spite of shipwreck he reaches the haven of silence where he would be. What else could his world-wearied flesh desire?

But *we* desire more; and we receive it. As those mysterious words, 'The rest is silence', die upon Hamlet's lips, Horatio answers:

> Now cracks a noble heart. Good night, sweet prince,
> And flights of angels sing thee to thy rest.

Why did Shakespeare here, so much against his custom, introduce this reference to another life? Did he remember that Hamlet is the only one of his tragic heroes whom he has not allowed us to see in the days when this life smiled on him? Did he feel that, while for the others we might be content to imagine after life's fitful fever nothing more than release and silence, we must ask more for one whose 'godlike reason' and passionate love of goodness have only gleamed upon us through the heavy clouds of melancholy, and yet have left us murmuring, as we bow our heads, 'This was the noblest spirit of them all'?

2

How many things still remain to say of Hamlet! Before I touch on his relation to Ophelia, I will choose but two. Neither of them, compared with the matters so far considered, is of great consequence, but both are interesting, and the first seems to have quite escaped observation.

(1) Most people have, beside their more essential traits of character, little peculiarities which, for their intimates, form an indissoluble part of their personality. In comedy, and in other humorous works of fiction, such peculiarities often figure prominently, but they rarely do so, I think, in tragedy. Shakespeare, however, seems to have given one such idiosyncrasy to Hamlet.

It is a trick of speech, a habit of repetition. And these are simple examples of it from the first soliloquy:

> O *God! God!*
> How weary, stale, flat and unprofitable
> Seem to me all the uses of this world!
> *Fie* on't! ah *fie!*

Now I ask your patience. You will say: 'There is nothing individual here. Everybody repeats words thus. And the tendency, in particular, to use such repetitions in moments of great emotion is well known, and frequently illustrated in literature – for example, in David's cry of lament for Absalom.'*

This is perfectly true, and plenty of examples could be drawn from Shakespeare himself. But what we find in Hamlet's case is, I believe, *not* common. In the first place, this repetition is a *habit* with him. Here are some more instances: 'Thrift, thrift, Horatio'; 'Indeed, indeed, sirs, but this troubles me'; 'Come, deal justly with me: come, come'; 'Wormwood, wormwood!' I do not profess to have made an exhaustive search, but I am much mistaken if this *habit* is to be found in any other serious character of Shakespeare.[15]

And, in the second place – and here I appeal with confidence to lovers of Hamlet – some of these repetitions strike us as intensely characteristic. Some even of those already quoted strike one thus, and still more do the following:

(*a*)   *Horatio.*   It would have much amazed you.
       Hamlet.   Very like, very like. Stay'd it long?
(*b*)   *Polonius.*   What do you read, my lord?
       Hamlet.   Words, words, words.
(*c*)   *Polonius.*   My honourable lord, I will most humbly take my leave of you.
       Hamlet.   You cannot, sir, take from me anything that I will more willingly part withal: except my life, except my life, except my life.

(*d*)   *Ophelia.*   Good my lord,
                  How does your honour for this many a day?
       Hamlet.   I humbly thank you, well, well, well.

Is there anything that Hamlet says or does in the whole play more unmistakably individual than these replies?[16]

---

[15] It should be observed also that many of Hamlet's repetitions can hardly be said to occur at moments of great emotion, like Cordelia's 'And so I am, I am', and 'No cause, no cause'. Of course, a habit of repetition quite as marked as Hamlet's may be found in comic persons, *e.g.* Justice Shallow in 2 *Henry IV*.

[16] Perhaps it is from noticing this trait that I find something characteristic too in this co-incidence of phrase: 'Alas, poor ghost!' (I.v.4). 'Alas, poor Yorick!' (V.i.202).

(2) Hamlet, everyone has noticed, is fond of quibbles and word-play, and of 'conceits' and turns of thought such as are common in the poets whom Johnson called Metaphysical. Sometimes, no doubt, he plays with words and ideas chiefly in order to mystify, thwart and annoy. To some extent, again, as we may see from the conversation where Rosencrantz and Guildenstern first present themselves (II.ii. 227), he is merely following the fashion of the young courtiers about him, just as in his love-letter to Ophelia[17] he uses for the most part the fantastic language of Court Euphuism. Nevertheless in this trait there is something very characteristic. We should be greatly surprised to find it marked in Othello or Lear or Timon, in Macbeth or Antony or Coriolanus; and, in fact, we find it in them hardly at all. One reason of this may perhaps be that these characters are all later creations than Hamlet, and that Shakespeare's own fondness for this kind of play, like the fondness of the theatrical audience for it, diminished with time. But the main reason is surely that this tendency, as we see it in Hamlet, betokens a nimbleness and flexibility of mind which is characteristic of him and not of the later less many-sided heroes. Macbeth, for instance, has an imagination quite as sensitive as Hamlet's to certain impressions, but he has none of Hamlet's delight in freaks and twists of thought, or of his tendency to perceive and play with resemblances in the most diverse objects and ideas. Though Romeo shows this tendency, the only tragic hero who approaches Hamlet here is Richard II, who indeed in several ways recalls the emasculated Hamlet of some critics, and may, like the real Hamlet, have owed his existence in part to Shakespeare's personal familiarity with the weaknesses and dangers of an imaginative temperament.

That Shakespeare meant this trait to be characteristic of Hamlet is beyond question. The very first line the hero speaks contains a play on words:

A little more than kin and less than kind.

The fact is significant, though the pun itself is not specially charac-teristic. Much more so, and indeed absolutely individual, are the uses of word-play in moments of extreme excitement. Remember the awe

---

[17] This letter, of course, was written before the time when the action of the drama begins, for we know that Ophelia, after her father's commands in I.iii., received no more letters (II.i.109).

and terror of the scene where the Ghost beckons Hamlet to leave his friends and follow him into the darkness, and then consider this dialogue:

Hamlet.	It waves me still.
	Go on; I'll follow thee.
Marcellus.	You shall not go, my lord.
Hamlet.	Hold off your hands.
Horatio.	Be ruled; you shall not go.
Hamlet.	My fate cries out,

> And makes each petty artery in this body
> As hardy as the Nemean lion's nerve.
> Still am I called. Unhand me, gentlemen.
> *By heaven I'll make a ghost of him that lets me.*

Would any other character in Shakespeare have used those words? And, again, where is Hamlet more Hamlet than when he accompanies with a pun the furious action by which he compels his enemy to drink the 'poison tempered by himself?

> Here, thou incestuous, murderous, damn'd Dane,
> Drink off this potion. Is thy union here?
> Follow my mother.

The 'union' was the pearl which Claudius professed to throw into the cup, and in place of which (as Hamlet supposes) he dropped poison in. But the 'union' is also that incestuous marriage which must not be broken by his remaining alive now that his partner is dead. What rage there is in the words, and what a strange lightning of the mind!

Much of Hamlet's play with words and ideas is imaginatively humorous. That of Richard II is fanciful, but rarely, if ever, humorous. Antony has touches of humour, and Richard III has more; but Hamlet, we may safely assert, is the only one of the tragic heroes who can be called a humorist, his humour being first cousin to that speculative tendency which keeps his mental world in perpetual movement. Some of his quips are, of course, poor enough, and many are not distinctive. Those of his retorts which strike one as perfectly individual do so, I think, chiefly because they suddenly reveal the misery and bitterness below the surface; as when, to Rosencrantz's message from his mother, 'She desires to speak with you in her closet, ere you go to bed,' he answers, 'We shall obey, were she ten times our mother'; or as when he replies, to Polonius's invitation, 'Will you walk out of the air, my lord?' with words that suddenly turn one cold, 'Into my grave'. Otherwise, what we justly call Hamlet's characteristic humour is not his exclusive property, but appears in passages spoken by persons as different as Mercutio, Falstaff and Rosalind. The truth probably is that it was the kind of humour most natural to Shakespeare himself, and that here, as in some other traits of the poet's greatest creation, we come into close contact with Shakespeare the man.

3

The actor who plays the part of Hamlet must make up his mind as to the interpretation of every word and deed of the character. Even if at some point he feels no certainty as to which of two interpretations is right, he must still choose one or the other. The mere critic is not obliged to do this. Where he remains in doubt he may say so, and, if the matter is of importance, he ought to say so.

This is the position in which I find myself in regard to Hamlet's love for Ophelia. I am unable to arrive at a conviction as to the meaning of some of his words and deeds, and I question whether from the mere text of the play a sure interpretation of them can be drawn. For this reason I have reserved the subject for separate treatment, and have, so far as possible, kept it out of the general discussion of Hamlet's character.

On two points no reasonable doubt can, I think, be felt. (1) Hamlet was at one time sincerely and ardently in love with Ophelia. For she herself says that he had importuned her with love in honourable fashion, and had given countenance to his speech with almost all the holy vows of heaven (I.iii.110 f.). (2) When at Ophelia's grave, he declared,

> I loved Ophelia; forty thousand brothers
> Could not, with all their quantity of love,
> Make up my sum,

he must have spoken sincerely; and, further, we may take it for granted that he used the past tense, 'loved', merely because Ophelia was dead, and not to imply that he had once loved her but no longer did so.

So much being assumed, we come to what is doubtful, and I will begin by stating what is probably the most popular view. According to this view, Hamlet's love for Ophelia never changed. On the revelation made by the Ghost, however, he felt that he must put aside all thoughts of it; and it also seemed to him necessary to convince Ophelia, as well as others, that he was insane, and so to destroy her hopes of any happy issue to their love. This was the purpose of his appearance in her chamber, though he was probably influenced also by a longing to see her and bid her a silent farewell, and possibly by a faint hope that he might safely entrust his secret to her. If he entertained any such hope his study of her face dispelled it; and thereafter, as in the Nunnery-scene (III.i.) and again at the play-scene, he not only feigned madness, but, to convince her that he had quite lost his love for her, he also addressed her in bitter and insulting language. In all this he was acting a part intensely painful to himself; the very violence of his language in the Nunnery-scene arose from this pain; and so the actor should make him show, in that scene, occasional signs of a tenderness which with all his efforts he cannot wholly conceal. Finally, over her grave the truth bursts from him in the declaration quoted just now, though it is still impossible for him to explain to others why he who loved her so profoundly was forced to wring her heart.

Now this theory, if the view of Hamlet's character which I have taken is anywhere near the truth, is certainly wrong at one point, viz., in so far as it supposes that Hamlet's bitterness to Ophelia was a *mere* pretence forced on him by his design of feigning to be insane; and I proceed to call attention to certain facts and considerations, of which the theory seems to take no account.

1. How is it that in his first soliloquy Hamlet makes no reference whatever to Ophelia?

2. How is it that in his second soliloquy, on the departure of the Ghost, he again says nothing about her? When the lover is feeling that he must make a complete break with his past, why does it not occur to him at once that he must give up his hopes of happiness in love?

3. Hamlet does not, as the popular theory supposes, break with Ophelia directly after the Ghost appears to him; on the contrary, he tries to see her and sends letters to her (II.i.109). What really happens is that Ophelia suddenly repels his visits and letters. Now, *we* know that she is simply obeying her father's order; but how would her action appear to Hamlet, already sick at heart because of his mother's

frailty,[18] and now finding that, the moment fortune has turned against him, the woman who had welcomed his love turns against him too? Even if he divined (as his insults to Polonius suggest) that her father was concerned in this change, would he not still, in that morbid condition of mind, certainly suspect her of being less simple than she had appeared to him?[19] Even if he remained free from *this* suspicion, and merely thought her deplorably weak, would he not probably feel anger against *her*, an anger like that of the hero of *Locksley Hall* against his Amy?

4. When Hamlet made his way into Ophelia's room, why did he go in the garb, the conventionally recognized garb, of the distracted *lover*? If it was necessary to convince Ophelia of his insanity, how was it necessary to convince her that disappointment in *love* was the cause of his insanity? His *main* object in the visit appears to have been to convince *others*, through her, that his insanity was not due to any mysterious unknown cause, but to this disappointment, and so to allay the suspicions of the King. But if his feeling for her had been simply that of love, however unhappy, and had not been in any degree that of suspicion or resentment, would he have adopted a plan which must involve her in so much suffering?[20]

---

[18] 'Frailty, thy name is woman!' he had exclaimed in the first soliloquy. Cf. what he says of his mother's act (III.iv.40):

> Such an act
> That blurs the grace and blush of modesty,
> Calls virtue hypocrite, takes off the rose
> From the fair forehead of an innocent love
> And sets a blister there.

[19] There are signs that Hamlet was haunted by the horrible idea that he had been deceived in Ophelia as he had been in his mother; that she was shallow and artificial, and even that what had seemed simple and affectionate love might really have been something very different. The grossness of his language at the play-scene, and some lines in the Nunnery-scene, suggest this; and, considering the state of his mind, there is nothing unnatural in his suffering from such a suspicion. I do not suggest that he *believed* in it, and in the Nunnery-scene it is clear that his healthy perception of her innocence is in conflict with it.

He seems to have divined that Polonius suspected him of dishonourable intentions towards Ophelia; and there are also traces of the idea that Polonius had been quite ready to let his daughter run the risk as long as Hamlet was prosperous. But it is dangerous, of course, to lay stress on inferences drawn from his conversations with Polonius.

[20] Many readers and critics imagine that Hamlet went straight to Ophelia's room after his interview with the Ghost. But we have just seen that on the contrary he tried to visit her and was repelled, and it is absolutely certain that a long interval separates the events of I.v. and II.i. They think also, of course, that Hamlet's visit to Ophelia was the first announcement of his madness. But the text flatly contradicts that idea also. Hamlet has for some time appeared totally changed (II.ii.1–10); the King is very uneasy at his 'transformation', and has sent for his school-

5. In what way are Hamlet's insults to Ophelia at the play-scene necessary either to his purpose of convincing her of his insanity or to his purpose of revenge? And, even if he did regard them as somehow means to these ends, is it conceivable that he would have uttered them, if his feeling for her were one of hopeless but unmingled love?

6. How is it that neither when he kills Polonius, nor afterwards, does he appear to reflect that he has killed Ophelia's father, or what the effect on Ophelia is likely to be?

7. We have seen that there is no reference to Ophelia in the soliloquies of the First Act. Neither is there the faintest allusion to her in any one of the soliloquies of the subsequent Acts, unless possibly in the words (III.i.72) 'the pangs of despised love'.[21] If the popular theory is true, is not this an astonishing fact?

8. Considering this fact, is there no significance in the further fact (which, by itself, would present no difficulty) that in speaking to Horatio Hamlet never alludes to Ophelia, and that at his death he says nothing of her?

9. If the popular theory is true, how is it that neither in the Nunnery-scene nor at the play-scene does Shakespeare insert anything to make the truth plain? Four words like Othello's 'O hardness to dissemble' would have sufficed.

These considerations, coupled with others as to Hamlet's state of mind, seem to point to two conclusions. They suggest, first, that Hamlet's love, though never lost, was, after Ophelia's apparent rejection of him, mingled with suspicion and resentment, and that his treatment of her was due in part to this cause. And I find it impossible to resist this conclusion. But the question how much of his harshness is meant to be real, and how much assumed, seems to me impossible in some places to answer. For example, his behaviour at the play-scene seems to me to show an intention to hurt and insult; but in the Nunnery-scene (which cannot be discussed briefly) he is

---

fellows in order to discover its cause. Polonius now, after Ophelia has told him of the interview, comes to announce his discovery, not of Hamlet's madness, but of its cause (II.ii.49). That, it would seem, was the effect Hamlet aimed at in his interview. I may add that Ophelia's description of his intent examination of her face suggests doubt rather as to her 'honesty' or sincerity than as to her strength of mind. I cannot believe that he ever dreamed of confiding his secret to her.

[21] If this *is* an allusion to his own love, the adjective 'despised' is significant. But I doubt the allusion. The other calamities mentioned by Hamlet, 'the oppressor's wrong, the proud man's contumely, the law's delay, the insolence of office, and the spurns that patient merit of the unworthy takes', are not at all specially his own.

evidently acting a part and suffering acutely, while at the same time his invective, however exaggerated, seems to spring from real feelings; and what is pretence, and what sincerity, appears to me an insoluble problem. Something depends here on the further question whether or not Hamlet suspects or detects the presence of listeners; but, in the absence of an authentic stage tradition, this question too seems to be unanswerable.

But something further seems to follow from the considerations adduced. Hamlet's love, they seem to show, was not only mingled with bitterness, it was also, like all his healthy feelings, weakened and deadened by his melancholy.[22] It was far from being extinguished; probably it was *one* of the causes which drove him to force his way to Ophelia; whenever he saw Ophelia, it awoke and, the circumstances being what they were, tormented him. But it was not an absorbing passion; it did not habitually occupy his thoughts; and when he declared that it was such a love as forty thousand brothers could not equal, he spoke sincerely indeed but not truly. What he said was true, if I may put it thus, of the inner healthy self which doubtless in time would have fully reasserted itself; but it was only partly true of the Hamlet whom we see in the play. And the morbid influence of his melancholy on his love is the cause of those strange facts, that he never alludes to her in his soliloquies, and that he appears not to realize how the death of her father must affect her.

The facts seem almost to force this idea on us. That it is less 'romantic' than the popular view is no argument against it. And psychologically it is quite sound, for a frequent symptom of such melancholy as Hamlet's is a more or less complete paralysis, or even perversion, of the emotion of love. And yet, while feeling no doubt that up to a certain point it is true, I confess I am not satisfied that the explanation of Hamlet's silence regarding Ophelia lies in it. And the reason of this uncertainty is that scarcely any spectators or readers of *Hamlet* notice this silence at all; that I never noticed it myself till I began to try to solve the problem of Hamlet's relation to Ophelia; and that even now, when I read the play through without pausing to consider particular questions, it scarcely strikes me. Now Shakespeare wrote primarily for the theatre and not for students, and therefore

---

[22] It should be noticed that it was not apparently of long standing. See the words 'of late' in I.iii.91, 99.

great weight should be attached to the immediate impressions made by his works. And so it seems at least possible that the explanation of Hamlet's silence may be that Shakespeare, having already a very difficult task to perform in the soliloquies – that of showing the state of mind which caused Hamlet to delay his vengeance – did not choose to make his task more difficult by introducing matter which would not only add to the complexity of the subject but might, from its 'sentimental' interest, distract attention from the main point; while, from his theatrical experience, he knew that the audience would not observe how unnatural it was that a man deeply in love, and forced not only to renounce but to wound the woman he loved, should not think of her when he was alone. But, as this explanation is no more completely convincing to me than the other, I am driven to suspend judgment, and also to suspect that the text admits of no sure interpretation.

This result may seem to imply a serious accusation against Shakespeare. But it must be remembered that if we could see a contemporary representation of *Hamlet*, our doubts would probably disappear. The actor, instructed by the author, would make it clear to us by looks, tones, gestures, and by-play how far Hamlet's feigned harshness to Ophelia was mingled with real bitterness, and again how far his melancholy had deadened his love.

4

As we have seen, all the persons in *Hamlet* except the hero are minor characters, who fail to rise to the tragic level. They are not less interesting on that account, but the hero has occupied us so long that I shall refer only to those in regard to whom Shakespeare's intention appears to be not seldom misunderstood or overlooked.

It may seem strange that Ophelia should be one of these; and yet Shakespearean literature and the experience of teachers show that there is much difference of opinion regarding her, and in particular that a large number of readers feel a kind of personal irritation against her. They seem unable to forgive her for not having been a heroine, and they fancy her much weaker than she was. They think she ought to have been able to help Hamlet to fulfil his task. And they betray, it appears to me, the strangest misconceptions as to what she actually did.

Now it was essential to Shakespeare's purpose that too great an interest should not be aroused in the love-story; essential, therefore, that Ophelia should be merely one of the subordinate characters; and necessary, accordingly, that she should not be the equal, in spirit, power or intelligence, of his famous heroines. If she had been an Imogen, a Cordelia, even a Portia or a Juliet, the story must have taken another shape. Hamlet would either have been stimulated to do his duty, or (which is more likely) he would have gone mad, or (which is likeliest) he would have killed himself in despair. Ophelia, therefore, was made a character who could not help Hamlet, and for whom on the other hand he would not naturally feel a passion so vehement or profound as to interfere with the main motive of the play.[23] And in the love and the fate of Ophelia herself there was introduced an element, not of deep tragedy, but of pathetic beauty, which makes the analysis of her character seem almost a desecration.

Ophelia is plainly quite young and inexperienced. She has lost her mother, and has only a father and a brother, affectionate but worldly, to take care of her. Everyone in the drama who has any heart is drawn to her. To the persons in the play, as to the readers of it, she brings the thought of flowers. 'Rose of May' Laertes names her.

> Lay her in the earth,
> And from her fair and unpolluted flesh
> May violets spring!

– so he prays at her burial. 'Sweets to the sweet' the Queen murmurs, as she scatters flowers on the grave; and the flowers which Ophelia herself gathered – those which she gave to others, and those which floated about her in the brook – glimmer in the picture of the mind. Her affection for her brother is shown in two or three delicate strokes. Her love for her father is deep, though mingled with fear. For Hamlet she has, some say, no deep love – and perhaps she is so near childhood that old affections have still the strongest hold; but certainly she has given to Hamlet all the love of which her nature is as yet capable. Beyond these three beloved ones she seems to have eyes and ears for no one. The Queen is fond of her, but there is no sign of her returning the Queen's affection. Her existence is wrapped up in these three.

On this childlike nature and on Ophelia's inexperience everything

---

[23] This, I think, may be said on almost any sane view of Hamlet's love.

depends. The knowledge that 'there's tricks in the world' has reached her only as a vague report. Her father and brother are jealously anxious for her because of her ignorance and innocence; and we resent their anxiety chiefly because we know Hamlet better than they. Her whole character is that of simple unselfish affection. Naturally she is incapable of understanding Hamlet's mind, though she can feel its beauty. Naturally, too, she obeys her father when she is forbidden to receive Hamlet's visits and letters. If we remember not what *we* know but what *she* knows of her lover and her father; if we remember that she had not, like Juliet, confessed her love; and if we remember that she was much below her suitor in station, her compliance surely must seem perfectly natural, apart from the fact that the standard of obedience to a father was in Shakespeare's day higher than in ours.

'But she does more than obey,' we are told; 'she runs off frightened to report to her father Hamlet's strange visit and behaviour; she shows to her father one of Hamlet's letters, and tells him[24] the whole story of the courtship; and she joins in a plot to win Hamlet's secret from him.' One must remember, however, that she had never read the tragedy. Consider for a moment how matters looked to *her*. She knows nothing about the Ghost and its disclosures. She has undergone for some time the pain of repelling her lover and appearing to have turned against him. She sees him, or hears of him, sinking daily into deeper gloom, and so transformed from what he was that he is considered to be out of his mind. She hears the question constantly discussed what the cause of this sad change can be; and her heart tells her – how can it fail to tell her? – that her unkindness is the chief cause. Suddenly Hamlet forces his way into her chamber; and his appearance and his behaviour are those of a man crazed with love. She is frightened – why not? She is not Lady Macbeth. Rosalind would have been frightened. Which of her censors would be wholly unmoved if his room were invaded by a lunatic? She is frightened, then; frightened, if you will, like a child. Yes, but, observe, her one idea is to help Hamlet. She goes, therefore, at once to her father. To whom else should she go? Her brother is away. Her father, whom she saw with her own eyes and not with Shakespeare's, is kind, and the wisest of men, and concerned about Hamlet's state. Her father finds,

---

[24] Polonius says so, and it *may* be true.

in her report, the solution of the mystery: Hamlet is mad because she has repulsed him. Why should she not tell her father the whole story and give him an old letter which may help to convince the King and the Queen? Nay, why should she not allow herself to be used as a 'decoy' to settle the question why Hamlet is mad? It is all-important that it should be settled, in order that he may be cured; all her seniors are simply and solely anxious for his welfare; and, if her unkindness is the cause of his sad state, they will permit her to restore him by kindness (III.i.40). Was she to refuse to play a part just because it would be painful to her to do so? I find in her joining the 'plot' (as it is absurdly called) a sign not of weakness, but of unselfishness and strength.

'But she practised deception; she even told a lie. Hamlet asked her where her father was, and she said he was at home, when he was really listening behind a curtain.' Poor Ophelia! It is considered angelic in Desdemona to say untruly that she killed herself, but most immoral or pusillanimous in Ophelia to tell *her* lie. I will not discuss these casuistical problems; but, if ever an angry lunatic asks me a question which I cannot answer truly without great danger to him and to one of my relations, I hope that grace may be given me to imitate Ophelia. Seriously, at such a terrible moment was it weak, was it not rather heroic, in a simple girl not to lose her presence of mind and not to flinch, but to go through her task for Hamlet's sake and her father's? And, finally, is it really a thing to be taken as matter of course, and no matter for admiration, in this girl that, from beginning to end, and after a storm of utterly unjust reproach, not a thought of resentment should even cross her mind?

Still, we are told, it was ridiculously weak in her to lose her reason. And here again her critics seem hardly to realize the situation, hardly to put themselves in the place of a girl whose lover, estranged from her, goes mad and kills her father. They seem to forget also that Ophelia must have believed that these frightful calamities were not mere calamities, but followed from *her* action in repelling her lover. Nor do they realize the utter loneliness that must have fallen on her. Of the three persons who were all the world to her, her father has been killed, Hamlet has been sent out of the country insane, and her brother is abroad. Horatio, when her mind gives way, tries to befriend her, but there is no sign of any previous relation between them, or of Hamlet's having commended her to his friend's care. What support

she can gain from the Queen we can guess from the Queen's character, and from the fact that, when Ophelia is most helpless, the Queen
shrinks from the very sight of her (IV.v.1). She was left, thus,
absolutely alone, and if she looked for her brother's return (as she did,
IV.v.70), she might reflect that it would mean danger to Hamlet.

Whether this idea occurred to her we cannot tell. In any case it was
well for her that her mind gave way before Laertes reached Elsinore;
and pathetic as Ophelia's madness is, it is also, we feel, the kindest
stroke that now could fall on her. It is evident, I think, that this was
the effect Shakespeare intended to produce. In her madness Ophelia
continues sweet and lovable.

> Thought and affliction, passion, hell itself,
> She turns to favour and to prettiness.

In her wanderings we hear from time to time an undertone of the
deepest sorrow, but never the agonized cry of fear or horror which
makes madness dreadful or shocking.[25] And the picture of her death,
if our eyes grow dim in watching it, is still purely beautiful. Coleridge
was true to Shakespeare when he wrote of 'the affecting death of
Ophelia – who in the beginning lay like a little projection of land into
a lake or stream covered with spray-flowers quietly reflected in the
quiet waters, but at length is undermined or loosened, and becomes a
fairy isle, and after a brief vagrancy sinks almost without an eddy'.[26]

---

[25] I have heard an actress in this part utter such a cry as is described above, but there is
absolutely nothing in the text to justify her rendering. Even the exclamation 'O, ho!' found in
the Quartos at IV.v.33, but omitted in the Folios and by almost all modern editors, coming as
it does after the stanza, 'He is dead and gone, lady,' evidently expresses grief, not terror.

[26] In the remarks above I have not attempted, of course, a complete view of the character,
which has often been well described; but I cannot forbear a reference to one point which I do
not remember to have seen noticed. In the Nunnery-scene Ophelia's first words pathetically
betray her own feeling:

> Good my lord,
> How does your honour *for this many a day?*

She then offers to return Hamlet's presents. This has not been suggested to her by her father: it
is her own thought. And the next lines, in which she refers to the sweet words which accompanied those gifts, and to the unkindness which has succeeded that kindness, imply a reproach. So
again do those most touching little speeches:

> *Hamlet.* . . . I did love you once.
> *Ophelia.* Indeed, my lord, you made me believe so.
> *Hamlet.* You should not have believed me . . . I loved you not.
> *Ophelia.* I was the more deceived.

5

I reluctantly pass by Polonius, Laertes and the beautiful character of Horatio, to say something in conclusion of the Queen and the King.

The answers to two questions asked about the Queen are, it seems to me, practically certain. (1) She did not merely marry a second time with indecent haste; she was false to her husband while he lived. This is surely the most natural interpretation of the words of the Ghost (I.v. 41 f.), coming, as they do, before his account of the murder. And against this testimony what force has the objection that the queen in the 'Murder of Gonzago' is not represented as an adulteress? Hamlet's mark in arranging the play-scene was not his mother, whom besides he had been expressly ordered to spare (I.v.84 f.).

(2) On the other hand, she was *not* privy to the murder of her husband, either before the deed or after it. There is no sign of her being so, and there are clear signs that she was not. The representation of the murder in the play-scene does not move her; and when her husband starts from his throne, she innocently asks him, 'How fares my lord?' In the interview with Hamlet, when her son says of his slaughter of Polonius,

> 'A bloody deed!' Almost as bad, good mother,
> As kill a king and marry with his brother,

the astonishment of her repetition 'As kill a king!' is evidently genuine; and, if it had not been so, she would never have had the hardihood to exclaim:

> What have I done, that thou darest wag thy tongue
> In noise so rude against me?

Further, it is most significant that when she and the King speak

---

Now the obvious surface fact was not that Hamlet had forsaken her, but that *she* had repulsed *him*; and here, with his usual unobtrusive subtlety, Shakespeare shows how Ophelia, even though she may have accepted from her elders the theory that her unkindness has driven Hamlet mad, knows within herself that she is forsaken, and cannot repress the timid attempt to win her lover back by showing that her own heart is unchanged.

I will add one note. There are critics who, after all the help given them in different ways by Goethe and Coleridge, and Mrs. Jameson, still shake their heads over Ophelia's song, 'To-morrow is Saint Valentine's day'. Probably they are incurable, but they may be asked to consider that Shakespeare makes Desdemona, 'as chaste as ice, as pure as snow', sing an old song containing the line,

If I court moe women, you'll couch with moe men.

together alone, nothing that is said by her or to her implies her knowledge of the secret.

The Queen was not a bad-hearted woman, not at all the woman to think little of murder. But she had a soft animal nature, and was very dull and very shallow. She loved to be happy, like a sheep in the sun; and, to do her justice, it pleased her to see others happy, like more sheep in the sun. She never saw that drunkenness is disgusting till Hamlet told her so; and, though she knew that he considered her marriage 'o'er-hasty' (II.ii.57), she was untroubled by any shame at the feelings which had led to it. It was pleasant to sit upon her throne and see smiling faces round her, and foolish and unkind in Hamlet to persist in grieving for his father instead of marrying Ophelia and making everything comfortable. She was fond of Ophelia and genuinely attached to her son (though willing to see her lover exclude him from the throne); and, no doubt, she considered equality of rank a mere trifle compared with the claims of love. The belief at the bottom of her heart was that the world is a place constructed simply that people may be happy in it in a good-humoured sensual fashion.

Her only chance was to be made unhappy. When affliction comes to her, the good in her nature struggles to the surface through the heavy mass of sloth. Like other faulty characters in Shakespeare's tragedies, she dies a better woman than she had lived. When Hamlet shows her what she has done she feels genuine remorse. It is true, Hamlet fears it will not last, and so at the end of the interview (III.iv. 80 ff.) he adds a warning that, if she betrays him, she will ruin herself as well.[27] It is true too that there is no sign of her obeying Hamlet in breaking off her most intimate connection with the King. Still she does feel remorse; and she loves her son, and does not betray him. She gives her husband a false account of Polonius's death, and is silent about the appearance of the Ghost. She becomes miserable;

> To her sick soul, as sin's true nature is,
> Each toy seems prologue to some great amiss.

She shows spirit when Laertes raises the mob, and one respects her for standing up for her husband when she can do nothing to help her son. If she had sense to realize Hamlet's purpose, or the probability of the

---

[27] I.e. the King will kill *her* to make all sure.

King's taking some desperate step to foil it, she must have suffered torture in those days. But perhaps she was too dull.

The last we see of her, at the fencing-match, is most characteristic. She is perfectly serene. Things have slipped back into their groove, and she has no apprehensions. She is, however, disturbed and full of sympathy for her son, who is out of condition and pants and perspires. These are afflictions she can thoroughly feel for, though they are even more common than the death of a father. But then she meets her death because she cannot resist the wish to please her son by drinking to his success. And more: when she falls dying, and the King tries to make out that she is merely swooning at the sight of blood, she collects her energies to deny it and to warn Hamlet:

> No, no, the drink, the drink, – O my dear Hamlet, –
> The drink, the drink! I am poison'd.   [*Dies.*

Was ever any other writer at once so pitiless and so just as Shakespeare? Did ever any other mingle the grotesque and the pathetic with a realism so daring and yet so true to 'the modesty of nature'?

King Claudius rarely gets from the reader the attention he deserves. But he is very interesting, both psychologically and dramatically. On the one hand, he is not without respectable qualities. As a king he is courteous and never undignified; he performs his ceremonial duties efficiently; and he takes good care of the national interests. He nowhere shows cowardice, and when Laertes and the mob force their way into the palace, he confronts a dangerous situation with coolness and address. His love for his ill-gotten wife seems to be quite genuine, and there is no ground for suspecting him of having used her as a mere means to the crown.[28] His conscience, though ineffective, is far from being dead. In spite of its reproaches he plots new crimes to ensure the prize of the old one; but still it makes him unhappy (III.i.49 f., III.iii.35 f.). Nor is he cruel or malevolent.

On the other hand, he is no tragic character. He had a small nature. If Hamlet may be trusted, he was a man of mean appearance – a mildewed ear, a toad, a bat; and he was also bloated by excess in drink-

---

[28] I do not rely so much on his own statement to Laertes (IV.vii.12 f.) as on the absence of contrary indications, on his tone in speaking to her, and on such signs as his mention of her in soliloquy (III.iii.55).

ing. People made mouths at him in contempt while his brother lived; and though, when he came to the throne, they spent large sums in buying his portrait, he evidently put little reliance on their loyalty. He was no villain of force, who thought of winning his brother's crown by a bold and open stroke, but a cut-purse who stole the diadem from a shelf and put it in his pocket. He had the inclination of natures physically weak and morally small towards intrigue and crooked dealing. His instinctive predilection was for poison: this was the means he used in his first murder, and he at once recurred to it when he had failed to get Hamlet executed by deputy. Though in danger he showed no cowardice, his first thought was always for himself.

> I like him not, nor stands it safe with *us*
> To let his madness range,

– these are the first words we hear him speak after the play-scene. His first comment on the death of Polonius is,

> It had been so with *us* had we been there;

and his second is,

> Alas, how shall this bloody deed be answered?
> It will be laid to *us*.

He was not, however, stupid, but rather quick-witted and adroit. He won the Queen partly indeed by presents (how pitifully characteristic of her!), but also by 'witch-craft of his wit' or intellect. He seems to have been soft-spoken, ingratiating in manner, and given to smiling on the person he addressed ('that one may smile, and smile, and be a villain'). We see this in his speech to Laertes about the young man's desire to return to Paris (I.ii.42 f.). Hamlet scarcely ever speaks to him without an insult, but he never shows resentment, hardly even annoyance. He makes use of Laertes with great dexterity. He had evidently found that a clear head, a general complaisance, a willingness to bend and oblige where he could not overawe, would lead him to his objects – that he could trick men and manage them. Unfortunately he imagined he could trick something more than men.

This error, together with a decided trait of temperament, leads him to his ruin. He has a sanguine disposition. When first we see him, all has fallen out to his wishes, and he confidently looks forward to a happy life. He believes his secret to be absolutely safe, and he is quite ready to be kind to Hamlet, in whose melancholy he sees only excess of grief. He has no desire to see him leave the court; he promises him his voice for the succession (I.ii.108, III.ii.355); he will be a father to him. Before long, indeed, he becomes very uneasy, and then more and more alarmed; but when, much later, he has contrived Hamlet's death in England, he has still no suspicion that he need not hope for happiness:

> till I know 'tis done,
> Howe'er my haps, my *joys* were ne'er begun.

Nay, his very last words show that he goes to death unchanged:

> Oh yet defend me, friends, I am but hurt [= wounded],

he cries, although in half a minute he is dead. That his crime has failed, and that it could do nothing else, never once comes home to him. He thinks he can over-reach Heaven. When he is praying for pardon, he is all the while perfectly determined to keep his crown; and he knows it. More – it is one of the grimmest things in Shakespeare, but he puts such things so quietly that we are apt to miss them – when the King is praying for pardon for his first murder he has just made his final arrangements for a second, the murder of Hamlet. But he does not allude to that fact in his prayer. If Hamlet had really wished to kill him at a moment that had no relish of salvation in it, he had no need to wait.[29] So we are inclined to say; and yet it was not so. For this was the crisis for Claudius as well as Hamlet. He had better have died at once, before he had added to his guilt a share in the responsibility for all the woe and death that followed. And so, we may allow ourselves to say, here also Hamlet's indiscretion served him well. The power that shaped his end shaped the King's no less.

For – to return in conclusion to the action of the play – in all that happens or is done we seem to apprehend some vaster power. We do not define it, or even name it, or perhaps even say to ourselves that it is there; but our imagination is haunted by the sense of it, as it

---

[29] This also is quietly indicated. Hamlet spares the King, he says, because if the King is killed praying he will *go to heaven*. On Hamlet's departure, the King rises from his knees, and mutters:

> My words fly up, my thoughts remain below:
> Words without thoughts *never to heaven go.*

works its way through the deeds or the delays of men to its inevitable end. And most of all do we feel this in regard to Hamlet and the King. For these two, the one by his shrinking from his appointed task, and the other by efforts growing ever more feverish to rid himself of his enemy, seem to be bent on avoiding each other. But they cannot. Through devious paths, the very paths they take in order to escape, something is pushing them silently step by step towards one another, until they meet and it puts the sword into Hamlet's hand. He himself must die, for he needed this compulsion before he could fulfil the demand of destiny; but he *must* fulfil it. And the King too, turn and twist as he may, must reach the appointed goal, and is only hastening to it by the windings which seem to lead elsewhere. Concentration on the character of the hero is apt to withdraw our attention from this aspect of the drama; but in no other tragedy of Shakespeare's, not even in *Macbeth*, is this aspect so impressive.[30]

I mention *Macbeth* for a further reason. In *Macbeth* and *Hamlet* not only is the feeling of a supreme power or destiny peculiarly marked, but it has also at times a peculiar tone, which may be called, in a sense, religious. I cannot make my meaning clear without using language too definite to describe truly the imaginative impression produced; but it is roughly true that, while we do not imagine the supreme power as a divine being who avenges crime, or as a providence which supernaturally interferes, our sense of it is influenced by the fact that Shakespeare uses current religious ideas here much more decidedly than in *Othello* or *King Lear.* The horror in Macbeth's soul is more than once represented as desperation at the thought that he is eternally 'lost'; the same idea appears in the attempt of Claudius at repentance; and as *Hamlet* nears its close the 'religious' tone of the tragedy is deepened in two ways. In the first place, 'accident' is introduced into the plot in its barest and least dramatic form, when Hamlet is brought back to Denmark by the chance of the meeting with the pirate ship. This incident has been therefore severely criticized as a lame expedient,[31] but it appears probable that the 'accident' is meant to impress the imagination as the very reverse of accidental, and with many readers it certainly does so. And that this

---

[30] I am indebted to Werder in this paragraph.

[31] The attempt to explain this meeting as pre-arranged by Hamlet is scarcely worth mention.

was the intention is made the more likely by a second fact, the fact that in connection with the events of the voyage Shakespeare introduces that feeling, on Hamlet's part, of his being in the hands of Providence. The repeated expressions of this feeling are not, I have maintained, a sign that Hamlet has now formed a fixed resolution to do his duty forthwith; but their effect is to strengthen in the spectator the feeling that, whatever may become of Hamlet, and whether he wills it or not, his task will surely be accomplished, because it is the purpose of a power against which both he and his enemy are impotent, and which makes of them the instruments of its own will.

Observing this, we may remember another significant point of resemblance between *Hamlet* and *Macbeth*, the appearance in each play of a Ghost – a figure which seems quite in place in either, whereas it would seem utterly out of place in *Othello* or *King Lear*. Much might be said of the Ghost in *Hamlet*, but I confine myself to the matter which we are now considering. What is the effect of the appearance of the Ghost? And, in particular, why does Shakespeare make this Ghost so *majestical* a phantom, giving it that measured and solemn utterance, and that air of impersonal abstraction which forbids, for example, all expression of affection for Hamlet and checks in Hamlet the outburst of pity for his father? Whatever the intention may have been, the result is that the Ghost affects imagination not simply as the apparition of a dead king who desires the accomplishment of *his* purposes, but also as the representative of that hidden ultimate power, the messenger of divine justice set upon the expiation of offences which it appeared impossible for man to discover and avenge, a reminder of a symbol of the connection of the limited world of ordinary experience with the vaster life of which it is but a partial appearance. And as, at the beginning of the play, we have this intimation, conveyed through the medium of the received religious idea of a soul come from purgatory, so at the end, conveyed through the similar idea of a soul carried by angels to its rest, we have an intimation of the same character, and a reminder that the apparent failure of Hamlet's life is not the ultimate truth concerning him.

If these various peculiarities of the tragedy are considered, it will be agreed that, while *Hamlet* certainly cannot be called in the specific sense a 'religious drama', there is in it nevertheless both a freer use of popular religious ideas, and a more decided, though always imaginative, intimation of a supreme power concerned in human evil and good, than can be found in any other of Shakespeare's tragedies. And this is probably one of the causes of the special popularity of this play, just as *Macbeth*, the tragedy which in these respects most nearly approaches it, has also the place next to it in general esteem.

LECTURE V

OTHELLO

There is practically no doubt that *Othello* was the tragedy written next after *Hamlet*. Such external evidence as we possess points to this conclusion, and it is confirmed by similarities of style, diction and versification, and also by the fact that ideas and phrases of the earlier play are echoed in the later.[1] There is, further (not to speak of one curious point, to be considered when we come to Iago), a certain resemblance in the subjects. The heroes of the two plays are doubtless extremely unlike, so unlike that each could have dealt without much difficulty with the situation which proved fatal to the other; but still each is a man exceptionally noble and trustful, and each endures the shock of a terrible disillusionment. This theme is treated by Shakespeare for the first time in *Hamlet*, for the second in *Othello*. It recurs with modifications in *King Lear*, and it probably formed the attraction which drew Shakespeare to refashion in part another writer's tragedy of *Timon*. These four dramas may so far be grouped together in distinction from the remaining tragedies.

But in point of substance, and, in certain respects, in point of style, the unlikeness of *Othello* to *Hamlet* is much greater than the likeness, and the later play belongs decidedly to one group with its successors. We have seen that, like them, it is a tragedy of passion, a description inapplicable to *Julius Caesar* or *Hamlet*. And with this change goes another, an enlargement in the stature of the hero. There is in most of the later heroes something colossal, something which reminds us of Michael Angelo's figures. They are not merely exceptional men, they are huge men; as it were, survivors of the heroic age living in a later and smaller world. We do not receive this impression from Romeo or Brutus or Hamlet, nor did it lie in Shakespeare's design to allow more

---

[1] One instance is worth pointing out, because the passage in *Othello* has, oddly enough, given trouble. Desdemona says of the maid Barbara: 'She was in love, and he she loved proved mad And did forsake her.' Theobald* changed 'mad' to 'bad'. Warburton* read 'and he she loved forsook her, And she proved mad'! Johnson said 'mad' meant only 'wild, frantic, uncertain'. But what Desdemona says of Barbara is just what Ophelia might have said of herself.

than touches of this trait to Julius Caesar himself; but it is strongly marked in Lear and Coriolanus, and quite distinct in Macbeth and even in Antony. Othello is the first of these men, a being essentially large and grand, towering above his fellows, holding a volume of force which in repose ensures pre-eminence without an effort, and in commotion reminds us rather of the fury of the elements than of the tumult of common human passion.

1

What is the peculiarity of *Othello*? What is the distinctive impression that it leaves? Of all Shakespeare's tragedies, I would answer, not even excepting *King Lear*, *Othello* is the most painfully exciting and the most terrible. From the moment when the temptation of the hero begins, the reader's heart and mind are held in a vice, experiencing the extremes of pity and fear, sympathy and repulsion, sickening hope and dreadful expectation. Evil is displayed before him, not indeed with the profusion found in *King Lear*, but forming, as it were, the soul of a single character, and united with an intellectual superiority so great that he watches its advance fascinated and appalled. He sees it, in itself almost irresistible, aided at every step by fortunate accidents and the innocent mistakes of its victims. He seems to breathe an atmosphere as fateful as that of *King Lear*, but more confined and oppressive, the darkness not of night but of a close-shut murderous room. His imagination is excited to intense activity, but it is the activity of concentration rather than dilation.

I will not dwell now on aspects of the play which modify this impression, and I reserve for later discussion one of its principal sources, the character of Iago. But if we glance at some of its other sources, we shall find at the same time certain distinguishing characteristics of *Othello*.

(1) One of these has been already mentioned in our discussion of Shakespeare's technique. *Othello* is not only the most masterly of the tragedies in point of construction, but its method of construction is unusual. And this method, by which the conflict begins late, and advances without appreciable pause and with accelerating speed to the catastrophe, is a main cause of the painful tension just described. To this may be added that, after the conflict has begun, there is very little relief by way of the ridiculous. Henceforward at any rate Iago's

humour never raises a smile. The clown is a poor one; we hardly attend to him and quickly forget him; I believe most readers of Shakespeare, if asked whether there is a clown in *Othello*, would answer No.

(2) In the second place, there is no subject more exciting than sexual jealousy rising to the pitch of passion; and there can hardly be any spectacle at once so engrossing and so painful as that of a great nature suffering the torment of this passion, and driven by it to a crime which is also a hideous blunder. Such a passion as ambition, however terrible its results, is not itself ignoble; if we separate it in thought from the conditions which make it guilty, it does not appear despicable; it is not a kind of suffering, its nature is active; and therefore we can watch its course without shrinking. But jealousy, and especially sexual jealousy, brings with it a sense of shame and humiliation. For this reason it is generally hidden; if we perceive it we ourselves are ashamed and turn our eyes away; and when it is not hidden it commonly stirs contempt as well as pity. Nor is this all. Such jealousy as Othello's converts human nature into chaos, and liberates the beast in man; and it does this in relation to one of the most intense and also the most ideal of human feelings. What spectacle can be more painful than that of this feeling turned into a tortured mixture of longing and loathing, the 'golden purity' of passion split by poison into fragments, the animal in man forcing itself into his consciousness in naked grossness, and he writhing before it but powerless to deny it entrance, gasping inarticulate images of pollution, and finding relief only in a bestial thirst for blood? This is what we have to witness in one who was indeed 'great of heart' and no less pure and tender than he was great. And this, with what it leads to, the blow to Desdemona, and the scene where she is treated as the inmate of a brothel, a scene far more painful than the murder scene, is another cause of the special effect of this tragedy.[2]

(3) The mere mention of these scenes will remind us painfully of a third cause; and perhaps it is the most potent of all. I mean the suffering of Desdemona. This is, unless I mistake, the most nearly intolerable spectacle that Shakespeare offers us. For one thing, it is *mere*

---

[2] The whole force of the passages referred to can be felt only by a reader. The Othello of our stage can never be Shakespeare's Othello, any more than the Cleopatra of our stage can be his Cleopatra.

suffering; and, *ceteris paribus*,* that is much worse to witness than suffering that issues in action. Desdemona is helplessly passive. She can do nothing whatever. She cannot retaliate even in speech; no, not even in silent feeling. And the chief reason of her helplessness only makes the sight of her suffering more exquisitely painful. She is helpless because her nature is infinitely sweet and her love absolute. I would not challenge Mr. Swinburne's* statement that we *pity* Othello even more than Desdemona; but we watch Desdemona with more unmitigated distress. We are never wholly uninfluenced by the feeling that Othello is a man contending with another man; but Desdemona's suffering is like that of the most loving of dumb creatures tortured without cause by the being he adores.

(4) Turning from the hero and heroine to the third principal character, we observe (what has often been pointed out) that the action and catastrophe of *Othello* depend largely on intrigue. We must not say more than this. We must not call the play a tragedy of intrigue as distinguished from a tragedy of character. Iago's plot is Iago's character in action; and it is built on his knowledge of Othello's character, and could not otherwise have succeeded. Still it remains true that an elaborate plot was necessary to elicit the catastrophe; for Othello was no Leontes, and his was the last nature to engender such jealousy from itself. Accordingly Iago's intrigue occupies a position in the drama for which no parallel can be found in the other tragedies; the only approach, and that a distant one, being the intrigue of Edmund in the secondary plot of *King Lear*. Now in any novel or play, even if the persons rouse little interest and are never in serious danger, a skilfully-worked intrigue will excite eager attention and suspense. And where, as in *Othello*, the persons inspire the keenest sympathy and antipathy, and life and death depend on the intrigue, it becomes the source of a tension in which pain almost overpowers pleasure. Nowhere else in Shakespeare do we hold our breath in such anxiety and for so long a time as in the later Acts of *Othello*.

(5) One result of the prominence of the element of intrigue is that *Othello* is less unlike a story of private life than any other of the great tragedies. And this impression is strengthened in further ways. In the other great tragedies the action is placed in a distant period, so that its general significance is perceived through a thin veil which separates the persons from ourselves and our own world. But *Othello* is a drama of modern life; when it first appeared it was a drama almost of

contemporary life, for the date of the Turkish attack on Cyprus is 1570. The characters come close to us, and the application of the drama to ourselves (if the phrase may be pardoned) is more immediate than it can be in *Hamlet* or *Lear*. Besides this, their fortunes affect us as those of private individuals more than is possible in any of the later tragedies with the exception of *Timon*. I have not forgotten the Senate, nor Othello's position, nor his service to the State;[3] but his deed and his death have not that influence on the interests of a nation or an empire which serves to idealize, and to remove far from our own sphere, the stories of Hamlet and Macbeth, of Coriolanus and Antony. Indeed he is already superseded at Cyprus when his fate is consummated, and as we leave him no vision rises on us, as in other tragedies, of peace descending on a distracted land.

(6) The peculiarities so far considered combine with others to produce those feelings of oppression, of confinement to a comparatively narrow world, and of dark fatality, which haunt us in reading *Othello*. In *Macbeth* the fate which works itself out alike in the external conflict and in the hero's soul, is obviously hostile to evil; and the imagination is dilated both by the consciousness of its presence and by the appearance of supernatural agencies. These, as we have seen, produce in *Hamlet* a somewhat similar effect, which is increased by the hero's acceptance of the accidents as a providential shaping of his end. *King Lear* is undoubtedly the tragedy which comes nearest to *Othello* in the impression of darkness and fatefulness, and in the absence of direct indications of any guiding power.[4] But in *King Lear*, apart from other differences to be considered later, the conflict assumes proportions so vast that the imagination seems, as in *Paradise Lost*, to traverse spaces wider than the earth. In reading *Othello* the mind is not thus distended. It is more bound down to the spectacle of noble beings caught in toils from which there is no escape; while the

---

[3] See p. 4.

[4] Even here, however, there is a great difference; for although the idea of such a power is not suggested by *King Lear* as it is by *Hamlet* and *Macbeth*, it is repeatedly expressed by persons *in* the drama. Of such references there are very few in *Othello*. But for somewhat frequent allusions to hell and the devil the view of the characters is almost strictly secular. Desdemona's sweetness and forgivingness are not based on religion, and her only way of accounting for her undeserved suffering is by an appeal to Fortune: 'It is my wretched fortune' (IV.ii.128). In like manner Othello can only appeal to Fate (V.ii.264):

> but, oh vain boast!
> Who can control his fate?

prominence of the intrigue diminishes the sense of the dependence of the catastrophe on character, and the part played by accident[5] in this catastrophe accentuates the feeling of fate. This influence of accident is keenly felt in *King Lear* only once, and at the very end of the play. In *Othello*, after the temptation has begun, it is incessant and terrible. The skill of Iago was extraordinary, but so was his good fortune. Again and again a chance word from Desdemona, a chance meeting of Othello and Cassio, a question which starts to our lips and which anyone but Othello would have asked, would have destroyed Iago's plot and ended his life. In their stead, Desdemona drops her handkerchief at the moment most favourable to him,[6] Cassio blunders into the presence of Othello only to find him in a swoon, Bianca arrives precisely when she is wanted to complete Othello's deception and incense his anger into fury. All this and much more seems to us quite natural, so potent is the art of the dramatist; but it confounds us with a feeling, such as we experience in the *Oedipus Tyrannus,** that for these star-crossed mortals – both δυσδαίμονες* – there is no escape from fate, and even with a feeling, absent from that play, that fate has taken sides with villainy.[7] It is not surprising, therefore, that *Othello* should affect us as *Hamlet* and *Macbeth* never do, and as *King Lear* does only in slighter measure. On the contrary, it is marvellous that, before the tragedy is over, Shakespeare should have succeeded in toning down this impression into harmony with others more solemn and serene.

---

[5] Ulrici* has good remarks, though he exaggerates, on this point and the element of intrigue.

[6] And neither she nor Othello observes what handkerchief it is. Else she would have remembered how she came to lose it, and would have told Othello; and Othello, too, would at once have detected Iago's lie (III.iii.438) that he had seen Cassio wipe his beard with the handkerchief, 'today'. For in fact the handkerchief has been lost *not an hour* before Iago told that lie (line 288 of the *same scene*), and it was at that moment in his pocket. He lied therefore most rashly, but with his usual luck.

[7] For those who know the end of the story there is a terrible irony in the enthusiasm with which Cassio greets the arrival of Desdemona in Cyprus. Her ship (which is also Iago's) sets out from Venice a week later than the others, but reaches Cyprus on the same day with them:

> Tempests themselves, high seas and howling winds
> The gutter'd rocks and congregated sands –
> Traitors ensteep'd to clog the guiltless keel –
> As having sense of beauty, do omit
> Their mortal natures, letting go safely by
> The divine Desdemona.

So swiftly does Fate conduct her to her doom.

But has he wholly succeeded? Or is there a justification for the fact – a fact it certainly is – that some readers, while acknowledging, of course, the immense power of *Othello*, and even admitting that it is dramatically perhaps Shakespeare's greatest triumph, still regard it with a certain distaste, or, at any rate, hardly allow it a place in their minds beside *Hamlet, King Lear* and *Macbeth*.

The distaste to which I refer is due chiefly to two causes. First, to many readers in our time, men as well as women, the subject of sexual jealousy, treated with Elizabethan fullness and frankness, is not merely painful but so repulsive that not even the intense tragic emotions which the story generates can overcome this repulsion. But while it is easy to understand a dislike of *Othello* thus caused, it does not seem necessary to discuss it, for it may fairly be called personal or subjective. It would become more than this, and would amount to a criticism of the play, only if those who feel it maintained that the fullness and frankness which are disagreeable to them are also needless from a dramatic point of view, or betray a design of appealing to unpoetic feelings in the audience. But I do not think that this is maintained, or that such a view would be plausible.

To some readers, again, parts of *Othello* appear shocking or even horrible. They think – if I may formulate their objection – that in these parts Shakespeare has sinned against the canons of art, by representing on the stage a violence or brutality the effect of which is unnecessarily painful and rather sensational than tragic. The passages which thus give offence are probably those already referred to – that where Othello strikes Desdemona (IV.i.251), that where he affects to treat her as an inmate of a house of ill-fame (IV.ii.), and finally the scene of her death.

The issues thus raised ought not to be ignored or impatiently dismissed, but they cannot be decided, it seems to me, by argument. All we can profitably do is to consider narrowly our experience, and to ask ourselves this question: If we feel these objections, do we feel them when we are reading the play with all our force, or only when we are reading it in a half-hearted manner? For, however matters may stand in the former case, in the latter case evidently the fault is ours and not Shakespeare's. And if we try the question thus, I believe we shall find that on the whole the fault is ours. The first, and least important, of the three passages – that of the blow – seems to me the most doubtful. I confess that, do what I will, I cannot reconcile myself with it. It seems certain that the blow is by no means a tap on the shoulder with a roll of paper, as some actors, feeling the repulsiveness of the passage, have made it. It must occur, too, on the open stage. And there is not, I think, a sufficiently overwhelming tragic feeling in the passage to make it bearable. But in the other two scenes the case is different. There, it seems to me, if we fully imagine the inward tragedy in the souls of the persons as we read, the more obvious and almost physical sensations of pain or horror do not appear in their own likeness, and only serve to intensify the tragic feelings in which they are absorbed. Whether this would be so in the murder-scene if Desdemona had to be imagined as dragged about the open stage (as in some modern performances) may be doubtful; but there is absolutely no warrant in the text for imagining this, and it is also quite clear that the bed where she is stifled was within the curtains,[8] and so, presumably, in part, concealed.

Here, then, *Othello* does not appear to be, unless perhaps at one point,[9] open to criticism, though it has more passages than the other three tragedies where, if imagination is not fully exerted, it is shocked or else sensationally excited. If nevertheless we feel it to occupy a place in our minds a little lower than the other three (and I believe this feeling, though not general, is not rare), the reason lies not here but in another characteristic, to which I have already referred – the comparative confinement of the imaginative atmosphere. *Othello* has not equally with the other three the power of dilating the imagination by vague suggestions of huge universal powers working in the world of individual fate and passion. It is, in a sense, less 'symbolic'. We seem to be aware in it of a certain limitation, a partial suppression of that element in Shakespeare's mind which unites him with the mystical poets and with the great musicians and philosophers. In one or two of his plays, notably in *Troilus and Cressida,* we are almost painfully conscious of this suppression; we feel an intense intellectual activity, but at the same time a certain coldness and hardness, as though some power in his soul, at once the highest and the sweetest, were for a time in abeyance. In other plays, notably in the *Tempest,* we are constantly

---

[8] The dead bodies are not carried out at the end, as they must have been if the bed had been on the main stage (for this had no front curtain). The curtains within which the bed stood were drawn together at the words, 'Let it be hid' (V.ii.365).

[9] Against which may be set the scene of the blinding of Gloster in *King Lear.*

aware of the presence of this power; and in such cases we seem to be peculiarly near to Shakespeare himself. Now this is so in *Hamlet* and *King Lear*, and, in a slighter degree, in *Macbeth*; but it is much less so in *Othello*. I do not mean that in *Othello* the suppression is marked, or that, as in *Troilus and Cressida*, it strikes us as due to some unpleasant mood; it seems rather to follow simply from the design of a play on a contemporary and wholly mundane subject. Still it makes a difference of the kind I have attempted to indicate, and it leaves an impression that in *Othello* we are not in contact with the whole of Shakespeare. And it is perhaps significant in this respect that the hero himself strikes us as having, probably, less of the poet's personality in him than many characters far inferior both as dramatic creations and as men.

2

The character of Othello is comparatively simple, but, as I have dwelt on the prominence of intrigue and accident in the play, it is desirable to show how essentially the success of Iago's plot is connected with this character. Othello's description of himself as

> one not easily jealous, but, being wrought,
> Perplexed in the extreme,

is perfectly just. His tragedy lies in this – that his whole nature was indisposed to jealousy, and yet was such that he was unusually open to deception, and, if once wrought to passion, likely to act with little reflection, with no delay, and in the most decisive manner conceivable.

Let me first set aside a mistaken view. I do not mean the ridiculous notion that Othello was jealous by temperament, but the idea, which has some little plausibility, that the play is primarily a study of a noble barbarian, who has become a Christian and has imbibed some of the civilization of his employers, but who retains beneath the surface the savage passions of his Moorish blood and also the suspiciousness regarding female chastity common among Oriental peoples, and that the last three Acts depict the outburst of these original feelings through the thin crust of Venetian culture. It would take too long to discuss this idea,[10] and it would perhaps be useless to do so, for all

---

[10] The reader who is tempted by it should, however, first ask himself whether Othello does act like a barbarian, or like a man who, though wrought almost to madness, does 'all in honour'.

arguments against it must end in an appeal to the reader's under-standing of Shakespeare. If he thinks it is like Shakespeare to look at things in this manner; that he had a historical mind and occupied himself with problems of 'Culturgeschichte';* that he laboured to make his Romans perfectly Roman, to give a correct view of the Britons in the days of Lear or Cymbeline, to portray in Hamlet a stage of the moral consciousness not yet reached by the people around him, the reader will also think this interpretation of *Othello* probable. To me it appears hopelessly un-Shakespearean. I could as easily believe that Chaucer meant the Wife of Bath* for a study of the peculiarities of Somersetshire. I do not mean that Othello's race is a matter of no account. It has, as we shall presently see, its importance in the play. It makes a difference to our idea of him; it makes a difference to the action and catastrophe. But in regard to the essentials of his character it is not important; and if anyone had told Shakespeare that no Englishman would have acted like the Moor, and had congratulated him on the accuracy of his racial psychology, I am sure he would have laughed.

Othello is, in one sense of the word, by far the most romantic figure among Shakespeare's heroes; and he is so partly from the strange life of war and adventure which he has lived from childhood. He does not belong to our world, and he seems to enter it we know not whence – almost as if from wonderland. There is something mysterious in his descent from men of royal siege; in his wanderings in vast deserts and among marvellous peoples; in his tales of magic handkerchiefs and prophetic Sibyls; in the sudden vague glimpses we get of numberless battles and sieges in which he has played the hero and has borne a charmed life; even in chance references to his baptism, his being sold to slavery, his sojourn in Aleppo.

And he is not merely a romantic figure; his own nature is roman-tic. He has not indeed, the meditative or speculative imagination of Hamlet; but in the strictest sense of the word he is more poetic than Hamlet. Indeed, if one recalls Othello's most famous speeches – those that begin, 'Her father loved me', 'O now for ever', 'Never, Iago', 'Had it pleased Heaven', 'It is the cause', 'Behold, I have a weapon', 'Soft you, a word or two before you go' – and if one places side by side with these speeches an equal number by any other hero, one will not doubt that Othello is the greatest poet of them all. There is the same poetry in his casual phrases – like 'These nine moons wasted', 'Keep up your bright swords, for the dew will rust them', 'You chaste stars', 'It is a sword of Spain, the ice-brook's temper', 'It is the very error of the moon' – and in those brief expressions of intense feeling which ever since have been taken as the absolute expression, like

> If it were now to die,
> 'Twere now to be most happy; for, I fear,
> My soul hath her content so absolute
> That not another comfort like to this
> Succeeds in unknown fate,

or

> If she be false, O then Heaven mocks itself,
> I'll not believe it;

or

> No, my heart is turned to stone; I strike it, and it hurts my hand,

or

> But yet the pity of it, Iago! O Iago, the pity of it, Iago!

or

> O thou weed,
> Who are so lovely fair and smell'st so sweet
> That the sense aches at thee, would thou hadst ne'er been born.

And this imagination, we feel, has accompanied his whole life. He has watched with a poet's eye the Arabian trees dropping their med'cinable gum, and the Indian throwing away his chance-found pearl; and has gazed in a fascinated dream at the Pontic sea rushing, never to return, to the Propontic and the Hellespont; and has felt as no other man ever felt (for he speaks of it as none other ever did) the poetry of the pride, pomp, and circumstance of glorious war.

So he comes before us, dark and grand, with a light upon him from the sun where he was born; but no longer young, and now grave, self-controlled, steeled by the experience of countless perils, hardships and vicissitudes, at once simple and stately in bearing and in speech, a great man naturally modest but fully conscious of his worth, proud of his services to the state, unawed by dignitaries and unelated by honours, secure, it would seem, against all dangers from without and all rebellion from within. And he comes to have his life crowned with the final glory of love, a love as strange, adventurous and romantic as any passage of his eventful history, filling his heart with tenderness and his imagination with ecstasy. For there is no love, not that of Romeo in his youth, more steeped in imagination than Othello's.

The sources of danger in this character are revealed but too clearly by the story. In the first place, Othello's mind, for all its poetry, is very simple. He is not observant. His nature tends outward. He is quite free from introspection, and is not given to reflection. Emotion excites his imagination, but it confuses and dulls his intellect. On this side he is the very opposite of Hamlet, with whom, however, he shares a great openness and trustfulness of nature. In addition, he has little experience of the corrupt products of civilized life, and is ignorant of European women.

In the second place, for all his dignity and massive calm (and he has greater dignity than any other of Shakespeare's men), he is by nature full of the most vehement passion. Shakespeare emphasizes his self-control, not only by the wonderful pictures of the First Act, but by references to the past. Lodovico, amazed at his violence, exclaims:

> Is this the noble Moor whom our full Senate
> Call all in all sufficient? Is this the nature
> Whom passion could not shake? whose solid virtue
> The shot of accident nor dart of chance
> Could neither graze nor pierce?

Iago, who has here no motive for lying, asks:

> Can he be angry? I have seen the cannon
> When it hath blown his ranks into the air,
> And, like the devil, from his very arm
> Puffed his own brother – and can he be angry?[11]

This, and other aspects of his character, are best exhibited by a single line – one of Shakespeare's miracles – the words by which Othello silences in a moment the night-brawl between his attendants and those of Brabantio:

> Keep up your bright swords, for the dew will rust them.

---

[11] For the actor, then, to represent him as violently angry when he cashiers Cassio is an utter mistake.

And the same self-control is strikingly shown where Othello endeav-
ours to elicit some explanation of the fight between Cassio and
Montano. Here, however, there occur ominous words, which make us
feel how necessary was this self-control, and make us admire it the
more:

> Now, by heaven,
> My blood begins my safer guides to rule,
> And passion, having my best judgment collied,
> Assays to lead the way.

We remember these words later, when the sun of reason is 'collied',
blackened and blotted out in total eclipse.

Lastly, Othello's nature is all of one piece. His trust, where he
trusts, is absolute. Hesitation is almost impossible to him. He is
extremely self-reliant, and decides and acts instantaneously. If stirred
to indignation, as 'in Aleppo once', he answers with one lightning
stroke. Love, if he loves, must be to him the heaven where either he
must live or bear no life. If such a passion as jealousy seizes him, it will
swell into a well-nigh incontrollable flood. He will press for immediate conviction or immediate relief. Convinced, he will act with the
authority of a judge and the swiftness of a man in mortal pain.
Undeceived, he will do like execution on himself.

This character is so noble, Othello's feelings and actions follow so
inevitably from it and from the forces brought to bear on it, and his
sufferings are so heart-rending, that he stirs, I believe, in most readers
a passion of mingled love and pity which they feel for no other hero
in Shakespeare, and to which not even Mr. Swinburne can do more
than justice. Yet there are some critics and not a few readers who cherish a grudge against him. They do not merely think that in the later
stages of his temptation he showed a certain obtuseness, and that, to
speak pedantically, he acted with unjustifiable precipitance and
violence; no one, I suppose, denies that. But, even when they admit
that he was not of a jealous temper, they consider that he *was* 'easily
jealous'; they seem to think that it was inexcusable in him to feel any
suspicion of his wife at all; and they blame him for never suspecting
Iago or asking him for evidence. I refer to this attitude of mind chiefly
in order to draw attention to certain points in the story. It comes
partly from mere inattention (for Othello did suspect Iago and did ask
him for evidence); partly from a misconstruction of the text which

makes Othello appear jealous long before he really is so;[12] and partly from failure to realize certain essential facts. I will begin with these.

(1) Othello, we have seen, was trustful, and thorough in his trust. He put entire confidence in the honesty of Iago, who had not only been his companion in arms, but, as he believed, had just proved his faithfulness in the matter of the marriage. This confidence was misplaced, and we happen to know it; but it was no sign of stupidity in Othello. For his opinion of Iago was the opinion of practically everyone who knew him: and that opinion was that Iago was before all things 'honest', his very faults being those of excess in honesty. This being so, even if Othello had not been trustful and simple, it would have been quite unnatural in him to be unmoved by the warnings of so honest a friend, warnings offered with extreme reluctance and manifestly from a sense of a friend's duty.[13] *Any* husband would have been troubled by them.

(2) Iago does not bring these warnings to a husband who had lived with a wife for months and years and knew her like his sister or his bosom-friend. Nor is there any ground in Othello's character for supposing that, if he had been such a man, he would have felt and acted as he does in the play. But he was newly married; in the circumstances he cannot have known much of Desdemona before his marriage; and further he was conscious of being under the spell of a feeling which can give glory to the truth but can also give it to a dream.

(3) This consciousness in any imaginative man is enough, in such circumstances, to destroy his confidence in his powers of perception. In Othello's case, after a long and most artful preparation, there now come, to reinforce its effect, the suggestions that he is not an Italian, nor even a European; that he is totally ignorant of the thoughts and the customary morality of Venetian women,[14] that he had himself seen in Desdemona's deception of her father how perfect an actress

---

[12] I cannot deal fully with this point in the lecture. See Note L.

[13] It is important to observe that, in his attempt to arrive at the facts about Cassio's drunken misdemeanour, Othello had just had an example of Iago's unwillingness to tell the whole truth where it must injure a friend. No wonder he feels in the Temptation-scene that 'this honest creature doubtless Sees and knows more, much more, than he unfolds'.

[14] To represent that Venetian women do not regard adultery so seriously as Othello does, and again that Othello would be wise to accept the situation like an Italian husband, is one of Iago's most artful and most maddening devices.

she could be. As he listens in horror, for a moment at least the past is revealed to him in a new and dreadful light, and the ground seems to sink under his feet. These suggestions are followed by a tentative but hideous and humiliating insinuation of what his honest and much-experienced friend fears may be the true explanation of Desdemona's rejection of acceptable suitors, and of her strange, and naturally temporary, preference for a black man. Here Iago goes too far. He sees something in Othello's face that frightens him, and he breaks off. Nor does this idea take any hold of Othello's mind. But it is not surprising that his utter powerlessness to repel it on the ground of knowledge of his wife, or even of that instinctive interpretation of character which is possible between persons of the same race,[15] should complete his misery, so that he feels he can bear no more, and abruptly dismisses his friend (III.iii.238).

Now I repeat that *any* man situated as Othello was would have been disturbed by Iago's communications, and I add that many men would have been made wildly jealous. But up to this point, where Iago is dismissed, Othello, I must maintain, does not show jealousy. His confidence is shaken, he is confused and deeply troubled, he feels even horror; but he is not yet jealous in the proper sense of that word. In his soliloquy (III.iii.258 ff.) the beginning of this passion may be traced; but it is only after an interval of solitude, when he has had time to dwell on the idea presented to him, and especially after statements of fact, not mere general grounds of suspicion, are offered, that the passion lays hold of him. Even then, however, and indeed to the very end, he is quite unlike the essentially jealous man, quite unlike Leontes. No doubt the thought of another man's possessing the woman he loves is intolerable to him; no doubt the sense of insult and the impulse of revenge are at times most violent; and these are the feelings of jealousy proper. But these are not the chief or the deepest source of Othello's suffering. It is the wreck of his faith and his love. It is the feeling,

---

[15] If the reader has ever chanced to see an African violently excited, he may have been startled to observe how completely at a loss he was to interpret those bodily expressions of passion which in a fellow-countryman he understands at once, and in a European foreigner with somewhat less certainty. The effect of difference in blood in increasing Othello's bewilderment regarding his wife is not sufficiently realized. The same effect has to be remembered in regard to Desdemona's mistakes in dealing with Othello in his anger.

If she be false, oh then Heaven mocks itself;

the feeling,

> O Iago, the pity of it, Iago!

the feeling,

> But there where I have garner'd up my heart,
> Where either I must live, or bear no life;
> The fountain from the which my current runs,
> Or else dries up – to be discarded thence.

You will find nothing like this in Leontes.

Up to this point, it appears to me, there is not a syllable to be said against Othello. But the play is a tragedy, and from this point we may abandon the ungrateful and undramatic task of awarding praise and blame. When Othello, after a brief interval, re-enters (III.iii.330), we see at once that the poison has been at work, and 'burns like the mines of sulphur'.

> Look where he comes! Not poppy, nor mandragora,
> Nor all the drowsy syrups of the world,
> Shall ever medicine thee to that sweet sleep
> Which thou owedst yesterday.

He is 'on the rack', in an agony so unbearable that he cannot endure the sight of Iago. Anticipating the probability that Iago has spared him the whole truth, he feels that in that case his life is over and his 'occupation gone' with all its glories. But he has not abandoned hope. The bare possibility that his friend is deliberately deceiving him – though such a deception would be a thing so monstrously wicked that he can hardly conceive it credible – is a kind of hope. He furiously demands proof, ocular proof. And when he is compelled to see that he is demanding an impossibility he still demands evidence. He forces it from the unwilling witness, and hears the maddening tale of Cassio's dream. It is enough. And if it were not enough, has he not sometimes seen a handkerchief spotted with strawberries in his wife's hand? Yes, it was his first gift to her.

> I know not that; but such a handkerchief –
> I am sure it was your wife's – did I to-day
> See Cassio wipe his beard with.

'If it be that,' he answers – but what need to test the fact? The 'madness of revenge' is in his blood, and hesitation is a thing he never knew. He passes judgment, and controls himself only to make his sentence a solemn vow.

The Othello of the Fourth Act is Othello in his fall. His fall is never complete, but he is much changed. Towards the close of the Temptation-scene he becomes at times most terrible, but his grandeur remains almost undiminished. Even in the following scene (III.iv.), where he goes to test Desdemona in the matter of the handkerchief, and receives a fatal confirmation of her guilt, our sympathy with him is hardly touched by any feeling of humiliation. But in the Fourth Act 'Chaos has come'. A slight interval of time may be admitted here. It is but slight; for it was necessary for Iago to hurry on, and terribly dangerous to leave a chance for a meeting of Cassio with Othello; and his insight into Othello's nature taught him that his plan was to deliver blow on blow, and never to allow his victim to recover from the confusion of the first shock. Still there is a slight interval; and when Othello reappears we see at a glance that he is a changed man. He is physically exhausted, and his mind is dazed.[16] He sees everything blurred through a mist of blood and tears. He has actually forgotten the incident of the handkerchief, and has to be reminded of it. When Iago, perceiving that he can now risk almost any lie, tells him that Cassio has confessed his guilt, Othello, the hero who has seemed to us only second to Coriolanus in physical power, trembles all over; he mutters disjointed words; a blackness suddenly intervenes between his eyes and the world; he takes it for the shuddering testimony of nature to the horror he has just heard,[17] and he falls senseless to the ground. When he recovers it is to watch Cassio, as he imagines, laughing over his shame. It is an imposition so gross, and

---

[16] See Note M.

[17] Cf. *Winter's Tale*, I.ii.137 ff.:

> Can thy dam? – may't be? –
> Affection! thy intention stabs the centre:
> Thou dost make possible things not so held,
> Communicatest with dreams; – how can this be?
> With what's unreal thou coactive art,
> And fellow'st nothing: then 'tis very credent
> Thou may'st cojoin with something; and thou dost,
> And that beyond commission, and I find it,
> And that to the infection of my brains
> And hardening of my brows.

should have been one so perilous, that Iago would never have ventured it before. But he is safe now. The sight only adds to the confusion of intellect the madness of rage; and a ravenous thirst for revenge, contending with motions of infinite longing and regret, conquers them. The delay till night-fall is torture to him. His self-control has wholly deserted him, and he strikes his wife in the presence of the Venetian envoy. He is so lost to all sense of reality that he never asks himself what will follow the deaths of Cassio and his wife. An ineradicable instinct of justice, rather than any last quiver of hope, leads him to question Emilia; but nothing could convince him now, and there follows the dreadful scene of accusation; and then, to allow us the relief of burning hatred and burning tears, the interview of Desdemona with Iago, and that last talk of hers with Emilia, and her last song.

But before the end there is again a change. The supposed death of Cassio (V.i.) satiates the thirst for vengeance. The Othello who enters the bed-chamber with the words,

> It is the cause, it is the cause, my soul,

is not the man of the Fourth Act. The deed he is bound to do is no murder, but a sacrifice. He is to save Desdemona from herself, not in hate but in honour; in honour, and also in love. His anger has passed; a boundless sorrow has taken its place; and

> this sorrow's heavenly:
> It strikes where it doth love.

Even when, at the sight of her apparent obduracy, and at the hearing of words which by a crowning fatality can only reconvince him of her guilt, these feelings give way to others, it is to righteous indignation they give way, not to rage; and, terribly painful as this scene is, there is almost nothing here to diminish the admiration and love which heighten pity.[18] And pity itself vanishes, and love and admiration alone remain, in the majestic dignity and sovereign ascendancy of the close. Chaos has come and gone; and the Othello of the Council-chamber and the quay of Cyprus has returned, or a greater and nobler Othello still. As he speaks those final words in which all the glory and agony of his life – long ago in India and Arabia and Aleppo, and

---

[18] See Note O.

afterwards in Venice, and now in Cyprus – seem to pass before us, like the pictures that flash before the eyes of a drowning man, a triumphant scorn for the fetters of the flesh and the littleness of all the lives that must survive him sweeps our grief away, and when he dies upon a kiss the most painful of all tragedies leaves us for the moment free from pain, and exulting in the power of 'love and man's unconquerable mind'.

3

The words just quoted come from Wordsworth's sonnet to Toussaint L'Ouverture.* Toussaint was a Negro; and there is a question, which, though of little consequence, is not without dramatic interest, whether Shakespeare imagined Othello as a Negro or as a Moor. Now I will not say that Shakespeare imagined him as a Negro and not as a Moor, for that might imply that he distinguished Negroes and Moors precisely as we do; but what appears to me nearly certain is that he imagined Othello as a black man, and not as a light-brown one.

In the first place, we must remember that the brown or bronze, to which we are now accustomed in the Othellos of our theatres is a recent innovation. Down to Edmund Kean's time, so far as is known, Othello was always quite black. This stage-tradition goes back to the Restoration, and it almost settles our question. For it is impossible that the colour of the original Othello should have been forgotten so soon after Shakespeare's time, and most improbable that it should have been changed from brown to black.

If we turn to the play itself, we find many references to Othello's colour and appearance. Most of these are indecisive; for the word 'black' was of course used then where we should speak of a 'dark' complexion now; and even the nickname 'thick-lips', appealed to as proof that Othello was a Negro, might have been applied by an enemy to what we call a Moor. On the other hand, it is hard to believe that, if Othello had been light brown, Brabantio would have taunted him with having a 'sooty bosom', or that (as Mr. Furness observes) he himself would have used the words,

> her name, that was as fresh
> As Dian's visage, is now begrimed and black
> As mine own face.

These arguments cannot be met by pointing out that Othello was of royal blood, is not called an Ethiopian, is called a Barbary horse, and is said to be going to Mauritania. All this would be of importance if we had reason to believe that Shakespeare shared our ideas, knowledge and terms. Otherwise it proves nothing. And we know that sixteenth-century writers called any dark North African a Moor, or a black Moor, or a blackamoor. Sir Thomas Elyot,* according to Hunter,[19]* calls Ethiopians Moors; and the following are the first two illustrations of 'Blackamoor' in the Oxford *English Dictionary*. 1547, 'I am a blake More borne in Barbary'; 1548, '*Ethiopo*, a blake More, or a man of Ethiope'. Thus geographical names can tell us nothing about the question how Shakespeare imagined Othello. He may have known that a Mauritanian is not a Negro nor black, but we cannot assume that he did. He may have known, again, that the Prince of Morocco, who is described in the *Merchant of Venice* as having, like Othello, the complexion of a devil, was no Negro. But we cannot tell: nor is there any reason why he should not have imagined the Prince as a brown Moor and Othello as a Blackamoor.

Titus Andronicus appeared in the Folio among Shakespeare's works. It is believed by some good critics to be his: hardly anyone doubts that he had a hand in it: it is certain that he knew it, for reminiscences of it are scattered through his plays. Now no one who reads *Titus Andronicus* with an open mind can doubt that Aaron was, in our sense, black; and he appears to have been a Negro. To mention nothing else, he is twice called 'coal-black'; his colour is compared with that of a raven and a swan's legs; his child is coal-black and thick-lipped; he himself has a 'fleece of woolly hair'. Yet he is 'Aaron the Moor', just as Othello is 'Othello the Moor'. In the *Battle of Alcazar** (Dyce's *Peele*, p. 421) Muly the Moor is called 'the negro'; and Shakespeare himself in a single line uses 'negro' and 'Moor' of the same person (*Merchant of Venice*, III.v.42).

The horror of most American critics (Mr. Furness is a bright exception) at the idea of a black Othello is very amusing, and their arguments are highly instructive. But they were anticipated, I regret to say, by Coleridge, and we will hear him. 'No doubt Desdemona saw Othello's visage in his mind; yet, as we are constituted, and most surely as an English audience was disposed in the beginning of the seventeenth century, it would be something monstrous to conceive

---

[19] New Illustrations, ii.281.

this beautiful Venetian girl falling in love with a veritable negro. It would argue a disproportionateness, a want of balance, in Desdemona, which Shakespeare does not appear to have in the least contemplated.'[20] Could any argument be more self-destructive? It actually *did* appear to Brabantio 'something monstrous to conceive' his daughter falling in love with Othello – so monstrous that he could account for her love only by drugs and foul charms. And the suggestion that such love would argue 'disproportionateness' is precisely the suggestion that Iago *did* make in Desdemona's case:

> Foh! one may smell in such a will most rank,
> Foul *disproportion*, thoughts unnatural.

In fact he spoke of the marriage exactly as a filthy-minded cynic might now speak of the marriage of an English lady to a negro like Toussaint. Thus the argument of Coleridge and others points straight to the conclusion against which they argue.

But this is not all. The question whether to Shakespeare Othello was black or brown is not a mere question of isolated fact or historical curiosity; it concerns the character of Desdemona. Coleridge, and still more the American writers, regard her love, in effect, as Brabantio regarded it, and not as Shakespeare conceived it. They are simply blurring this glorious conception when they try to lessen the distance between her and Othello, and to smooth away the obstacle which his 'visage' offered to her romantic passion for a hero. Desdemona, the 'eternal womanly' in its most lovely and adorable form, simple and innocent as a child, ardent with the courage and idealism of a saint, radiant with that heavenly purity of heart which men worship the more because nature so rarely permits it to themselves, had no theories about universal brotherhood, and no phrases about 'one blood in all the nations of the earth' or 'barbarian, Scythian, bond and free'; but when her soul came in sight of the noblest soul on earth, she made nothing of the shrinking of her senses, but followed her soul until her senses took part with it, and 'loved him with the love which was her doom'. It was not prudent. It even turned out tragically. She met in life with the reward of those who rise too far above our common level; and we continue to allot her the same reward when we consent to

---

[20] *Lectures on Shakespeare*, ed. Ashe, p. 386.

forgive her for loving a brown man, but find it monstrous that she should love a black one.[21]

There is perhaps a certain excuse for our failure to rise to Shakespeare's meaning, and to realize how extraordinary and splendid a thing it was in a gentle Venetian girl to love Othello, and to assail fortune with such a 'downright violence and storm' as is expected only in a hero. It is that when first we hear of her marriage we have not yet seen the Desdemona of the later Acts; and therefore we do not perceive how astonishing this love and boldness must have been in a maiden so quiet and submissive. And when we watch her in her suffering and death we are so penetrated by the sense of her heavenly sweetness and self-surrender that we almost forget that she had shown herself quite as exceptional in the active assertion of her own soul and will. She tends to become to us predominantly pathetic, the sweetest and most pathetic of Shakespeare's women, as innocent as Miranda and as loving as Viola, yet suffering more deeply than Cordelia or Imogen. And she seems to lack that independence and strength of spirit which Cordelia and Imogen possess, and which in a manner raises them above suffering. She appears passive and defenceless, and can oppose to wrong nothing but the infinite endurance and forgiveness of a love that knows not how to resist or resent. She thus becomes at once the most beautiful example of this love, and the most pathetic heroine in Shakespeare's world. If her part were acted by an artist equal to Salvini, and with a Salvini for Othello, I doubt if the spectacle of the last two Acts would not be pronounced intolerable.

---

[21] I will not discuss the further question whether, granted that to Shakespeare Othello was a black, he should be represented as a black in our theatres now. I dare say not. We do not like the real Shakespeare. We like to have his language pruned and his conceptions flattened into something that suits our mouths and minds. And even if we were prepared to make an effort, still, as Lamb* observes, to imagine is one thing and to see is another. Perhaps if we saw Othello coal-black with the bodily eye, the aversion of our blood, an aversion which comes as near to being merely physical as anything human can, would overpower our imagination and sink us below not Shakespeare only but the audiences of the seventeenth and eighteenth centuries.

As I have mentioned Lamb, I may observe that he differed from Coleridge as to Othello's colour, but, I am sorry to add, thought Desdemona to stand in need of excuse. 'This noble lady, with a singularity rather to be wondered at than imitated, had chosen for the object of her affections a Moor, a black. . . . Neither is Desdemona to be altogether condemned for the unsuitableness of the person whom she selected for her lover' (*Tales from Shakespeare*). Others, of course, have gone much further and have treated all the calamities of the tragedy as a sort of judgment on Desdemona's rashness, wilfulness and undutifulness. There is no arguing with opinions like this; but I cannot believe that even Lamb is true to Shakespeare in implying that Desdemona is in some degree to be condemned. What is there in the play to show that Shakespeare regarded her marriage differently from Imogen's?

Of course this later impression of Desdemona is perfectly right, but it must be carried back and united with the earlier before we can see what Shakespeare imagined. Evidently, we are to understand, innocence, gentleness, sweetness, lovingness were the salient and, in a sense, the principal traits in Desdemona's character. She was, as her father supposed her to be,

> a maiden never bold,
> Of spirit so still and quiet that her motion
> Blushed at herself.

But suddenly there appeared something quite different – something which could never have appeared, for example, in Ophelia – a love not only full of romance but showing a strange freedom and energy of spirit, and leading to a most unusual boldness of action; and this action was carried through with a confidence and decision worthy of Juliet or Cordelia. Desdemona does not shrink before the Senate; and her language to her father, though deeply respectful, is firm enough to stir in us some sympathy with the old man who could not survive his daughter's loss. This then, we must understand, was the emergence in Desdemona, as she passed from girlhood to womanhood, of an individuality and strength which if she had lived would have been gradually fused with her more obvious qualities and have issued in a thousand actions, sweet and good, but surprising to her conventional or timid neighbours. And, indeed, we have already a slight example in her overflowing kindness, her boldness and her ill-fated persistence in pleading Cassio's cause. But the full ripening of her lovely and noble nature was not to be. In her brief wedded life she appeared again chiefly as the sweet and submissive being of her girlhood; and the strength of her soul, first evoked by love, found scope to show itself only in a love which, when harshly repulsed, blamed only its own pain; when bruised, only gave forth a more exquisite fragrance; and when rewarded with death, summoned its last labouring breath to save its murderer.

Many traits in Desdemona's character have been described with sympathetic insight by Mrs. Jameson,* and I will pass them by and add but a few words on the connection between this character and the catastrophe of *Othello*. Desdemona, as Mrs. Jameson remarks, shows less quickness of intellect and less tendency to reflection than most of Shakespeare's heroines; but I question whether the critic is right in adding that she shows much of the 'unconscious address common in women'. She seems to me deficient in this address, having in its place a frank childlike boldness and persistency, which are full of charm but are unhappily united with a certain want of perception. And these graces and this deficiency appear to be inextricably intertwined, and in the circumstances conspire tragically against her. They, with her innocence, hinder her from understanding Othello's state of mind, and lead her to the most unlucky acts and words; and unkindness or anger subdues her so completely that she becomes passive and seems to drift helplessly towards the cataract in front.

In Desdemona's incapacity to resist there is also, in addition to her perfect love, something which is very characteristic. She is, in a sense, a child of nature. That deep inward division which leads to clear and conscious oppositions of right and wrong, duty and inclination, justice and injustice, is alien to her beautiful soul. She is not good, kind and true in spite of a temptation to be otherwise, any more than she is charming in spite of a temptation to be otherwise. She seems to know evil only by name, and, her inclinations being good, she acts on inclination. This trait, with its results, may be seen if we compare her, at the crises of the story, with Cordelia. In Desdemona's place, Cordelia, however frightened at Othello's anger about the lost handkerchief, would not have denied its loss. Painful experience had produced in her a conscious principle of rectitude and a proud hatred of falseness, which would have made a lie, even one wholly innocent in spirit, impossible to her; and the clear sense of justice and right would have led her, instead, to require an explanation of Othello's agitation which would have broken Iago's plot to pieces. In the same way, at the final crisis, no instinctive terror of death would have compelled Cordelia suddenly to relinquish her demand for justice and to plead for life. But these moments are fatal to Desdemona, who acts precisely as if she were guilty; and they are fatal because they ask for something which, it seems to us, could hardly be united with the peculiar beauty of her nature.

This beauty is all her own. Something as beautiful may be found in Cordelia, but not the same beauty. Desdemona, confronted with Lear's foolish but pathetic demand for a profession of love, could have done, I think, what Cordelia could not do – could have refused to compete with her sisters, and yet have made her father feel that she loved him well. And I doubt if Cordelia, 'falsely murdered', would have been capable of those last words of Desdemona – her answer to Emilia's 'O, who hath done this deed?'

> Nobody: I myself. Farewell.
> Commend me to my kind lord. O, farewell!

Were we intended to remember, as we hear this last 'falsehood', that other falsehood, 'It is not lost', and to feel that, alike in the momentary child's fear and the deathless woman's love, Desdemona is herself and herself alone?[22]

---

[22] When Desdemona spoke her last words, perhaps that line of the ballad which she sang an hour before her death was still busy in her brain,

> Let nobody blame him: his scorn I approve.

Nature plays such strange tricks, and Shakespeare almost alone among poets seems to create in somewhat the same manner as Nature. In the same way, as Malone* pointed out, Othello's exclamation, 'Goats and monkeys!' (IV.i.274) is an unconscious reminiscence of Iago's words at III.iii.403.

LECTURE VI

OTHELLO

1

Evil has nowhere else been portrayed with such mastery as in the character of Iago. Richard III, for example, beside being less subtly conceived, is a far greater figure and a less repellent. His physical deformity, separating him from other men, seems to offer some excuse for his egoism. In spite of his egoism, too, he appears to us more than a mere individual; he is the representative of his family, the Fury of the House of York. Nor is he so negative as Iago: he has strong passions, he has admirations, and his conscience disturbs him. There is the glory of power about him. Though an excellent actor, he prefers force to fraud, and in his world there is no general illusion as to his true nature. Again, to compare Iago with the Satan of *Paradise Lost* seems almost absurd, so immensely does Shakespeare's man exceed Milton's Fiend in evil. That mighty Spirit, whose

> form had yet not lost
> All her original brightness, nor appeared
> Less than archangel ruined and the excess
> Of glory obscured;*

who knew loyalty to comrades and pity for victims; who

> felt how awful goodness is, and saw
> Virtue in her shape how lovely; saw, and pined
> His loss;*

who could still weep – how much further distant is he than Iago from spiritual death, even when, in procuring the fall of Man, he completes his own fall! It is only in Goethe's Mephistopheles that a fit companion for Iago can be found. Here there is something of the same deadly coldness, the same gaiety in destruction. But then Mephistopheles, like so many scores of literary villains, has Iago for his father. And Mephistopheles, besides, is not, in the strict sense, a character. He is half person, half symbol. A metaphysical idea speaks through him. He is earthy, but could never live upon the earth.

Of Shakespeare's characters Falstaff, Hamlet, Iago, and Cleopatra (I name them in the order of their births) are probably the most wonderful. Of these, again, Hamlet and Iago, whose births come nearest together, are perhaps the most subtle. And if Iago had been a person as attractive as Hamlet, as many thousands of pages might have been written about him, containing as much criticism good and bad. As it is, the majority of interpretations of his character are inadequate not only to Shakespeare's conception, but, I believe, to the impressions of most readers of taste who are bewildered by analysis. These false interpretations, if we set aside the usual lunacies,[1] fall into two groups. The first contains views which reduce Shakespeare to common-place. In different ways and degrees they convert his Iago into an ordinary villain. Their Iago is simply a man who has been slighted and revenges himself; or a husband who believes he has been wronged, and will make his enemy suffer a jealousy worse than his own; or an ambitious man determined to ruin his successful rival – one of these, or a combination of these, endowed with unusual ability and cruelty. These are the more popular views. The second group of false interpretations is much smaller, but it contains much weightier matter than the first. Here Iago is a being who hates good simply because it is good, and loves evil purely for itself. His action is not prompted by any plain motive like revenge, jealousy or ambition. It springs from a 'motiveless malignity', or a disinterested delight in the pain of others; and Othello, Cassio and Desdemona, are scarcely more than the material requisite for the full attainment of this delight. This second Iago, evidently, is no conventional villain, and he is much nearer to Shakespeare's Iago than the first. Only he is, if not a psychological impossibility, at any rate, not a *human* being. He might be in place, therefore, in a symbolical poem like *Faust*, but in a purely human drama like *Othello* he would be a ruinous blunder. Moreover, he is not in *Othello*: he is a product of imperfect observation and analysis.

Coleridge, the author of that misleading phrase 'motiveless malignity', has some fine remarks on Iago; and the essence of the character

---

[1] It has been held, for example, that Othello treated Iago abominably in preferring Cassio to him; that he *did* seduce Emilia; that he and Desdemona were too familiar before marriage; and that in any case his fate was a moral judgment on his sins, and Iago a righteous, if sharp, instrument of Providence.

has been described, first in some of the best lines Hazlitt* ever wrote, and then rather more fully by Mr. Swinburne – so admirably described that I am tempted merely to read and illustrate these two criticisms. This plan, however, would make it difficult to introduce all that I wish to say. I propose, therefore, to approach the subject directly, and, first, to consider how Iago appeared to those who knew him, and what inferences may be drawn from their illusions; and then to ask what, if we judge from the play, his character really was. And I will indicate the points where I am directly indebted to the criticisms just mentioned.

But two warnings are first required. One of these concerns Iago's nationality. It has been held that he is a study of that peculiarly Italian form of villainy which is considered both too clever and too diaboli-cal for an Englishman. I doubt if there is much more to be said for this idea than for the notion that Othello is a study of Moorish char-acter. No doubt the belief in that Italian villainy was prevalent in Shakespeare's time, and it may perhaps have influenced him in some slight degree both here and in drawing the character of Iachimo in *Cymbeline*. But even this slight influence seems to be doubtful. If Don John in *Much Ado* had been an Englishman, critics would have admired Shakespeare's discernment in making his English villain sulky and stupid. If Edmund's father had been Duke of Ferrara instead of Earl of Gloster, they would have said that Edmund could have been nothing but an Italian. Change the name and country of Richard III, and he would be called a typical despot of the Italian Renaissance. Change those of Juliet, and we should find her whole-some English nature contrasted with the southern dreaminess of Romeo. But this way of interpreting Shakespeare is not Shakespearean. With him the differences of period, race, nationality, and locality have little bearing on the inward character, though they sometimes have a good deal on the total imaginative effect, of his figures. When he does lay stress on such differences his intention is at once obvious, as in characters like Fluellen or Sir Hugh Evans, or in the talk of the French princes before the battle of Agincourt. I may add that Iago certainly cannot be taken to exemplify the popular Elizabethan idea of a disciple of Macchiavelli.* There is no sign that he is in theory an atheist or even an unbeliever in the received religion. On the contrary, he uses its language, and says nothing resembling the words of the prologue of the *Jew of Malta*:*

I count religion but a childish toy,
And hold there is no sin but ignorance.

Aaron in *Titus Andronicus* might have said this (and is not more likely
to be Shakespeare's creation on that account), but not Iago.

I come to a second warning. One must constantly remember not
to believe a syllable that Iago utters on any subject, including himself,
until one has tested his statement by comparing it with known facts
and with other statements of his own or of other people, and by
considering whether he had in the particular circumstances any reason
for telling a lie or for telling the truth. The implicit confidence which
his acquaintances placed in his integrity has descended to most of his
critics; and this, reinforcing the comical habit of quoting as
Shakespeare's own statement everything said by his characters, has
been a fruitful source of misinterpretation. I will take as an instance
the very first assertions made by Iago. In the opening scene he tells his
dupe Roderigo that three great men of Venice went to Othello and
begged him to make Iago his lieutenant; that Othello, out of pride
and obstinacy, refused; that in refusing he talked a deal of military
rigmarole, and ended by declaring (falsely, we are to understand) that
he had already filled up the vacancy; that Cassio, whom he chose, had
absolutely no practical knowledge of war, nothing but bookish theo-
ric, mere prattle, arithmetic, whereas Iago himself had often fought by
Othello's side, and by 'old gradation' too ought to have been
preferred. Most or all of this is repeated by some critics as though it
were information given by Shakespeare, and the conclusion is quite
naturally drawn that Iago had some reason to feel aggrieved. But if we
ask ourselves how much of all this is true we shall answer, I believe, as
follows. It is absolutely certain that Othello appointed Cassio his lieutenant, and *nothing* else is absolutely certain. But there is no reason to
doubt the statement that Iago had seen service with him, nor is there
anything inherently improbable in the statement that he was solicited
by three great personages on Iago's behalf. On the other hand, the
suggestions that he refused out of pride and obstinacy, and that he lied
in saying he had already chosen his officer, have no verisimilitude; and
if there is any fact at all (as there probably is) behind Iago's account of
the conversation, it doubtless is the fact that Iago himself was ignorant of military science, while Cassio was an expert, and that Othello
explained this to the great personages. That Cassio, again, was an

interloper and a mere closet-student without experience of war is incredible, considering first that Othello chose him for lieutenant, and secondly that the senate appointed him to succeed Othello in command at Cyprus; and we have direct evidence that part of Iago's statement is a lie, for Desdemona happens to mention that Cassio was a man who 'all his time' had founded his good fortunes on Othello's love and had 'shared dangers' with him (III.iv.93). There remains only the implied assertion that, if promotion had gone by old gradation, Iago, as the senior, would have been preferred. It may be true: Othello was not the man to hesitate to promote a junior for good reasons. But it is just as likely to be a pure invention; and, though Cassio was young, there is nothing to show that he was younger, in years or in service, than Iago. Iago, for instance, never calls him 'young', as he does Roderigo; and a mere youth would not have been made Governor of Cyprus. What is certain, finally, in the whole business is that Othello's mind was perfectly at ease about the appointment, and that he never dreamed of Iago's being discontented at it, not even when the intrigue was disclosed and he asked himself how he had offended Iago.

2

It is necessary to examine in this manner every statement made by Iago. But it is not necessary to do so in public, and I proceed to the question what impression he made on his friends and acquaintances. In the main there is here no room for doubt. Nothing could be less like Iago than the melodramatic villain so often substituted for him on the stage, a person whom everyone in the theatre knows for a scoundrel at the first glance. Iago, we gather, was a Venetian[2] soldier, eight-and-twenty years of age, who had seen a good deal of service and had a high reputation for courage. Of his origin we are ignorant, but, unless I am mistaken, he was not of gentle birth or breeding.[3] He does

---

[2] See III.iii.201, V.i.89 f. The statements are his own, but he has no particular reason for lying. One reason of his disgust at Cassio's appointment was that Cassio was a Florentine (I.i.20). When Cassio says (III.i.42) 'I never knew a Florentine more kind and honest,' of course he means, not that Iago is a Florentine, but that he could not be kinder and honester if he were one.

[3] I am here merely recording a general impression. There is no specific evidence, unless we take Cassio's language in his drink (II.ii.105 f.) to imply that Iago was not a 'man of quality'

not strike one as a degraded man of culture: for all his great powers, he is vulgar, and his probable want of military science may well be significant. He was married to a wife who evidently lacked refinement, and who appears in the drama almost in the relation of a servant to Desdemona. His manner was that of a blunt, bluff soldier, who spoke his mind freely and plainly. He was often hearty, and could be thoroughly jovial; but he was not seldom rather rough and caustic of speech, and he was given to making remarks somewhat disparaging to human nature. He was aware of this trait in himself, and frankly admitted that he was nothing if not critical, and that it was his nature to spy into abuses. In these admissions he characteristically exaggerated his fault, as plain-dealers are apt to do; and he was liked none the less for it, seeing that his satire was humorous, that on serious matters he did not speak lightly (III.iii.119), and that the one thing perfectly obvious about him was his honesty. 'Honest' is the word that springs to the lips of everyone who speaks of him. It is applied to him some fifteen times in the play, not to mention some half-dozen where he employs it, in derision, of himself. In fact he was one of those sterling men who, in disgust at gush, say cynical things which they do not believe, and then, the moment you are in trouble, put in practice the very sentiment they had laughed at. On such occasions he showed the kindliest sympathy and the most eager desire to help. When Cassio misbehaved so dreadfully and was found fighting with Montano, did not Othello see that 'honest Iago looked dead with grieving'? With what difficulty was he induced, nay, compelled, to speak the truth against the lieutenant! Another man might have felt a touch of satisfaction at the thought that the post he had coveted was now vacant; but Iago not only comforted Cassio, talking to him cynically about reputation, just to help him over his shame, but he set his wits to work and at once perceived that the right plan for Cassio to get his post again was to ask Desdemona to intercede. So troubled was he at his friend's disgrace that his own wife was sure 'it grieved her husband as if the case was his'. What wonder that anyone in sore trouble, like

---

like himself. I do not know if it has been observed that Iago uses more nautical phrases and metaphors than is at all usual with Shakespeare's characters. This might naturally be explained by his roving military life, but it is curious that almost all the examples occur in the earlier scenes (see *e.g.* I.i.30, 153, 157; I.ii.17, 50; I.iii.343; II.iii.65), so that the use of these phrases and metaphors may not be characteristic of Iago but symptomatic of a particular state of Shakespeare's mind.

Desdemona, should send at once for Iago (IV.ii.106)? If this rough diamond had any flaw, it was that Iago's warm loyal heart incited him to too impulsive action. If he merely heard a friend like Othello calumniated, his hand flew to his sword; and though he restrained himself he almost regretted his own virtue (I.ii.1–10).

Such seemed Iago to the people about him, even to those who, like Othello, had known him for some time. And it is a fact too little noticed but most remarkable, that he presented an appearance not very different to his wife. There is no sign either that Emilia's marriage was downright unhappy, or that she suspected the true nature of her husband.[4] No doubt she knew rather more of him than others. Thus we gather that he was given to chiding and sometimes spoke shortly and sharply to her (III.iii.300 f.); and it is quite likely that she gave him a good deal of her tongue in exchange (II.i.101 f.). He was also unreasonably jealous; for his own statement that he was jealous of Othello is confirmed by Emilia herself, and must therefore be believed (IV.ii.145).[5] But it seems clear that these defects of his had not seriously impaired Emilia's confidence in her husband or her affection for him. She knew in addition that he was not quite so honest as he seemed, for he had often begged her to steal Desdemona's handkerchief. But Emilia's nature was not very delicate or scrupulous about trifles. She thought her husband odd and 'wayward', and looked on his fancy for the handkerchief as an instance of this (III.iii.292); but she never dreamed he was a villain, and there is no reason to doubt the sincerity of her belief that he was heartily sorry for Cassio's disgrace. Her failure, on seeing Othello's agitation about the handkerchief, to form any suspicion of an intrigue, shows how little she doubted her husband. Even when, later, the idea strikes her that some scoundrel has poisoned Othello's mind, the tone of all her speeches, and her mention of the rogue who (she believes) had stirred up Iago's jealousy of her, prove beyond doubt that the thought of Iago's being the scoundrel has not crossed her mind (IV.ii.115–47). And if any hesitation on the subject could remain, surely it must be dispelled by the thrice-repeated cry of astonishment and horror, 'My husband!',

---

[4] See further Note P.

[5] But it by no means follows that we are to believe his statement that there was a report abroad about an intrigue between his wife and Othello (I.iii.393), or his statement (which may be divined from IV.ii.145) that someone had spoken to him on the subject.

which follows Othello's words, 'Thy husband knew it all'; and by the choking indignation and desperate hope which we hear in her appeal when Iago comes in:

> Disprove this villain, if thou be'st a man:
> He says thou told'st him that his wife was false:
> I know thou did'st not, thou'rt not such a villain:
> Speak, for my heart is full.

Even if Iago *had* betrayed much more of his true self to his wife than to others, it would make no difference to the contrast between his true self and the self he presented to the world in general. But he never did so. Only the feeble eyes of the poor gull Roderigo were allowed a glimpse into that pit.

The bearing of this contrast upon the apparently excessive credulity of Othello has been already pointed out. What further conclusions can be drawn from it? Obviously, to begin with, the inference, which is accompanied by a thrill of admiration, that Iago's powers of dissimilation and of self-control must have been prodigious: for he was not a youth, like Edmund, but had worn this mask for years, and he had apparently never enjoyed, like Richard, occasional explosions of the reality within him. In fact so prodigious does his self-control appear that a reader might be excused for feeling a doubt of its possibility. But there are certain observations and further inferences which, apart from confidence in Shakespeare, would remove this doubt. It is to be observed, first, that Iago was able to find a certain relief from the discomfort of hypocrisy in those caustic or cynical speeches which, being misinterpreted, only heightened confidence in his honesty. They acted as a safety valve, very much as Hamlet's pretended insanity did. Next, I would infer from the entire success of his hypocrisy – what may also be inferred on other grounds, and is of great importance – that he was by no means a man of strong feelings and passions, like Richard, but decidedly cold by temperament. Even so, his self-control was wonderful, but there never was in him any violent storm to be controlled. Thirdly, I would suggest that Iago, though thoroughly selfish and unfeeling, was not by nature malignant, nor even morose, but that, on the contrary, he had a superficial good-nature, the kind of good-nature that wins popularity and is often taken as the sign, not of a good digestion, but of a good heart. And lastly, it may be inferred that, before the giant crime which we witness, Iago had never been detected in any serious offence and may even never have been guilty of one, but had pursued a selfish but outwardly decent life, enjoying the excitement of war and of casual pleasures, but never yet meeting with any sufficient temptation to risk his position and advancement by a dangerous crime. So that, in fact, the tragedy of *Othello* is in a sense his tragedy too. It shows us not a violent man, like Richard, who spends his life in murder, but a thoroughly bad, *cold* man, who is at last tempted to let loose the forces within him, and is at once destroyed.

3

In order to see how this tragedy arises let us now look more closely into Iago's inner man. We find here, in the first place, as has been implied in part, very remarkable powers both of intellect and of will. Iago's insight, within certain limits, into human nature; his ingenuity and address in working upon it; his quickness and versatility in dealing with sudden difficulties and unforeseen opportunities, have probably no parallel among dramatic characters. Equally remarkable is his strength of will. Not Socrates* himself, not the ideal sage of the Stoics, was more lord of himself than Iago appears to be. It is not merely that he never betrays his true nature; he seems to be master of *all* the motions that might affect his will. In the most dangerous moments of his plot, when the least slip or accident would be fatal, he never shows a trace of nervousness. When Othello takes him by the throat he merely shifts his part with his usual instantaneous adroitness. When he is attacked and wounded at the end he is perfectly unmoved. As Mr. Swinburne says, you cannot believe for a moment that the pain of torture will ever open Iago's lips. He is equally unassailable by the temptations of indolence or of sensuality. It is difficult to imagine him inactive; and though he has an obscene mind, and doubtless took his pleasures when and how he chose, he certainly took them by choice and not from weakness, and if pleasure interfered with his purposes the holiest of ascetics would not put it more resolutely by. 'What should I do?' Roderigo whimpers to him; 'I confess it is my shame to be so fond; but it is not in my virtue to amend it'. He answers: 'Virtue! a fig! 'tis in ourselves that we are thus and thus'. It all depends on our will. Love is 'merely a lust of the blood and a permission of the will. Come, be a man. . . . Ere I would say I would drown myself for the love of a guinea-hen, I would change my humanity with a baboon'. Forget for a moment that love is for Iago the appetite of a baboon; forget that he is as little assailable by pity as by fear or pleasure; and you will acknowledge that this lordship of the will, which is his practice as well as his doctrine, is great, almost sublime. Indeed, in intellect (always within certain limits) and in will (considered as a mere power, and without regard to its objects) Iago *is* great.

To what end does he use these great powers? His creed – for he is no sceptic, he has a definite creed – is that absolute egoism is the only rational and proper attitude, and that conscience or honour or any kind of regard for others is an absurdity. He does not deny that this absurdity exists. He does not suppose that most people secretly share his creed, while pretending to hold up and practise another. On the contrary, he regards most people as honest fools. He declares that he has never yet met a man who knew how to love himself; and his one expression of admiration in the play is for servants

> Who trimmed in forms and visages of duty,
> Keep yet their hearts attending on themselves.

'These fellows,' he says, 'have some soul.' He professes to stand, and he attempts to stand, wholly outside the world of morality.

The existence of Iago's creed and of his corresponding practice is evidently connected with a characteristic in which he surpasses nearly all the other inhabitants of Shakespeare's world. Whatever he may once have been, he appears, when we meet him, to be almost destitute of humanity, of sympathetic or social feeling. He shows no trace of affection, and in presence of the most terrible suffering he shows either pleasure or an indifference which, if not complete, is nearly so. Here, however, we must be careful. It is important to realize, and few readers are in danger of ignoring, this extraordinary deadness of feeling, but it is also important not to confuse it with a general positive ill-will. When Iago has no dislike or hostility to a person he does *not* show pleasure in the suffering of that person: he shows at most the absence of pain. There is, for instance, not the least sign of his enjoying the distress of Desdemona. But his sympathetic feelings are so abnormally feeble and cold that, when his dislike is roused, or when an indifferent person comes in the way of his purpose, there is scarcely anything within him to prevent his applying the torture.

What is it that provokes his dislike or hostility? Here again we must look closely. Iago has been represented as an incarnation of envy, as a man who, being determined to get on in the world, regards everyone else with enmity as his rival. But this idea, though containing truth, seems much exaggerated. Certainly he is devoted to himself; but if he were an eagerly ambitious man, surely we should see much more positive signs of this ambition; and surely too, with his great powers, he would already have risen high, instead of being a mere ensign, short of money, and playing Captain Rook to Roderigo's Mr. Pigeon.* Taking all the facts, one must conclude that his desires were comparatively moderate and his ambition weak; that he probably enjoyed war keenly, but, if he had money enough, did not exert himself greatly to acquire reputation or position; and, therefore, that he was not habitually burning with envy and actively hostile to other men as possible competitors.

But what is clear is that Iago is keenly sensitive to anything that touches his pride or self-esteem. It would be most unjust to call him vain, but he has a high opinion of himself and a great contempt for others. He is quite aware of his superiority to them in certain respects; and he either disbelieves in or despises the qualities in which they are superior to him. Whatever disturbs or wounds his sense of superiority irritates him at once; and in *that* sense he is highly competitive. This is why the appointment of Cassio provokes him. This is why Cassio's scientific attainments provoke him. This is the reason of his jealousy of Emilia. He does not care for his wife; but the fear of another man's getting the better of him, and exposing him to pity or derision as an unfortunate husband, is wormwood to him; and as he is sure that no woman is virtuous at heart, this fear is ever with him. For much the same reason he has a spite against goodness in men (for it is characteristic that he is less blind to its existence in men, the stronger, than in women, the weaker). He has a spite against it, not from any love of evil for evil's sake, but partly because it annoys his intellect as a stupidity; partly (though he hardly knows this) because it weakens his satisfaction with himself, and disturbs his faith that egoism is the right and proper thing; partly because, the world being such a fool, goodness is popular and prospers. But he, a man ten times as able as Cassio or even Othello, does not greatly prosper. Somehow, for all the stupidity of these open and generous people, they get on better than the 'fellow of some soul'. And this, though he is not particularly eager to get on, wounds his pride. Goodness therefore annoys him. He is always ready to scoff at it, and would like to strike at it. In ordinary circumstances these feelings of irritation are not vivid in Iago – *no* feeling is so – but they are constantly present.

4

Our task of analysis is not finished; but we are now in a position to consider the rise of Iago's tragedy. Why did he act as we see him acting in the play? What is the answer to that appeal of Othello's:

> Will you, I pray, demand that demi-devil
> Why he hath thus ensnared my soul and body?

This question Why? is *the* question about Iago, just as the question Why did Hamlet delay? is *the* question about Hamlet. Iago refused to answer it; but I will venture to say that he *could* not have answered it, any more than Hamlet could tell why he delayed. But Shakespeare knew the answer, and if these characters are great creations and not blunders we ought to be able to find it too.

Is it possible to elicit it from Iago himself against his will? He makes various statements to Roderigo, and he has several soliloquies. From these sources, and especially from the latter, we should learn something. For with Shakespeare soliloquy generally gives information regarding the secret springs as well as the outward course of the plot; and, moreover, it is a curious point of technique with him that the soliloquies of his villains sometimes read almost like explanations offered to the audience.[6] Now Iago repeatedly offers explanations either to Roderigo or to himself. In the first place, he says more than once that he 'hates' Othello. He gives two reasons for his hatred. Othello has made Cassio lieutenant; and he suspects, and has heard it reported, that Othello has an intrigue with Emilia. Next there is Cassio. He never says he hates Cassio, but he finds in him three causes of offence: Cassio has been preferred to him; he suspects *him* too of an intrigue with Emilia; and, lastly, Cassio has a daily beauty in his life which makes Iago ugly. In addition to these annoyances he wants Cassio's place. As for Roderigo, he calls him a snipe, and who can hate a snipe? But Roderigo knows too much; and he is becoming a

---

[6] See, for instance, Aaron in *Titus Andronicus*, II.iii.; Richard in 3 *Henry VI*, III.ii. and V.vi., and in *Richard III*, I.i. (twice), I.ii.; Edmund in *King Lear*, I.ii. (twice), III.iii. and V.v.i.

nuisance, getting angry, and asking for the gold and jewels he handed to Iago to give to Desdemona. So Iago kills Roderigo. Then for Desdemona: a fig's-end for her virtue! but he has no ill-will to her. In fact he 'loves' her, though he is good enough to explain, varying the word, that his 'lust' is mixed with a desire to pay Othello in his own coin. To be sure she must die, and so must Emilia, and so would Bianca if only the authorities saw things in their true light; but he did not set out with any hostile design against these persons.

Is the account which Iago gives of the causes of his action the true account? The answer of the most popular view will be, 'Yes. Iago was, as he says, chiefly incited by two things, the desire of advancement, and a hatred of Othello due principally to the affair of the lieutenancy. These are perfectly intelligible causes; we have only to add to them unusual ability and cruelty, and all is explained. Why should Coleridge and Hazlitt and Swinburne go further afield?' To which last question I will at once oppose these: If your view is correct, why should Iago be considered an extraordinary creation; and is it not odd that the people who reject it are the people who elsewhere show an exceptional understanding of Shakespeare?

The difficulty about this popular view is, in the first place, that it attributes to Iago what cannot be found in the Iago of the play. Its Iago is impelled by *passions*, a passion of ambition and a passion of hatred; for no ambition or hatred short of passion could drive a man who is evidently so clear-sighted, and who must hitherto have been so prudent, into a plot so extremely hazardous. Why, then, in the Iago of the play do we find no sign of these passions or of anything approaching to them? Why, if Shakespeare meant that Iago was impelled by them, does he suppress the signs of them? Surely not from want of ability to display them. The poet who painted Macbeth and Shylock understood his business. Who ever doubted Macbeth's ambition or Shylock's hate? And what resemblance is there between these passions and any feeling that we can trace in Iago? The resemblance between a volcano in eruption and a flameless fire of coke; the resemblance between a consuming desire to hack and hew your enemy's flesh, and the resentful wish, only too familiar in common life, to inflict pain in return for a slight. Passion, in Shakespeare's plays, is perfectly easy to recognize. What vestige of it, of passion unsatisfied or of passion gratified, is visible in Iago? None: that is the very horror of him. He has *less* passion than an ordinary man, and yet he does these frightful things. The only ground for attributing to him, I do not say a passionate hatred, but anything deserving the name of hatred at all, is his own statement, 'I hate Othello'; and we know what his statements are worth.

But the popular view, besides attributing to Iago what he does not show, ignores what he does show. It selects from his own account of his motives one or two, and drops the rest; and so it makes everything natural. But it fails to perceive how unnatural, how strange and suspicious, his own account is. Certainly he assigns motives enough; the difficulty is that he assigns so many. A man moved by simple passions due to simple causes does not stand fingering his feelings, industriously enumerating their sources, and groping about for new ones. But this is what Iago does. And this is not all. These motives appear and disappear in the most extraordinary manner. Resentment at Cassio's appointment is expressed in the first conversation with Roderigo, and from that moment is never once mentioned again in the whole play. Hatred of Othello is expressed in the First Act alone. Desire to get Cassio's place scarcely appears after the first soliloquy, and when it is gratified Iago does not refer to it by a single word. The suspicion of Cassio's intrigue with Emilia emerges suddenly, as an after-thought, not in the first soliloquy but the second, and then disappears for ever.[7] Iago's 'love' of Desdemona is alluded to in the second soliloquy; there is not the faintest trace of it in word or deed either before or after. The mention of jealousy of Othello is followed by declarations that Othello is infatuated about Desdemona and is of a constant nature, and during Othello's sufferings Iago never shows a sign of the idea that he is now paying his rival in his own coin. In the second soliloquy he declares that he quite believes Cassio to be in love with Desdemona: it is obvious that he believes no such thing, for he never alludes to the idea again, and within a few hours describes Cassio in soliloquy as an honest fool. This final reason for ill-will to Cassio never appears till the Fifth Act.

What is the meaning of all this? Unless Shakespeare was out of his mind, it must have a meaning. And certainly this meaning is not contained in any of the popular accounts of Iago.

Is it contained then in Coleridge's word 'motive-hunting'? Yes,

---

[7] See, further, Note Q.

'motive-hunting' exactly answers to the impression that Iago's soliloquies produce. He is pondering his design, and unconsciously trying to justify it to himself. He speaks of one or two real feelings, such as resentment against Othello, and he mentions one or two real causes of these feelings. But these are not enough for him. Along with them, or alone, there come into his head, only to leave it again, ideas and suspicions, the creations of his own baseness or uneasiness, some old, some new, caressed for a moment to feed his purpose and give it a reasonable look, but never really believed in, and never the main forces which are determining his action. In fact, I would venture to describe Iago in these soliloquies as a man setting out on a project which strongly attracts his desire, but at the same time conscious of a resistance to the desire, and unconsciously trying to argue the resistance away by assigning reasons for the project. He is the counterpart of Hamlet, who tried to find reasons for his delay in pursuing a design which excites his aversion. And most of Iago's reasons for actions are no more the real ones than Hamlet's reasons for delay were the real ones. Each is moved by forces which he does not understand; and it is probably no accident that these two studies of states psychologically so similar were produced at about the same period.

What then were the real moving forces of Iago's action? Are we to fall back on the idea of a 'motiveless malignity';[8] that is to say, a disinterested love of evil, or a delight in the pain of others as simple and direct as the delight in one's own pleasure? Surely not. I will not insist that this thing or these things are inconceivable, mere phrases, not ideas; for, even so, it would remain possible that Shakespeare had tried to represent an inconceivability. But there is not the slightest reason to suppose that he did so. Iago's action is intelligible; and indeed the popular view contains enough truth to refute this desperate theory. It greatly exaggerates his desire for advancement, and the ill-will caused by his disappointment, and it ignores other forces more important than these; but it is right in insisting on the presence of this desire and this ill-will, and their presence is enough to destroy Iago's claims to be more than a demi-devil. For love of the evil that advances my interest and hurts a person I dislike, is a very different thing from love of evil simply as evil; and pleasure in the pain of a person disliked or regarded

---

[8] On the meaning which this phrase had for its author, Coleridge, see note on p. 170.

as a competitor is quite distinct from pleasure in the pain of others simply as others. The first is intelligible, and we find it in Iago. The second, even if it were intelligible, we do not find in Iago.

Still, desire of advancement and resentment about the lieutenancy, though factors and indispensable factors in the cause of Iago's action, are neither the principal nor the most characteristic factors. To find these, let us return to our half-completed analysis of the character. Let us remember especially the keen sense of superiority, the contempt of others, the sensitiveness to everything which wounds these feelings, the spite against goodness in men as a thing not only stupid but, both in its nature and by its success, contrary to Iago's nature and irritating to his pride. Let us remember in addition the annoyance of having always to play a part, the consciousness of exceptional but unused ingenuity and address, the enjoyment of action, and the absence of fear. And let us ask what would be the greatest pleasure of such a man, and what the situation which might tempt him to abandon his habitual prudence and pursue this pleasure. Hazlitt and Mr. Swinburne do not put this question, but the answer I proceed to give to it is in principle theirs.[9]

The most delightful thing to such a man would be something that gave an extreme satisfaction to his sense of power and superiority; and if it involved, secondly, the triumphant exertion of his abilities, and, thirdly, the excitement of danger, his delight would be consummated. And the moment most dangerous to such a man would be one when his sense of superiority had met with an affront, so that its habitual crazing was reinforced by resentment, while at the same time he saw an opportunity of satisfying it by subjecting to his will the very persons who had affronted it. Now, this is the temptation that comes to Iago. Othello's eminence, Othello's goodness, and his own dependence on Othello, must have been a perpetual annoyance to him. At *any* time he would have enjoyed befooling and tormenting Othello. Under ordinary circumstances he was restrained, chiefly by self-interest, in some

---

[9] Coleridge's view is not materially different, though less complete. When he speaks of 'the motive-hunting of a motiveless malignity', he does not mean by the last two words that 'disinterested love of evil' or 'love of evil for evil's sake' of which I spoke just now, and which other critics attribute to Iago. He means really that Iago's malignity does not spring from the causes to which Iago himself refers it, nor from any 'motive' in the sense of an idea present to consciousness. But unfortunately his phrase suggests the theory which has been criticized above. On the question whether there is such a thing as this supposed pure malignity, the reader may refer to a discussion between Professor Bain and F. H. Bradley* in *Mind*, vol. viii.

slight degree perhaps by the faintest pulsations of conscience or humanity. But disappointment at the loss of the lieutenancy supplied the touch of lively resentment that was required to overcome these obstacles; and the prospect of satisfying the sense of power by mastering Othello through an intricate and hazardous intrigue now became irresistible. Iago did not clearly understand what was moving his desire; though he tried to give himself reasons for his action, even those that had some reality made but a small part of the motive force; one may almost say they were no more than the turning of the handle which admits the driving power into the machine. Only once does he appear to see something of the truth. It is when he uses the phrase 'to *plume up my will* in double knavery'.

To 'plume up the will', to heighten the sense of power or superiority – this seems to be the unconscious motive of many acts of cruelty which evidently do not spring chiefly from ill-will, and which therefore puzzle and sometimes horrify us most. It is often this that makes a man bully the wife or children of whom he is fond. The boy who torments another boy, as we say, 'for no reason', or who without any hatred for frogs tortures a frog, is pleased with his victim's pain, not from any disinterested love of evil or pleasure in pain, but mainly because this pain is the unmistakable proof of his own power over his victim. So it is with Iago. His thwarted sense of superiority wants satisfaction. What fuller satisfaction could it find than the consciousness that he is the master of the General who has undervalued him and of the rival who has been preferred to him; that these worthy people, who are so successful and popular and stupid, are mere puppets in his hands, but living puppets, who at the motion of his finger must contort themselves in agony while all the time they believe that he is their one true friend and comforter? It must have been an ecstasy of bliss to him. And this, granted a most abnormal deadness of human feeling, is, however horrible, perfectly intelligible. There is no mystery in the psychology of Iago; the mystery lies in a further question, which the drama has not to answer, the question why such a being should exist.

Iago's longing to satisfy the sense of power is, I think, the strongest of the forces that drive him on. But there are two others to be noticed. One is the pleasure in an action very difficult and perilous and, therefore, intensely exciting. This action sets all his powers on the strain. He feels the delight of one who executes successfully a feat thoroughly congenial to his special aptitude, and only just within his compass; and, as he is fearless by nature, the fact that a single slip will cost him his life only increases his pleasure. His exhilaration breaks out in the ghastly words with which he greets the sunrise after the night of the drunken tumult which has led to Cassio's disgrace: 'By the mass, 'tis morning. Pleasure and action make the hours seem short'. Here, however, the joy in exciting action is quickened by other feelings. It appears more simply elsewhere in such a way as to suggest that nothing but such actions gave him happiness, and that his happiness was greater if the action was destructive as well as exciting. We find it, for instance, in his gleeful cry to Roderigo, who proposes to shout to Brabantio in order to wake him and tell him of his daughter's flight:

> Do, with like timorous[10] accent and dire yell
> As when, by night and negligence, the fire
> Is spied in populous cities.

All through that scene; again, in the scene where Cassio is attacked and Roderigo murdered; everywhere where Iago is in physical action, we catch this sound of almost feverish enjoyment. His blood, usually so cold and slow, is racing through his veins.

But Iago, finally, is not simply a man of action; he is an artist. His action is a plot, the intricate plot of a drama, and in the conception and execution of it he experiences the tension and the joy of artistic creation. 'He is,' says Hazlitt, 'an amateur of tragedy in real life; and, instead of employing his invention on imaginary characters or long-forgotten incidents, he takes the bolder and more dangerous course of getting up his plot at home, casts the principal parts among his nearest friends and connections, and rehearses it in downright earnest, with steady nerves and unabated resolution.' Mr. Swinburne lays even greater stress on this aspect of Iago's character, and even declares that 'the very subtlest and strongest component of his complex nature' is 'the instinct of what Mr. Carlyle* would call an inarticulate poet'. And those to whom this idea is unfamiliar, and who may suspect it at first sight of being fanciful, will find, if they examine the play in the light of Mr. Swinburne's exposition, that it rests on a true and deep perception, will stand scrutiny, and might easily be illustrated. They may observe, to take only one point, the curious analogy between the early

---

[10] I.e. terrifying.

stages of dramatic composition and those soliloquies in which Iago broods over his plot, drawing at first only an outline, puzzled how to fix more than the main idea, and gradually seeing it develop and clarify as he works upon it or lets it work. Here at any rate Shakespeare put a good deal of himself into Iago. But the tragedian in real life was not the equal of the tragic poet. His psychology, as we shall see, was at fault, at a critical point, as Shakespeare's never was. And so his catastrophe came out wrong, and his piece was ruined.

Such, then, seem to be the chief ingredients of the force which, liberated by his resentment at Cassio's promotion, drives Iago from inactivity into action, and sustains him through it. And, to pass to a new point, this force completely possesses him; it is his fate. It is like the passion with which a tragic hero wholly identifies himself, and which bears him on to his doom. It is true that, once embarked on this course, Iago *could* not turn back, even if this passion did abate; and it is also true that he is compelled, by his success in convincing Othello, to advance to conclusions of which at the outset he did not dream. He is thus caught in his own web, and could not liberate himself if he would. But, in fact, he never shows a trace of wishing to do so, not a trace of hesitation, of looking back, or of fear, any more than of remorse; there is no ebb in the tide. As the crisis approaches there passes through his mind a fleeting doubt whether the deaths of Cassio and Roderigo are indispensable; but that uncertainty, which does not concern the main issue, is dismissed, and he goes forward with undiminished zest. Not even in his sleep – as in Richard's before his final battle – does any rebellion of outraged conscience or pity, or any foreboding of despair, force itself into clear consciousness. His fate – which is himself – has completely mastered him: so that, in the later scenes, where the improbability of the entire success of a design built on so many different falsehoods forces itself on the reader, Iago appears for moments not as a consummate schemer, but as a man absolutely infatuated and delivered over to certain destruction.

5

Iago stands supreme among Shakespeare's evil characters because the greatest intensity and subtlety of imagination have gone to his making, and because he illustrates in the most perfect combination the two facts concerning evil which seem to have impressed

Shakespeare most. The first of these is the fact that perfectly sane people exist in whom fellow-feeling of any kind is so weak that an almost absolute egoism becomes possible to them, and with it those hard vices – such as ingratitude and cruelty – which to Shakespeare were far the worst. The second is that such evil is compatible, and even appears to ally itself easily, with exceptional powers of will and intellect. In the latter respect Iago is nearly or quite the equal of Richard, in egoism he is the superior, and his inferiority in passion and massive force only makes him more repulsive. How is it then that we can bear to contemplate him; nay, that, if we really imagine him, we feel admiration and some kind of sympathy? Henry the Fifth tells us:

> There is some soul of goodness in things evil,
> Would men observingly distil it out;

but here, it may be said, we are shown a thing absolutely evil, and – what is more dreadful still – this absolute evil is united with supreme intellectual power. Why is the representation tolerable, and why do we not accuse its author either of untruth or of a desperate pessimism?

To these questions it might at once be replied: Iago does not stand alone; he is a factor in a whole; and we perceive him there and not in isolation, acted upon as well as acting, destroyed as well as destroying.[11] But, although this is true and important, I pass it by and, continuing to regard him by himself, I would make three remarks in answer to the questions.

In the first place, Iago is not merely negative or evil – far from it. Those very forces that moved him and made his fate – sense of power, delight in performing a difficult and dangerous action, delight in the exercise of artistic skill – are not at all evil things. We sympathize with one or other of them almost every day of our lives. And, accordingly, though in Iago they are combined with something detestable and so contribute to evil, our perception of them is accompanied with sympathy. In the same way, Iago's insight, dexterity, quickness, address, and the like, are in themselves admirable things; the perfect man would possess them. And certainly he would possess also Iago's courage and self-control, and, like Iago, would stand above the impulses of mere feeling, lord of his inner world. All this goes to evil

---

[11] Cf. note at end of lecture.

ends in Iago, but in itself it has a great worth; and, although in reading, of course, we do not sift it out and regard it separately, it inevitably affects us and mingles admiration with our hatred or horror.

All this, however, might apparently co-exist with absolute egoism and total want of humanity. But in the second place, it is not true that in Iago this egoism and this want are absolute, and that in this sense he is a thing of mere evil. They are frightful, but if they were absolute Iago would be a monster, not a man. The fact is, he *tries* to make them absolute and cannot succeed; and the traces of conscience, shame and humanity, though faint, are discernible. If his egoism were absolute he would be perfectly indifferent to the opinion of others; and he clearly is not so. His very irritation at goodness, again, is a sign that his faith in his creed is not entirely firm; and it is not entirely firm because he himself has a perception, however dim, of the goodness of goodness. What is the meaning of the last reason he gives himself for killing Cassio:

> He hath a daily beauty in his life
> That makes me ugly?

Does he mean that he is ugly to others? Then he is not an absolute egoist. Does he mean that he is ugly to himself? Then he makes an open confession of moral sense. And, once more, if he really possessed no moral sense, we should never have heard those soliloquies which so clearly betray his uneasiness and his unconscious desire to persuade himself that he has some excuse for the villainy he contemplates. These seem to be indubitable proofs that, against his will, Iago is a little better than his creed, and has failed to withdraw himself wholly from the human atmosphere about him. And to these proofs I would add, though with less confidence, two others. Iago's momentary doubt towards the end whether Roderigo and Cassio must be killed has always surprised me. As a mere matter of calculation it is perfectly obvious that they must; and I believe his hesitation is not merely intellectual, it is another symptom of the obscure working of conscience or humanity. Lastly, is it not significant that, when once his plot has begun to develop, Iago never seeks the presence of Desdemona; that he seems to leave her as quickly as he can (III.iv.138); and that, when he is fetched by Emilia to see her in her distress (IV.ii.110ff.), we fail to catch in his words any sign of the pleasure he shows in Othello's misery, and seem rather to perceive a certain discomfort, and, if one dare say it, a faint touch of shame or remorse? This interpretation of the passage, I admit, is not inevitable, but to my mind (quite apart from any theorizing about Iago) it seems the natural one.[12] And if it is right, Iago's discomfort is easily understood; for Desdemona is the one person concerned against whom it is impossible for him even to imagine a ground of resentment, and so an excuse for cruelty.[13]

There remains, thirdly, the idea that Iago is a man of supreme intellect who is at the same time supremely wicked. That he is supremely wicked nobody will doubt; and I have claimed for him nothing that will interfere with his right to that title. But to say that his intellectual power is supreme is to make a great mistake. Within certain limits he has indeed extraordinary penetration, quickness, inventiveness, adaptiveness; but the limits are defined with the hardest of lines, and they are narrow limits. It would scarcely be unjust to call him simply astonishingly clever, or simply a consummate master of intrigue. But compare him with one who may perhaps be roughly called a bad man of supreme intellectual power, Napoleon,* and you see how small and negative Iago's mind is, incapable of Napoleon's military achievements, and much more incapable of his political constructions. Or, to keep within the Shakespearean world, compare him with Hamlet, and you perceive how miserably close is his intellectual horizon; that such a thing as a thought beyond the reaches of his soul has never come near him; that he is prosaic through and through, deaf and blind to all but a tiny fragment of the meaning of things. Is it not quite absurd, then, to call him a man of supreme intellect?

And observe, lastly, that his failure in perception is closely connected with his badness. He was destroyed by the power that he attacked, the power of love; and he was destroyed by it because he could not understand it; and he could not understand it because it was not in him. Iago never meant his plot to be so dangerous to himself. He knew that jealousy is painful, but the jealousy of a love

---

[12] It was suggested to me by a Glasgow student.

[13] A curious proof of Iago's inability to hold by his creed that absolute egoism is the only proper attitude, and that loyalty and affection are mere stupidity or want of spirit, may be found in his one moment of real passion, where he rushes at Emilia with the cry, 'Villainous whore!' (V.ii.229). There is more than fury in his cry, there is indignation. She has been false to him, she has betrayed him. Well, but why should she not, if his creed is true? And what a melancholy exhibition of human inconsistency it is that he should use as terms of reproach words which, according to him, should be quite neutral, if not complimentary!

like Othello's he could not imagine, and he found himself involved in murders which were no part of his original design. That difficulty he surmounted, and his changed plot still seemed to prosper. Roderigo and Cassio and Desdemona once dead, all will be well. Nay, when he fails to kill Cassio, all may still be well. He will avow that he told Othello of the adultery, and persist that he told the truth, and Cassio will deny it in vain. And then, in a moment, his plot is shattered by a blow from a quarter where he never dreamt of danger. He knows his wife, he thinks. She is not over-scrupulous, she will do anything to please him, and she has learnt obedience. But one thing in her he does not know – that she *loves* her mistress and would face a hundred deaths sooner than see her fair fame darkened. There is genuine aston-ishment in his outburst 'What! Are you mad?' as it dawns upon him that she means to speak the truth about the handkerchief. But he might well have applied to himself the words she flings at Othello,

> O gull! O dolt!
> As ignorant as dirt!

The foulness of his own soul made him so ignorant that he built into the marvellous structure of his plot a piece of crass stupidity.

To the thinking mind the divorce of unusual intellect from good-ness is a thing to startle; and Shakespeare clearly felt it so. The combi-nation of unusual intellect with extreme evil is more than startling, it is frightful. It is rare, but it exists; and Shakespeare represented it in Iago. But the alliance of evil like Iago's with *supreme* intellect is an impossible fiction; and Shakespeare's fictions were truth.

6

The characters of Cassio and Emilia hardly require analysis, and I will touch on them only from a single point of view. In their combination of excellences and defects they are good examples of that truth to nature which in dramatic art is the one unfailing source of moral instruction.

Cassio is a handsome, light-hearted, good-natured young fellow, who takes life gaily, and is evidently very attractive and popular. Othello, who calls him by his Christian name, is fond of him; Desdemona likes him much; Emilia at once interests herself on his behalf. He has warm, generous feelings, an enthusiastic admiration for the General, and a chivalrous adoration for his peerless wife. But he is too easy-going. He finds it hard to say No; and accordingly, although he is aware that he has a very weak head, and that the occasion is one on which he is bound to run no risk, he gets drunk – not disgustingly so, but ludicrously so.[14] And, besides, he amuses himself without any scruple by frequenting the company of a woman of more than doubtful reputation, who has fallen in love with his good looks. Moralizing critics point out that he pays for the first offence by losing his post, and for the second by nearly losing his life. They are quite entitled to do so, though the careful reader will not forget Iago's part in these transactions. But they ought also to point out that Cassio's looseness does not in the least disturb our confidence in him in his relations with Desdemona and Othello. He is loose, and we are sorry for it; but we never doubt that there was 'a daily beauty in his life', or that his rapturous admiration of Desdemona was as wholly beautiful a thing as it appears, or that Othello was perfectly safe when in his courtship he employed Cassio to 'go between' Desdemona and himself. It is fortunately a fact in human nature that these aspects of Cassio's character are quite compatible. Shakespeare simply sets it down; and it is just because he is truthful in these smaller things that in greater things we trust him absolutely never to pervert the truth for the sake of some doctrine or purpose of his own.

There is something very lovable about Cassio, with his fresh eager feelings; his distress at his disgrace and still more at having lost Othello's trust; his hero-worship; and at the end his sorrow and pity, which are at first too acute for words. He is carried in, wounded, on a chair. He looks at Othello and cannot speak. His first words came later when, to Lodovico's question, 'Did you and he consent in Cassio's death?' Othello answers 'Ay.' Then he falters out, 'Dear General, I never gave you cause.' One is sure he had never used that adjective before. The love in it makes it beautiful, but there is something else in it, unknown to Cassio, which goes to one's heart. It tells us that his hero is no longer unapproachably above him.

Few of Shakespeare's minor characters are more distinct than Emilia, and towards few do our feelings change so much within the

---

[14] Cassio's invective against drink may be compared with Hamlet's expressions of disgust at his uncle's drunkenness. Possibly the subject may for some reason have been prominent in Shakespeare's mind about this time.

course of a play. Till close to the end she frequently sets one's teeth on edge; and at the end one is ready to worship her. She nowhere shows any sign of having a bad heart; but she is common, sometimes vulgar, in minor matters far from scrupulous, blunt in perception and feeling, and quite destitute of imagination. She let Iago take the handkerchief though she knew how much its loss would distress Desdemona; and she said nothing about it though she saw that Othello was jealous. We rightly resent her unkindness in permitting the theft, but – it is an important point – we are apt to misconstrue her subsequent silence, because we know that Othello's jealousy was intimately connected with the loss of the handkerchief. Emilia, however, certainly failed to perceive this; for otherwise, when Othello's anger showed itself violently and she was really distressed for her mistress, she could not have failed to think of the handkerchief, and would, I believe, undoubtedly have told the truth about it. But, in fact, she never thought of it, although she guessed that Othello was being deceived by some scoundrel. Even after Desdemona's death, nay, even when she knew that Iago had brought it about, she still did not remember the handkerchief; and when Othello at last mentions, as a proof of his wife's guilt, that he had seen the handkerchief in Cassio's hand, the truth falls on Emilia like a thunder-bolt. 'O God!' she bursts out, 'O heavenly God!'[15] Her stupidity in this matter is gross, but it is stupidity and nothing worse.

But along with it goes a certain coarseness of nature. The contrast between Emilia and Desdemona in their conversation about the infidelity of wives (IV.iii.) is too famous to need a word – unless it be a word of warning against critics who take her light talk too seriously. But the contrast in the preceding scene is hardly less remarkable. Othello, affecting to treat Emilia as the keeper of a brothel, sends her away, bidding her shut the door behind her; and then he proceeds to torture himself as well as Desdemona by accusations of adultery. But, as a critic has pointed out, Emilia listens at the door, for we find, as soon as Othello is gone and Iago has been summoned, that she knows what Othello has said to Desdemona. And what could better illustrate those defects of hers which make one wince, than her repeating again and again in Desdemona's presence the word Desdemona could not

---

[15] So the Quarto, and certainly rightly, though modern editors reprint the feeble alteration of the Folio, due to fear of the Censor, 'O heaven! O heavenly Powers!'

repeat; than her talking before Desdemona of Iago's suspicions regarding Othello and herself; than her speaking to Desdemona of husbands who strike their wives; than the expression of her honest indignation in the words,

> Has she forsook so many noble matches,
> Her father and her country and her friends,
> To be called whore?

If one were capable of laughing or even of smiling when this point in the play is reached, the difference between Desdemona's anguish at the loss of Othello's love, and Emilia's recollection of the noble matches she might have secured, would be irresistibly ludicrous.

And yet how all this, and all her defects, vanish into nothingness when we see her face to face with that which she can understand and feel! From the moment of her appearance after the murder to the moment of her death she is transfigured; and yet she remains perfectly true to herself, and we would not have her one atom less herself. She is the only person who utters for us the violent common emotions which we feel, together with those more tragic emotions which she does not comprehend. She has done this once already, to our great comfort. When she suggests that some villain has poisoned Othello's mind, and Iago answers,

> Fie, there is no such man; it is impossible;

and Desdemona answers,

> If any such there be, Heaven pardon him;

Emilia's retort,

> A halter pardon him, and Hell gnaw his bones,

says what we long to say, and helps us. And who has not felt in the last scene how her glorious carelessness of her own life, and her outbursts against Othello – even that most characteristic one,

> She was too fond of her most filthy bargain –

lift the overwhelming weight of calamity that oppresses us, and bring us an extraordinary lightening of the heart? Terror and pity are here too much to bear; we long to be allowed to feel also indignation, if not rage; and Emilia lets us feel them and gives them words. She

brings us too the relief of joy and admiration, – a joy that is not less-
ened by her death. Why should she live? If she lived for ever she never
could soar a higher pitch, and nothing in her life became her like the
losing it.[16]

---

[16] The feelings evoked by Emilia are one of the causes which mitigate the excess of tragic
pain at the conclusion. Others are the downfall of Iago, and the fact, already alluded to, that
both Desdemona and Othello show themselves at their noblest just before death.

LECTURE VII

KING LEAR

King Lear has again and again been described as Shakespeare's greatest work, the best of his plays, the tragedy in which he exhibits most fully his multitudinous powers; and if we were doomed to lose all his dramas except one, probably the majority of those who know and appreciate him best would pronounce for keeping *King Lear*.

Yet this tragedy is certainly the least popular of the famous four. The 'general reader' reads it less often than the others, and, though he acknowledges its greatness, he will sometimes speak of it with a certain distaste. It is also the least often presented on the stage, and the least successful there. And when we look back on its history, we find a curious fact. Some twenty years after the Restoration, Nahum Tate* altered *King Lear* for the stage, giving it a happy ending, and putting Edgar in the place of the King of France as Cordelia's lover. From that time Shakespeare's tragedy in its original form was never seen on the stage for a century and a half. Betterton* acted Tate's version; Garrick* acted it and Dr. Johnson approved it. Kemble* acted it, Kean* acted it. In 1823 Kean, 'stimulated by Hazlitt's remonstrances and Charles Lamb's essays', restored the original tragic ending. At last, in 1838, Macready* returned to Shakespeare's text throughout.

What is the meaning of these opposite sets of facts? Are the lovers of Shakespeare wholly in the right; and is the general reader and playgoer, were even Tate and Dr. Johnson, altogether in the wrong? I venture to doubt it. When I read *King Lear* two impressions are left on my mind, which seem to answer roughly to the two sets of facts. *King Lear* seems to me Shakespeare's greatest achievement, but it seems to me *not* his best play. And I find that I tend to consider it from two rather different points of view. When I regard it strictly as a drama, it appears to me, though in certain parts overwhelming, decidedly inferior as a whole to *Hamlet, Othello* and *Macbeth*. When I am feeling that it is greater than any of these, and the fullest revelation of Shakespeare's power, I find I am not regarding it simply as a drama, but am grouping it in my mind with works like the *Prometheus*

*Vinctus** and the *Divine Comedy*, and even with the greatest symphonies of Beethoven* and the statues in the Medici Chapel.*

This two-fold character of the play is to some extent illustrated by the affinities and the probable chronological position of *King Lear*. It is allied with two tragedies, *Othello* and *Timon of Athens*, and these two tragedies are utterly unlike.[1] *Othello* was probably composed about 1604, and *King Lear* about 1605; and though there is a somewhat marked change in style and versification, there are obvious resemblances between the two. The most important have been touched on already: these are the most painful and the most pathetic of the four tragedies, those in which evil appears in its coldest and most inhuman forms, and those which exclude the supernatural from the action. But there is also in *King Lear* a good deal which sounds like an echo of *Othello*, – a fact which should not surprise us, since there are other instances where the matter of a play seems to go on working in Shakespeare's mind and re-appears, generally in a weaker form, in his next play. So, in *King Lear*, the conception of Edmund is not so fresh as that of Goneril. Goneril has no predecessor; but Edmund, though of course essentially distinguished from Iago, often reminds us of him, and the soliloquy, 'This is the excellent foppery of the world', is in the very tone of Iago's discourse on the sovereignty of the will. The gulling of Gloster, again, recalls the gulling of Othello. Even Edmund's idea (not carried out) of making his father witness, without overhearing, his conversation with Edgar, reproduces the idea of the passage where Othello watches Iago and Cassio talking about Bianca; and the conclusion of the temptation, where Gloster says to Edmund:

> and of my land,
> Loyal and natural boy, I'll work the means
> To make thee capable,

reminds us of Othello's last words in the scene of temptation, 'Now art thou my lieutenant'. This list might be extended; and the appearance of certain unusual words and phrases in both the plays increases the likelihood that the composition of the one followed at no great distance on that of the other.[2]

---

[1] I leave undiscussed the position of *King Lear* in relation to the 'comedies' of *Measure for Measure*, *Troilus and Cressida* and *All's Well*.

[2] See Note R.

When we turn from *Othello* to *Timon of Athens* we find a play of quite another kind. *Othello* is dramatically the most perfect of the tragedies. *Timon*, on the contrary, is weak, ill-constructed and confused; and, though care might have made it clear, no mere care could make it really dramatic. Yet it is undoubtedly Shakespearean in part, probably in great part; and it immediately reminds us of *King Lear*. Both plays deal with the tragic effects of ingratitude. In both the victim is exceptionally unsuspicious, soft-hearted and vehement. In both he is completely overwhelmed, passing through fury to madness in the one case, to suicide in the other. Famous passages in both plays are curses. The misanthropy of Timon pours itself out in a torrent of maledictions on the whole race of man; and these at once recall, alike by their form and their substance, the most powerful speeches uttered by Lear in his madness. In both plays occur repeated comparisons between man and the beasts; the idea that 'the strain of man's bred out into baboon', wolf, tiger, fox; the idea that this bestial degradation will end in a furious struggle of all with all, in which the race will perish. The 'pessimistic' strain in *Timon* suggests to many readers, even more imperatively than *King Lear*, the notion that Shakespeare was giving vent to some personal feeling, whether present or past; for the signs of his hand appear most unmistakably when the hero begins to pour the vials of his wrath upon mankind. *Timon*, lastly, in some of the unquestionably Shakespearean parts, bears (as it appears to me) so strong a resemblance to *King Lear* in style and in versification that it is hard to understand how competent judges can suppose that it belongs to a time at all near that of the final romances, or even that it was written so late as the last Roman plays. It is more likely to have been composed immediately after *King Lear* and before *Macbeth*.[3]

Drawing these comparisons together, we may say that, while as a work of art and in tragic power *King Lear* is infinitely nearer to *Othello* than to *Timon*, in its spirit and substance its affinity with *Timon* is a good deal the stronger. And, returning to the point from which these comparisons began, I would now add that there is in *King Lear* a reflection or anticipation, however faint, of the structural weakness of *Timon*. This weakness in *King Lear* is not due, however, to anything intrinsically undramatic in the story, but to characteristics which were

---

[3] On some of the points mentioned in this paragraph see Note S.

necessary to an effect not wholly dramatic. The stage is the test of strictly dramatic quality, and *King Lear* is too huge for the stage. Of course, I am not denying that it is a great stage-play. It has scenes immensely effective in the theatre; three of them – the two between Lear and Goneril and between Lear, Goneril and Regan, and the ineffably beautiful scene in the Fourth Act between Lear and Cordelia – lose in the theatre very little of the spell they have for imagination; and the gradual interweaving of the two plots is almost as masterly as in *Much Ado*. But (not to speak of defects due to mere carelessness) that which makes the *peculiar* greatness of King Lear – the immense scope of the work; the mass and variety of intense experience which it contains; the interpenetration of sublime imagination, piercing pathos, and humour almost as moving as the pathos; the vastness of the convulsion both of nature and of human passion; the vagueness of the scene where the action takes place, and of the movements of the figures which cross this scene; the strange atmosphere, cold and dark, which strikes on us as we enter this scene, enfolding these figures and magnifying their dim outlines like a winter mist; the half-realized suggestions of vast universal powers working in the world of individual fates and passions – all this interferes with dramatic clearness even when the play is read, and in the theatre not only refuses to reveal itself fully through the senses but seems to be almost in contradiction with their reports. This is not so with the other great tragedies. No doubt, as Lamb declared, theatrical representation gives only a part of what we imagine when we read them; but there is no *conflict* between the representation and the imagination, because these tragedies are, in essentials, perfectly dramatic. But *King Lear*, as a whole, is imperfectly dramatic, and there is something in its very essence which is at war with the senses, and demands a purely imaginative realization. It is therefore Shakespeare's greatest work, but it is not what Hazlitt called it, the best of his plays; and its comparative unpopularity is due, not merely to the extreme painfulness of the catastrophe, but in part to its dramatic defects, and in part to a failure in many readers to catch the peculiar effects to which I have referred – a failure which is natural because the appeal is made not so much to dramatic perception as to a rarer and more strictly poetic kind of imagination. For this reason, too, even the best attempts at exposition of *King Lear* are disappointing; they remind us of attempts to reduce to prose the impalpable spirit of the *Tempest*.

I propose to develop some of these ideas by considering, first, the dramatic defects of the play, and then some of the causes of its extraordinary imaginative effect.

1

We may begin, however, by referring to two passages which have often been criticized with injustice. The first is that where the blinded Gloster, believing that he is going to leap down Dover cliff, does in fact fall flat on the ground at his feet, and then is persuaded that he *has* leaped down Dover cliff but has been miraculously preserved. Imagine this incident transferred to *Othello*, and you realize how completely the two tragedies differ in dramatic atmosphere. In *Othello* it would be a shocking or a ludicrous dissonance, but it is in harmony with the spirit of *King Lear*. And not only is this so, but, contrary to expectation, it is not, if properly acted, in the least absurd on the stage. The imagination and the feelings have been worked upon with such effect by the description of the cliff, and by the portrayal of the old man's despair and his son's courageous and loving wisdom, that we are unconscious of the grotesqueness of the incident for common sense.

The second passage is more important, for it deals with the origin of the whole conflict. The oft-repeated judgment that the first scene of *King Lear* is absurdly improbable, and that no sane man would think of dividing his kingdom among his daughters in proportion to the strength of their several protestations of love, is much too harsh and is based upon a strange misunderstanding. This scene acts effectively, and to imagination the story is not at all incredible. It is merely strange, like so many of the stories on which our romantic dramas are based. Shakespeare, besides, has done a good deal to soften the improbability of the legend, and he has done much more than the casual reader perceives. The very first words of the drama, as Coleridge pointed out, tell us that the division of the kingdom is already settled in all its details, so that only the public announcement of it remains.[4] Later we find that the lines of division have already

---

[4] '*Kent.*   I thought the king had more affected the Duke of Albany than Cornwall.
      Glos.   It did always seem so to us: but now, in the division of the kingdom, it appears
              not which of the dukes he values most.'

For (Gloster goes on to say) their shares are exactly equal in value. And if the shares of the two elder daughters are fixed, obviously that of the third is so too.

been drawn on the map of Britain (l. 38), and again that Cordelia's share, which is her dowry, is perfectly well known to Burgundy, if not to France (ll. 197, 245). That then which is censured as absurd, the dependence of the division on the speeches of the daughters, was in Lear's intention a mere form, devised as a childish scheme to gratify his love of absolute power and his hunger for assurances of devotion. And this scheme is perfectly in character. We may even say that the main cause of its failure was not that Goneril and Regan were exceptionally hypocritical, but that Cordelia was exceptionally sincere and unbending. And it is essential to observe that its failure, and the consequent necessity of publicly reversing his whole well-known intention, is one source of Lear's extreme anger. He loved Cordelia most and knew that she loved him best, and the supreme moment to which he looked forward was that in which she should outdo her sisters in expressions of affection, and should be rewarded by that 'third' of the kingdom which was the most 'opulent'. And then – so it naturally seemed to him – she put him to open shame.

There is a further point, which seems to have escaped the attention of Coleridge and others. Part of the absurdity of Lear's plan is taken to be his idea of living with his three daughters in turn. But he never meant to do this. He meant to live with Cordelia, and with her alone.[5] The scheme of his alternate monthly stay with Goneril and Regan is forced on him at the moment by what he thinks the undutifulness of his favourite child. In fact his whole original plan, though foolish and rash, was not a 'hideous rashness'[6] or incredible folly. If carried out it would have had no such consequences as followed its alteration. It would probably have led quickly to war,[7] but not to the agony which culminated in the storm upon the heath. The first scene, therefore, is not absurd, though it must be pronounced dramatically faulty in so far as it discloses the true position of affairs only to an attention more alert than can be expected in a theatrical audience or has been found in many critics of the play.

Let us turn next to two passages of another kind, the two which are mainly responsible for the accusation of excessive painfulness, and so

---

5 I loved her most, and thought to set my rest
  On her kind nursery.

6 It is to Lear's altered plan that Kent applies these words.

7 There is talk of a war between Goneril and Regan within a fortnight of the division of the kingdom (II.i.11 f.).

for the distaste of many readers and the long theatrical eclipse of *King Lear*. The first of these is much the less important; it is the scene of the blinding of Gloster. The blinding of Gloster on the stage has been condemned almost universally; and surely with justice, because the mere physical horror of such a spectacle would in the theatre be a sensation so violent as to overpower the purely tragic emotions, and therefore the spectacle would seem revolting or shocking. But it is otherwise in reading. For mere imagination the physical horror, though not lost, is so far deadened that it can do its duty as a stimulus to pity, and to that appalled dismay at the extremity of human cruelty which it is of the essence of the tragedy to excite. Thus the blinding of Gloster belongs rightly to *King Lear* in its proper world of imagination; it is a blot upon *King Lear* as a stage-play.

But what are we to say of the second and far more important passage, the conclusion of the tragedy, the 'unhappy ending', as it is called, though the word 'unhappy' sounds almost ironical in its weakness? Is this too a blot upon *King Lear* as a stage-play? The question is not so easily answered as might appear. Doubtless we are right when we turn with disgust from Tate's sentimental alterations, from his marriage of Edgar and Cordelia, and from that cheap moral which every one of Shakespeare's tragedies contradicts, 'that Truth and Virtue shall at last succeed'.* But are we so sure that we are right when we unreservedly condemn the feeling which prompted these alterations, or at all events the feeling which beyond question comes naturally to many readers of *King Lear* who would like Tate as little as we? What they wish, though they have not always the courage to confess it even to themselves, is that the deaths of Edmund, Goneril, Regan and Gloster should be followed by the escape of Lear and Cordelia from death, and that we should be allowed to imagine the poor old King passing quietly in the home of his beloved child to the end which cannot be far off. Now, I do not dream of saying that we ought to wish this, so long as we regard *King Lear* simply as a work of poetic imagination. But if *King Lear* is to be considered strictly as a drama, or simply as we consider *Othello*, it is not so clear that the wish is unjustified. In fact I will take my courage in both hands and say boldly that I share it, and also that I believe Shakespeare would have ended his play thus had he taken the subject in hand a few years later, in the days of *Cymbeline* and the *Winter's Tale*. If I read *King Lear* simply as a drama, I find that my feelings call for this 'happy ending'.

I do not mean the human, the philanthropic, feelings, but the dramatic sense. The former wish Hamlet and Othello to escape their doom; the latter does not; but it does wish Lear and Cordelia to be saved. Surely, it says, the tragic emotions have been sufficiently stirred already. Surely the tragic outcome of Lear's error and his daughters' ingratitude has been made clear enough and moving enough. And, still more surely, such a tragic catastrophe as this should seem *inevitable*. But this catastrophe, unlike those of all the other mature tragedies, does not seem at all inevitable. It is not even satisfactorily motived.[8] In fact it seems expressly designed to fall suddenly like a bolt from a sky cleared by the vanished storm. And although from a wider point of view one may fully recognize the value of this effect, and may even reject with horror the wish for a 'happy ending', this wider point of view, I must maintain, is not strictly dramatic or tragic.

Of course this is a heresy and all the best authority is against it. But then the best authority, it seems to me, is either influenced unconsciously by disgust at Tate's sentimentalism or unconsciously takes that wider point of view. When Lamb – there is no higher authority – writes, 'A happy ending! – as if the living martyrdom that Lear had

---

[8] I mean that no sufficiently clear reason is supplied for Edmund's delay in attempting to save Cordelia and Lear. The matter stands thus. Edmund, after the defeat of the opposing army, sends Lear and Cordelia to prison. Then, in accordance with a plan agreed on between himself and Goneril, he despatches a captain with secret orders to put them both to death *instantly* (V.iii.26–37, 244, 252). He then has to fight with the disguised Edgar. He is mortally wounded, and, as he lies dying, he says to Edgar (at line 162, *more than a hundred lines* after he gave that commission to the captain):

What you have charged me with, that have I done;
And more, much more; the time will bring it out;
'Tis past, and so am I.

In 'more, much more' he seems to be thinking of the order for the deaths of Lear and Cordelia (what else remained undisclosed?); yet he says nothing about it. A few lines later he recognizes the justice of his fate, yet still says nothing. Then he hears the story of his father's death, says it has moved him and 'shall perchance do good' (what good except saving his victims?); yet he still says nothing. Even when he hears that Goneril is dead and Regan poisoned, he *still* says nothing. It is only when he is directly questioned about Lear and Cordelia that he tries to save the victims who were to be killed 'instantly' (242). How can we explain his delay? Perhaps, thinking the deaths of Lear and Cordelia would be of use to Goneril and Regan, he will not speak till he is sure that both the sisters are dead. Or perhaps, though he can recognize the justice of his fate and can be touched by the account of his father's death, he is still too self-absorbed to rise to the active effort to 'do some good, despite of his own nature'. But, while either of these conjectures is possible, it is surely far from satisfactory that we should be left to mere conjecture as to the cause of the delay which permits the catastrophe to take place. The *real* cause lies outside the dramatic *nexus*. It is Shakespeare's wish to deliver a sudden and crushing blow to the hopes which he has excited.

gone through, the flaying of his feelings alive, did not make a fair dismissal from the stage of life the only decorous thing for him', I answer, first, that it is precisely this *fair* dismissal which we desire for him instead of renewed anguish; and, secondly, that what we desire for him during the brief remainder of his days is not 'the childish pleasure of getting his gilt robes and sceptre again', not what Tate gives him, but what Shakespeare himself might have given him – peace and happiness by Cordelia's fireside. And if I am told that he has suffered too much for this, how can I possibly believe it with these words ringing in my ears:

> Come, let's away to prison:
> We two alone will sing like birds i' the cage.
> When thou dost ask me blessing, I'll kneel down,
> And ask of thee forgiveness: so we'll live,
> And pray, and sing, and tell old tales, and laugh
> At gilded butterflies?

And again when Schlegel declares that, if Lear were saved, 'the whole' would 'lose its significance', because it would no longer show us that the belief in Providence 'requires a wider range than the dark pilgrimage on earth to be established in its whole extent', I answer that, if the drama does show us that, it takes us beyond the strictly tragic point of view.[9]

A dramatic mistake in regard to the catastrophe, however, even supposing it to exist, would not seriously affect the whole play. The principal structural weakness of *King Lear* lies elsewhere. It is felt to some extent in the earlier Acts, but still more (as from our study of Shakespeare's technique we have learnt to expect) in the Fourth and the first part of the Fifth. And it arises chiefly from the double action, which is a peculiarity of *King Lear* among the tragedies. By the side of Lear, his daughters, Kent, and the Fool, who are the principal figures in the main plot, stand Gloster and his two sons, the chief persons of the secondary plot. Now by means of this double action Shakespeare secured certain results highly advantageous even from the strictly dramatic point of view, and easy to perceive. But the disadvantages were dramatically greater. The number of essential characters is so large, their actions and movements are so complicated, and events

---

[9] Everything in these paragraphs must, of course, be taken in connection with later remarks.

towards the close crowd on one another so thickly, that the reader's attention,[10] rapidly transferred from one centre of interest to another, is overstrained. He becomes, if not intellectually confused, at least emotionally fatigued. The battle, on which everything turns, scarcely affects him. The deaths of Edmund, Goneril, Regan and Gloster seem 'but trifles here'; and anything short of the incomparable pathos of the close would leave him cold. There is something almost ludicrous in the insignificance of this battle, when it is compared with the corresponding battles in *Julius Caesar* and *Macbeth*; and though there may have been further reasons for its insignificance, the main one is simply that there was no room to give it its due effect among such a host of competing interests.[11]

A comparison of the last two Acts of *Othello* with the last two Acts of *King Lear* would show how unfavourable to dramatic clearness is a multiplicity of figures. But that this multiplicity is not in itself a fatal obstacle is evident from the last two Acts of *Hamlet*, and especially from the final scene. This is in all respects one of Shakespeare's triumphs, yet the stage is crowded with characters. Only they are not *leading* characters. The plot is single; Hamlet and the King are the 'mighty opposites'; and Ophelia, the only other person in whom we are obliged to take a vivid interest, has already disappeared. It is therefore natural and right that the deaths of Laertes and the Queen should affect us comparatively little. But in *King Lear*, because the plot is double, we have present in the last scene no less than five persons who are technically of the first importance – Lear, his three daughters and Edmund; not to speak of Kent and Edgar, of whom the latter at any rate is technically quite as important as Laertes. And again, owing to the pressure of persons and events, and owing to the concentration of our anxiety on Lear and Cordelia, the combat of Edgar and Edmund, which occupies so considerable a space, fails to excite a tithe of the interest of the fencing-match in *Hamlet*. The truth is that all through these Acts Shakespeare has too vast a material to use with complete

---

10 I say 'the reader's,' because on the stage, whenever I have seen *King Lear*, the 'cuts' necessitated by modern scenery would have made this part of the play absolutely unintelligible to me if I had not been familiar with it. It is significant that Lamb in his *Tale of King Lear** almost omits the subplot.

11 Even if Cordelia had won the battle, Shakespeare would probably have hesitated to concentrate interest on it, for her victory would have been a British defeat. On Spedding's* view, that he did mean to make the battle more interesting, and that his purpose has been defeated by our wrong division of Acts IV. and V., see Note X.

dramatic effectiveness, however essential this very vastness was for effects of another kind.

Added to these defects there are others, which suggest that in *King Lear* Shakespeare was less concerned than usual with dramatic fitness; improbabilities, inconsistencies, sayings and doings which suggest questions only to be answered by conjecture. The improbabilities in *King Lear* surely far surpass those of the other great tragedies in number and in grossness. And they are particularly noticeable in the secondary plot. For example, no sort of reason is given why Edgar, who lives in the same house with Edmund, should write a letter to him instead of speaking; and this is a letter absolutely damning to his character. Gloster was very foolish, but surely not so foolish as to pass unnoticed this improbability; or, if so foolish, what need for Edmund to forge a letter rather than a conversation, especially as Gloster appears to be unacquainted with his son's handwriting?[12] Is it in character that Edgar should be persuaded without the slightest demur to avoid his father instead of confronting him and asking him the cause of his anger? Why in the world should Gloster, when expelled from his castle, wander painfully all the way to Dover simply in order to destroy himself (IV.i.80)? And is it not extraordinary that, after Gloster's attempted suicide, Edgar should first talk to him in the language of a gentleman, then to Oswald in his presence in broad peasant dialect, then again to Gloster in gentle language, and yet that Gloster should not manifest the least surprise?

Again, to take three instances of another kind: (*a*) only a fortnight seems to have elapsed between the first scene and the breach with Goneril; yet already there are rumours not only of war between Goneril and Regan but of the coming of a French army; and this, Kent says, is perhaps connected with the harshness of *both* the sisters to their father, although Regan has apparently had no opportunity of showing any harshness till the day before. (*b*) In the quarrel with Goneril Lear speaks of his having to dismiss fifty of his followers at a clap, yet she has neither mentioned any number nor had any opportunity of mentioning it off the stage. (*c*) Lear and Goneril, intending to hurry to Regan, both send off messengers to her, and both tell the messengers to bring back an answer. But it does not appear either how

---

[12] It is vain to suggest that Edmund has only just come home, and that the letter is supposed to have been sent to him when he was 'out'. See I.ii.38–40, 65 f.

the messengers *could* return or what answer could be required, as their superiors are following them with the greatest speed.

Once more, (*a*) why does Edgar not reveal himself to his blind father, as he truly says he ought to have done? The answer is left to mere conjecture. (*b*) Why does Kent so carefully preserve his incognito till the last scene? He says he does it for an important purpose, but what the purpose is we have to guess. (*c*) Why Burgundy rather than France should have first choice of Cordelia's hand is a question we cannot help asking, but there is no hint of any answer.[13] (*d*) I have referred already to the strange obscurity regarding Edmund's delay in trying to save his victims, and I will not extend this list of examples. No one of such defects is surprising when considered by itself, but their number is surely significant. Taken in conjunction with other symptoms it means that Shakespeare, set upon the dramatic effect of the great scenes and upon certain effects not wholly dramatic, was exceptionally careless of probability, clearness and consistency in smaller matters, introducing what was convenient or striking for a momentary purpose without troubling himself about anything more than the moment. In presence of these signs it seems doubtful whether his failure to give information about the fate of the Fool was due to anything more than carelessness or an impatient desire to reduce his overloaded material.[14]

Before I turn to the other side of the subject I will refer to one more characteristic of this play which is dramatically disadvantageous. In Shakespeare's dramas, owing to the absence of scenery from the Elizabethan stage, the question, so vexatious to editors, of the exact locality of a particular scene is usually unimportant and often unanswerable; but, as a rule, we know, broadly speaking, where the persons live and what their journeys are. The text makes this plain, for example, almost throughout *Hamlet, Othello* and *Macbeth,* and the imagination is therefore untroubled. But in *King Lear* the indications are so scanty that the reader's mind is left not seldom both vague and bewildered.

---

[13] The idea in scene i., perhaps, is that Cordelia's marriage, like the division of the kingdom, has really been pre-arranged, and that the ceremony of choosing between France and Burgundy (I.i.46 f.) is a mere fiction. Burgundy is to be her husband, and that is why, when Lear has cast her off, he offers her to Burgundy first (l.192 ff.). It might seem from 211 ff. that Lear's reason for doing so is that he prefers France, or thinks him the greater man, and therefore will not offer him first what is worthless: but the language of France (240 ff.) seems to show that he recognizes a prior right in Burgundy.

[14] See Note T. and pp. 238–9.

Nothing enables us to imagine whereabouts in Britain Lear's palace lies, or where the Duke of Albany lives. In referring to the dividing-lines on the map, Lear tells us of shadowy forests and plenteous rivers, but, unlike Hotspur and his companions, he studiously avoids proper names. The Duke of Cornwall, we presume in the absence of information, is likely to live in Cornwall; but we suddenly find, from the introduction of a place-name which all readers take at first for a surname, that he lives at Gloster (I.v.1).[15] This seems likely to be also the home of the Earl of Gloster, to whom Cornwall is patron. But no: it is a night's journey from Cornwall's 'house' to Gloster's, and Gloster's is in the middle of an uninhabited heath.[16] Here, for the purpose of the crisis, nearly all the persons assemble, but they do so in a manner which no casual spectator or reader could follow. Afterwards they all drift towards Dover for the purpose of the catas-trophe; but again the localities and movements are unusually indefi-nite. And this indefiniteness is found in smaller matters. One cannot help asking, for example, and yet one feels one had better not ask, where that 'lodging' of Edmund's can be, in which he hides Edgar from his father, and whether Edgar is mad that he should return from his hollow tree (in a district where 'for many miles about there's scarce a bush') to his father's castle in order to soliloquize (II.iii.): – for the favourite stage-direction, 'a wood' (which is more than 'a bush'), however convenient to imagination, is scarcely compatible with the presence of Kent asleep in the stocks.[17] Something of the confusion which bewilders the reader's mind in *King Lear* recurs in *Antony and Cleopatra*, the most faultily constructed of all the tragedies; but there it is due not so much to the absence or vagueness of the indications as to the necessity of taking frequent and fatiguing journeys over thou-sands of miles. Shakespeare could not help himself in the Roman play: in *King Lear* he did not choose to help himself, perhaps deliberately chose to be vague.

From these defects, or from some of them, follows one result which must be familiar to many readers of *King Lear*. It is far more difficult to retrace in memory the steps of the action in this tragedy than in

---

[15] See Note U.

[16] The word 'heath' in the stage-directions of the storm-scenes is, I may remark, Rowe's,* not Shakespeare's, who never used the word till he wrote *Macbeth*.

[17] It is pointed out in Note V. that what modern editors call Scenes ii., iii., iv. of Act II are really one scene, for Kent is on the stage through them all.

Hamlet, Othello, or *Macbeth.* The outline is of course quite clear; anyone could write an 'argument' of the play. But when an attempt is made to fill in the detail, it issues sooner or later in confusion even with readers whose dramatic memory is unusually strong.[18]

2

How is it, now, that this defective drama so overpowers us that we are either unconscious of its blemishes or regard them as almost irrelevant? As soon as we turn to this question we recognize, not merely that *King Lear* possesses purely dramatic qualities which far outweigh its defects, but that its greatness consists partly in imaginative effects of a wider kind. And, looking for the sources of these effects, we find among them some of those very things which appeared to us dramatically faulty or injurious. Thus, to take at once two of the simplest examples of this, that very vagueness in the sense of locality which we have just considered, and again that excess in the bulk of the material and the number of figures, events and movements, while they interfere with the clearness of vision, have at the same time a positive value for imagination. They give the feeling of vastness, the feeling not of a scene or particular place, but of a world; or, to speak more accurately, of a particular place which is also a world. This world is dim to us, partly from its immensity, and partly because it is filled with gloom; and in the gloom shapes approach and recede, whose half-seen faces and motions touch us with dread, horror, or the most painful pity – sympathies and antipathies which we seem to be feeling not only for them but for the whole race. This world, we are told, is called Britain; but we should no more look for it in an atlas than for the place, called Caucasus,* where Prometheus was chained by Strength and Force and comforted by the daughters of Ocean, or the place where Farinata stands erect in his glowing tomb, 'Come avesse lo Inferno in gran dispitto.'*

Consider next the double action. It has certain strictly dramatic advantages, and may well have had its origin in purely dramatic considerations. To go no further, the secondary plot fills out a story which would by itself have been somewhat thin, and it provides a

---

18 [On the locality of Act I., Sc. ii., see *Modern Language Review* for Oct., 1908, and Jan., 1909.]

most effective contrast between its personages and those of the main plot, the tragic strength and stature of the latter being heightened by comparison with the slighter build of the former. But its chief value lies elsewhere, and is not merely dramatic. It lies in the fact – in Shakespeare without a parallel – that the sub-plot simply repeats the theme of the main story. Here, as there, we see an old man 'with a white beard'. He, like Lear, is affectionate, unsuspicious, foolish, and self-willed. He, too, wrongs deeply a child who loves him not less for the wrong. He, too, meets with monstrous ingratitude from the child whom he favours, and is tortured and driven to death. This repetition does not simply double the pain with which the tragedy is witnessed: it startles and terrifies by suggesting that the folly of Lear and the ingratitude of his daughters are no accidents or merely individual aberrations, but that in that dark cold world some fateful malignant influence is abroad, turning the hearts of the fathers against their children and of the children against their fathers, smiting the earth with a curse, so that the brother gives the brother to death and the father the son, blinding the eyes, maddening the brain, freezing the springs of pity, numbing all powers except the nerves of anguish and the dull lust of life.[19]

Hence, too, as well as from other sources, comes that feeling which haunts us in *King Lear*, as though we were witnessing something universal – a conflict not so much of particular persons as of the powers of good and evil in the world. And the treatment of many of the characters confirms this feeling. Considered simply as psychological studies few of them, surely, are of the highest interest. Fine and subtle touches could not be absent from a work of Shakespeare's maturity; but, with the possible exception of Lear himself, no one of the characters strikes us as psychologically a *wonderful* creation, like Hamlet or Iago or even Macbeth; one or two seem even to be somewhat faint and thin. And, what is more significant, it is not quite natural to us to regard them from this point of view at all. Rather we observe a most unusual circumstance. If Lear, Gloster and Albany are set apart, the rest fall into two distinct groups, which are strongly, even violently, contrasted: Cordelia, Kent, Edgar, the Fool on one side, Goneril, Regan, Edmund, Cornwall, Oswald on the other. These

---

[19] This effect of the double action seems to have been pointed out first by Schlegel.

characters are in various degrees individualized, most of them completely so; but still in each group there is a quality common to all the members, or one spirit breathing through them all. Here we have unselfish and devoted love, there hard self-seeking. On both sides, further, the common quality takes an extreme form; the love is incapable of being chilled by injury, the selfishness of being softened by pity; and, it may be added, this tendency to extremes is found again in the characters of Lear and Gloster, and is the main source of the accusations of improbability directed against their conduct at certain points. Hence the members of each group tend to appear, at least in part, as varieties of one species; the radical differences of the two species are emphasized in broad hard strokes; and the two are set in conflict, almost as if Shakespeare, like Empedocles,* were regarding Love and Hate as the two ultimate forces of the universe.

The presence in *King Lear* of so large a number of characters in whom love or self-seeking is so extreme, has another effect. They do not merely inspire in us emotions of unusual strength, but they also stir the intellect to wonder and speculation. How can there be such men and women? we ask ourselves. How comes it that humanity can take such absolutely opposite forms? And, in particular, to what omission of elements which should be present in human nature, or, if there is no omission, to what distortion of these elements is it due that such beings as some of these come to exist? This is a question which Iago (and perhaps no previous creation of Shakespeare's) forces us to ask, but in *King Lear* it is provoked again and again. And more, it seems to us that the author himself is asking this question. 'Then let them anatomize Regan, see what breeds about her heart. Is there any cause in nature that makes these hard hearts?' – the strain of thought which appears here seems to be present in some degree throughout the play. We seem to trace the tendency which, a few years later, produced Ariel and Caliban, the tendency of imagination to analyse and abstract, to decompose human nature into its constituent factors, and then to construct beings in whom one or more of these factors is absent or atrophied or only incipient. This, of course, is a tendency which produces symbols, allegories, personifications of qualities and abstract ideas; and we are accustomed to think it quite foreign to Shakespeare's genius, which was in the highest degree concrete. No doubt in the main we are right here; but it is hazardous to set limits to that genius. The Sonnets, if nothing else, may show us how easy it was to

Shakespeare's mind to move in a world of 'Platonic' ideas;[20]* and, while it would be going too far to suggest that he was employing conscious symbolism or allegory in *King Lear*, it does appear to disclose a mode of imagination not so very far removed from the mode with which, we must remember, Shakespeare was perfectly familiar in Morality plays and in the *Fairy Queen*.*

This same tendency shows itself in *King Lear* in other forms. To it is due the idea of monstrosity – of beings, actions, states of mind, which appear not only abnormal but absolutely contrary to nature; an idea, which, of course, is common enough in Shakespeare, but appears with unusual frequency in *King Lear*, for instance in the lines:

> Ingratitude, thou marble-hearted fiend,
> More hideous when thou show'st thee in a child
> Than the sea-monster!

or in the exclamation,

> Filial ingratitude!
> Is it not as this mouth should tear this hand
> For lifting food to't?

It appears in another shape in that most vivid passage where Albany, as he looks at the face which had bewitched him, now distorted with dreadful passions, suddenly sees it in a new light and exclaims in horror:

> Thou changed and self-cover'd thing, for shame
> Bemonster not thy feature. Were't my fitness
> To let these hands obey my blood,
> They are apt enough to dislocate and tear
> Thy flesh and bones: howe'er thou art a fiend,
> A woman's shape doth shield thee.[21]

It appears once more in that exclamation of Kent's, as he listens to the description of Cordelia's grief:

---

[20] How prevalent these are is not recognized by readers familiar only with English poetry. See Simpson's *Introduction to the Philosophy of Shakespeare's Sonnets* (1868) and Mr. Wyndham's* edition of Shakespeare's Poems. Perhaps both writers overstate, and Simpson's interpretations are often forced or arbitrary, but his book is valuable and ought not to remain out of print.

[21] The monstrosity here is a being with a woman's body and a fiend's soul. For the interpretation of the lines see Note Y.

> It is the stars,
> The stars above us, govern our conditions;
> Else one self mate and mate could not beget
> Such different issues.

(This is not the only sign that Shakespeare had been musing over heredity, and wondering how it comes about that the composition of two strains of blood or two parent souls can produce such astonishingly different products.)

This mode of thought is responsible, lastly, for a very striking characteristic of *King Lear* – one in which it has no parallel except *Timon* – the incessant references to the lower animals[22] and man's likeness to them. These references are scattered broadcast through the whole play as though Shakespeare's mind were so busy with the subject that he could hardly write a page without some allusion to it. The dog, the horse, the cow, the sheep, the hog, the lion, the bear, the wolf, the fox, the monkey, the pole-cat, the civet-cat, the pelican, the owl, the crow, the chough, the wren, the fly, the butterfly, the rat, the mouse, the frog, the tadpole, the wall-newt, the water-newt, the worm – I am sure I cannot have completed the list, and some of them are mentioned again and again. Often, of course, and especially in the talk of Edgar as the Bedlam, they have no symbolical meaning; but not seldom, even in his talk, they are expressly referred to for their typical qualities – 'hog in sloth, fox in stealth, wolf in greediness, dog in madness, lion in prey', 'The fitchew nor the soiled horse goes to't With a more riotous appetite'. Sometimes a person in the drama is compared, openly or implicitly, with one of them. Goneril is a kite: her ingratitude has a serpent's tooth: she has struck her father most serpent-like upon the very heart: her visage is wolvish: she has tied sharp-toothed unkindness like a vulture on her father's breast: for her husband she is a gilded serpent: to Gloster her cruelty seems to have the fangs of a boar. She and Regan are dog-hearted: they are tigers, not daughters: each is an adder to the other: the flesh of each is covered with the fell of a beast. Oswald is a mongrel, and the son and heir of a mongrel: ducking to everyone in power, he is a wag-tail: white with fear, he is a goose. Gloster, for Regan, is an ingrateful fox: Albany, for

---

[22] Since this paragraph was written I have found that the abundance of these references has been pointed out and commented on by J. Kirkman, *New Shaks. Soc. Trans.*, 1877.

his wife, has a cowish spirit and is milk-liver'd: when Edgar as the
Bedlam first appeared to Lear he made him think a man a worm. As
we read, the souls of all the beasts in turn seem to us to have entered
the bodies of these mortals; horrible in their venom, savagery, lust,
deceitfulness, sloth, cruelty, filthiness; miserable in their feebleness,
nakedness, defencelessness, blindness; and man, 'consider him well', is
even what they are. Shakespeare, to whom the idea of the transmigra-
tion of souls was familiar and had once been material for jest,[23] seems
to have been brooding on humanity in the light of it. It is remarkable,
and somewhat sad, that he seems to find none of man's better qualities in the world of the brutes (though he might well have found the
prototype of the self-less love of Kent and Cordelia in the dog whom
he so habitually maligns);[24] but he seems to have been asking himself
whether that which he loathes in man may not be due to some strange
wrenching of this frame of things, through which the lower animal
souls have found a lodgment in human forms, and there found – to
the horror and confusion of the thinking mind – brains to forge,
tongues to speak, and hands to act, enormities which no mere brute
can conceive or execute. He shows us in *King Lear* these terrible forces
bursting into monstrous life and flinging themselves upon those

---

[23] *E.g.* in *As You Like It*, III.ii.187, 'I was never so berhymed since Pythagoras' time, that I
was an Irish rat, which I can hardly remember'; *Twelfth Night*, IV.ii.55, '*Clown.* What is the
opinion of Pythagoras concerning wild fowl? *Mal.* That the soul of our grandam might haply
inhabit a bird. *Clown.* What thinkest thou of his opinion? *Mal.* I think nobly of the soul, and
no way approve his opinion,' etc. But earlier comes a passage which reminds us of *King Lear*,
Merchant of Venice, IV.i.128:

> O be thou damn'd, inexecrable dog!
> And for thy life let justice be accused.
> Thou almost makest me waver in my faith
> To hold opinion with Pythagoras,
> That souls of animals infuse themselves
> Into the trunks of men: thy currish spirit
> Govern'd a wolf, who, hang'd for human slaughter,
> Even from the gallows did his fell soul fleet,
> And, whilst thou lay'st in thy unhallow'd dam,
> Infused itself in thee; for thy desires
> Are wolvish, bloody, starved and ravenous.

[24] I fear it is not possible, however, to refute, on the whole, one charge – that the dog is a
snob, in the sense that he respects power and prosperity, and objects to the poor and despised.
It is curious that Shakespeare refers to this trait three times in *King Lear*, as if he were feeling a
peculiar disgust at it. See III.vi.65, 'The little dogs and all', etc.: IV.vi.159, 'Thou hast seen a
farmer's dog bark at a beggar . . . and the creature run from the cur? There thou mightst behold
the great image of authority': V.iii.186, 'taught me to shift Into a madman's rags: to assume a
semblance That very dogs disdain'd'. Cf. *Oxford Lectures*, p. 341.

human beings who are weak and defenceless, partly from old age, but partly because they *are* human and lack the dreadful undivided energy of the beast. And the only comfort he might seem to hold out to us is the prospect that at least this bestial race, strong only where it is vile, cannot endure: though stars and gods are powerless, or careless, or empty dreams, yet there must be an end of this horrible world:

> It will come;
> Humanity must perforce prey on itself
> Like monsters of the deep.[25]

The influence of all this on imagination as we read *King Lear* is very great; and it combines with other influences to convey to us, not in the form of distinct ideas but in the manner proper to poetry, the wider or universal significance of the spectacle presented to the inward eye. But the effect of theatrical exhibition is precisely the reverse. There the poetic atmosphere is dissipated; the meaning of the very words which create it passes half-realized; in obedience to the tyranny of the eye we conceive the characters as mere particular men and women; and all that mass of vague suggestion, if it enters the mind at all, appears in the shape of an allegory which we immediately reject. A similar conflict between imagination and sense will be found if we consider the dramatic centre of the whole tragedy, the Storm-scenes. The temptation of Othello and the scene of Duncan's murder may lose upon the stage, but they do not lose their essence, and they gain as well as lose. The Storm-scenes in *King Lear* gain nothing and

---

[25] With this compare the following lines in the great speech on 'degree' in *Troilus and Cressida*, I.iii.:

> Take but degree away, untune that string,
> And, hark, what discord follows! Each thing meets
> In mere oppugnancy: the bounded, waters
> Should lift their bosoms higher than the shores
> And make a sop of all this solid globe:
> Strength should be lord of imbecility,
> And the rude son should strike his father dead:
> Force should be right; or, rather, right and wrong,
> Between whose endless jar justice resides,
> Should lose their names, and so should justice too.
> Then everything includes itself in power,
> Power into will, will into appetite;
> And appetite, an universal wolf,
> So doubly seconded with will and power,
> Must make perforce an universal prey,
> And last eat up himself.

their very essence is destroyed. It is comparatively a small thing that the theatrical storm, not to drown the dialogue, must be silent whenever a human being wishes to speak, and is wretchedly inferior to many a storm we have witnessed. Nor is it simply that, as Lamb observed, the corporal presence of Lear, 'an old man tottering about the stage with a walking-stick', disturbs and depresses that sense of the greatness of his mind which fills the imagination. There is a further reason, which is not expressed, but still emerges, in these words of Lamb's: 'the explosions of his passion are terrible as a volcano: they are storms turning up and disclosing to the bottom that sea, his mind, with all its vast riches'. Yes, 'they are *storms*'. For imagination, that is to say, the explosions of Lear's passion, and the bursts of rain and thunder, are not, what for the senses they must be, two things, but manifestations of one thing. It is the powers of the tormented soul that we hear and see in the 'groans of roaring wind and rain' and the 'sheets of fire'; and they that, at intervals almost more overwhelming, sink back into darkness and silence. Nor yet is even this all; but, as those incessant references to wolf and tiger made us see humanity 'reeling back into the beast' and ravening against itself, so in the storm we seem to see Nature herself convulsed by the same horrible passions; the 'common mother',

> Whose womb immeasureable and infinite breast
> Teems and feeds all,

turning on her children, to complete the ruin they have wrought upon themselves. Surely something not less, but much more, than these helpless words convey, is what comes to us in these astounding scenes; and if, translated thus into the language of prose, it becomes confused and inconsistent, the reason is simply that it itself is poetry, and such poetry as cannot be transferred to the space behind the footlights, but has its being only in imagination. Here then is Shakespeare at his very greatest, but not the mere dramatist Shakespeare.[26]

---

[26] Nor is it believable that Shakespeare, whose means of imitating a storm were so greatly inferior even to ours, had the stage-performance only or chiefly in view in composing these scenes. He may not have thought of readers (or he may), but he must in any case have written to satisfy his own imagination. I have taken no notice of the part played in these scenes by anyone except Lear. The matter is too huge, and too strictly poetic, for analysis. I may observe that in our present theatres, owing to the use of elaborate scenery, the three Storm-scenes are usually combined, with disastrous effect. Shakespeare, as we saw (p. 33), interposed between them short scenes of much lower tone.

And now we may say this also of the catastrophe, which we found questionable from the strictly dramatic point of view. Its purpose is not merely dramatic. This sudden blow out of the darkness, which seems so far from inevitable, and which strikes down our reviving hopes for the victims of so much cruelty, seems now only what we might have expected in a world so wild and monstrous. It is as if Shakespeare said to us: 'Did you think weakness and innocence have any chance here? Were you beginning to dream that? I will show you it is not so.'

I come to a last point. As we contemplate this world, the question presses on us What can be the ultimate power that moves it, that excites this gigantic war and waste, or, perhaps, that suffers them and overrules them? And in *King Lear* this question is not left to us to ask, it is raised by the characters themselves. References to religious or irreligious beliefs and feelings are more frequent than is usual in Shakespeare's tragedies, as frequent perhaps as in his final plays. He introduces characteristic differences in the language of the different persons about fortune or the stars or the gods, and shows how the question What rules the world? is forced upon their minds. They answer it in their turn: Kent, for instance:

> It is the stars,
> The stars above us, govern our condition:

Edmund:

> Thou, nature, art my goddess; to thy law
> My services are bound:

and again,

> This is the excellent foppery of the world, that, when we are sick in fortune – often the surfeit of our own behaviour – we make guilty of our disasters the sun, the moon and the stars; as if we were villains by necessity, fools by heavenly compulsion, . . . and all that we are evil in by a divine thrusting on:

Gloster:

> As flies to wanton boys are we to the gods;
> They kill us for their sport;

Edgar:

> Think that the clearest gods, who make them honours
> Of men's impossibilities, have preserved thee.

Here we have four distinct theories of the nature of the ruling power. And besides this, in such of the characters as have any belief in gods who love good and hate evil, the spectacle of triumphant injustice or cruelty provokes questionings like those of Job,* or else the thought, often repeated, of divine retribution. To Lear at one moment the storm seems the messenger of heaven:

> Let the great gods,
> That keep this dreadful pother o'er our heads,
> Find out their enemies now. Tremble, thou wretch,
> That hast within thee undivulged crimes. . . .

At another moment those habitual miseries of the poor, of which he has taken too little account, seem to him to accuse the gods of injustice:

> Take physic, pomp;
> Expose thyself to feel what wretches feel,
> That thou mayst shake the superflux to them
> And show the heavens more just;

and Gloster has almost the same thought (IV.i.67 ff.). Gloster again, thinking of the cruelty of Lear's daughters, breaks out,

> but I shall see
> The winged vengeance overtake such children.

The servants who have witnessed the blinding of Gloster by Cornwall and Regan, cannot believe that cruelty so atrocious will pass unpunished. One cries,

> I'll never care what wickedness I do,
> If this man come to good;

and another,

> if she live long,
> And in the end meet the old course of death,
> Women will all turn monsters.

Albany greets the news of Cornwall's death with the exclamation,

> This shows you are above,
> You justicers, that these our nether crimes
> So speedily can venge;

and the news of the deaths of the sisters with the words,

This judgment[27] of the heavens, that makes us tremble,
Touches us not with pity.

Edgar, speaking to Edmund of their father, declares

The gods are just, and of our pleasant vices
Make instruments to plague us,

and Edmund himself assents. Almost throughout the latter half of the drama we note in most of the better characters a preoccupation with the question of the ultimate power, and a passionate need to explain by reference to it what otherwise would drive them to despair. And the influence of this preoccupation and need joins with other influences in affecting the imagination, and in causing it to receive from *King Lear* an impression which is at least as near of kin to the *Divine Comedy* as to *Othello*.

3

For Dante that which is recorded in the *Divine Comedy* was the justice and love of God. What did *King Lear* record for Shakespeare? Something, it would seem, very different. This is certainly the most terrible picture that Shakespeare painted of the world. In no other of his tragedies does humanity appear more pitiably infirm or more hopelessly bad. What is Iago's malignity against an envied stranger compared with the cruelty of the son of Gloster and the daughters of Lear? What are the sufferings of a strong man like Othello to those of helpless age? Much too that we have already observed – the repetition of the main theme in that of the under-plot, the comparisons of man with the most wretched and the most horrible of the beasts, the impression of Nature's hostility to him, the irony of the unexpected catastrophe – these, with much else, seem even to indicate an intention to show things at their worst, and to return the sternest of replies to that question of the ultimate power and those appeals for retribution. Is it an accident, for example, that Lear's first appeal to something beyond the earth,

O heavens,
If you do love old men, if your sweet sway

---

[27] 'justice', Qq.

> Allow[28] obedience, if yourselves are old,
> Make it your cause:

is immediately answered by the iron voices of his daughters, raising by
turns the conditions on which they will give him a humiliating
harbourage; or that his second appeal, heart-rending in its piteousness,

> You see me here, you gods, a poor old man,
> As full of grief as age; wretched in both:

is immediately answered from the heavens by the sound of the breaking storm?[29] Albany and Edgar may moralize on the divine justice as
they will, but how, in the face of all that we see, shall we believe that
they speak Shakespeare's mind? Is not his mind rather expressed in the
bitter contrast between their faith and the events we witness, or in the
scornful rebuke of those who take upon them the mystery of things as
if they were God's spies?[30] Is it not Shakespeare's judgment on his
kind that we hear in Lear's appeal:

> And thou, all-shaking thunder,
> Smite flat the thick rotundity o' the world!
> Crack nature's moulds, all germens spill at once,
> That make ingrateful man!

and Shakespeare's judgment on the worth of existence that we hear in
Lear's agonized cry, 'No, no, no life!'?

Beyond doubt, I think, some such feelings as these possess us, and,
if we follow Shakespeare, ought to possess us, from time to time as we
read *King Lear*. And some readers will go further and maintain that
this is also the ultimate and total impression left by the tragedy. *King
Lear* has been held to be profoundly 'pessimistic' in the full meaning
of that word – the record of a time when contempt and loathing for
his kind had overmastered the poet's soul, and in despair he
pronounced man's life to be simply hateful and hideous. And if we
exclude the biographical part of this view,[31] the rest may claim some

---

[28] = approve.

[29] The direction 'Storm and tempest' at the end of this speech is not modern, it is in the
Folio.

[30] The gods are mentioned many times in *King Lear*, but 'God' only here (V.ii.16).

[31] The whole question how far Shakespeare's works represent his personal feelings and attitude, and the changes in them, would carry us so far beyond the bounds of the four tragedies,
is so needless for the understanding of them, and is so little capable of decision, that I have

support even from the greatest of Shakespearean critics since the days of Coleridge, Hazlitt and Lamb. Mr. Swinburne, after observing that *King Lear* is 'by far the most Aeschylean' of Shakespeare's works, proceeds thus:

'But in one main point it differs radically from the work and the spirit of Aeschylus.* Its fatalism is of a darker and harder nature. To Prometheus the fetters of the lord and enemy of mankind were bitter;

---

excluded it from these lectures; and I will add here a note on it only as it concerns the 'tragic period'.

There are here two distinct sets of facts, equally important. (1) On the one side there is the fact that, so far as we can make out, after *Twelfth Night* Shakespeare wrote, for seven or eight years, no play which, like many of his earlier works, can be called happy, much less merry or sunny. He wrote tragedies; and if the chronological order *Hamlet, Othello, King Lear, Timon, Macbeth*, is correct, these tragedies show for some time a deepening darkness, and *King Lear* and *Timon* lie at the nadir. He wrote also in these years (probably in the earlier of them) certain 'comedies', *Measure for Measure* and *Troilus and Cressida* and perhaps *All's Well*. But about these comedies there is a peculiar air of coldness; there is humour, of course, but little mirth; in *Measure for Measure* perhaps, certainly in *Troilus and Cressida*, a spirit of bitterness and contempt seems to pervade an intellectual atmosphere of an intense but hard clearness. With *Macbeth* perhaps, and more decidedly in the two Roman tragedies which followed, the gloom seems to lift; and the final romances show a mellow serenity which sometimes warms into radiant sympathy, and even into a mirth almost as light-hearted as that of younger days. When we consider these facts, not as barely stated thus but as they affect us in reading the plays, it is, to my mind, very hard to believe that their origin was simply and solely a change in dramatic methods or choice of subjects, or even merely such inward changes as may be expected to accompany the arrival and progress of middle age.

(2) On the other side, and over against these facts, we have to set the multitudinousness of Shakespeare's genius, and his almost unlimited power of conceiving and expressing human experience of all kinds. And we have to set more. Apparently during this period of years he never ceased to write busily, or to exhibit in his writings the greatest mental activity. He wrote also either nothing or very little (*Troilus and Cressida* and his part of *Timon* are the possible exceptions) in which there is any appearance of personal feeling overcoming or seriously endangering the self-control or 'objectivity' of the artist. And finally it is not possible to make out any continuously deepening *personal* note: for although *Othello* is darker than *Hamlet* it surely strikes one as about as impersonal as a play can be; and, on grounds of style and versification, it appears (to me, at least) impossible to bring *Troilus and Cressida* chronologically close to *King Lear* and *Timon*; even if parts of it are later than others, the late parts must be decidedly earlier than those plays.

The conclusion we may very tentatively draw from these sets of facts would seem to be as follows. Shakespeare during these years was probably not a happy man, and it is quite likely that he felt at times even an intense melancholy, bitterness, contempt, anger, possibly even loathing and despair. It is quite likely too that he used these experiences of his in writing such plays as *Hamlet, Troilus and Cressida, King Lear, Timon*. But it is evident that he cannot have been for any considerable time, if ever, overwhelmed by such feelings, and there is no appearance of their having issued in any settled 'pessimistic' conviction which coloured his whole imagination and expressed itself in his works. The choice of the subject of ingratitude, for instance, in *King Lear* and *Timon*, and the method of handling it, may have been due in part to personal feeling; but it does not follow that his feeling was particularly acute at this particular time, and, even if it was, it certainly was not so absorbing as to hinder Shakespeare from representing in the most sympathetic manner aspects of life the very reverse of pessimistic. Whether the total impression of *King Lear* can be called pessimistic is a further question, which is considered in the text.

upon Orestes* the hand of heaven was laid too heavily to bear; yet in the not utterly infinite or everlasting distance we see beyond them the promise of the morning on which mystery and justice shall be made one; when righteousness and omnipotence at last shall kiss each other. But on the horizon of Shakespeare's tragic fatalism we see no such twilight of atonement, such pledge of reconciliation as this. Requital, redemption, amends, equity, explanation, pity and mercy, are words without a meaning here.

> As flies to wanton boys are we to the gods;
> They kill us for their sport.

Here is no need of the Eumenides,* children of Night everlasting; for here is very Night herself.

'The words just cited are not casual or episodical; they strike the keynote of the whole poem, lay the keystone of the whole arch of thought. There is no contest of conflicting forces, no judgment so much as by casting of lots: far less is there any light of heavenly harmony or of heavenly wisdom, of Apollo* or Athene* from above. We have heard much and often from theologians of the light of revelation: and some such thing indeed we find in Aeschylus; but the darkness of revelation is here.'[32]

It is hard to refuse assent to these eloquent words, for they express in the language of a poet what we feel at times in reading *King Lear* but cannot express. But do they represent the total and final impression produced by the play? If they do, this impression, so far as the substance of the drama is concerned (and nothing else is in question here), must, it would seem, be one composed almost wholly of painful feelings – utter depression, or indignant rebellion, or appalled despair. And that would surely be strange. For *King Lear* is admittedly one of the world's greatest poems, and yet there is surely no other of these poems which produces on the whole this effect, and we regard it as a very serious flaw in any considerable work of art that this should be its ultimate effect.[33] So that Mr. Swinburne's description, if taken as final, and any description of *King Lear* as 'pessimistic' in the proper-

---

[32] *A Study of Shakespeare*, pp. 171, 172.

[33] A flaw, I mean, in a work of art considered not as a moral or theological document but as a work of art – an aesthetic flaw. I add the word 'considerable' because we do not regard the effect in question as a flaw in a work like a lyric or a short piece of music, which may naturally be taken as expressions merely of a mood or a subordinate aspect of things.

sense of that word, would imply a criticism which is not intended, and which would make it difficult to leave the work in the position almost universally assigned to it.

But in fact these descriptions, like most of the remarks made on *King Lear* in the present lecture, emphasize only certain aspects of the play and certain elements in the total impression; and in that impression the effect of these aspects, though far from being lost, is modified by that of others. I do not mean that the final effect resembles that of the *Divine Comedy* or the *Oresteia*: how should it, when the first of these can be called by its author a 'Comedy', and when the second, ending (as doubtless the *Prometheus* trilogy also ended) with a solution, is not in the Shakespearean sense a tragedy at all?[34] Nor do I mean that *King Lear* contains a revelation of righteous omnipotence or heavenly harmony, or even a promise of the reconciliation of mystery and justice. But then, as we saw, neither do Shakespeare's other tragedies contain these things. Any theological interpretation of the world on the author's part is excluded from them, and their effect would be disordered or destroyed equally by the ideas of righteous or of unrighteous omnipotence. Nor, in reading them, do we think of 'justice' or 'equity' in the sense of a strict requital or such an adjustment of merit and prosperity as our moral sense is said to demand; and there never was vainer labour than that of critics who try to make out that the persons in these dramas meet with 'justice' or their 'deserts'.[35] But, on the other hand, man is not represented in these tragedies as the mere plaything of a blind or capricious power, suffering woes which have no relation to his character and actions; nor is the world represented as given over to darkness. And in these respects

---

[34] Caution is very necessary in making comparisons between Shakespeare and the Greek dramatists. A tragedy like the *Antigone* stands, in spite of differences, on the same ground as a Shakespearean tragedy; it is a self-contained whole with a catastrophe. A drama like the *Philoctetes* is a self-contained whole, but, ending with a solution, it corresponds not with a Shakespearean tragedy but with a play like *Cymbeline*. A drama like the *Agamemnon* or the *Prometheus Vinctus* answers to no Shakespearean form of play. It is not a self-contained whole, but a part of a trilogy. If the trilogy is considered as a unit, it answers not to *Hamlet* but to *Cymbeline*. If the part is considered as a whole, it answers to *Hamlet*, but may then be open to serious criticism. Shakespeare never made a tragedy end with the complete triumph of the worse side: the *Agamemnon* and *Prometheus*, if wrongly taken as wholes, would do this, and would so far, I must think, be bad tragedies. [It can scarcely be necessary to remind the reader that, in point of 'self-containedness', there is a difference of degree between the pure tragedies of Shakespeare and some of the historical.]

[35] I leave it to better authorities to say how far these remarks apply also to Greek Tragedy, however much the language of 'justice' may be used there.

King Lear, though the most terrible of these works, does not differ in essence from the rest. Its keynote is surely to be heard neither in the words wrung from Gloster in his anguish, nor in Edgar's words 'the gods are just'. Its final and total result is one in which pity and terror, carried perhaps to the extreme limits of art, are so blended with a sense of law and beauty that we feel at last, not depression and much less despair, but a consciousness of greatness in pain, and of solemnity in the mystery we cannot fathom.

LECTURE VIII

KING LEAR

We have now to look at the characters in *King Lear*; and I propose to consider them to some extent from the point of view indicated at the close of the last lecture, partly because we have so far been regarding the tragedy mainly from an opposite point of view, and partly because these characters are so numerous that it would not be possible within our limits to examine them fully.

1

The position of the hero in this tragedy is in one important respect peculiar. The reader of *Hamlet, Othello,* or *Macbeth,* is in no danger of forgetting, when the catastrophe is reached, the part played by the hero in bringing it on. His fatal weakness, error, wrong-doing, continues almost to the end. It is otherwise with *King Lear.* When the conclusion arrives, the old King has for a long while been passive. We have long regarded him not only as 'a man more sinned against than sinning', but almost wholly as a sufferer, hardly at all as an agent. His sufferings too have been so cruel, and our indignation against those who inflicted them has been so intense, that recollection of the wrong he did to Cordelia, to Kent, and to his realm, has been well-nigh effaced. Lastly, for nearly four Acts he has inspired in us, together with this pity, much admiration and affection. The force of his passion has made us feel that his nature was great; and his frankness and generosity, his heroic efforts to be patient, the depth of his shame and repentance, and the ecstasy of his re-union with Cordelia, have melted our very hearts. Naturally, therefore, at the close we are in some danger of forgetting that the storm which has overwhelmed him was liberated by his own deed.

Yet it is essential that Lear's contribution to the action of the drama should be remembered; not at all in order that we may feel that he 'deserved' what he suffered, but because otherwise his fate would appear to us at best pathetic, at worst shocking, but certainly not tragic. And when we were reading the earlier scenes of the play we

211

recognized this contribution clearly enough. At the very beginning, it is true, we are inclined to feel merely pity and misgivings. The first lines tell us that Lear's mind is beginning to fail with age.[1] Formerly he had perceived how different were the characters of Albany and Cornwall, but now he seems either to have lost this perception or to be unwisely ignoring it. The rashness of his division of the kingdom troubles us, and we cannot but see with concern that its motive is mainly selfish. The absurdity of the pretence of making the division depend on protestations of love from his daughters, his complete blindness to the hypocrisy which is patent to us at a glance, his piteous delight in these protestations, the openness of his expressions of preference for his youngest daughter – all make us smile, but all pain us. But pity begins to give way to another feeling when we witness the precipitance, the despotism, the uncontrolled anger of his injustice to Cordelia and Kent, and the 'hideous rashness' of his persistence in dividing the kingdom after the rejection of his one dutiful child. We feel now the presence of force as well as weakness, but we feel also the presence of the tragic ὕβρις.* Lear, we see, is generous and unsuspicious, of an open and free nature, like Hamlet and Othello, and indeed most of Shakespeare's heroes, who in this, according to Ben Jonson, resemble the poet who made them. Lear, we see, is also choleric by temperament – the first of Shakespeare's heroes who is so. And a long life of absolute power, in which he has been flattered to the top of his bent, has produced in him that blindness to human limitations, and that presumptuous self-will, which in Greek tragedy we have so often seen stumbling against the altar of Nemesis. Our consciousness that the decay of old age contributes to this condition deepens our pity and our sense of human infirmity, but certainly does not lead us to regard the old King as irresponsible, and so to sever the tragic *nexus* which binds together his error and his calamities.

The magnitude of this first error is generally fully recognized by the reader owing to his sympathy with Cordelia, though, as we have seen, he often loses the memory of it as the play advances. But this is not so, I think, with the repetition of this error, in the quarrel with Goneril. Here the daughter excites so much detestation, and the father so much sympathy, that we often fail to receive the due impres-

---

[1] Of course I do not mean that he is beginning to be insane, and still less that he *is* insane (as some medical critics suggest).

sion of his violence. There is not here, of course, the *injustice* of his rejection of Cordelia, but there is precisely the same ὕβρις. This had been shown most strikingly in the first scene when *immediately* upon the apparently cold words of Cordelia, 'So young, my lord, and true', there comes this dreadful answer:

> Let it be so; thy truth then be thy dower.
> For, by the sacred radiance of the sun,
> The mysteries of Hecate and the night;
> By all the operation of the orbs
> From whom we do exist and cease to be;
> Here I disclaim all my paternal care,
> Propinquity and property of blood,
> And as a stranger to my heart and me
> Hold thee from this for ever. The barbarous Scythian,
> Or he that makes his generation messes
> To gorge his appetite, shall to my bosom
> Be as well neighbour'd, pitied and relieved,
> As thou my sometime daughter.

Now the dramatic effect of this passage is exactly, and doubtless intentionally, repeated in the curse pronounced against Goneril. This does not come after the daughters have openly and wholly turned against their father. Up to the moment of its utterance Goneril has done no more than to require him 'a little to disquantity' and reform his train of knights. Certainly her manner and spirit in making this demand are hateful, and probably her accusations against the knights are false; and we should expect from any father in Lear's position passionate distress and indignation. But surely the famous words which form Lear's immediate reply were meant to be nothing short of frightful:

> Hear, nature, hear; dear goddess, hear!
> Suspend thy purpose, if thou didst intend
> To make this creature fruitful!
> Into her womb convey sterility!
> Dry up in her the organs of increase;
> And from her derogate body never spring
> A babe to honour her! If she must teem,
> Create her child of spleen; that it may live,
> And be a thwart disnatured torment to her!
> Let it stamp wrinkles in her brow of youth;
> With cadent tears fret channels in her cheeks;

Turn all her mother's pains and benefits
To laughter and contempt; that she may feel
How sharper than a serpent's tooth it is
To have a thankless child!

The question is not whether Goneril deserves these appalling impre-
cations, but what they tell us about Lear. They show that, although he
has already recognized his injustice towards Cordelia, is secretly blaming himself, and is endeavouring to do better, the disposition from
which his first error sprang is still unchanged. And it is precisely the
disposition to give rise, in evil surroundings, to calamities dreadful
but at the same time tragic, because due in some measure to the
person who endures them.

The perception of this connection, if it is not lost as the play
advances, does not at all diminish our pity for Lear, but it makes it
impossible for us permanently to regard the world displayed in this
tragedy as subject to a mere arbitrary or malicious power. It makes us
feel that this world is so far at least a rational and a moral order, that
there holds in it the law, not of proportionate requital, but of strict
connection between act and consequence. It is, so far, the world of all
Shakespeare's tragedies.

But there is another aspect of Lear's story, the influence of which
modifies, in a way quite different and more peculiar to this tragedy,
the impressions called pessimistic and even this impression of law.
There is nothing more noble and beautiful in literature than
Shakespeare's exposition of the effect of suffering in reviving the greatness and eliciting the sweetness of Lear's nature. The occasional recurrence, during his madness, of autocratic impatience or of desire for
revenge serves only to heighten this effect, and the moments when his
insanity becomes merely infinitely piteous do not weaken it. The old
King who in pleading with his daughters feels so intensely his own
humiliation and their horrible ingratitude, and who yet, at fourscore
and upward, constrains himself to practise a self-control and patience
so many years disused; who out of old affection for his Fool, and in
repentance for his injustice to the Fool's beloved mistress, tolerates
incessant and cutting reminders of his own folly and wrong; in whom
the rage of the storm awakes a power and a poetic grandeur surpass-
ing even that of Othello's anguish; who comes in his affliction to
think of others first, and to seek, in tender solicitude for his poor boy,

the shelter he scorns for his own bare head; who learns to feel and to pray for the miserable and houseless poor, to discern the falseness of flattery and the brutality of authority, and to pierce below the differences of rank and raiment to the common humanity beneath; whose sight is so purged by scalding tears that it sees at last how power and place and all things in the world are vanity except love; who tastes in his last hours the extremes both of love's rapture and of its agony, but could never, if he lived on or lived again, care a jot for aught beside – there is no figure, surely, in the world of poetry at once so grand, so pathetic, and so beautiful as his. Well, but Lear owes the whole of this to those sufferings which made us doubt whether life were not simply evil, and men like the flies which wanton boys torture for their sport. Should we not be at least as near the truth if we called this poem *The Redemption of King Lear*, and declared that the business of 'the gods' with him was neither to torment him, nor to teach him a 'noble anger', but to lead him to attain through apparently hopeless failure the very end and aim of life? One can believe that Shakespeare had been tempted at times to feel misanthropy and despair, but it is quite impossible that he can have been mastered by such feelings at the time when he produced this conception.

To dwell on the stages of this process of purification (the word is Professor Dowden's) is impossible here; and there are scenes, such as that of the meeting of Lear and Cordelia, which it seems almost a profanity to touch.[2] But I will refer to two scenes which may remind us more in detail of some of the points just mentioned. The third and fourth scenes of Act III. present one of those contrasts which speak as eloquently even as Shakespeare's words, and which were made possible in his theatre by the absence of scenery and the consequent absence of intervals between the scenes. First, in a scene of twenty-three lines, mostly in prose, Gloster is shown, telling his son Edmund how Goneril and Regan have forbidden him on pain of death to succour the houseless King; how a secret letter has reached him, announcing the arrival of a French force; and how, whatever the consequences may be, he is determined to relieve his old master. Edmund, left alone, soliloquizes in words which seem to freeze one's blood:

---

[2] I must however point out that the modern stage-directions are most unfortunate in concealing the fact that here Cordelia sees her father again *for the first time*. See Note W.

This courtesy, forbid thee, shall the duke
Instantly know; and of that letter too:
This seems a fair deserving, and must draw me
That which my father loses; no less than all:
The younger rises when the old doth fall.

He goes out; and the next moment, as the fourth scene opens, we find ourselves in the icy storm with Lear, Kent and the Fool, and yet in the inmost shrine of love. I am not speaking of the devotion of the others to Lear, but of Lear himself. He had consented, merely for the Fool's sake, to seek shelter in the hovel:

Come, your hovel.
Poor fool and knave, I have one part in my heart
That's sorry for thee.

But on the way he has broken down and has been weeping (III.iv. 17), and now he resists Kent's efforts to persuade him to enter. He does not feel the storm:

when the mind's free
The body's delicate: the tempest in my mind
Doth from my senses take all feeling else
Save what beats there:

and the thoughts that will drive him mad are burning in his brain:

Filial ingratitude!
Is it not as this mouth should tear this hand
For lifting food to't? But I will punish home.
No, I will weep no more. In such a night
To shut me out! Pour on; I will endure.
In such a night as this! O Regan, Goneril!
Your old kind father, whose frank heart gave all, –
O, that way madness lies; let me shun that;
No more of that.

And then suddenly, as he controls himself, the blessed spirit of kindness breathes on him 'like a meadow gale of spring', and he turns gently to Kent:

Prithee, go in thyself; seek thine own ease:
This tempest will not give me leave to ponder
On things would hurt me more. But I'll go in.
In, boy; go first. You houseless poverty –
Nay, get thee in. I'll pray, and then I'll sleep.

But his prayer is not for himself.

> Poor naked wretches, whereso'er you are,

it begins, and I need not quote more. This is one of those passages which make one worship Shakespeare.[3]

Much has been written on the representation of insanity in *King Lear*, and I will confine myself to one or two points which may have escaped notice. The most obvious symptom of Lear's insanity, especially in its first stages, is of course the domination of a fixed idea. Whatever presents itself to his senses, is seized on by this idea and compelled to express it; as for example in those words, already quoted, which first show that his mind has actually given way:

> Hast thou given all
> To thy two daughters? And art thou come to this?[4]

But it is remarkable that what we have here is only, in an exaggerated and perverted form, the very same action of imagination that, just before the breakdown of reason, produced those sublime appeals:

> O heavens,
> If you do love old men, if your sweet sway
> Allow obedience, if yourselves are old,
> Make it your cause;

---

[3] What immediately follows is as striking an illustration of quite another quality, and of the effects which make us think of Lear as pursued by a relentless fate. If he could go in and sleep after his prayer, as he intends, one feels, might be saved: so far there has been only the menace of madness. But from within the hovel Edgar – the last man who would willingly have injured Lear – cries, 'Fathom and half, fathom and half! Poor Tom!'; the Fool runs out terrified; Edgar, summoned by Kent, follows him; and, at sight of Edgar, in a moment something gives way in Lear's brain, and he exclaims:

> Hast thou given all
> To thy two daughters? And art thou come to this?

Henceforth he is mad. And they remain out in the storm.

I have not seen it noticed that this stroke of fate is repeated – surely intentionally – in the sixth scene. Gloster has succeeded in persuading Lear to come into the 'house'; he then leaves, and Kent after much difficulty induces Lear to lie down and rest upon the cushions. Sleep begins to come to him again, and he murmurs,

> 'Make no noise, make no noise; draw the curtains; so, so, so. We'll go to supper i' the morning. So, so, so.'

At that moment Gloster enters with the news that he has discovered a plot to kill the King; the rest that 'might yet have balm'd his broken senses' is again interrupted; and he is hurried away on a litter. (His recovery, it will be remembered, is due to a long sleep artificially induced.)

[4] III.iv.49. This is [1904] printed as prose in the Globe edition, but is surely verse. Lear has not yet spoken prose in this scene, and his next three speeches are in verse. The next is in prose, and, ending in his tearing off his clothes, shows the advance of insanity.

and:

> Rumble thy bellyful! Spit, fire! spout, rain!
> Nor rain, wind, thunder, fire, are my daughters:
> I tax not you, you elements, with unkindness;
> I never gave you kingdom, call'd you children,
> You owe me no subscription: then let fall
> Your horrible pleasure; here I stand, your slave,
> A poor, infirm, weak, and despised old man:
> But yet I call you servile ministers,
> That have with two pernicious daughters join'd
> Your high engender'd battles 'gainst a head
> So old and white as this. O! O! 'tis foul!

Shakespeare, long before this, in the *Midsummer Night's Dream*, had noticed the resemblance between the lunatic, the lover, and the poet; and the partial truth that genius is allied to insanity was quite familiar to him. But he presents here the supplementary half-truth that insanity is allied to genius.

He does not, however, put into the mouth of the insane Lear any such sublime passages as those just quoted. Lear's insanity, which destroys the coherence, also reduces the poetry of his imagination. What it stimulates is that power of moral perception and reflection which had already been quickened by his sufferings. This, however partial and however disconnectedly used, first appears, quite soon after the insanity has declared itself, in the idea that the naked beggar represents truth and reality, in contrast with those conventions, flatteries, and corruptions of the great world, by which Lear has so long been deceived and will never be deceived again:

> Is man no more than this? Consider him well. Thou owest the worm no
> silk, the beast no hide, the sheep no wool, the cat no perfume. Ha! here's
> three on's are sophisticated: thou art the thing itself.

Lear regards the beggar therefore with reverence and delight, as a person who is in the secret of things, and he longs to question him about their causes. It is this same strain of thought which much later (IV.vi.), gaining far greater force, though the insanity has otherwise advanced, issues in those famous Timon-like speeches which make us realize the original strength of the old King's mind. And when this strain, on his recovery, unites with the streams of repentance and love, it produces that serene renunciation of the world, with its power and glory and resentments and revenges, which is expressed in the speech (V.iii.):

> No, no, no, no! Come, let's away to prison:
> We two alone will sing like birds i' the cage:
> When thou dost ask me blessing, I'll kneel down,
> And ask of thee forgiveness: so we'll live,
> And pray, and sing, and tell old tales, and laugh
> At gilded butterflies, and hear poor rogues
> Talk of court news; and we'll talk with them too.
> Who loses, and who wins; who's in, who's out;
> And take upon's the mystery of things,
> As if we were God's spies: and we'll wear out,
> In a wall'd prison, packs and sets of great ones,
> That ebb and flow by the moon.

This is that renunciation which is at the same time a sacrifice offered to the gods, and on which the gods themselves throw incense; and, it may be, it would never have been offered but for the knowledge that came to Lear in his madness.

I spoke of Lear's 'recovery', but the word is too strong. The Lear of the Fifth Act is not indeed insane, but his mind is greatly enfeebled. The speech just quoted is followed by a sudden flash of the old passionate nature, reminding us most pathetically of Lear's efforts, just before his madness, to restrain his tears:

> Wipe thine eyes:
> The good-years shall devour them, flesh and fell,
> Ere they shall make us weep: we'll see 'em starve first.

And this weakness is still more pathetically shown in the blindness of the old King to his position now that he and Cordelia are made prisoners. It is evident that Cordelia knows well what mercy her father is likely to receive from her sisters; that is the reason of her weeping. But he does not understand her tears; it never crosses his mind that they have anything more than imprisonment to fear. And what is that to them? They have made that sacrifice, and all is well:

> Have I caught thee?
> He that parts us shall bring a brand from heaven,
> And fire us hence like foxes.

This blindness is most affecting to us, who know in what manner they will be parted; but it is also comforting. And we find the same mingling of effects in the overwhelming conclusion of the story. If to the reader, as to the bystanders, that scene brings one unbroken pain, it is not so with Lear himself. His shattered mind passes from the first transports of hope and despair, as he bends over Cordelia's body and holds the feather to her lips, into an absolute forgetfulness of the cause of these transports. This continues so long as he can converse with Kent; becomes an almost complete vacancy; and is disturbed only to yield, as his eyes suddenly fall again on his child's corpse, to an agony which at once breaks his heart. And, finally, though he is killed by an agony of pain, the agony in which he actually dies is one not of pain but of ecstasy. Suddenly, with a cry represented in the oldest text by a four-times repeated 'O', he exclaims:

> Do you see this? Look on her, look, her lips,
> Look there, look there!

These are the last words of Lear. He is sure, at last, that she *lives*: and what had he said when he was still in doubt?

> She lives! if it be so,
> It is a chance which does redeem all sorrows
> That ever I have felt!

To us, perhaps, the knowledge that he is deceived may bring a culmination of pain: but, if it brings *only* that, I believe we are false to Shakespeare, and it seems almost beyond question that any actor is false to the text who does not attempt to express, in Lear's last accents and gestures and look, an unbearable *joy*.[5]

---

[5] [Lear's death is thus, I am reminded, like *père* Goriot's.] This interpretation may be condemned as fantastic, but the text, it appears to me, will bear no other. This is the whole speech (in the Globe* text):

> And my poor fool is hang'd! No, no, no life!
> Why should a dog, a horse, a rat, have life,
> And thou no breath at all? Thou'lt come no more,
> Never, never, never, never, never!
> Pray you, undo this button: thank you, sir.
> Do you see this? Look on her, look, her lips,
> Look there, look there!

The transition at 'Do you see this?' from despair to something more than hope is exactly the same as in the preceding passage at the word 'Ha!':

> A plague upon you, murderers, traitors all!
> I might have saved her; now she's gone for ever!

To dwell on the pathos of Lear's last speech would be an impertinence, but I may add a remark on the speech from the literary point of view. In the simplicity of its language, which consists almost wholly of monosyllables of native origin, composed in very brief sentences of the plainest structure, it presents an extraordinary contrast to the dying speech of Hamlet and the last words of Othello to the bystanders. The fact that Lear speaks in passion is one cause of the difference, but not the sole cause. The language is more than simple, it is familiar. And this familiarity is characteristic of Lear (except at certain moments, already referred to) from the time of his madness onwards, and is the source of the peculiarly poignant effect of some of his sentences (such as 'The little dogs and all . . .'). We feel in them the loss of power to sustain his royal dignity; we feel also that everything external has become nothingness to him, and that what remains is 'the thing itself', the soul in its bare greatness. Hence also it is that two lines in this last speech show, better perhaps than any other passage of poetry, one of the qualities we have in mind when we distinguish poetry as 'romantic'. Nothing like Hamlet's mysterious sigh 'The rest is silence', nothing like Othello's memories of his life of marvel and achievement, was possible to Lear. Those last thoughts are romantic in their strangeness: Lear's five-times repeated 'Never', in which the simplest and most unanswerable cry of anguish rises note by note till the heart breaks, is romantic in its naturalism; and to make a verse out of this one word required the boldness as well as the inspiration which came infallibly to Shakespeare at the greatest moments. But the familiarity, boldness and inspiration are surpassed (if that can be) by the next line, which shows the bodily oppression asking for bodily relief. The imagination that produced Lear's curse or his defiance of the storm may be paralleled in its kind, but where else are we

---

Cordelia, Cordelia, stay a little.
Ha!
What is't thou say'st? Her voice was ever soft,
Gentle, and low, an excellent thing in woman.

As to any other remarks, I will ask the reader to notice that the passage from Lear's entrance with the body of Cordelia to the stage-direction *He dies* (which probably comes a few lines too soon) is 54 lines in length, and that 30 of them represent the interval during which he has absolutely forgotten Cordelia. (It begins when he looks up at the Captain's words, line 275.) To make Lear during this interval turn continually in anguish to the corpse, is to act the passage in a manner irreconcilable with the text, and insufferable in its effect. I speak from experience. I have seen the passage acted thus, and my sympathies were so exhausted long before Lear's death that his last speech, the most pathetic speech ever written, left me disappointed and weary.

to seek the imagination that could venture to follow that cry of
'Never' with such a phrase as 'undo this button', and yet could leave
us on the topmost peaks of poetry?[6]

2

Gloster and Albany are the two neutral characters of the tragedy. The
parallel between Lear and Gloster, already noticed, is, up to a certain
point, so marked that it cannot possibly be accidental. Both are old
white-haired men (III.vii.37); both, it would seem, widowers, with
children comparatively young. Like Lear, Gloster is tormented, and
his life is sought, by the child whom he favours; he is tended and
healed by the child whom he has wronged. His sufferings, like Lear's,
are partly traceable to his own extreme folly and injustice, and, it may
be added, to a selfish pursuit of his own pleasure.[7] His sufferings,
again, like Lear's, purify and enlighten him: he dies a better and wiser
man than he showed himself at first. They even learn the same lesson,
and Gloster's repetition (noticed and blamed by Johnson) of the
thought in a famous speech of Lear's is surely intentional.[8] And,

---

[6] The Quartos give the 'Never' only thrice (surely wrongly), and all the actors I have heard
have preferred this easier task. I ought perhaps to add that the Quartos give the words 'Break,
heart; I prithee, break!' to Lear, not Kent. They and the Folio are at odds throughout the last
sixty lines of *King Lear*, and all good modern texts are eclectic.

[7] The connection of these sufferings with the sin of earlier days (not, it should be noticed,
of youth) is almost thrust upon our notice by the levity of Gloster's own reference to the subject
in the first scene, and by Edgar's often quoted words 'The gods are just', etc. The following
collocation, also, may be intentional (III.iv.116):

> *Fool.* Now a little fire in a wild field were like an old lecher's heart; a small spark, all the
> rest on's body cold. Look, here comes a walking fire. [*Enter* GLOSTER with a torch.]

Pope destroyed the collocation by transferring the stage-direction to a point some dozen lines
later.

[8] The passages are here printed together (III.iv.28 ff. and IV.i.67 ff.):

> *Lear.* Poor naked wretches, whereso'er you are,
> That bide the pelting of this pitiless storm,
> How shall your houseless heads and unfed sides,
> Your loop'd and window'd raggedness, defend you
> From seasons such as these? O, I have ta'en
> Too little care of this! Take physic, pomp;
> Expose thyself to feel what wretches feel,
> That thou mayst shake the superflux to them,
> And show the heavens just.
>   *Glo.* Here, take this purse, thou whom the heavens' plagues
> Have humbled to all strokes: that I am wretched

finally, Gloster dies almost as Lear dies. Edgar reveals himself to him and asks his blessing (as Cordelia asks Lear's)

> but his flaw'd heart –
> Alack, too weak the conflict to support –
> 'Twixt two extremes of passion, joy and grief,
> Burst smilingly.

So far, the resemblance of the two stories, and also of the ways in which their painful effect is modified, is curiously close. And in character too Gloster is, like his master, affectionate,[9] credulous and hasty. But otherwise he is sharply contrasted with the tragic Lear, who is a towering figure, every inch a king,[10] while Gloster is built on a much smaller scale, and has infinitely less force and fire. He is, indeed, a decidedly weak though good-hearted man; and, failing wholly to support Kent in resisting Lear's original folly and injustice,[11] he only gradually takes the better part. Nor is his character either very interesting or very distinct. He often gives one the impression of being wanted mainly to fill a place in the scheme of the play; and, though it would be easy to give a long list of his characteristics, they scarcely, it seems to me, compose an individual, a person whom we are sure we should recognize at once. If this is so, the fact is curious, considering how much we see and hear of him.

I will add a single note. Gloster is the superstitious character of the drama – the only one. He thinks much of 'these late eclipses in the sun and moon'. His two sons, from opposite points of view, make

---

Makes thee the happier: heavens, deal so still!
Let the superfluous and lust-dieted man,
That slaves your ordinance, that will not see
Because he cloth not feel, feel your power quickly;
So distribution should undo excess,
And each man have enough.

[9] Schmidt's idea* – based partly on the omission from the Folios at I.ii.103 (see Furness' Variorum) of the words 'To his father that so tenderly and entirely loves him' – that Gloster loved neither of his sons, is surely an entire mistake. See, not to speak of general impressions, III.iv.171 ff.

[10] Imagination demands for Lear, even more than for Othello, majesty of stature and mien. Tourgénief felt this and made his 'Lear of the Steppes' a *gigantic* peasant. If Shakespeare's texts give no express authority for ideas like these, the reason probably is that he wrote primarily for the theatre, where the principal actor might not be a large man.

[11] He is not present, of course, till France and Burgundy enter; but while he is present he says not a word beyond 'Here's France and Burgundy, my noble lord'. For some remarks on the possibility that Shakespeare imagined him as having encouraged Lear in his idea of dividing the kingdom see Note T. It must be remembered that Cornwall was Gloster's 'arch and patron'.

nothing of them. His easy acceptance of the calumny against Edgar is partly due to this weakness, and Edmund builds upon it, for an evil purpose, when he describes Edgar thus:

> Here stood he in the dark, his sharp sword out,
> Mumbling of wicked charms, conjuring the moon,
> To prove's auspicious mistress.

Edgar in turn builds upon it, for a good purpose, when he persuades his blind father that he was led to jump down Dover cliff by the temptation of a fiend in the form of a beggar, and was saved by a miracle:

> As I stood here below, methought his eyes
> Were two full moons; he had a thousand noses,
> Horns whelk'd and waved like the enridged sea:
> It was some fiend; therefore, thou happy father,
> Think that the clearest gods, who make them honours
> Of men's impossibilities, have preserved thee.

This passage is odd in its collocation of the thousand noses and the clearest gods, of grotesque absurdity and extreme seriousness. Edgar knew that the 'fiend' was really Gloster's 'worser spirit', and that 'the gods' were himself. Doubtless, however – for he is the most religious person in the play – he thought that it *was* the gods who, through him, had preserved his father; but he knew that the truth could only enter this superstitious mind in a superstitious form.

The combination of parallelism and contrast that we observe in Lear and Gloster, and again in the attitude of the two brothers to their father's superstition, is one of many indications that in *King Lear* Shakespeare was working more than usual on a basis of conscious and reflective ideas. Perhaps it is not by accident, then, that he makes Edgar and Lear preach to Gloster in precisely the same strain. Lear says to him:

> If thou wilt weep my fortunes, take my eyes.
> I know thee well enough; thy name is Gloster:
> Thou must be patient; we came crying hither:
> Thou know'st, the first time that we smell the air,
> We wawl and cry. I will preach to thee: mark.

Edgar's last words to him are:

> What, in ill thoughts again? Men must endure

Their going hence, even as their coming hither:
Ripeness is all.

Albany is merely sketched, and he is so generally neglected that a few words about him may be in place. He too ends a better and wiser man than he began. When the play opens he is, of course, only just married to Goneril; and the idea is, I think, that he has been bewitched by her fiery beauty not less than by her dowry. He is an inoffensive peace-loving man, and is overborne at first by his 'great love' for his wife and by her imperious will. He is not free from responsibility for the treatment which the King receives in his house; the Knight says to Lear, 'there's a great abatement of kindness appears as well in the general dependants as in *the duke himself also* and your daughter'. But he takes no part in the quarrel, and doubtless speaks truly when he protests that he is as guiltless as ignorant of the cause of Lear's violent passion. When the King departs, he begins to remonstrate with Goneril, but shrinks in a cowardly manner, which is a trifle comical, from contest with her. She leaves him behind when she goes to join Regan, and he is not further responsible for what follows. When he hears of it, he is struck with horror: the scales drop from his eyes, Goneril becomes hateful to him, he determines to revenge Gloster's eyes. His position is however very difficult, as he is willing to fight against Cordelia in so far as her army is French, and unwilling in so far as she represents her father. This difficulty, and his natural inferiority to Edmund in force and ability, pushes him into the background; the battle is not won by him but by Edmund; and but for Edgar he would certainly have fallen a victim to the murderous plot against him. When it is discovered, however, he is fearless and resolute enough, besides being full of kind feeling towards Kent and Edgar, and of sympathetic distress at Gloster's death. And one would be sure that he is meant to retain this strength till the end, but for his last words. He has announced his intention of resigning, during Lear's life, the 'absolute power' which has come to him; and that may be right. But after Lear's death he says to Kent and Edgar:

> Friends of my soul, you twain
> Rule in this realm, and the gored state sustain.

If this means that he wishes to hand over his absolute power to them, Shakespeare's intention is certainly to mark the feebleness of a well-meaning but weak man. But possibly he means by 'this realm' only that half of Britain which had belonged to Cornwall and Regan.

3

I turn now to those two strongly contrasted groups of good and evil beings; and to the evil first. The members of this group are by no means on a level. Far the most contemptible of them is Oswald, and Kent has fortunately expressed our feelings towards him. Yet twice we are able to feel sympathy with him. Regan cannot tempt him to let her open Goneril's letter to Edmund; and his last thought as he dies is given to the fulfilment of his trust. It is to a monster that he is faithful, and he is faithful to her in a monstrous design. Still faithfulness is faithfulness, and he is not wholly worthless. Dr. Johnson says: 'I know not well why Shakespeare gives to Oswald, who is a mere factor of wickedness, so much fidelity'; but in any other tragedy this touch, so true to human nature, is only what we should expect. If it surprises us in *King Lear*, the reason is that Shakespeare, in dealing with the other members of the group, seems to have been less concerned than usual with such mingling of light with darkness, and intent rather on making the shadows as utterly black as a regard for truth would permit.

Cornwall seems to have been a fit mate for Regan; and what worse can be said of him? It is a great satisfaction to think that he endured what to him must have seemed the dreadful disgrace of being killed by a servant. He shows, I believe, no redeeming trait, and he is a coward, as may be seen from the sudden rise in his courage when Goneril arrives at the castle and supports him and Regan against Lear (II.iv.202). But as his cruelties are not aimed at a blood-relation, he is not, in this sense, a 'monster', like the remaining three.

Which of these three is the least and which the most detestable there can surely be no question. For Edmund, not to mention other alleviations, is at any rate not a woman. And the differences between the sisters, which are distinctly marked and need not be exhibited once more in full, are all in favour of 'the elder and more terrible'. That Regan did not commit adultery, did not murder her sister or plot to murder her husband, did not join her name with Edmund's on the order for the deaths of Cordelia and Lear, and in other respects failed to take quite so active a part as Goneril in atrocious wickedness, is quite true but not in the least to her credit. It only means that she had much less force, courage and initiative than her sister, and for that reason is less formidable and more loathsome. Edmund judged right when, caring for neither sister but aiming at the crown, he preferred Goneril, for he could trust her to remove the living impediments to her desires. The scornful and fearless exclamation, 'An interlude!' with which she greets the exposure of her design, was quite beyond Regan. Her unhesitating suicide was perhaps no less so. She would not have condescended to the lie which Regan so needlessly tells to Oswald:

> It was great ignorance, Gloster's eyes being out,
> To let him live: where he arrives he moves
> All hearts against us: Edmund, I think, is gone,
> *In pity of his misery*, to dispatch
> His nighted life.

Her father's curse is nothing to her. She scorns even to mention the gods.[12] Horrible as she is, she is almost awful. But, to set against Regan's inferiority in power, there is nothing: she is superior only in a venomous meanness which is almost as hateful as her cruelty. She is the most hideous human being (if she is one) that Shakespeare ever drew.

I have already noticed the resemblance between Edmund and Iago in one point; and Edmund recalls his greater forerunner also in courage, strength of will, address, egoism, an abnormal want of feeling, and the possession of a sense of humour. But here the likeness ends. Indeed a decided difference is observable even in the humour. Edmund is apparently a good deal younger than Iago. He has a lighter and more superficial nature, and there is a certain genuine gaiety in him which makes one smile not unsympathetically as one listens to his first soliloquy, with its cheery conclusion, so unlike Iago's references to the powers of darkness,

---

[12] In this she stands alone among the more notable characters of the play. Doubtless Regan's exclamation 'O the blest gods' means nothing, but the fact that it is given to her means something. For some further remarks on Goneril see Note T. I may add that touches of Goneril reappear in the heroine of the next tragedy, *Macbeth*; and that we are sometimes reminded of her again by the character of the Queen in *Cymbeline*, who bewitched the feeble King by her beauty, and married him for greatness while she abhorred his person (*Cymbeline*, V.v.62 f., 31 f.); who tried to poison her step-daughter and intended to poison her husband; who died despairing because she could not execute all the evil she purposed; and who inspirited her husband to defy the Romans by words that still stir the blood (*Cymbeline*, III.i.14 f. Cf. *King Lear*, IV.ii.50 f.).

Now, gods, stand up for bastards!

Even after we have witnessed his dreadful deeds, a touch of this sympathy is felt again when we hear his nonchalant reflections before the battle:

> To both these sisters have I sworn my love:
> Each jealous of the other, as the stung
> Are of the adder. Which of them shall I take?
> Both? one? or neither?

Besides, there is nothing in Edmund of Iago's motive-hunting and very little of any of the secret forces which impelled Iago. He is comparatively a straightforward character, as straightforward as the Iago of some critics. He moves wonder and horror merely because the fact that a man so young can have a nature so bad is a dark mystery.

Edmund is an adventurer pure and simple. He acts in pursuance of a purpose, and, if he has any affections or dislikes, ignores them. He is determined to make his way, first to his brother's lands, then – as the prospect widens – to the crown; and he regards men and women, with their virtues and vices, together with the bonds of kinship, friendship, or allegiance, merely as hindrances or helps to his end. They are for him divested of all quality except their relation to this end; as indifferent as mathematical quantities or mere physical agents.

> A credulous father and a brother noble,
> . . . I see the business,

he says, as if he were talking of x and y.

> This seems a fair deserving, and must draw me
> That which my father loses; no less than all:
> The younger rises when the old doth fall:

he meditates, as if he were considering a problem in mechanics. He preserves this attitude with perfect consistency until the possibility of attaining his end is snatched from him by death.

Like the deformity of Richard, Edmund's illegitimacy furnishes, of course, no excuse for his villainy, but it somewhat influences our feelings. It is no fault of his, and yet it separates him from other men. He is the product of Nature – of a natural appetite asserting itself against the social order; and he has no recognized place within this order. So he devotes himself to Nature, whose law is that of the stronger, and who does not recognize those moral obligations which exist only by convention – by 'custom' or 'the curiosity of nations'.[13] Practically, his attitude is that of a professional criminal. 'You tell me I do not belong to you,' he seems to say to society: 'very well: I will make my way into your treasure-house if I can. And if I have to take life in doing so, that is your affair.' How far he is serious in this attitude, and really indignant at the brand of bastardy, how far his indignation is a half-conscious self-excuse for his meditated villainy, it is hard to say; but the end shows that he is not entirely in earnest.

As he is an adventurer, with no more ill-will to anyone than good-will, it is natural that, when he has lost the game, he should accept his failure without showing personal animosity. But he does more. He admits the truth of Edgar's words about the justice of the gods, and applies them to his own case (though the fact that he himself refers to fortune's wheel rather than to the gods may be significant). He shows too that he is not destitute of feeling; for he is touched by the story of his father's death, and at last 'pants for life' in the effort to do 'some good' by saving Lear and Cordelia. There is something pathetic here which tempts one to dream that, if Edmund had been whole brother to Edgar, and had been at home during those 'nine years' when he was 'out', he might have been a very different man. But perhaps his words,

> Some good I mean to do,
> *Despite of mine own nature,*

suggest rather that Shakespeare is emphasizing the mysterious fact, commented on by Kent in the case of the three daughters of Lear, of an immense original difference between children of one father. Stranger than this emergence of better feelings, and curiously pathetic, is the pleasure of the dying man in the thought that he was loved by both the women whose corpses are almost the last sight he is to see. Perhaps, as we conjectured, the cause of his delay in saving Lear and Cordelia even after he hears of the deaths of the sisters is that he is sunk in dreamy reflections on his past. When he murmurs, 'Yet Edmund was beloved', one is almost in danger of forgetting that he

---

[13] I.ii.1 f. Shakespeare seems to have in mind the idea expressed in the speech of Ulysses about the dependence of the world on degree, order, system, custom, and about the chaos which would result from the free action of appetite, the 'universal wolf' (*Troilus and Cr.* I.iii.83 f.). Cf. the contrast between 'particular will' and 'the moral laws of nature and of nations', II.ii.53, 185 ('nature' here of course is the opposite of the 'nature' of Edmund's speech).

had done much more than reject the love of his father and half-brother. The passage is one of several in Shakespeare's plays where it strikes us that he is recording some fact about human nature with which he had actually met, and which had seemed to him peculiarly strange.

What are we to say of the world which contains these five beings, Goneril, Regan, Edmund, Cornwall, Oswald? I have tried to answer this question in our first lecture; for in its representation of evil *King Lear* differs from the other tragedies only in degree and manner. It is the tragedy in which evil is shown in the greatest abundance; and the evil characters are peculiarly repellent from their hard savagery, and because so little good is mingled with their evil. The effect is therefore more startling than elsewhere; it is even appalling. But in substance it is the same as elsewhere; and accordingly, although it may be useful to recall here our previous discussion, I will do so only by the briefest statement.

On the one hand we see a world which generates terrible evil in profusion. Further, the beings in whom this evil appears at its strongest are able, to a certain extent, to thrive. They are not unhappy, and they have power to spread misery and destruction around them. All this is undeniable fact.

On the other hand this evil is *merely* destructive: it founds nothing, and seems capable of existing only on foundations laid by its opposite. It is also self-destructive: it sets those beings at enmity; they can scarcely unite against a common and pressing danger; if it were averted they would be at each other's throats in a moment; the sisters do not even wait till it is past. Finally, these beings, all five of them, are dead a few weeks after we see them first; three at least die young; the outburst of their evil is fatal to them. These also are undeniable facts; and, in face of them, it seems odd to describe *King Lear* as 'a play in which the wicked prosper' (Johnson).

Thus the world in which evil appears seems to be at heart unfriendly to it. And this impression is confirmed by the fact that the convulsion of this world is due to evil, mainly in the worst forms here considered, partly in the milder forms which we call the errors or defects of the better characters. Good, in the widest sense, seems thus to be the principle of life and health in the world; evil, at least in these worst forms, to be a poison. The world reacts against it violently, and, in the struggle to expel it, is driven to devastate itself.

If we ask why the world should generate that which convulses and wastes it, the tragedy gives no answer, and we are trying to go beyond tragedy in seeking one. But the world, in this tragic picture, is convulsed by evil, and rejects it.

4

And if here there is 'very Night herself', she comes 'with stars in her raiment'. Cordelia, Kent, Edgar, the Fool – these form a group not less remarkable than that which we have just left. There is in the world of *King Lear* the same abundance of extreme good as of extreme evil. It generates in profusion selfless devotion and unconquerable love. And the strange thing is that neither Shakespeare nor we are surprised. We approve these characters, admire them, love them; but we feel no mystery. We do not ask in bewilderment, Is there any cause in nature that makes these kind hearts? Such hardened optimists are we, and Shakespeare – and those who find the darkness of revelation in a tragedy which reveals Cordelia. Yet surely, if we condemn the universe for Cordelia's death, we ought also to remember that it gave her birth. The fact that Socrates was executed does not remove the fact that he lived, and the inference thence to be drawn about the world that produced him.

Of these four characters Edgar excites the least enthusiasm, but he is the one whose development is the most marked. His behaviour in the early part of the play, granted that it is not too improbable, is so foolish as to provoke one. But he learns by experience, and becomes the most capable person in the story, without losing any of his purity and nobility of mind. There remain in him, however, touches which a little chill one's feeling for him.

> The gods are just, and of our pleasant vices
> Make instruments to plague us:
> The dark and vicious place where thee he got
> Cost him his eyes:

– one wishes he had not said to his dying brother those words about their dead father. 'The gods are just' would have been enough.[14] It

---

[14] The line last quoted is continued by Edmund in the Folios thus: 'Th' hast spoken right; 'tis true,' but in the Quartos thus: 'Thou hast spoken truth,' which leaves the line

may be suggested that Shakespeare merely wished to introduce this moral somehow, and did not mean the speech to be characteristic of the speaker. But I doubt this: he might well have delivered it through Albany, if he was determined to deliver it. This trait in Edgar *is* characteristic. It seems to be connected with his pronounced and conscious religiousness. He interprets everything religiously, and is speaking here from an intense conviction which overrides personal feelings. With this religiousness, on the other side, is connected his cheerful and confident endurance, and his practical helpfulness and resource. He never thinks of despairing; in the worst circumstances he is sure there is something to be done to make things better. And he is sure of this, not only from temperament, but from faith in 'the clearest gods'. He is the man on whom we are to rely at the end for the recovery and welfare of the state: and we do rely on him.

I spoke of his temperament. There is in Edgar, with much else that is fine, something of that buoyancy of spirit which charms us in Imogen. Nothing can subdue in him the feeling that life is sweet and must be cherished. At his worst, misconstrued, contemned, exiled, under sentence of death, 'the lowest and most dejected thing of fortune', he keeps his head erect. The inextinguishable spirit of youth and delight is in him; he *embraces* the unsubstantial air which has blown him to the worst; for him 'the worst returns to laughter'.[15] 'Bear free and patient thoughts,' he says to his father. His own thoughts are more than patient, they are 'free', even joyous, in spite of the tender sympathies which strive in vain to overwhelm him. This ability to feel and offer great sympathy with distress, without losing through the sympathy any elasticity or strength, is a noble quality, sometimes found in souls like Edgar's, naturally buoyant and also religious. It may even be characteristic of him that, when Lear is sinking down in death, he tries to rouse him and bring him back to life. 'Look up, my lord!' he cries. It is Kent who feels that

---

imperfect. This, and the imperfect line 'Make instruments to plague us', suggest that Shakespeare wrote at first simply,

> Make instruments to plague us.
> *Edm.*   Th' hast spoken truth.

The Quartos show other variations which seem to point to the fact that the MS. was here difficult to make out.

[15] IV.i.1–9. I am indebted here to Koppel,* *Verbesserungsvorschläge zu den Erläuterungen und der Textlesung des Lear* (1899).

> he hates him,
> That would upon the rack of this tough world
> Stretch him out longer.

Kent is one of the best-loved characters in Shakespeare. He is beloved for his own sake, and also for the sake of Cordelia and of Lear. We are grateful to him because he stands up for Cordelia, and because, when she is out of sight, he constantly keeps her in our minds. And how well these two love each other we see when they meet. Yet it is not Cordelia who is dearest to Kent. His love for Lear is the passion of his life: it is his life. At the beginning he braves Lear's wrath even more for Lear's sake than Cordelia's.[16] At the end he seems to realize Cordelia's death only as it is reflected in Lear's agony. Nor does he merely love his master passionately, as Cordelia loves her father. That word 'master', and Kent's appeal to the 'authority' he saw in the old King's face, are significant. He belongs to Lear, body and soul, as a dog does to his master and god. The King is not to him old, wayward, unreasonable, piteous: he is still terrible, grand, the king of men. Through his eyes we see the Lear of Lear's prime, whom Cordelia never saw. Kent never forgets this Lear. In the Storm-scenes, even after the King becomes insane, Kent never addresses him without the old terms of respect, 'your grace', 'my lord', 'sir'. How characteristic it is that in the scene of Lear's recovery Kent speaks to him but once: it is when the King asks 'Am I in France?' and he answers 'In your own kingdom, sir'.

In acting the part of a blunt and eccentric serving-man Kent retains much of his natural character. The eccentricity seems to be put on, but the plainness which gets him set in the stocks is but an exaggeration of his plainness in the opening scene, and Shakespeare certainly meant him for one of those characters whom we love none the less for their defects. He is hot and rash; noble but far from skilful in his resistance to the King; he might well have chosen wiser words to gain his

---

[16] See I.i.142 ff. Kent speaks, not of the *injustice* of Lear's action, but of its 'folly', its 'hideous rashness'. When the King exclaims 'Kent, on thy life, no more', he answers:

> My life I never held but as a pawn
> To wage against thy enemies, nor fear to lose it,
> *Thy safety being the motive.*

(The first Folio omits 'a', and in the next line reads 'nere' for 'nor'. Perhaps the first line should read 'My life I ne'er held but as pawn to wage'.)

point. But, as he himself says, he has more man than wit about him. He shows this again when he rejoins Lear as a servant, for he at once brings the quarrel with Goneril to a head; and, later, by falling upon Oswald, whom he so detests that he cannot keep his hands off him, he provides Regan and Cornwall with a pretext for their inhospitality. One has not the heart to wish him different, but he illustrates the truth that to run one's head unselfishly against a wall is not the best way to help one's friends.

One fact about Kent is often overlooked. He is an old man. He tells Lear that he is eight and forty, but it is clear that he is much older; not so old as his master, who was 'four-score and upward' and whom he 'loved as his father', but, one may suppose, three-score and upward. From the first scene we get this impression, and in the scene with Oswald it is repeatedly confirmed. His beard is grey. 'Ancient ruffian', 'old fellow', 'you stubborn ancient knave, you reverent brag-gart' – these are some of the expressions applied to him. 'Sir,' he says to Cornwall, 'I am too old to learn.' If his age is not remembered, we fail to realize the full beauty of his thoughtlessness of himself, his incessant care of the King, his light-hearted indifference to fortune or fate.[17] We lose also some of the naturalness and pathos of his feeling that his task is nearly done. Even at the end of the Fourth Act we find him saying,

> My point and period will be thoroughly wrought
> Or well or ill, as this day's battle's fought.

His heart is ready to break when he falls with his strong arms about Edgar's neck; bellows out as he'd burst heaven (how like him!);

> threw him on my father,
> Told the most piteous tale of Lear and him
> That ever ear received; which in recounting
> His grief grew puissant, and the strings of life
> Began to crack. Twice then the trumpet sounded,
> And there I left him tranced;

and a little after, when he enters, we hear the sound of death in his voice:

---

[17] See II.ii.162 to end. The light-heartedness disappears, of course, as Lear's misfortunes thicken.

> I am come
> To bid my king and master aye goodnight.

This desire possesses him wholly. When the bodies of Goneril and Regan are brought in he asks merely, 'Alack, why thus?' How can he care? He is waiting for one thing alone. He cannot but yearn for recognition, cannot but beg for it even when Lear is bending over the body of Cordelia; and even in that scene of unmatched pathos we feel a sharp pang at his failure to receive it. It is of himself he is speaking, perhaps, when he murmurs, as his master dies, 'Break, heart, I prithee, break!' He puts aside Albany's invitation to take part in the government; his task is over:

> I have a journey, sir, shortly to go:
> My master calls me; I must not say no.

Kent in his devotion, his self-effacement, his cheerful stoicism, his desire to follow his dead lord, has been well likened to Horatio. But Horatio is not old; nor is he hot-headed; and though he is stoical he is also religious. Kent, as compared with him and with Edgar, is not so. He has not Edgar's ever-present faith in the 'clearest gods'. He refers to them, in fact, less often than to fortune or the stars. He lives mainly by the love in his own heart.[18]

The theatrical fool or clown (we need not distinguish them here) was a sore trial to the cultured poet and spectator in Shakespeare's day. He came down from the Morality plays, and was beloved of the groundlings. His antics, his songs, his dances, his jests, too often unclean, delighted them, and did something to make the drama, what the vulgar, poor or rich, like it to be, a variety entertainment. Even if he confined himself to what was set down for him he often disturbed the dramatic unity of the piece; and the temptation to 'gag' was too strong for him to resist. Shakespeare makes Hamlet object to it in emphatic terms. The more learned critics and poets went further and would have abolished the fool altogether. His part declines as the drama advances, diminishing markedly at the end of the sixteenth

---

[18] This difference, however, must not be pressed too far; nor must we take Kent's retort,

> Now by Apollo, king,
> Thou swear'st thy gods in vain,

for a sign of disbelief. He twice speaks of the gods in another manner (I.i.185, III.vi.5), and he was accustomed to think of Lear in his 'prayers' (I.i.144).

century. Jonson and Massinger* exclude him. Shakespeare used him –
we know to what effect – as he used all the other popular elements of
the drama; but he abstained from introducing him into the Roman
plays,[19] and there is no fool in the last of the pure tragedies, *Macbeth.*

But the Fool is one of Shakespeare's triumphs in *King Lear.* Imagine
the tragedy without him, and you hardly know it. To remove him
would spoil its harmony, as the harmony of a picture would be spoiled
if one of the colours were extracted. One can almost imagine that
Shakespeare, going home from an evening at the Mermaid, where he
had listened to Jonson fulminating against fools in general and
perhaps criticizing the Clown in *Twelfth Night* in particular, had said
to himself: 'Come, my friends, I will show you once for all that the
mischief is in you, and not in the fool or the audience. I will have a
fool in the most tragic of my tragedies. He shall not play a little part.
He shall keep from first to last the company in which you most object
to see him, the company of a king. Instead of amusing the king's idle
hours, he shall stand by him in the very tempest and whirlwind of
passion. Before I have done you shall confess, between laughter and
tears, that he is of the very essence of life, that you have known him
all your days though you never recognized him till now, and that you
would as soon go without Hamlet as miss him.'

The Fool in *King Lear* has been so favourite a subject with good critics that I will confine myself to one or two points on which a difference of opinion is possible. To suppose that the Fool is, like many a
domestic fool at that time, a perfectly sane man pretending to be half-
witted, is surely a most prosaic blunder. There is no difficulty in imagining that, being slightly touched in the brain, and holding the office
of fool, he performs the duties of his office intentionally as well as
involuntarily: it is evident that he does so. But unless we suppose that
he *is* touched in the brain we lose half the effect of his appearance in
the Storm-scenes. The effect of those scenes (to state the matter as
plainly as possible) depends largely on the presence of three characters,
and on the affinities and contrasts between them; on our perception
that the differences of station in King, Fool, and beggar-noble, are

---

[19] The 'clown' in *Antony and Cleopatra* is merely an old peasant. There is a fool in *Timon of Athens*, however, and he appears in a scene (II.ii.) generally attributed to Shakespeare. His talk sometimes reminds one of Lear's fool; and Kent's remark, 'This is not altogether fool, my lord,' is repeated in *Timon*, II.ii.122, 'Thou art not altogether a fool.'

levelled by one blast of calamity; but also on our perception of the differences between these three in one respect – viz. in regard to the peculiar affliction of insanity. The insanity of the King differs widely in its nature from that of the Fool, and that of the Fool from that of the beggar. But the insanity of the King differs from that of the beggar not only in its nature, but also in the fact that one is real and the other simply a pretence. Are we to suppose then that the insanity of the third character, the Fool, is, in this respect, a mere repetition of that of the second, the beggar – that it too is *mere* pretence? To suppose this is not only to impoverish miserably the impression made by the trio as a whole, it is also to diminish the heroic and pathetic effect of the character of the Fool. For his heroism consists largely in this, that his efforts to outjest his master's injuries are the efforts of a being to whom a responsible and consistent course of action, nay even a responsible use of language, is at the best of times difficult, and from whom it is never at the best of times expected. It is a heroism something like that of Lear himself in his endeavour to learn patience at the age of eighty. But arguments against the idea that the Fool is wholly sane are either needless or futile; for in the end they are appeals to the perception that this idea almost destroys the poetry of the character.

This is not the case with another question, the question whether the Fool is a man or a boy. Here the evidence and the grounds for discussion are more tangible. He is frequently addressed as 'boy'. This is not decisive; but Lear's first words to him, 'How now, my pretty knave, how dost thou?' are difficult to reconcile with the idea of his being a man, and the use of this phrase on his first entrance may show Shakespeare's desire to prevent any mistake on the point. As a boy, too, he would be more strongly contrasted in the Storm-scenes with Edgar as well as with Lear; his faithfulness and courage would be even more heroic and touching; his devotion to Cordelia, and the consequent bitterness of some of his speeches to Lear, would be even more natural. Nor does he seem to show a knowledge of the world impossible to a quick-witted though not whole-witted lad who had lived at Court. The only serious obstacle to this view, I think, is the fact that he is not known to have been represented as a boy or youth till Macready produced *King Lear*.[20]

---

[20] [This is no obstacle. There could hardly be a stage tradition hostile to his youth, since he does not appear in Tate's version, which alone was acted during the century and a half before

But even if this obstacle were serious and the Fool were imagined as a grown man, we may still insist that he must also be imagined as a timid, delicate and frail being, who on that account and from the expression of his face has a boyish look.[21] He pines away when Cordelia goes to France. Though he takes great liberties with his master he is frightened by Goneril, and becomes quite silent when the quarrel rises high. In the terrible scene between Lear and his two daughters and Cornwall (II.iv.129–289), he says not a word; we have almost forgotten his presence when, at the topmost pitch of passion, Lear suddenly turns to him from the hateful faces that encompass him:

> You think I'll weep;
> No, I'll not weep:
> I have full cause of weeping; but this heart
> Shall break into a hundred thousand flaws
> Or ere I'll weep. O fool, I shall go mad.

From the beginning of the Storm-scenes, though he thinks of his master alone, we perceive from his words that the cold and rain are almost more than he can bear. His childishness comes home to us when he runs out of the hovel, terrified by the madman and crying out to the King 'Help me, help me', and the good Kent takes him by the hand and draws him to his side. A little later he exclaims, 'This cold night will turn us all to fools and madmen'; and almost from that point he leaves the King to Edgar, speaking only once again in the remaining hundred lines of the scene. In the shelter of the 'farm-house' (III.vi.) he revives, and resumes his office of love; but I think that critic is right who considers his last words significant. 'We'll go to supper i' the morning', says Lear; and the Fool answers, 'And I'll go to bed at noon', as though he felt he had taken his death. When, a little later, the King is being carried away on a litter, the Fool sits idle. He is so benumbed and worn out that he scarcely notices what is going on. Kent has to rouse him with the words,

---

Macready's production. I had forgotten this; and my memory must also have been at fault regarding an engraving to which I referred in the first edition. Both mistakes were pointed out by Mr. Archer.*]

[21] In parts of what follows I am indebted to remarks by Cowden Clarke,* quoted by Furness on I.iv.91.

> Come, help to bear thy master,
> Thou must not stay behind.

We know no more. For the famous exclamation 'And my poor fool is hanged' unquestionably refers to Cordelia; and even if it is intended to show a confused association in Lear's mind between his child and the Fool who so loved her (as a very old man may confuse two of his children), still it tells us nothing of the Fool's fate. It seems strange indeed that Shakespeare should have left us thus in ignorance. But we have seen that there are many marks of haste and carelessness in *King Lear*, and it may also be observed that, if the poet imagined the Fool dying on the way to Dover of the effects of that night upon the heath, he could perhaps convey this idea to the audience by instructing the actor who took the part to show, as he left the stage for the last time, the recognized tokens of approaching death.[22]

Something has now been said of the four characters, Lear, Edgar, Kent and the Fool, who are together in the storm upon the heath. I have made no attempt to analyse the whole effect of these scenes, but one remark may be added. These scenes, as we observed, suggest the idea of a convulsion in which Nature herself joins with the forces of evil in man to overpower the weak; and they are thus one of the main sources of the more terrible impressions produced by *King Lear*. But they have at the same time an effect of a totally different kind, because in them are exhibited also the strength and the beauty of Lear's nature, and, in Kent and the Fool and Edgar, the ideal of faithful devoted love. Hence from the beginning to the end of these scenes we have, mingled with pain and awe and a sense of man's infirmity, an equally strong feeling of his greatness; and this becomes at times even an exulting sense of the powerlessness of outward calamity or the malice of others against his soul. And this is one reason why imagination and emotion are never here pressed painfully inward, as in the scenes between Lear and his daughters, but are liberated and dilated.

5

The character of Cordelia is not a masterpiece of invention or subtlety like that of Cleopatra; yet in its own way it is a creation as wonderful.

---

[22] See also Note T.

Cordelia appears in only four of the twenty-six scenes of *King Lear*; she speaks – it is hard to believe it – scarcely more than a hundred lines; and yet no character in Shakespeare is more absolutely individual or more ineffaceably stamped on the memory of his readers. There is a harmony, strange but perhaps the result of intention, between the character itself and this reserved or parsimonious method of depicting it. An expressiveness almost inexhaustible gained through paucity of expression; the suggestion of infinite wealth and beauty conveyed by the very refusal to reveal this beauty in expansive speech – this is at once the nature of Cordelia herself and the chief characteristic of Shakespeare's art in representing it. Perhaps it is not fanciful to find a parallel in his drawing of a person very different, Hamlet. It was natural to Hamlet to examine himself minutely, to discuss himself at large, and yet to remain a mystery to himself; and Shakespeare's method of drawing the character answers to it; it is extremely detailed and searching, and yet its effect is to enhance the sense of mystery. The results in the two cases differ correspondingly. No one hesitates to enlarge upon Hamlet, who speaks of himself so much; but to use many words about Cordelia seems to be a kind of impiety.

I am obliged to speak of her chiefly because the devotion she inspires almost inevitably obscures her part in the tragedy. This devotion is composed, so to speak, of two contrary elements, reverence and pity. The first, because Cordelia's is a higher nature than that of most even of Shakespeare's heroines. With the tenderness of Viola or Desdemona she unites something of the resolution, power, and dignity of Hermione, and reminds us sometimes of Helena, sometimes of Isabella, though she has none of the traits which prevent Isabella from winning our hearts. Her assertion of truth and right, her allegiance to them, even the touch of severity that accompanies it, instead of compelling mere respect or admiration, become adorable in a nature so loving as Cordelia's. She is a thing enskyed and sainted, and yet we feel no incongruity in the love of the King of France for her as we do in the love of the Duke for Isabella.

But with this reverence or worship is combined in the reader's mind a passion of championship, of pity, even of protecting pity. She is so deeply wronged, and she appears, for all her strength, so defenceless. We think of her as unable to speak for herself. We think of her as quite young, and as slight and small.[23] 'Her voice was ever soft, gentle, and low'; ever so, whether the tone was that of resolution, or rebuke, or love.[24] Of all Shakespeare's heroines she knew least of joy. She grew up with Goneril and Regan for sisters. Even her love for her father must have been mingled with pain and anxiety. She must early have learned to school and repress emotion. She never knew the bliss of young love: there is no trace of such love for the King of France. She had knowingly to wound most deeply the being dearest to her. He cast her off; and, after suffering an agony for him, and before she could see him safe in death, she was brutally murdered. We have to thank the poet for passing lightly over the circumstances of her death. We do not think of them. Her image comes before us calm and bright and still.

The memory of Cordelia thus becomes detached in a manner from the action of the drama. The reader refuses to admit into it any idea of imperfection, and is outraged when any share in her father's sufferings is attributed to the part she plays in the opening scene. Because she was deeply wronged he is ready to insist that she was wholly right. He refuses, that is, to take the tragic point of view, and, when it is taken, he imagines that Cordelia is being attacked, or is being declared to have 'deserved' all that befell her. But Shakespeare's was the tragic point of view. He exhibits in the opening scene a situation tragic for Cordelia as well as for Lear. At a moment where terrible issues join, Fate makes on her the one demand which she is unable to meet. As I have already remarked in speaking of Desdemona, it was a demand which other heroines of Shakespeare could have met. Without loss of self-respect, and refusing even to appear to compete for a reward, they could have made the unreasonable old King feel that he was fondly loved. Cordelia cannot, because she is Cordelia. And so she is not merely rejected and banished, but her father is left to the mercies of her sisters. And the cause of her failure – a failure a thousand-fold redeemed – is a compound in which imperfection appears so intimately mingled

---

[23] 'Our last and least' (according to the Folio reading). Lear speaks again of 'this little seeming substance'. He can carry her dead body in his arms.

[24] Perhaps then the 'low sound' is not merely metaphorical in Kent's speech in I.i.153 f.:

> answer my life my judgment,
> Thy youngest daughter does not love thee least;
> Nor are those empty-hearted whose low sound
> Reverbs no hollowness.

with the noblest qualities that – if we are true to Shakespeare – we do not think either of justifying her or of blaming her: we feel simply the tragic emotions of fear and pity.

In this failure a large part is played by that obvious characteristic to which I have already referred. Cordelia is not, indeed, always tongue-tied, as several passages in the drama, and even in this scene, clearly show. But tender emotion, and especially a tender love for the person to whom she has to speak, makes her dumb. Her love, as she says, is more ponderous than her tongue:[25]

> Unhappy that I am, I cannot heave
> My heart into my mouth.

This expressive word 'heave' is repeated in the passage which describes her reception of Kent's letter:

> Faith, once or twice she heaved the name of 'Father'
> Pantingly forth, as if it press'd her heart:

two or three broken ejaculations escape her lips, and she 'starts' away 'to deal with grief alone'. The same trait reappears with an ineffable beauty in the stifled repetitions with which she attempts to answer her father in the moment of his restoration:

> *Lear.*   Do not laugh at me;
>   For, as I am a man, I think this lady
>   To be my child Cordelia.
> *Cor.*   And so I am, I am.
> *Lear.*   Be your tears wet? yes, faith. I pray, weep not;
>   If you have poison for me, I will drink it.
>   I know you do not love me; for your sisters
>   Have, as I so remember, done me wrong:
>   You have some cause, they have not.
> *Cor.*   No cause, no cause.

We see this trait for the last time, marked by Shakespeare with a decision clearly intentional, in her inability to answer one syllable to the last words we hear her father speak to her:

---

[25] I.i.80. 'More ponderous' is the reading of the Folios, 'more richer' that of the Quartos. The latter is usually preferred, and Mr. Aldis Wright says 'more ponderous' has the appearance of being a player's correction to avoid a piece of imaginary bad grammar. Does it not sound more like the .author's improvement of a phrase that he thought a little flat? And, apart from that, is it not significant that it expresses the same idea of weight that appears in the phrase 'I cannot heave my heart into my mouth'?

No, no, no, no! Come, let's away to prison:
We two alone will sing like birds i' the cage:
When thou dost ask me blessing, I'll kneel down,
And ask of thee forgiveness: so we'll live,
And pray, and sing, and tell old tales, and laugh
At gilded butterflies. . . .

She stands and weeps, and goes out with him silent. And we see her alive no more.

But (I am forced to dwell on the point, because I am sure to slur it over is to be false to Shakespeare) this dumbness of love was not the sole source of misunderstanding. If this had been all, even Lear could have seen the love in Cordelia's eyes when, to his question 'What can you say to draw a third more opulent than your sisters?' she answered 'Nothing'. But it did not shine there. She is not merely silent, nor does she merely answer 'Nothing'. She tells him that she loves him 'according to her bond, nor more nor less'; and his answer,

How now, Cordelia! mend your speech a little,
Lest it may mar your fortunes,

so intensifies her horror at the hypocrisy of her sisters that she replies,

Good my lord,
You have begot me, bred me, loved me: I
Return those duties back as are right fit,
Obey you, love you, and most honour you.
Why have my sisters husbands, if they say
They love you all? Haply, when I shall wed,
That lord whose hand must take my plight shall carry
Half my love with him, half my care and duty:
Sure, I shall never marry like my sisters,
To love my father all.

What words for the ear of an old father, unreasonable, despotic, but fondly loving, indecent in his own expressions of preference, and blind to the indecency of his appeal for protestations of fondness! Blank astonishment, anger, wounded love, contend within him; but for the moment he restrains himself and asks,

But goes thy heart with this?

Imagine Imogen's reply! But Cordelia answers,

Ay, good my lord.
Lear. So young, and so untender?
Cor. So young, my lord, and true.

Yes, 'heavenly true'. But truth is not the only good in the world, nor is the obligation to tell truth the only obligation. The matter here was to keep it inviolate, but also to preserve a father. And even if truth *were* the one and only obligation, to tell much less than truth is not to tell it. And Cordelia's speech not only tells much less than truth about her love, it actually perverts the truth when it implies that to give love to a husband is to take it from a father. There surely never was a more unhappy speech.

When Isabella goes to plead with Angelo for her brother's life, her horror of her brother's sin is so intense, and her perception of the justice of Angelo's reasons for refusing her is so clear and keen, that she is ready to abandon her appeal before it is well begun; she would actually do so but that the warm-hearted profligate Lucio reproaches her for her coldness and urges her on. Cordelia's hatred of hypocrisy and of the faintest appearance of mercenary professions reminds us of Isabella's hatred of impurity; but Cordelia's position is infinitely more difficult, and on the other hand there is mingled with her hatred a touch of personal antagonism and of pride. Lear's words,

Let pride, which she calls plainness, marry her![26]

are monstrously unjust, but they contain one grain of truth; and indeed it was scarcely possible that a nature so strong as Cordelia's, and with so keen a sense of dignity, should feel here nothing whatever of pride and resentment. This side of her character is emphatically shown in her language to her sisters in the first scene – language perfectly just, but little adapted to soften their hearts towards their father – and again in the very last words we hear her speak. She and her father are brought in, prisoners, to the enemy's camp; but she sees only Edmund, not those 'greater' ones on whose pleasure hangs her father's fate and her own. For her own she is little concerned; she knows how to meet adversity:

---

[26] Cf. Cornwall's satirical remarks on Kent's 'plainness' in II.ii.101 ff. – a plainness which did no service to Kent's master. (As a matter of fact, Cordelia had said nothing about 'plainness'.)

For thee, oppressed king, am I cast down;
Myself could else out-frown false fortune's frown.

Yes, that is how she would meet fortune, frowning it down, even as Goneril would have met it; nor, if her father had been already dead, would there have been any great improbability in the false story that was to be told of her death, that, like Goneril, she 'fordid herself'. Then, after those austere words about fortune, she suddenly asks,

Shall we not see these daughters and these sisters?

Strange last words for us to hear from a being so worshipped and beloved; but how characteristic! Their tone is unmistakable. I doubt if she could have brought herself to plead with her sisters for her father's life; and if she had attempted the task, she would have performed it but ill. Nor is our feeling towards her altered one whit by that. But what is true of Kent and the Fool[27] is, in its measure, true of her. Any one of them would gladly have died a hundred deaths to help King Lear; and they do help his soul; but they harm his cause. They are all involved in tragedy.

Why does Cordelia die? I suppose no reader ever failed to ask that question, and to ask it with something more than pain – to ask it, if only for a moment, in bewilderment or dismay, and even perhaps in tones of protest. These feelings are probably evoked more strongly here than at the death of any other notable character in Shakespeare; and it may sound a wilful paradox to assert that the slightest element of reconciliation is mingled with them or succeeds them. Yet it seems to me indubitable that such an element is present, though difficult to make out with certainty what it is or whence it proceeds. And I will try to make this out, and to state it methodically.

(*a*) It is not due in any perceptible degree to the fact, which we have just been examining, that Cordelia through her tragic imperfection contributes something to the conflict and catastrophe; and I drew attention to that imperfection without any view to our present problem. The critics who emphasize it at this point in the drama are surely untrue to Shakespeare's mind; and still more completely astray are those who lay stress on the idea that Cordelia in bringing a foreign army to help her father was guilty of treason to her country. When she dies we regard her, practically speaking, simply as we regard Ophelia

---

[27] Who, like Kent, hastens on the quarrel with Goneril.

or Desdemona, as an innocent victim swept away in the convulsion caused by the error or guilt of others.

(*b*) Now this destruction of the good through the evil of others is one of the tragic facts of life, and no one can object to the use of it, within certain limits, in tragic art. And, further, those who because of it declaim against the nature of things, declaim without thinking. It is obviously the other side of the fact that the effects of good spread far and wide beyond the doer of good; and we should ask ourselves whether we really could wish (supposing it conceivable) to see this doubled-sided fact abolished. Nevertheless the touch of reconciliation that we feel in contemplating the death of Cordelia is not due, or is due only in some slight degree, to a perception that the event is true to life, admissible in tragedy, and a case of a law which we cannot seriously desire to see abrogated.

(*c*) What then is this feeling, and whence does it come? I believe that we shall find that it is a feeling not confined to *King Lear*, but present at the close of other tragedies; and that the reason why it has an exceptional tone or force at the close of *King Lear*, lies in that very peculiarity of the close which also – at least for the moment – excites bewilderment, dismay, or protest. The feeling I mean is the impression that the heroic being, though in one sense and outwardly he has failed, is yet in another sense superior to the world in which he appears; is, in some way which we do not seek to define, untouched by the doom that overtakes him; and is rather set free from life than deprived of it. Some such feeling as this – some feeling which, from this description of it, may be recognized as their own even by those who would dissent from the description – we surely have in various degrees at the deaths of Hamlet and Othello and Lear, and of Antony and Cleopatra and Coriolanus.[28] It accompanies the more prominent tragic impressions, and, regarded alone, could hardly be called tragic. For it seems to imply (though we are probably quite unconscious of the implication) an idea which, if developed, would transform the tragic view of things. It implies that the tragic world, if taken as it is presented, with all its error, guilt, failure, woe and waste, is no final reality, but only a part of reality taken for the whole, and, when so taken, illusive; and that if we

---

[28] I do not wish to complicate the discussion by examining the differences, in degree or otherwise, in the various cases, or by introducing numerous qualifications; and therefore I do not add the names of Macbeth and Lady Macbeth.

could see the whole, and the tragic facts in their true place in it, we should find them, not abolished, of course, but so transmuted that they had ceased to be strictly tragic – find, perhaps, the suffering and death counting for little or nothing, the greatness of the soul for much or all, and the heroic spirit, in spite of failure, nearer to the heart of things than the smaller, more circumspect, and perhaps even 'better' beings who survived the catastrophe. The feeling which I have tried to describe, as accompanying the more obvious tragic emotions at the deaths of heroes, corresponds with some such idea as this.[29]

Now this feeling is evoked with a quite exceptional strength by the death of Cordelia.[30] It is not due to the perception that she, like Lear, has attained through suffering; we know that she had suffered and attained in his days of prosperity. It is simply the feeling that what happens to such a being does not matter; all that matters is what she is. How this can be when, for anything the tragedy tells us, she has ceased to exist, we do not ask; but the tragedy itself makes us feel that somehow it is so. And the force with which this impression is conveyed depends largely on the very fact which excites our bewilderment and protest, that her death, following on the deaths of all the evil characters, and brought about by an unexplained delay in Edmund's effort to save her, comes on us, not as an inevitable conclusion to the sequence of events, but as the sudden stroke of mere fate or chance. The force of the impression, that is to say, depends on the very violence of the contrast between the outward and the inward, Cordelia's death and Cordelia's soul. The more unmotived, unmerited, senseless, monstrous, her fate, the more do we feel that it does not concern her. The extremity of the disproportion between prosperity and goodness first shocks us, and then flashes on us the conviction that our whole attitude in asking or expecting that goodness should be prosperous is wrong; that, if only we could see things as they are, we should see that the outward is nothing and the inward is all.

---

[29] It follows from the above that, if this idea were made explicit and accompanied our reading of a tragedy throughout, it would confuse or even destroy the tragic impression. So would the constant presence of Christian beliefs. The reader most attached to these beliefs holds them in temporary suspension while he is immersed in a Shakespearean tragedy. Such tragedy assumes that the world, as it is presented, is the truth, though it also provokes feelings which imply that this world is not the whole truth, and therefore not the truth.

[30] Though Cordelia, of course, does not occupy the position of the hero.

And some such thought as this (which, to bring it clearly out, I have stated, and still state, in a form both exaggerated and much too explicit) is really present through the whole play. Whether Shakespeare knew it or not, it is present. I might almost say that the 'moral' of *King Lear* is presented in the irony of this collocation:

> *Albany.*   The gods defend her!
> *Enter Lear with Cordelia dead in his arms.*

The 'gods', it seems, do *not* show their approval by 'defending' their own from adversity or death, or by giving them power and prosperity. These, on the contrary, are worthless, or worse; it is not on them, but on the renunciation of them, that the gods throw incense. They breed lust, pride, hardness of heart, the insolence of office, cruelty, scorn, hypocrisy, contention, war, murder, self-destruction. The whole story beats this indictment of prosperity into the brain. Lear's great speeches in his madness proclaim it like the curses of Timon on life and man. But here, as in *Timon,* the poor and humble are, almost without exception, sound and sweet at heart, faithful and pitiful.[31] And here adversity, to the blessed in spirit, is blessed. It wins fragrance from the crushed flower. It melts in aged hearts sympathies which prosperity had frozen. It purges the soul's sight by blinding that of the eyes.[32] Throughout that stupendous Third Act the good are seen growing better through suffering, and the bad worse through success. The warm castle is a room in hell, the storm-swept heath a sanctuary. The judgment of this world is a lie; its goods, which we covet, corrupt us; its ills, which break our bodies, set our souls free;

> Our means secure us,[33] and our mere defects
> Prove our commodities.

---

[31]   *E.g.* in *King Lear* the servants, and the old man who succours Gloster and brings to the naked beggar 'the best 'parel that he has, come on't what will', *i.e.* whatever vengeance Regan can inflict. Cf. the Steward and the Servants in *Timon.* Cf. there also (V.i.23), 'Promising is the very air o' the time . . . performance is ever the duller for his act; and, *but in the plainer and simpler kind of people,* the deed of saying [performance of promises] is quite out of use.' Shakespeare's feeling on this subject, though apparently specially keen at this time of his life, is much the same throughout (cf. Adam in *As You Like It*). He has no respect for the plainer and simpler kind of people as politicians, but a great respect and regard for their hearts.

[32]   'I stumbled when I saw,' says Gloster.

[33]   Our advantages give us a blind confidence in our security. Cf. *Timon,* IV.iii.76,

> *Alc.*   I have heard in some sort of thy miseries.
> *Tim.*   Thou saw'st them when I had prosperity.

Let us renounce the world, hate it, and lose it gladly. The only real thing in it is the soul, with its courage, patience, devotion. And nothing outward can touch that.

This, if we like to use the word, is Shakespeare's 'pessimism' in *King Lear*. As we have seen, it is not by any means the whole spirit of the tragedy, which presents the world as a place where heavenly good grows side by side with evil, where extreme evil cannot long endure, and where all that survives the storm is good, if not great. But still this strain of thought, to which the world appears as the kingdom of evil and therefore worthless, is in the tragedy, and may well be the record of many hours of exasperated feeling and troubled brooding. Pursued further and allowed to dominate, it would destroy the tragedy; for it is necessary to tragedy that we should feel that suffering and death do matter greatly, and that happiness and life are not to be renounced as worthless. Pursued further, again, it leads to the idea that the world, in that obvious appearance of it which tragedy cannot dissolve without dissolving itself, is illusive. And its tendency towards this idea is traceable in *King Lear*, in the shape of the notion that this 'great world' is transitory, or 'will wear out to nought' like the little world called 'man' (IV.vi.137), or that humanity will destroy itself.[34] In later days, in the drama that was probably Shakespeare's last complete work, the *Tempest*, this notion of the transitoriness of things appears, side by side with the simpler feeling that man's life is an illusion or dream, in some of the most famous lines he ever wrote:

> Our revels now are ended. These our actors,
> As I foretold you, were all spirits and
> Are melted into air, into thin air:
> And, like the baseless fabric of this vision,
> The cloud-capp'd towers, the gorgeous palaces,
> The solemn temples, the great globe itself,
> Yea, all which it inherit, shall dissolve

---

[34] Biblical ideas seem to have been floating in Shakespeare's mind. Cf. the words of Kent, when Lear enters with Cordelia's body, 'Is this the promised end?' and Edgar's answer, 'Or image of that horror?' The 'promised end' is certainly the end of the world (cf. with 'image' 'the great doom's image,' *Macbeth*, II.iii.83); and the next words, Albany's 'Fall and cease', *may* be addressed to the heavens or stars, not to Lear. It seems probable that in writing Gloster's speech about the predicted horrors to follow 'these late eclipses' Shakespeare had a vague recollection of the passage in *Matthew* xxiv., or of that in *Mark* xiii., about the tribulations which were to be the sign of 'the end of the world'. (I do not mean, of course, that the 'prediction' of i.ii.119 is the prediction to be found in one of these passages.)

And, like this insubstantial pageant faded,
Leave not a rack behind. We are such stuff
As dreams are made on, and our little life
Is rounded with a sleep.

These lines, detached from their context, are familiar to everyone; but, in the *Tempest*, they are dramatic as well as poetical. The sudden emergence of the thought expressed in them has a specific and most significant cause; and as I have not seen it remarked I will point it out.

Prospero, by means of his spirits, has been exhibiting to Ferdinand and Miranda a masque in which goddesses appear, and which is so majestic and harmonious that to the young man, standing beside such a father and such a wife, the place seems Paradise – as perhaps the world once seemed to Shakespeare. Then, at the bidding of Iris, there begins a dance of Nymphs with Reapers, sunburnt, weary of their August labour, but now in their holiday garb. But, as this is nearing its end, Prospero 'starts suddenly, and speaks'; and the visions vanish. And what he 'speaks' is shown in these lines, which introduce the famous passage just quoted:

> *Pros.*   [Aside] I had forgot that foul conspiracy
> Of the beast Caliban and his confederates
> Against my life: the minute of their plot
> Is almost come. [*To the Spirits.*] Well done! avoid; no more.
> *Fer.*   This is strange; your father's in some passion
> That works him strongly.
> *Mir.*   Never till this day
> Saw I him touch'd with anger so distemper'd.
> *Pros.*   You do look, my son, in a moved sort,
> As if you were dismay'd: be cheerful, sir.
> Our revels. . . .

And then, after the famous lines, follow these:

>   Sir, I am vex'd:
> Bear with my weakness; my old brain is troubled;
> Be not disturb'd with my infirmity;
> If you be pleased, retire into my cell
> And there repose: a turn or two I'll walk,
> To still my beating mind.

We seem to see here the whole mind of Shakespeare in his last years. That which provokes in Prospero first a 'passion' of anger, and, a moment later, that melancholy and mystical thought that the great world must perish utterly and that man is but a dream, is the sudden recollection of gross and apparently incurable evil in the 'monster' whom he had tried in vain to raise and soften, and in the monster's human confederates. It is this, which is but the repetition of his earlier experience of treachery and ingratitude, that troubles his old brain, makes his mind 'beat',[35] and forces on him the sense of unreality and evanescence in the world and the life that are haunted by such evil. Nor, though Prospero can spare and forgive, is there any sign to the end that he believed the evil curable either in the monster, the 'born devil', or in the more monstrous villains, the 'worse than devils', whom he so sternly dismisses. But he has learned patience, has come to regard his anger and loathing as a weakness or infirmity, and would not have it disturb the young and innocent. And so, in the days of *King Lear*, it was chiefly the power of 'monstrous' and apparently cureless evil in the 'great world' that filled Shakespeare's soul with horror, and perhaps forced him sometimes to yield to the infirmity of misanthropy and despair, to cry 'No, no, no life', and to take refuge in the thought that this fitful fever is a dream that must soon fade into a dreamless sleep; until, to free himself from the perilous stuff that weighed upon his heart, he summoned to his aid his 'so potent art', and wrought this stuff into the stormy music of his greatest poem, which seems to cry,

You heavens, give me that patience, patience I need,

and, like the *Tempest*, seems to preach to us from end to end, 'Thou must be patient', 'Bear free and patient thoughts'.[36]

---

[35] Cf. *Hamlet*, III.i.181:

This something-settled matter in his heart,
Whereon his brains still beating puts him thus
From fashion of himself.

[36] I believe the criticism of *King Lear* which has influenced me most is that in Prof. Dowden's *Shakespere, his Mind and Art* (though, when I wrote my lectures, I had not read that criticism for many years); and I am glad that this acknowledgment gives me the opportunity of repeating in print an opinion which I have often expressed to students, that anyone entering on the study of Shakespeare, and unable or unwilling to read much criticism, would do best to take Prof. Dowden for his guide.

LECTURE IX

MACBETH

Macbeth, it is probable, was the last-written of the four great tragedies, and immediately preceded *Antony and Cleopatra.*[1] In that play Shakespeare's final style appears for the first time completely formed, and the transition to this style is much more decidedly visible in *Macbeth* than in *King Lear.* Yet in certain respects *Macbeth* recalls *Hamlet* rather than *Othello* or *King Lear.* In the heroes of both plays the passage from thought to a critical resolution and action is difficult, and excites the keenest interest. In neither play, as in *Othello* and *King Lear*, is painful pathos one of the main effects. Evil, again, though it shows in *Macbeth* a prodigious energy, is not the icy or stony inhumanity of Iago or Goneril; and, as in *Hamlet*, it is pursued by remorse. Finally, Shakespeare no longer restricts the action to purely human agencies, as in the two preceding tragedies; portents once more fill the heavens, ghosts rise from their graves, an unearthly light flickers about the head of the doomed man. The special popularity of *Hamlet* and *Macbeth* is due in part to some of these common characteristics, notably to the fascination of the supernatural, the absence of the spectacle of extreme undeserved suffering, the absence of characters which horrify and repel and yet are destitute of grandeur. The reader who looks unwillingly at Iago gazes at Lady Macbeth in awe, because though she is dreadful she is also sublime. The whole tragedy is sublime.

In this, however, and in other respects, *Macbeth* makes an impression quite different from that of *Hamlet.* The dimensions of the principal characters, the rate of movement in the action, the supernatural effect, the style, the versification, are all changed; and they are all changed in much the same manner. In many parts of *Macbeth* there is in the language a peculiar compression, pregnancy, energy, even violence; the harmonious grace and even flow, often conspicuous in *Hamlet*, have almost disappeared. The chief characters, built on a scale

---

[1] See note BB.

at least as large as that of *Othello*, seem to attain at times an almost superhuman stature. The diction has in places a huge and rugged grandeur, which degenerates here and there into tumidity. The solemn majesty of the royal Ghost in *Hamlet*, appearing in armour and standing silent in the moonlight, is exchanged for shapes of horror, dimly seen in the murky air or revealed by the glare of the caldron fire in a dark cavern, or for the ghastly face of Banquo badged with blood and staring with blank eyes. The other three tragedies all open with conversations which lead into the action: here the action bursts into wild life amidst the sounds of a thunderstorm and the echoes of a distant battle. It hurries through seven very brief scenes of mounting suspense to a terrible crisis, which is reached, in the murder of Duncan, at the beginning of the Second Act. Pausing a moment and changing its shape, it hastes again with scarcely diminished speed to fresh horrors. And even when the speed of the outward action is slackened, the same effect is continued in another form: we are shown a soul tortured by an agony which admits not a moment's repose, and rushing in frenzy towards its doom. *Macbeth* is very much shorter than the other three tragedies, but our experience in traversing it is so crowded and intense that it leaves an impression not of brevity but of speed. It is the most vehement, the most concentrated, perhaps we may say the most tremendous, of the tragedies.

1

A Shakespearean tragedy, as a rule, has a special tone or atmosphere of its own, quite perceptible, however difficult to describe. The effect of this atmosphere is marked with unusual strength in *Macbeth*. It is due to a variety of influences which combine with those just noticed, so that, acting and reacting, they form a whole; and the desolation of the blasted heath, the design of the Witches, the guilt in the hero's soul, the darkness of the night, seem to emanate from one and the same source. This effect is strengthened by a multitude of small touches, which at the moment may be little noticed but still leave their mark on the imagination. We may approach the consideration of the characters and the action by distinguishing some of the ingredients of this general effect.

Darkness, we may even say blackness, broods over this tragedy. It is remarkable that almost all the scenes which at once recur to memory take place either at night or in some dark spot. The vision of the dagger, the murder of Duncan, the murder of Banquo, the sleep-walking of Lady Macbeth, all come in night-scenes. The Witches dance in the thick air of a storm, or, 'black and midnight hags', receive Macbeth in a cavern. The blackness of night is to the hero a thing of fear, even of horror; and that which he feels becomes the spirit of the play. The faint glimmerings of the western sky at twilight are here menacing: it is the hour when the traveller hastens to reach safety in his inn and when Banquo rides homeward to meet his assassins; the hour when 'light thickens', when 'night's black agents to their prey do rouse', when the wolf begins to howl, and the owl to scream, and withered murder steals forth to his work. Macbeth bids the stars hide their fires that his 'black' desires may be concealed; Lady Macbeth calls on thick night to come, palled in the dunnest smoke of hell. The moon is down and no stars shine when Banquo, dreading the dreams of the coming night, goes unwillingly to bed, and leaves Macbeth to wait for the summons of the little bell. When the next day should dawn, its light is 'strangled', and 'darkness does the face of earth entomb'. In the whole drama the sun seems to shine only twice; first, in the beautiful but ironical passage where Duncan sees the swallows flitting round the castle of death; and, afterwards, when at the close the avenging army gathers to rid the earth of its shame. Of the many slighter touches which deepen this effect I notice only one. The failure of nature in Lady Macbeth is marked by her fear of darkness; 'she has light by her continually'. And in the one phrase of fear that escapes her lips even in sleep, it is of the darkness of the place of torment that she speaks.[2]

The atmosphere of *Macbeth*, however, is not that of unrelieved blackness. On the contrary, as compared with *King Lear* and its cold dim gloom, *Macbeth* leaves a decided impression of colour; it is really the impression of a black night broken by flashes of light and colour, sometimes vivid and even glaring. They are the lights and colours of the thunderstorm in the first scene; of the dagger hanging before Macbeth's eyes and glittering alone in the midnight air; of the torch borne by the servant when he and his lord come upon Banquo cross-

---

[2] 'Hell is murky' (V.i.35). This, surely, is not meant for a scornful repetition of something said long ago by Macbeth. He would hardly in those days have used an argument or expressed a fear that could provoke nothing but contempt.

ing the castle-court to his room; of the torch, again, which Fleance carried to light his father to death, and which was dashed out by one of the murderers; of the torches that flared in the hall on the face of the Ghost and the blanched cheeks of Macbeth; of the flames beneath the boiling caldron from which the apparitions in the cavern rose; of the taper which showed to the Doctor and Gentlewoman the wasted face and blank eyes of Lady Macbeth. And, above all, the colour is the colour of blood. It cannot be an accident that the image of blood is forced upon us continually, not merely by the events themselves, but by full descriptions, and even by reiteration of the word in unlikely parts of the dialogue. The Witches, after their first wild appearance, have hardly quitted the stage when there staggers onto it a 'bloody man', gashed with wounds. His tale is of a hero whose 'brandished steel smoked with bloody execution', 'carved out a passage' to his enemy, and 'unseam'd him from the nave to the chaps'. And then he tells of a second battle so bloody that the combatants seemed as if they 'meant to bathe in reeking wounds'. What metaphors! What a dreadful image is that with which Lady Macbeth greets us almost as she enters, when she prays the spirits of cruelty so to thicken her blood that pity cannot flow along her veins! What pictures are those of the murderer appearing at the door of the banquet-room with Banquo's 'blood upon his face'; of Banquo himself 'with twenty trenched gashes on his head', or 'blood-bolter'd' and smiling in derision at his murderer; of Macbeth, gazing at his hand, and watching it dye the whole green ocean red; of Lady Macbeth, gazing at hers, and stretching it away from her face to escape the smell of blood that all the perfumes of Arabia will not subdue! The most horrible lines in the whole tragedy are those of her shuddering cry, 'Yet who would have thought the old man to have had so much blood in him?' And it is not only at such moments that these images occur. Even in the quiet conversation of Malcolm and Macduff, Macbeth is imagined as holding a bloody sceptre, and Scotland as a country bleeding and receiving every day a new gash added to her wounds. It is as if the poet saw the whole story through an ensanguined mist, and as if it stained the very blackness of the night. When Macbeth, before Banquo's murder, invokes night to scarf up the tender eye of pitiful day, and to tear in pieces the great bond that keeps him pale, even the invisible hand that is to tear the bond is imagined as covered with blood.

Let us observe another point. The vividness, magnitude, and

violence of the imagery in some of these passages are characteristic of
Macbeth almost throughout; and their influence contributes to form
its atmosphere. Images like those of the babe torn smiling from the
breast and dashed to death; of pouring the sweet milk of concord into
hell; of the earth shaking in fever; of the frame of things disjointed; of
sorrows striking heaven on the face, so that it resounds and yells out
like syllables of dolour; of the mind lying in restless ecstasy on a rack;
of the mind full of scorpions; of the tale told by an idiot, full of sound
and fury; – all keep the imagination moving on a 'wild and violent
sea', while it is scarcely for a moment permitted to dwell on thoughts
of peace and beauty. In its language, as in its action, the drama is full
of tumult and storm. Whenever the Witches are present we see and
hear a thunder-storm: when they are absent we hear of shipwrecking
storms and direful thunders; of tempests that blow down trees and
churches, castles, palaces and pyramids; of the frightful hurricane of
the night when Duncan was murdered; of the blast on which pity
rides like a new-born babe, or on which Heaven's cherubim are
horsed. There is thus something magnificently appropriate in the cry
'Blow, wind! Come wrack!' with which Macbeth, turning from the
sight of the moving wood of Birnam, bursts from his castle. He was
borne to his throne on a whirlwind, and the fate he goes to meet
comes on the wings of storm.

Now all these agencies – darkness, the lights and colours that illu-
minate it, the storm that rushes through it, the violent and gigantic
images – conspire with the appearances of the Witches and the Ghost
to awaken horror, and in some degree also a supernatural dread. And
to this effect other influences contribute. The pictures called up by the
mere words of the Witches stir the same feelings – those, for example,
of the spell-bound sailor driven tempest-tost for nine times nine
weary weeks, and never visited by sleep night or day; of the drop of
poisonous foam that forms on the moon, and, falling to earth, is
collected for pernicious ends; of the sweltering venom of the toad, the
finger of the babe killed at its birth by its own mother, the tricklings
from the murderer's gibbet. In Nature, again, something is felt to be
at work, sympathetic with human guilt and supernatural malice. She
labours with portents.

> Lamentings heard in the air, strange screams of death,
> And prophesying with accents terrible,

burst from her. The owl clamours all through the night; Duncan's horses devour each other in frenzy; the dawn comes, but no light with it. Common sights and sounds, the crying of crickets, the croak of the raven, the light thickening after sunset, the home-coming of the rooks, are all ominous. Then, as if to deepen these impressions, Shakespeare has concentrated attention on the obscurer regions of man's being, on phenomena which make it seem that he is in the power of secret forces lurking below, and independent of his consciousness and will: such as the relapse of Macbeth from conversation into a reverie, during which he gazes fascinated at the image of murder drawing closer and closer; the writing on his face of strange things he never meant to show; the pressure of imagination heightening into illusion, like the vision of a dagger in the air, at first bright, then suddenly splashed with blood, or the sound of a voice that cried 'Sleep no more' and would not be silenced.[3] To these are added other, and constant, allusions to sleep, man's strange half-conscious life; to the misery of its withholding; to the terrible dreams of remorse; to the cursed thoughts from which Banquo is free by day, but which tempt him in his sleep: and again to abnormal disturbances of sleep; in the two men, of whom one during the murder of Duncan laughed in his sleep, and the other raised a cry of murder; and in Lady Macbeth, who rises to re-enact in somnambulism those scenes the memory of which is pushing her on to madness or suicide. All this has one effect, to excite supernatural alarm and, even more, a dread of the presence of evil not only in its recognized seat but all through and around our mysterious nature. Perhaps there is no other work equal to *Macbeth* in the production of this effect.[4]

It is enhanced – to take a last point – by the use of a literary expedient. Not even in *Richard III*, which in this, as in other respects, has resemblances to *Macbeth*, is there so much of Irony. I do not refer to irony in the ordinary sense; to speeches, for example, where the speaker is intentionally ironical, like that of Lennox in III.vi. I refer to irony on the part of the author himself, to ironical juxtapositions of persons and events, and especially to the 'Sophoclean irony' by which a speaker is made to use words bearing to the audience, in addition to his own meaning, a further and ominous sense, hidden from himself

---

[3] 'Whether Banquo's ghost is a mere illusion, like the dagger, is discussed in Note FF.

[4] In parts of this paragraph I am indebted to Hunter's *Illustrations of Shakespeare*.

and, usually, from the other persons on the stage. The very first words uttered by Macbeth,

So foul and fair a day I have not seen,

are an example to which attention has often been drawn; for they startle the reader by recalling the words of the Witches in the first scene,

Fair is foul, and foul is fair.

When Macbeth, emerging from his murderous reverie, turns to the nobles saying, 'Let us toward the King', his words are innocent, but to the reader have a double meaning. Duncan's comment on the treachery of Cawdor,

There's no art
To find the mind's construction in the face:
He was a gentleman on whom I built
An absolute trust,

is interrupted[5] by the entrance of the traitor Macbeth, who is greeted with effusive gratitude and a like 'absolute trust'. I have already referred to the ironical effect of the beautiful lines in which Duncan and Banquo describe the castle they are about to enter. To the reader Lady Macbeth's light words,

A little water clears us of this deed:
How easy is it then,

summon up the picture of the sleep-walking scene. The idea of the Porter's speech, in which he imagines himself the keeper of hell-gate, shows the same irony. So does the contrast between the obvious and the hidden meanings of the apparitions of the armed head, the bloody child, and the child with the tree in his hand. It would be easy to add further examples. Perhaps the most striking is the answer which Banquo, as he rides away, never to return alive, gives to Macbeth's reminder, 'Fail not our feast'. 'My lord, I will not,' he replies, and he keeps his promise. It cannot be by accident that Shakespeare so frequently in this play uses a device which contributes to excite the vague fear of hidden forces operating on minds unconscious of their influence.[6]

---

[5] The line is a foot short.
[6] It should be observed that in some cases the irony would escape an audience ignorant of

2

But of course he had for this purpose an agency more potent than any yet considered. It would be almost an impertinence to attempt to describe anew the influence of the Witch-scenes on the imagination of the reader.[7] Nor do I believe that among different readers this influence differs greatly except in degree. But when critics begin to analyse the imaginative effect, and still more when, going behind it, they try to determine the truth which lay for Shakespeare or lies for us in these creations, they too often offer us results which, either through perversion or through inadequacy, fail to correspond with that effect. This happens in opposite ways. On the one hand the Witches, whose contribution to the 'atmosphere' of *Macbeth* can hardly be exaggerated, are credited with far too great an influence upon the action; sometimes they are described as goddesses, or even as fates, whom Macbeth is powerless to resist. And this is perversion. On the other hand, we are told that, great as is their influence on the action, it is so because they are merely symbolic representations of the unconscious or half-conscious guilt in Macbeth himself. And this is inadequate. The few remarks I have to make may take the form of a criticism on these views.

(1) As to the former, Shakespeare took, as material for his purposes, the ideas about witch-craft that he found existing in people around him and in books like Reginald Scot's *Discovery* (1584).* And he used these ideas without changing their substance at all. He selected and improved, avoiding the merely ridiculous, dismissing (unlike Middleton*) the sexually loathsome or stimulating, rehandling and heightening whatever could touch the imagination with fear, horror, and mysterious attraction. The Witches, that is to say, are not goddesses, or fates, or, in any way whatever, supernatural beings. They are old women, poor and ragged, skinny and hideous, full of vulgar spite, occupied in killing their neighbours' swine or revenging themselves on sailors' wives who have refused them chestnuts. If Banquo considers their beards a proof that they are not women, that only shows his ignorance: Sir Hugh Evans would have

---

the story and watching the play for the first time, – another indication that Shakespeare did not write solely for immediate stage purposes.

[7] Their influence on spectators is, I believe, very inferior. These scenes, like the Storm-scenes in *King Lear*, belong properly to the world of imagination.

known better.[8] There is not a syllable in *Macbeth* to imply that they are anything but women. But, again in accordance with the popular ideas, they have received from evil spirits certain supernatural powers. They can 'raise haile, tempests, and hurtfull weather; as lightening, thunder, etc.' They can 'passe from place to place in the aire invisible'. They can 'keepe divels and spirits in the likenesse of todes and cats', Paddock or Graymalkin. They can 'transferre corne in the blade from one place to another'. They can 'manifest unto others things hidden and lost, and foreshew things to come, and see them as though they were present'. The reader will apply these phrases and sentences at once to passages in *Macbeth*. They are all taken from Scot's first chapter, where he is retailing the current superstitions of his time; and, in regard to the Witches, Shakespeare mentions scarcely anything, if anything, that was not to be found, of course in a more prosaic shape, either in Scot or in some other easily accessible authority.[9] He read, to be sure, in Holinshed, his main source for the story of Macbeth, that, according to the common opinion, the 'women' who met Macbeth 'were eyther the weird sisters, that is (as ye would say) yᵉ Goddesses of destinee, or els some Nimphes or Feiries'. But what does that matter? What he read in his authority was absolutely nothing to his audience, and remains nothing to us, unless he *used* what he read. And he did not use this idea. He used nothing but the phrase 'weird sisters',[10] which certainly no more suggested to a London audience the Parcae of one mythology or the Norns* of another than it does to-day. His Witches owe all their power to the spirits; they are *'instruments* of darkness'; the spirits are their 'masters' (IV.i.63). Fancy the fates having masters! Even if the passages where Hecate appears are

---

[8] 'By yea and no, I think the 'oman is a witch indeed: I like not when a oman has a great peard' (*Merry Wives*, IV.ii.202).

[9] Even the metaphor in the lines (II.iii.127),

What should be spoken here, where our fate,
Hid in an auger-hole, may rush and seize us?

was probably suggested by the words in Scot's first chapter, 'They can go in and out at awger-holes'.

[10] Once, 'weird women.' Whether Shakespeare knew that 'weird' signified 'fate' we cannot tell, but it is probable that he did. The word occurs six times in *Macbeth* (it does not occur elsewhere in Shakespeare). The first three times it is spelt in the Folio *weyward*, the last three *weyard*. This may suggest a miswriting or misprinting of *wayward*; but, as that word is always spelt in the Folio either rightly or *waiward*, it is more likely that the *weyward* and *weyard* of *Macbeth* are the copyist's or printer's misreading of Shakespeare's *weird* or *weyrd*.

Shakespeare's,[11] that will not help the Witches; for they are subject to
Hecate, who is herself a goddess or superior devil, not a fate.[12]

Next, while the influence of the Witches' prophecies on Macbeth
is very great, it is quite clearly shown to be an influence and nothing
more. There is no sign whatever in the play that Shakespeare meant
the actions of Macbeth to be forced on him by an external power,
whether that of the Witches, or of their 'masters', or of Hecate. It is
needless therefore to insist that such a conception would be in contradiction with his whole tragic practice. The prophecies of the Witches
are presented simply as dangerous circumstances with which Macbeth
has to deal: they are dramatically on the same level as the story of the
Ghost in *Hamlet*, or the falsehoods told by Iago to Othello. Macbeth
is, in the ordinary sense, perfectly free in regard to them: and if we
speak of degrees of freedom, he is even more free than Hamlet, who
was crippled by melancholy when the Ghost appeared to him. That
the influence of the first prophecies upon him came as much from
himself as from them, is made abundantly clear by the obviously
intentional contrast between him and Banquo. Banquo, ambitious
but perfectly honest, is scarcely even startled by them, and he remains
throughout the scene indifferent to them. But when Macbeth heard
them he was not an innocent man. Precisely how far his mind was
guilty may be a question; but no innocent man would have started, as
he did, with a start of *fear* at the mere prophecy of a crown, or have
conceived thereupon *immediately* the thought of murder. Either this
thought was not new to him,[13] or he had cherished at least some

---

[11] The doubt as to these passages (see Note Z) does not arise from the mere appearance of
this figure. The idea of Hecate's connection with witches appears also at II.i.52, and she is
mentioned again at III.ii.41 (cf. *Mid. Night's Dream*, V.i.391, for her connection with fairies).
It is part of the common traditional notion of the heathen gods being now devils. Scot refers to
it several times. See the notes in the Clarendon Press edition on III.v.1., or those in Furness's
Variorum.

Of course in the popular notion the witch's spirits are devils or servants of Satan. (If
Shakespeare openly introduces this idea only in such phrases as 'the instruments of darkness'
and 'what! can the devil speak true?' the reason is probably his unwillingness to give too much
prominence to distinctly religious ideas.

[12] If this paragraph is true, some of the statements even of Lamb and of Coleridge about the
Witches are, taken literally, incorrect. What these critics, and notably the former, describe so
well is the poetic aspect abstracted from the remainder; and in describing this they attribute to
the Witches themselves what belongs really to the complex of Witches, Spirits, and Hecate. For
the purpose of imagination, no doubt, this inaccuracy is of small consequence; and it is these
purposes that matter. [I have not attempted to fulfil them.]

[13] See Note CC.

vaguer dishonourable dream, the instantaneous recurrence of which, at the moment of his hearing the prophecy, revealed to him an inward and terrifying guilt. In either case not only was he free to accept or resist the temptation, but the temptation was already within him. We are admitting too much, therefore, when we compare him with Othello, for Othello's mind was perfectly free from suspicion when his temptation came to him. And we are admitting, again, too much when we use the word 'temptation' in reference to the first prophecies of the Witches. Speaking strictly we must affirm that he was tempted only by himself. *He* speaks indeed of their 'supernatural soliciting'; but in fact they did not solicit. They merely announced events: they hailed him as Thane of Glamis, Thane of Cawdor, and King hereafter. No connection of these announcements with any action of his was even hinted by them. For all that appears, the natural death of an old man might have fulfilled the prophecy any day.[14] In any case, the idea of fulfilling it by murder was entirely his own.[15]

When Macbeth sees the Witches again, after the murders of Duncan and Banquo, we observe, however, a striking change. They no longer need to go and meet him; he seeks them out. He has committed himself to his course of evil. Now accordingly they do 'solicit'. They prophesy, but they also give advice: they bid him be bloody, bold, and secure. We have no hope that he will reject their advice; but so far are they from having, even now, any power to compel him to accept it, that they make careful preparations to deceive him into doing so. And, almost as though to intimate how entirely the responsibility for his deeds still lies with Macbeth, Shakespeare makes his first act after this interview one for which his tempters gave him not a hint – the slaughter of Macduff's wife and children.

To all this we must add that Macbeth himself nowhere betrays a suspicion that his action is, or has been, thrust on him by an external power. He curses the Witches for deceiving him, but he never attempts to shift to them the burden of his guilt. Neither has

---

[14] The proclamation of Malcolm as Duncan's successor (I.iv.) changes the position, but the design of murder is prior to this.

[15] Schlegel's* assertion that the first thought of the murder comes from the Witches is thus in flat contradiction with the text. (The sentence in which he asserts this is, I may observe, badly mistranslated in the English version, which, wherever I have consulted the original, shows itself untrustworthy. It ought to be revised, for Schlegel is well worth reading.)

Shakespeare placed in the mouth of any other character in this play such fatalistic expressions as may be found in *King Lear* and occasionally elsewhere. He appears actually to have taken pains to make the natural psychological genesis of Macbeth's crimes perfectly clear, and it was a most unfortunate notion of Schlegel's that the Witches were required because natural agencies would have seemed too weak to drive such a man as Macbeth to his first murder.

'Still,' it may be said, 'the Witches did foreknow Macbeth's future; and what is foreknown is fixed; and how can a man be responsible when his future is fixed?' With this question, as a speculative one, we have no concern here; but, in so far as it relates to the play, I answer, first, that not one of the things foreknown is an action. This is just as true of the later prophecies as of the first. That Macbeth will be harmed by none of woman born, and will never be vanquished till Birnam Wood shall come against him, involves (so far as we are informed) no action of his. It may be doubted, indeed, whether Shakespeare would have introduced prophecies of Macbeth's deeds, even if it had been convenient to do so; he would probably have felt that to do so would interfere with the interest of the inward struggle and suffering. And, in the second place, *Macbeth* was not written for students of metaphysics or theology, but for people at large; and, however it may be with prophecies of actions, prophecies of mere events do not suggest to people at large any sort of difficulty about responsibility. Many people, perhaps most, habitually think of their 'future' as something fixed, and of themselves as 'free'. The Witches nowadays take a room in Bond Street and charge a guinea; and when the victim enters they hail him the possessor of £1,000 a year, or prophesy to him of journeys, wives, and children. But though he is struck dumb by their prescience, it does not even cross his mind that he is going to lose his glorious 'freedom' – not though journeys and marriages imply much more agency on his part than anything foretold to Macbeth. This whole difficulty is undramatic; and I may add that Shakespeare nowhere shows, like Chaucer, any interest in speculative problems concerning foreknowledge, predestination and freedom.

(2) We may deal more briefly with the opposite interpretation. According to it the Witches and their prophecies are to be taken merely as symbolical representations of thoughts and desires which have slumbered in Macbeth's breast and now rise into consciousness

and confront him. With this idea, which springs from the wish to get rid of a mere external supernaturalism, and to find a psychological and spiritual meaning in that which the groundlings probably received as hard facts, one may feel sympathy. But it is evident that it is rather a 'philosophy' of the Witches than an immediate dramatic apprehension of them; and even so it will be found both incomplete and, in other respects, inadequate.

It is incomplete because it cannot possibly be applied to all the facts. Let us grant that it will apply to the most important prophecy, that of the crown; and that the later warning which Macbeth receives, to beware of Macduff, also answers to something in his own breast and 'harps his fear aright'. But there we have to stop. Macbeth had evidently no suspicion of that treachery in Cawdor through which he himself became Thane; and who will suggest that he had any idea, however subconscious, about Birnam Wood or the man not born of woman? It may be held – and rightly, I think – that the prophecies which answer to nothing inward, the prophecies which are merely supernatural, produce, now at any rate, much less imaginative effect than the others, – even that they are in *Macbeth* an element which was of an age and not for all time; but still they are there, and they are essential to the plot.[16] And as the theory under consideration will not apply to them at all, it is not likely that it gives an adequate account even of those prophecies to which it can in some measure be applied.

It is inadequate here chiefly because it is much too narrow. The Witches and their prophecies, if they are to be rationalized or taken symbolically, must represent not only the evil slumbering in the hero's soul, but all those obscurer influences of the evil around him in the world which aid his own ambition and the incitements of his wife. Such influences, even if we put aside all belief in evil 'spirits', are as certain, momentous, and terrifying facts as the presence of inchoate evil in the soul itself; and if we exclude all reference to these facts from our idea of the Witches, it will be greatly impoverished and will certainly fail to correspond with the imaginative effect. The union of the outward and inward here may be compared with something of the

---

[16] It is noticeable that Dr. Forman,* who saw the play in 1610 and wrote a sketch of it in his journal, says nothing about the later prophecies. Perhaps he despised them as mere stuff for the groundlings. The reader will find, I think, that the great poetic effect of Act IV, Sc. i. depends much more on the 'charm' which precedes Macbeth's entrance, and on Macbeth himself, than on the predictions.

same kind in Greek poetry.[17] In the first book of the *Iliad** we are told that, when Agamemnon threatened to take Briseis from Achilles, 'grief came upon Peleus' son, and his heart within his shaggy breast was divided in counsel, whether to draw his keen blade from his thigh and set the company aside and so slay Atreides, or to assuage his anger and curb his soul. While yet he doubted thereof in heart and soul, and was drawing his great sword from his sheath, Athene came to him from heaven, sent forth of the white-armed goddess Hera, whose heart loved both alike and had care for them. She stood behind Peleus' son and caught him by his golden hair, to him only visible, and of the rest no man beheld her'. And at her bidding he mastered his wrath, 'and stayed his heavy hand on the silver hilt, and thrust the great sword back into the sheath, and was not disobedient to the saying of Athene'[18] The succour of the goddess here only strengthens an inward movement in the mind of Achilles, but we should lose something besides a poetic effect if for that reason we struck her out of the account. We should lose the idea that the inward powers of the soul answer in their essence to vaster powers without, which support them and assure the effect of their exertion. So it is in *Macbeth*.[19] The words of the Witches are fatal to the hero only because there is in him something which leaps into light at the sound of them; but they are at the same time the witness of forces which never cease to work in the world around him, and, on the instant of his surrender to them, entangle him inextricably in the web of Fate. If the inward connection is once realized (and Shakespeare has left us no excuse for missing it), we need not fear, and indeed shall scarcely be able, to exaggerate the effect of the Witch-scenes in heightening and deepening the sense of fear, horror, and mystery which pervades the atmosphere of the tragedy.

3

From this murky background stand out the two great terrible figures, who dwarf all the remaining characters of the drama. Both are

---

[17] This comparison was suggested by a passage in Hegel's *Aesthetik,* i.291 ff.

[18] *Il.*i.188 ff. (Leaf's translation).

[19] The supernaturalism of the modern poet, indeed, is more 'external' than that of the ancient. We have already had evidence of this, and shall find more when we come to the character of Banquo.

sublime, and both inspire, far more than the other tragic heroes, the feeling of awe. They are never detached in imagination from the atmosphere which surrounds them and adds to their grandeur and terror. It is, as it were, continued into their souls. For within them is all that we felt without – the darkness of night, lit with the flame of tempest and the hues of blood, and haunted by wild and direful shapes, 'murdering ministers', spirits of remorse, and maddening visions of peace lost and judgment to come. The way to be untrue to Shakespeare here, as always, is to relax the tension of imagination, to conventionalize, to conceive Macbeth, for example, as a half-hearted cowardly criminal, and Lady Macbeth as a whole-hearted fiend.

These two characters are fired by one and the same passion of ambition; and to a considerable extent they are alike. The disposition of each is high, proud, and commanding. They are born to rule, if not to reign. They are peremptory or contemptuous to their inferiors. They are not children of light, like Brutus and Hamlet; they are of the world. We observe in them no love of country, and no interest in the welfare of anyone outside their family. Their habitual thoughts and aims are, and, we imagine, long have been, all of station and power. And though in both there is something, and in one much, of what is higher – honour, conscience, humanity – they do not live consciously in the light of these things or speak their language. Not that they are egoists, like Iago; or, if they are egoists, theirs is an *egoïsme à deux.* They have no separate ambitions.[20] They support and love one another. They suffer together. And if, as time goes on, they drift a little apart, they are not vulgar souls, to be alienated and recriminate when they experience the fruitlessness of their ambition. They remain to the end tragic, even grand.

So far there is much likeness between them. Otherwise they are contrasted, and the action is built upon this contrast. Their attitudes towards the projected murder of Duncan are quite different; and it produces in them equally different effects. In consequence, they appear in the earlier part of the play as of equal importance, if indeed Lady Macbeth does not overshadow her husband; but afterwards she retires more and more into the background, and he becomes unmis-

---

[20] The assertion that Lady Macbeth sought a crown for herself, or sought anything for herself, apart from her husband, is absolutely unjustified by anything in the play. It is based on a sentence of Holinshed's* which Shakespeare did *not* use.

takably the leading figure. His is indeed far the more complex character: and I will speak of it first.

Macbeth, the cousin of a King mild, just, and beloved, but now too old to lead his army, is introduced to us as a general of extraordinary prowess, who has covered himself with glory in putting down a rebellion and repelling the invasion of a foreign army. In these conflicts he showed great personal courage, a quality which he continues to display throughout the drama in regard to all plain dangers. It is difficult to be sure of his customary demeanour, for in the play we see him either in what appears to be an exceptional relation to his wife, or else in the throes of remorse and desperation; but from his behaviour during his journey home after the war, from his *later* conversations with Lady Macbeth, and from his language to the murderers of Banquo and to others, we imagine him as a great warrior, somewhat masterful, rough, and abrupt, a man to inspire some fear and much admiration. He was thought 'honest', or honourable; he was trusted, apparently, by everyone; Macduff, a man of the highest integrity, 'loved him well'. And there was, in fact, much good in him. We have no warrant, I think, for describing him, with many writers, as of a 'noble' nature, like Hamlet or Othello;[21] but he had a keen sense both of humour and of the worth of a good name. The phrase, again, 'too full of the milk of human kindness', is applied to him in impatience by his wife, who did not fully understand him; but certainly he was far from devoid of humanity and pity.

At the same time he was exceedingly ambitious. He must have been so by temper. The tendency must have been greatly strengthened by his marriage. When we see him, it has been further stimulated by his remarkable success and by the consciousness of exceptional powers and merit. It becomes a passion. The course of action suggested by it is extremely perilous: it sets his good name, his position, and even his life on the hazard. It is also abhorrent to his better feelings. Their defeat in the struggle with ambition leaves him utterly wretched, and would have kept him so, however complete had been his outward success and security. On the other hand, his passion for power and his instinct of self-assertion are so vehement that no inward misery could

---

[21] The word is used of him (I.ii.67), but not in a way that decides this question or even bears on it.

persuade him to relinquish the fruits of crime, or to advance from remorse to repentance.

In the character as so far sketched there is nothing very peculiar, though the strength of the forces contending in it is unusual. But there is in Macbeth one marked peculiarity, the true apprehension of which is the key to Shakespeare's conception.[22] This bold ambitious man of action, has, within certain limits, the imagination of a poet – an imagination on the one hand extremely sensitive to impressions of a certain kind, and, on the other, productive of violent disturbance both of mind and body. Through it he is kept in contact with supernatural impressions and is liable to supernatural fears. And through it, especially, come to him the intimations of conscience and honour. Macbeth's better nature – to put the matter for clearness' sake too broadly – instead of speaking to him in the overt language of moral ideas, commands, and prohibitions, incorporates itself in images which alarm and horrify. His imagination is thus the best of him, something usually deeper and higher than his conscious thoughts; and if he had obeyed it he would have been safe. But his wife quite misunderstands it, and he himself understands it only in part. The terrifying images which deter him from crime and follow its commission, and which are really the protest of his deepest self, seem to his wife the creations of mere nervous fear, and are sometimes referred by himself to the dread of vengeance or the restlessness of insecurity.[23] His conscious or reflective mind, that is, moves chiefly among considerations of outward success and failure, while his inner being is convulsed by conscience. And his inability to understand himself is repeated and exaggerated in the interpretations of actors and critics, who represent him as a coward, cold-blooded, calculating, and pitiless, who shrinks from crime simply because it is dangerous, and suffers afterwards simply because he is not safe. In reality his courage is frightful. He strides from crime to crime, though his soul never ceases to bar his advance with shapes of terror, or to clamour in his ears that he is murdering his peace and casting away his 'eternal jewel'.

It is of the first importance to realize the strength, and also (what has not been so clearly recognized) the limits, of Macbeth's imagina-

---

[22] This view, thus generally stated, is not original, but I cannot say who first stated it.

[23] The latter, and more important, point was put quite clearly by Coleridge.

tion. It is not the universal meditative imagination of Hamlet. He came to see in man, as Hamlet sometimes did, the 'quintessence of dust'; but he must always have been incapable of Hamlet's reflections on man's noble reason and infinite faculty, or of seeing with Hamlet's eyes 'this brave o'erhanging firmament, this majestical roof fretted with golden fire'. Nor could he feel, like Othello, the romance of war or the infinity of love. He shows no sign of any unusual sensitiveness to the glory or beauty in the world or the soul; and it is partly for this reason that we have no inclination to love him, and that we regard him with more of awe than of pity. His imagination is excitable and intense, but narrow. That which stimulates it is, almost solely, that which thrills with sudden, startling, and often supernatural fear.[24] There is a famous passage late in the play (V.v.10) which is here very significant, because it refers to a time before his conscience was burdened, and so shows his native disposition:

> The time has been, my senses would have cool'd
> To hear a night-shriek; and my fell of hair
> Would at a dismal treatise rise and stir
> As life were in't.

This 'time' must have been in his youth, or at least before we see him. And, in the drama, everything which terrifies him is of this character, only it has now a deeper and a moral significance. Palpable dangers leave him unmoved or fill him with fire. He does himself mere justice when he asserts he 'dare do all that may become a man', or when he exclaims to Banquo's ghost,

> What man dare, I dare:
> Approach thou like the rugged Russian bear,
> The arm'd rhinoceros, or the Hyrcan tiger;
> Take any shape but that, and my firm nerves
> Shall never tremble.

What appals him is always the image of his own guilty heart or bloody deed, or some image which derives from them its terror or gloom. These, when they arise, hold him spellbound and possess him wholly, like a hypnotic trance which is at the same time the ecstasy of a poet.

---

[24] It is the consequent insistence on the idea of fear, and the frequent repetition of the word, that have principally led to misinterpretation.

As the first 'horrid image' of Duncan's murder – of himself murdering
Duncan – rises from unconsciousness and confronts him, his hair
stands on end and the outward scene vanishes from his eyes. Why?
For fear of 'consequences'? The idea is ridiculous. Or because the deed
is bloody? The man who with his 'smoking' steel 'carved out his
passage' to the rebel leader, and 'unseam'd him from the nave to the
chaps', would hardly be frightened by blood. How could fear of
consequences make the dagger he is to use hang suddenly glittering
before him in the air, and then as suddenly dash it with gouts of
blood? Even when he *talks* of consequences, and declares that if he
were safe against them he would 'jump the life to come', his imagination bears witness against him, and shows us that what really holds
him back is the hideous vileness of the deed:

> He's here in double trust;
> First, as I am his kinsman and his subject,
> Strong both against the deed; then, as his host,
> Who should against his murderer shut the door,
> Not bear the knife myself. Besides, this Duncan
> Hath borne his faculties so meek, hath been
> So clear in his great office, that his virtues
> Will plead like angels, trumpet-tongued, against
> The deep damnation of his taking-off;
> And pity, like a naked new-born babe,
> Striding the blast, or heaven's cherubim, horsed
> Upon the sightless couriers of the air,
> Shall blow the horrid deed in every eye,
> That tears shall drown the wind.

It may be said that he is here thinking of the horror that others will
feel at the deed – thinking therefore of consequences. Yes, but could
he realize thus how horrible the deed would look to others if it were
not equally horrible to himself?

It is the same when the murder is done. He is well-nigh mad with
horror, but it is not the horror of detection. It is not he who thinks
of washing his hands or getting his nightgown on. He has brought
away the daggers he should have left on the pillows of the grooms,
but what does he care for that? What *he* thinks of is that, when he
heard one of the men awaked from sleep say 'God bless us', he could
not say 'Amen'; for his imagination presents to him the parching of
his throat as an immediate judgment from heaven. His wife heard

the owl scream and the crickets cry; but what *he* heard was the voice that first cried 'Macbeth doth murder sleep', and then, a minute later, with a change of tense, denounced on him, as if his three names gave him three personalities to suffer in, the doom of sleep-lessness:

> Glamis hath murdered sleep, and therefore Cawdor
> Shall sleep no more, Macbeth shall sleep no more.

There comes a sound of knocking. It should be perfectly familiar to him; but he knows not whence, or from what world, it comes. He looks down at his hands, and starts violently: 'What hands are here?' For they seem alive, they move, they mean to pluck out his eyes. He looks at one of them again; it does not move; but the blood upon it is enough to dye the whole ocean red. What has all this to do with fear of 'consequences'? It is his soul speaking in the only shape in which it can speak freely, that of imagination.

So long as Macbeth's imagination is active, we watch him fasci-nated; we feel suspense, horror, awe; in which are latent, also, admi-ration and sympathy. But so soon as it is quiescent these feelings vanish. He is no longer 'infirm of purpose': he becomes domineering, even brutal, or he becomes a cool pitiless hypocrite. He is generally said to be a very bad actor, but this is not wholly true. Whenever his imagination stirs, he acts badly. It so possesses him, and is so much stronger than his reason, that his face betrays him, and his voice utters the most improbable untruths[25] or the most artificial rhetoric.[26] But when it is asleep he is firm, self-controlled and practical, as in the conversation where he skilfully elicits from Banquo that information about his movements which is required for the successful arrangement of his murder.[27] Here he is hateful; and so he is in the conversation with the murderers, who are not professional cut-throats but old soldiers, and whom, without a vestige of remorse, he beguiles with calumnies against Banquo and with such appeals as his wife had used

---

[25] *E.g.* I.iii.149, where he excuses his abstraction by saying that his 'dull brain was wrought with things forgotten', when nothing could be more natural than that he should be thinking of his new honour.

[26] *E.g.* in I.iv. This is so also in II.iii.114 ff., though here there is some real imaginative excitement mingled with the rhetorical antitheses and balanced clauses and forced bombast.

[27] III.i. Lady Macbeth herself could not more naturally have introduced at intervals the ques-tions 'Ride you this afternoon?' (l. 19), 'Is't far you ride?' (l. 24), 'Goes Fleance with you?' (l. 36).

to him.[28] On the other hand, we feel much pity as well as anxiety in the scene (I.vii) where she overcomes his opposition to the murder; and we feel it (though his imagination is not specially active) because this scene shows us how little he understands himself. This is his great misfortune here. Not that he fails to realize in reflection the baseness of the deed (the soliloquy with which the scene opens shows that he does not). But he has never, to put it pedantically, accepted as the principle of his conduct the morality which takes shape in his imaginative fears. Had he done so, and said plainly to his wife, 'The thing is vile, and, however much I have sworn to do it, I will not', she would have been helpless; for all her arguments proceed on the assumption that there is for them no such point of view. Macbeth does approach this position once, when, resenting the accusation of cowardice, he answers,

> I dare do all that may become a man;
> Who dares do more is none.

She feels in an instant that everything is at stake, and, ignoring the point, ¯overwhelms him with indignant and contemptuous personal reproach. But he yields to it because he is himself half-ashamed of that answer of his, and because, for want of habit, the simple idea which it expresses has no hold on him comparable to the force it acquires when it becomes incarnate in visionary fears and warnings.

---

[28] We feel here, however, an underlying subdued frenzy which awakes some sympathy. There is an almost unendurable impatience expressed even in the rhythm of many of the lines; e.g.:

> Well then, now
> Have you consider'd of my speeches? Know
> That it was he in the times past which held you
> So under fortune, which you thought had been
> Our innocent self: this I made good to you
> In our last conference, pass'd in probation with you,
> How you were borne in hand, how cross'd, the instruments,
> Who wrought with them, and all things else that might
> To half a soul and to a notion crazed
> Say, 'Thus did Banquo.'

This effect is heard to the end of the play in Macbeth's less poetic speeches, and leaves the same impression of burning energy, though not of imaginative exaltation, as his great speeches. In these we find either violent, huge, sublime imagery, or a torrent of figurative expressions (as in the famous lines about 'the innocent sleep'). Our impressions as to the diction of the play are largely derived from these speeches of the hero, but not wholly so. The writing almost throughout leaves an impression of intense, almost feverish, activity.

Yet these were so insistent, and they offered to his ambition a resistance so strong, that it is impossible to regard him as falling through the blindness or delusion of passion. On the contrary, he himself feels with such intensity the enormity of his purpose that, it seems clear, neither his ambition nor yet the prophecy of the Witches would ever without the aid of Lady Macbeth have overcome this feeling. As it is, the deed is done in horror and without the faintest desire or sense of glory – done, one may almost say, as if it were an appalling duty; and, the instant it is finished, its futility is revealed to Macbeth as clearly as its vileness had been revealed beforehand. As he staggers from the scene he mutters in despair,

Wake Duncan with thy knocking! I would thou could'st.

When, half an hour later, he returns with Lennox from the room of the murder, he breaks out:

Had I but died an hour before this chance,
I had lived a blessed time; for from this instant
There's nothing serious in mortality:
All is but toys: renown and grace is dead;
The wine of life is drawn, and the mere lees
Is left this vault to brag of.

This is no mere acting. The language here has none of the false rhetoric of his merely hypocritical speeches. It is meant to deceive, but it utters at the same time his profoundest feeling. And this he can henceforth never hide from himself for long. However he may try to drown it in further enormities, he hears it murmuring,

Duncan is in his grave:
After life's fitful fever he sleeps well:

or,

better be with the dead:

or,

I have lived long enough:

and it speaks its last words on the last day of his life:

Out, out, brief candle!
Life's but a walking shadow, a poor player

That struts and frets his hour upon the stage
And then is heard no more: it is a tale
Told by an idiot, full of sound and fury,
Signifying nothing.

How strange that this judgment on life, the despair of a man who had knowingly made mortal war on his own soul, should be frequently quoted as Shakespeare's own judgment, and should even be adduced, in serious criticism, as a proof of his pessimism!

It remains to look a little more fully at the history of Macbeth after the murder of Duncan. Unlike his first struggle this history excites little suspense or anxiety on his account: we have now no hope for him. But it is an engrossing spectacle, and psychologically it is perhaps the most remarkable exhibition of the *development* of a character to be found in Shakespeare's tragedies.

That heart-sickness which comes from Macbeth's perception of the futility of his crime, and which never leaves him for long, is not, however, his habitual state. It could not be so, for two reasons. In the first place the consciousness of guilt is stronger in him than the consciousness of failure; and it keeps him in a perpetual agony of restlessness, and forbids him simply to droop and pine. His mind is 'full of scorpions'. He cannot sleep. He 'keeps alone', moody and savage. 'All that is within him does condemn itself for being there.' There is a fever in his blood which urges him to ceaseless action in the search for oblivion. And, in the second place, ambition, the love of power, the instinct of self-assertion, are much too potent in Macbeth to permit him to resign, even in spirit, the prize for which he has put rancours in the vessel of his peace. The 'will to live' is mighty in him. The forces which impelled him to aim at the crown re-assert themselves. He faces the world, and his own conscience, desperate, but never dreaming of acknowledging defeat. He will see 'the frame of things disjoint' first. He challenges fate into the lists.

The result is frightful. He speaks no more, as before Duncan's murder, of honour or pity. That sleepless torture, he tells himself, is nothing but the sense of insecurity and the fear of retaliation. If only he were safe, it would vanish. And he looks about for the cause of his fear; and his eye falls on Banquo. Banquo, who cannot fail to suspect him, has not fled or turned against him: Banquo has become his chief counsellor. Why? Because, he answers, the kingdom was promised to

Banquo's children. Banquo, then, is waiting to attack him, to make a way for them. The 'bloody instructions' he himself taught when he murdered Duncan, are about to return, as he said they would, to plague the inventor. *This* then, he tells himself, is the fear that will not let him sleep; and it will die with Banquo. There is no hesitation now, and no remorse: he has nearly learned his lesson. He hastens feverishly, not to murder Banquo, but to procure his murder: some strange idea is in his mind that the thought of the dead man will not haunt him, like the memory of Duncan, if the deed is done by other hands.[29] The deed is done: but, instead of peace descending on him, from the depths of his nature his half-murdered conscience rises; his deed confronts him in the apparition of Banquo's Ghost, and the horror of the night of his first murder returns. But, alas, *it* has less power, and *he* has more will. Agonized and trembling, he still faces this rebel image, and it yields:

> Why, so: being gone,
> I am a man again.

Yes, but his secret is in the hands of the assembled lords. And, worse, this deed is as futile as the first. For, though Banquo is dead and even his Ghost is conquered, that inner torture is unassuaged. But he will not bear it. His guests have hardly left him when he turns roughly to his wife:

> How say'st thou, that Macduff denies his person
> At our great bidding?

Macduff it is that spoils his sleep. He shall perish – he and aught else that bars the road to peace.

> For mine own good
> All causes shall give way: I am in blood
> Stepp'd in so far that, should I wade no more,
> Returning were as tedious as go o'er:
> Strange things I have in head that will to hand,
> Which must be acted ere they may be scann'd.

She answers, sick at heart.

> You lack the season of all natures, sleep.

---

[29] See his first words to the Ghost: 'Thou canst not say I did it.'

No doubt: but he has found the way to it now:

> Come, we'll to sleep. My strange and self abuse
> Is the initiate fear that wants hard use:
> We are yet but young in deed.

What a change from the man who thought of Duncan's virtues, and of pity like a naked new-born babe! What a frightful clearness of self-consciousness in this descent to hell, and yet what a furious force in the instinct of life and self-assertion that drives him on!

He goes to seek the Witches. He will know, by the worst means, the worst. He has no longer any awe of them.

> How now, you secret, black and midnight hags!

– so he greets them, and at once he demands and threatens. They tell him he is right to fear Macduff. They tell him to fear nothing, for none of woman born can harm him. He feels that the two statements are at variance; infatuated, suspects no double meaning; but, that he may 'sleep in spite of thunder', determines not to spare Macduff. But his heart throbs to know one thing, and he forces from the Witches the vision of Banquo's children crowned. The old intolerable thought returns, 'for Banquo's issue have I filed my mind'; and with it, for all the absolute security apparently promised him, there returns that inward fever. Will nothing quiet it? Nothing but destruction. Macduff, one comes to tell him, has escaped him; but that does not matter: he can still destroy:[30]

> And even now,
> To crown my thoughts with acts, be it thought and done:
> The castle of Macduff I will surprise;
> Seize upon Fife; give to the edge o' the sword
> His wife, his babes, and all unfortunate souls
> That trace him in's line. No boasting like a fool;
> This deed I'll do before this purpose cool.
> But no more sights!

---

[30] For only in destroying I find ease
  To my relentless thoughts. – *Paradise Lost*, ix.129.

Milton's portrait of Satan's misery here, and at the beginning of Book IV., might well have been suggested by *Macbeth*. Coleridge, after quoting Duncan's speech, I.iv.35 ff., says: 'It is a fancy; but I can never read this, and the following speeches of Macbeth, without involuntarily thinking of the Miltonic Messiah and Satan.' I doubt if it was a mere fancy. (It will be remembered that Milton thought at one time of writing a tragedy on Macbeth.)

No, he need fear no more 'sights'. The Witches have done their work, and after this purposeless butchery his own imagination will trouble him no more.[31] He has dealt his last blow at the conscience and pity which spoke through it.

The whole flood of evil in his nature is now let loose. He becomes an open tyrant, dreaded by everyone about him, and a terror to his country. She 'sinks beneath the yoke'.

> Each new morn
> New widows howl, new orphans cry, new sorrows
> Strike heaven on the face.

She weeps, she bleeds, 'and each new day a gash is added to her wounds'. She is not the mother of her children, but their grave;

> where nothing,
> But who knows nothing, is once seen to smile:
> Where sighs and groans and shrieks that rend the air
> Are made, not mark'd.

For this wild rage and furious cruelty we are prepared; but vices of another kind start up as he plunges on his downward way.

> I grant him bloody,
> Luxurious, avaricious, false, deceitful,
> Sudden, malicious,

says Malcolm; and two of these epithets surprise us. Who would have expected avarice or lechery[32] in Macbeth? His ruin seems complete.

Yet it is never complete. To the end he never totally loses our sympathy; we never feel towards him as we do to those who appear the born children of darkness. There remains something sublime in the defiance with which, even when cheated of his last hope, he faces

---

[31] The immediate reference in 'But no more sights' is doubtless to the visions called up by the Witches; but one of these, the 'blood-bolter'd Banquo', recalls to him the vision of the preceding night, of which he had said,

> You make me strange
> Even to the disposition that I owe,
> When now I think you can behold such *sights*,
> And keep the natural ruby of your cheeks,
> When mine is blanch'd with fear.

[32] 'Luxurious' and 'luxury' are used by Shakespeare only in this older sense. It must be remembered that these lines are spoken by Malcolm, but it seems likely that they are meant to be taken as true throughout.

earth and hell and heaven. Nor would any soul to whom evil was congenial be capable of that heart sickness which overcomes him when he thinks of the 'honour, love, obedience, troops of friends' which 'he must not look to have' (and which Iago would never have cared to have), and contrasts with them

> Curses, not loud but deep, mouth-honour, breath,
> Which the poor heart would fain deny, and dare not,

(and which Iago would have accepted with indifference). Neither can I agree with those who find in his reception of the news of his wife's death proof of alienation or utter carelessness. There is no proof of these in the words,

> She should have died hereafter;
> There would have been a time for such a word,

spoken as they are by a man already in some measure prepared for such news, and now transported by the frenzy of his last fight for life. He has no time now to feel.[33] Only, as he thinks of the morrow when time to feel will come – if anything comes – the vanity of all hopes and forward-lookings sinks deep into his soul with an infinite weariness, and he murmurs,

> To-morrow, and to-morrow, and to-morrow,
> Creeps in this petty pace from day to day
> To the last syllable of recorded time,
> And all our yesterdays have lighted fools
> The way to dusty death.

In the very depths a gleam of his native love of goodness, and with it a touch of tragic grandeur, rests upon him. The evil he has desperately

---

[33] I do not at all suggest that his love for his wife remains what it was when he greeted her with the words 'My dearest love, Duncan comes here to-night'. He has greatly changed; she has ceased to help him, sunk in her own despair; and there is no intensity of anxiety in the questions he puts to the doctor about her. But his love for her was probably never unselfish, never the love of Brutus, who, in somewhat similar circumstances, uses, on the death of Cassius, words which remind us of Macbeth's:

> I shall find time, Cassius, I shall find time.

For the opposite strain of feeling cf. Sonnet 90:

> Then hate me if thou wilt; if ever, now,
> Now while the world is bent my deeds to cross.

embraced continues to madden or to wither his inmost heart. No experience in the world could bring him to glory in it or make his peace with it, or to forget what he once was and Iago and Goneril never were.

LECTURE X

MACBETH

1

To regard *Macbeth* as a play, like the love-tragedies *Romeo and Juliet* and *Antony and Cleopatra*, in which there are two central characters of equal importance, is certainly a mistake. But Shakespeare himself is in a measure responsible for it, because the first half of *Macbeth* is greater than the second, and in the first half Lady Macbeth not only appears more than in the second but exerts the ultimate deciding influence on the action. And, in the opening Act at least, Lady Macbeth is the most commanding and perhaps the most awe-inspiring figure that Shakespeare drew. Sharing, as we have seen, certain traits with her husband, she is at once clearly distinguished from him by an inflexibility of will, which appears to hold imagination, feeling, and conscience completely in check. To her the prophecy of things that will be becomes instantaneously the determination that they shall be:

> Glamis thou art, and Cawdor, and shalt be
> What thou art promised.

She knows her husband's weakness, how he scruples 'to catch the nearest way' to the object he desires; and she sets herself without a trace of doubt or conflict to counteract this weakness. To her there is no separation between will and deed; and, as the deed falls in part to her, she is sure it will be done:

> The raven himself is hoarse
> That croaks the fatal entrance of Duncan
> Under my battlements.

On the moment of Macbeth's rejoining her, after braving infinite dangers and winning infinite praise, without a syllable on these subjects or a word of affection, she goes straight to her purpose and permits him to speak of nothing else. She takes the superior position and assumes the direction of affairs – appears to assume it even more than she really can, that she may spur him on. She animates him by

picturing the deed as heroic, 'this night's *great* business', or 'our *great*
quell', while she ignores its cruelty and faithlessness. She bears down
his faint resistance by presenting him with a prepared scheme which
may remove from him the terror and danger of deliberation. She
rouses him with a taunt no man can bear, and least of all a soldier –
the word 'coward'. She appeals even to his love for her:

> from this time
> Such I account thy love;

– such, that is, as the protestations of a drunkard. Her seasonings are
mere sophisms; they could persuade no man. It is not by them, it is
by personal appeals, through the admiration she extorts from him,
and through sheer force of will, that she impels him to the deed. Her
eyes are fixed upon the crown and the means to it; she does not attend
to the consequences. Her plan of laying the guilt upon the chamberlains is invented on the spur of the moment, and simply to satisfy her
husband. Her true mind is heard in the ringing cry with which she
answers his question, 'Will it not be received . . . that they have done
it?'

> Who *dares* receive it other?

And this is repeated in the sleep-walking scene: 'What need we fear
who knows it, when none can call our power to account?' Her
passionate courage sweeps him off his feet. His decision is taken in a
moment of enthusiasm:

> Bring forth men-children only;
> For thy undaunted mettle should compose
> Nothing but males.

And even when passion has quite died away her will remains supreme.
In presence of overwhelming horror and danger, in the murder scene
and the banquet scene, her self-control is perfect. When the truth of
what she has done dawns on her, no word of complaint, scarcely a
word of her own suffering, not a single word of her own as apart from
his, escapes her when others are by. She helps him, but never asks his
help. She leans on nothing but herself. And from the beginning to the
end – though she makes once or twice a slip in acting her part – her
will never fails her. Its grasp upon her nature may destroy her, but it
is never relaxed. We are sure that she never betrayed her husband or

herself by a word or even a look, save in sleep. However appalling she may be, she is sublime.

In the earlier scenes of the play this aspect of Lady Macbeth's character is far the most prominent. And if she seems invincible she seems also inhuman. We find no trace of pity for the kind old king; no consciousness of the treachery and baseness of the murder; no sense of the value of the lives of the wretched men on whom the guilt is to be laid; no shrinking even from the condemnation or hatred of the world. Yet if the Lady Macbeth of these scenes were really utterly inhuman, or a 'fiend-like queen', as Malcolm calls her, the Lady Macbeth of the sleep-walking scene would be an impossibility. The one woman could never become the other. And in fact, if we look below the surface, there is evidence enough in the earlier scenes of preparation for the later. I do not mean that Lady Macbeth was naturally humane. There is nothing in the play to show this, and several passages subsequent to the murder-scene supply proof to the contrary. One is that where she exclaims, on being informed of Duncan's murder,

> Woe, alas!
> What, in our house?

This mistake in acting shows that she does not even know what the natural feeling in such circumstances would be; and Banquo's curt answer, 'Too cruel anywhere', is almost a reproof of her insensibility. But, admitting this, we have in the first place to remember, in imagining the opening scenes, that she is deliberately bent on counteracting the 'human kindness' of her husband, and also that she is evidently not merely inflexibly determined but in a condition of abnormal excitability. That exaltation in the project which is so entirely lacking in Macbeth is strongly marked in her. When she tries to help him by representing their enterprise as heroic, she is deceiving herself as much as him. Their attainment of the crown presents itself to her, perhaps has long presented itself, as something so glorious, and she has fixed her will upon it so completely, that for the time she sees the enterprise in no other light than that of its greatness. When she soliloquizes,

> Yet do I fear thy nature:
> It is too full o' the milk of human kindness

To catch the nearest way: thou wouldst be great;
Art not without ambition, but without
The illness should attend it; what thou wouldst highly,
That wouldst thou holily,

one sees that 'ambition' and 'great' and 'highly' and even 'illness' are
to her simply terms of praise, and 'holily' and 'human kindness'
simply terms of blame. Moral distinctions do not in this exaltation
exist for her; or rather they are inverted: 'good' means to her the
crown and whatever is required to obtain it, 'evil' whatever stands in
the way of its attainment. This attitude of mind is evident even when
she is alone, though it becomes still more pronounced when she has
to work upon her husband. And it persists until her end is attained.
But, without being exactly forced, it betrays a strain which could not
long endure.

Besides this, in these earlier scenes the traces of feminine weakness
and human feeling, which account for her later failure, are not absent.
Her will, it is clear, was exerted to overpower not only her husband's
resistance but some resistance in herself. Imagine Goneril uttering the
famous words,

Had he not resembled
My father as he slept, I had done 't.

They are spoken, I think, without any sentiment – impatiently, as
though she regretted her weakness: but it was there. And in reality,
quite apart from this recollection of her father, she could never have
done the murder if her husband had failed. She had to nerve herself
with wine to give her 'boldness' enough to go through her minor part.
That appalling invocation to the spirits of evil, to unsex her and fill
her from the crown to the toe topfull of direst cruelty, tells the same
tale of determination to crush the inward protest. Goneril had no
need of such a prayer. In the utterance of the frightful lines,

I have given suck, and know
How tender 'tis to love the babe that milks me:
I would, while it was smiling in my face,
Have pluck'd my nipple from his boneless gums,
And dash'd the brains out, had I so sworn as you
Have done to this,

her voice should doubtless rise until it reaches, in 'dash'd the brains out', an almost hysterical scream.[1] These lines show unmistakably that strained exaltation which, as soon as the end is reached, vanishes, never to return.

The greatness of Lady Macbeth lies almost wholly in courage and force of will. It is an error to regard her as remarkable on the intellectual side. In acting a part she shows immense self-control, but not much skill. Whatever may be thought of the plan of attributing the murder of Duncan to the chamberlains, to lay their bloody daggers on their pillows, as if they were determined to advertise their guilt, was a mistake which can be accounted for only by the excitement of the moment. But the limitations of her mind appear most in the point where she is most strongly contrasted with Macbeth, – in her comparative dullness of imagination. I say 'comparative', for she sometimes uses highly poetic language, as indeed does everyone in Shakespeare who has any greatness of soul. Nor is she perhaps less imaginative than the majority of his heroines. But as compared with her husband she has little imagination. It is not *simply* that she suppresses what she has. To her, things remain at the most terrible moment precisely what they were at the calmest, plain facts which stand in a given relation to a certain deed, not visions which tremble and flicker in the light of other worlds. The probability that the old king will sleep soundly after his long journey to Inverness is to her simply a fortunate circumstance; but one can fancy the shoot of horror across Macbeth's face as she mentions it. She uses familiar and prosaic illustrations, like

> Letting 'I dare not' wait upon 'I would',
> Like the poor cat i' the adage,

(the cat who wanted fish but did not like to wet her feet); or

> We fail?
> But screw your courage to the sticking-place,
> And we'll not fail;[2]

or,

---

[1] So Mrs. Siddons* is said to have given the passage.

[2] Surely the usual interpretation of 'We fail?' as a question of contemptuous astonishment, is right. 'We fail!' gives practically the same sense, but alters the punctuation of the first two Folios. In either case, 'But', I think, means 'Only'. On the other hand the proposal to read 'We fail'. with a full stop, as expressive of sublime acceptance of the possibility, seems to me, however attractive at first sight, quite out of harmony with Lady Macbeth's mood throughout these scenes.

> Was the hope drunk
> Wherein you dress'd yourself? hath it slept since?
> And wakes it now, to look so green and pale
> At what it did so freely?

The Witches are practically nothing to her. She feels no sympathy in Nature with her guilty purpose, and would never bid the earth not hear her steps, which way they walk. The noises before the murder, and during it, are heard by her as simple facts, and are referred to their true sources. The knocking has no mystery for her: it comes from 'the south entry'. She calculates on the drunkenness of the grooms, compares the different effects of wine on herself and on them, and listens to their snoring. To her the blood upon her husband's hands suggests only the taunt,

> My hands are of your colour, but I shame
> To wear a heart so white;

and the blood to her is merely 'this filthy witness' – words impossible to her husband, to whom it suggested something quite other than sensuous disgust or practical danger. The literalism of her mind appears fully in two contemptuous speeches where she dismisses his imaginings; in the murder scene:

> Infirm of purpose!
> Give me the daggers! The sleeping and the dead
> Are but as pictures: 'tis the eye of childhood
> That fears a painted devil;

and in the banquet scene:

> O these flaws and starts,
> Impostors to true fear, would well become
> A woman's story at a winter's fire,
> Authorised by her grandam. Shame itself!
> Why do you make such faces? When all's done,
> You look but on a stool.

Even in the awful scene where her imagination breaks loose in sleep she uses no such images as Macbeth's. It is the direct appeal of the facts to sense that has fastened on her memory. The ghastly realism of 'Yet who would have thought the old man to have had so much blood in him?' or 'Here's the smell of the blood still', is wholly unlike him.

Her most poetical words, 'All the perfumes of Arabia will not sweeten this little hand', are equally unlike his words about great Neptune's ocean. Hers, like some of her other speeches, are the more moving, from their greater simplicity and because they seem to tell of that self-restraint in suffering which is so totally lacking in him; but there is in them comparatively little of imagination. If we consider most of the passages to which I have referred, we shall find that the quality which moves our admiration is courage or force of will.

This want of imagination, though it helps to make Lady Macbeth strong for immediate action, is fatal to her. If she does not feel before-hand the cruelty of Duncan's murder, this is mainly because she hardly imagines the act, or at most imagines its outward show, 'the motion of a muscle this way or that'. Nor does she in the least foresee those inward consequences which reveal themselves immediately in her husband, and less quickly in herself. It is often said that she under-stands him well. Had she done so, she never would have urged him on. She knows that he is given to strange fancies; but, not realizing what they spring from, she has no idea either that they may gain such power as to ruin the scheme, or that, while they mean present weak-ness, they mean also perception of the future. At one point in the murder scene the force of his imagination impresses her, and for a moment she is startled; a light threatens to break on her:

> These deeds must not be thought
> After these ways: so, it will make us mad,

she says, with a sudden and great seriousness. And when he goes pant-ing on, 'Methought I heard a voice cry, "Sleep no more",' . . . she breaks in, 'What do you mean?' half-doubting whether this was not a real voice that he heard. Then, almost directly, she recovers herself, convinced of the vanity of his fancy. Nor does she understand herself any better than him. She never suspects that these deeds *must* be thought after these ways; that her facile realism,

> A little water clears us of this deed,

will one day be answered by herself, 'Will these hands ne'er be clean?' or that the fatal commonplace, 'What's done is done', will make way for her last despairing sentence, 'What's done cannot be undone'.

Hence the development of her character – perhaps it would be more strictly accurate to say, the change in her state of mind – is both inevitable, and the opposite of the development we traced in Macbeth. When the murder has been done, the discovery of its hideousness, first reflected in the faces of her guests, comes to Lady Macbeth with the shock of a sudden disclosure, and at once her nature begins to sink. The first intimation of the change is given when, in the scene of the discovery, she faints.[3] When next we see her, Queen of Scotland, the glory of her dream has faded. She enters, disillusioned, and weary with want of sleep: she has thrown away everything and gained nothing:

> Nought's had, all's spent,
> Where our desire is got without content:
> 'Tis safer to be that which we destroy
> Than by destruction dwell in doubtful joy.

Henceforth she has no initiative: the stem of her being seems to be cut through. Her husband, physically the stronger, maddened by pangs he had foreseen, but still flaming with life, comes into the foreground, and she retires. Her will remains, and she does her best to help him; but he rarely needs her help. Her chief anxiety appears to be that he should not betray his misery. He plans the murder of Banquo without her knowledge (not in order to spare her, I think, for he never shows love of this quality, but merely because he does not need her now); and even when she is told vaguely of his intention she appears but little interested. In the sudden emergency of the banquet scene she makes a prodigious and magnificent effort; her strength, and with it her ascendancy, returns, and she saves her husband at least from an open disclosure. But after this she takes no part whatever in the action. We only know from her shuddering words in the sleep-walking scene, 'The Thane of Fife had a wife: where is she now?' that she has even learned of her husband's worst crime; and in all the horrors of his tyranny over Scotland she has, so far as we hear, no part. Disillusionment and despair prey upon her more and more. That she should seek any relief in speech, or should ask for sympathy, would seem to her mere weakness, and would be to Macbeth's defiant fury an irritation. Thinking of the change in him, we imagine the bond between them slackened, and Lady Macbeth left much alone. She sinks slowly downward. She cannot bear darkness, and has light by

---

[3] See Note DD.

her continually: 'tis her command. At last her nature, not her will, gives way. The secrets of the past find vent in a disorder of sleep, the beginning perhaps of madness. What the doctor fears is clear. He reports to her husband no great physical mischief, but bids her attendant to remove from her all means by which she could harm herself, and to keep eyes on her constantly. It is in vain. Her death is announced by a cry from her women so sudden and direful that it would thrill her husband with horror if he were any longer capable of fear. In the last words of the play Malcolm tells us it is believed in the hostile army that she died by her own hand. And (not to speak of the indications just referred to) it is in accordance with her character that even in her weakest hour she should cut short by one determined stroke the agony of her life.

The sinking of Lady Macbeth's nature, and the marked change in her demeanour to her husband, are most strikingly shown in the conclusion of the banquet scene; and from this point pathos is mingled with awe. The guests are gone. She is completely exhausted, and answers Macbeth in listless, submissive words which seem to come with difficulty. How strange sounds the reply 'Did you send to him, sir?' to his imperious question about Macduff! And when he goes on, 'waxing desperate in imagination', to speak of new deeds of blood, she seems to sicken at the thought, and there is a deep pathos in that answer which tells at once of her care for him and of the misery she herself has silently endured,

> You lack the season of all natures, sleep.

We begin to think of her now less as the awful instigator of murder than as a woman with much that is grand in her, and much that is piteous. Strange and almost ludicrous as the statement may sound,[4] she is, up to her light, a perfect wife. She gives her husband the best she has; and the fact that she never uses to him the terms of affection which, up to this point in the play, he employs to her, is certainly no indication of want of love. She urges, appeals, reproaches, for a practical end, but she never recriminates. The harshness of her taunts is free from mere personal feeling, and also from any deep or more than momentary contempt. She despises what she thinks the weakness which stands in the way of her husband's ambition; but she does not

---

[4] It is not new.

despise *him*. She evidently admires him and thinks him a great man, for whom the throne is the proper place. Her commanding attitude in the moments of his hesitation or fear is probably confined to them. If we consider the peculiar circumstances of the earlier scenes and the banquet scene, and if we examine the language of the wife and husband at other times, we shall come, I think, to the conclusion that their habitual relations are better represented by the later scenes than by the earlier, though naturally they are not truly represented by either. Her ambition for her husband and herself (there was no distinction to her mind) proved fatal to him, far more so than the prophecies of the Witches; but even when she pushed him into murder she believed she was helping him to do what he merely lacked the nerve to attempt; and her part in the crime was so much less open-eyed than his, that, if the impossible and undramatic task of estimating degrees of culpability were forced on us, we should surely have to assign the larger share to Macbeth.

'Lady Macbeth,' says Dr. Johnson, 'is merely detested'; and for a long time critics generally spoke of her as though she were Malcolm's 'fiend-like queen'. In natural reaction we tend to insist, as I have been doing, on the other and less obvious side; and in the criticism of the last century there is even a tendency to sentimentalize the character. But it can hardly be doubted that Shakespeare meant the predominant impression to be one of awe, grandeur, and horror, and that he never meant this impression to be lost, however it might be modified, as Lady Macbeth's activity diminishes and her misery increases. I cannot believe that, when she said of Banquo and Fleance,

> But in them nature's copy's not eterne,

she meant only that they would some day die; or that she felt any surprise when Macbeth replied,

> There's comfort yet: they are assailable;

though I am sure no light came into her eyes when he added those dreadful words, 'Then be thou jocund'. She was listless. She herself would not have moved a finger against Banquo. But she thought his death, and his son's death, might ease her husband's mind, and she suggested the murders indifferently and without remorse. The sleep walking scene, again, inspires pity, but its main effect is one of awe. There is great horror in the references to blood, but it cannot be said that there is more than horror; and Campbell was surely right when, in alluding to Mrs. Jameson's analysis, he insisted that in Lady Macbeth's misery there is no trace of contrition.[5] Doubtless she would have given the world to undo what she had done; and the thought of it killed her; but, regarding her from the tragic point of view, we may truly say she was too great to repent.[6]

2

The main interest of the character of Banquo arises from the changes that take place in him, and from the influence of the Witches upon him. And it is curious that Shakespeare's intention here is so frequently missed. Banquo being at first strongly contrasted with Macbeth, as an innocent man with a guilty, it seems to be supposed that this contrast must be continued to his death; while, in reality, though it is never removed, it is gradually diminished. Banquo in fact

---

[5] The words about Lady Macduff are of course significant of natural human feeling, and may have been introduced expressly to mark it, but they do not, I think show any fundamental change in Lady Macbeth, for at no time would she have suggested or approved a *purposeless* atrocity. It is perhaps characteristic that this human feeling should show itself most clearly in reference to an act for which she was not directly responsible, and in regard to which therefore she does not feel the instinct of self-assertion.

[6] The tendency to sentimentalize Lady Macbeth is partly due to Mrs. Siddons's* fancy that she was a small, fair, blue-eyed woman, 'perhaps even fragile'. Dr. Bucknill,* who was unacquainted with this fancy, independently determined that she was 'beautiful and delicate', 'unoppressed by weight of flesh', 'probably small', but 'a tawny or brown blonde', with grey eyes: and Brandes* affirms that she was lean, slight, and hard. They know much more than Shakespeare, who tells us absolutely nothing on these subjects. That Lady Macbeth, after taking part in a murder, was so exhausted as to faint, will hardly demonstrate her fragility. That she must have been blue-eyed, fair, or red-haired, because she was a Celt, is a bold inference, and it is an idle dream that Shakespeare had any idea of making her or her husband characteristically Celtic. The only evidence ever offered to prove that she was small is the sentence, 'All the perfumes of Arabia will not sweeten this little hand'; and Goliath might have called his hand 'little' in contrast with all the perfumes of Arabia. One might as well propose to prove that Othello was a small man by quoting,

> I have seen the day,
> That, with this little arm and this good sword,
> I have made my way through more impediments
> Than twenty times your stop.

The reader is at liberty to imagine Lady Macbeth's person in the way that pleases him best, or to leave it, as Shakespeare very likely did, unimagined.

Perhaps it may be well to add that there is not the faintest trace in the play of the idea occasionally met with, and to some extent embodied in Madame Bernhardt's* impersonation of Lady Macbeth, that her hold upon her husband lay in seductive attractions deliberately exercised. Shakespeare was not unskilled or squeamish in indicating such ideas.

may be described much more truly than Macbeth as the victim of the Witches. If we follow his story this will be evident.

He bore a part only less distinguished than Macbeth's in the battles against Sweno and Macdonwald. He and Macbeth are called 'our captains', and when they meet the Witches they are traversing the 'blasted heath'[7] alone together. Banquo accosts the strange shapes without the slightest fear. They lay their fingers on their lips, as if to signify that they will not, or must not, speak to *him*. To Macbeth's brief appeal, 'Speak, if you can: what are you?' they at once reply, not by saying what they are, but by hailing him Thane of Glamis, Thane of Cawdor, and King hereafter. Banquo is greatly surprised that his partner should start as if in fear, and observes that he is at once 'rapt'; and he bids the Witches, if they know the future, to prophecy to *him*, who neither begs their favour nor fears their hate. Macbeth, looking back at a later time, remembers Banquo's daring, and how

> he chid the sisters,
> When first they put the name of king upon me,
> And bade them speak to him.

'Chid' is an exaggeration; but Banquo is evidently a bold man, probably an ambitious one, and certainly has no lurking guilt in his ambition. On hearing the predictions concerning himself and his descendants he makes no answer, and when the Witches are about to vanish he shows none of Macbeth's feverish anxiety to know more. On their vanishing he is simply amazed, wonders if they were anything but hallucinations, makes no reference to the predictions till Macbeth mentions them, and then answers lightly.

When Ross and Angus, entering, announce to Macbeth that he has been made Thane of Cawdor Banquo exclaims, aside, to himself or Macbeth, 'What! can the devil speak true?' He now believes that the Witches were real beings and the 'instruments of darkness'. When Macbeth, turning to him, whispers,

> Do you not hope your children shall be kings,
> When those that gave the Thane of Cawdor to me
> Promised no less to them?

---

[7] That it is Macbeth who feels the harmony between the desolation of the heath and the figures who appear on it is a characteristic touch.

he draws with the boldness of innocence the inference which is really occupying Macbeth, and answers,

> That, trusted home,
> Might yet enkindle you unto the crown
> Beside the thane of Cawdor.

Here he still speaks, I think, in a free, off-hand, even jesting,[8] manner ('enkindle' meaning merely 'excite you to *hope* for'). But then, possibly from noticing something in Macbeth's face, he becomes graver, and goes on, with a significant 'but'

> But 'tis strange:
> And oftentimes, to win us to our harm,
> The instruments of darkness tell us truths,
> Win us with honest trifles, to betray's
> In deepest consequence.

He afterwards observes for the second time that his partner is 'rapt'; but he explains his abstraction naturally and sincerely by referring to the surprise of his new honours; and at the close of the scene, when Macbeth proposes that they shall discuss the predictions together at some later time, he answers in the cheerful, rather bluff manner, which he has used almost throughout, 'Very gladly'. Nor was there any reason why Macbeth's rejoinder, 'Till then, enough', should excite misgivings in him, though it implied a request for silence, and though the whole behaviour of his partner during the scene must have looked very suspicious to him when the prediction of the crown was made good through the murder of Duncan.

In the next scene Macbeth and Banquo join the King, who welcomes them both with the kindest expressions of gratitude and with promises of favours to come. Macbeth has indeed already received a noble reward. Banquo, who is said by the King to have 'no less deserved', receives as yet mere thanks. His brief and frank acknowledgment is contrasted with Macbeth's laboured rhetoric; and, as Macbeth goes out, Banquo turns with hearty praises of him to the King.

And when next we see him, approaching Macbeth's castle in

---

8 So, in Holinshed, 'Banquho jested with him and sayde, now Makbeth thou haste obtayned those things which the twoo former sisters prophesied, there remayneth onely for thee to purchase that which the third sayd should come to passe'.

company with Duncan, there is still no sign of change. Indeed he gains on us. It is he who speaks the beautiful lines,

> This guest of summer,
> The temple-haunting martlet, does approve,
> By his loved mansionry, that the heaven's breath
> Smells wooingly here: no jutty, frieze,
> Buttress, nor coign of vantage, but this bird
> Hath made his pendent bed and procreant cradle:
> Where they most breed and haunt, I have observed,
> The air is delicate;

– lines which tell of that freedom of heart, and that sympathetic sense of peace and beauty, which the Macbeth of the tragedy could never feel.

But now Banquo's sky begins to darken. At the opening of the Second Act we see him with Fleance crossing the court of the castle on his way to bed. The blackness of the moonless, starless night seems to oppress him. And he is oppressed by something else.

> A heavy summons lies like lead upon me,
> And yet I would not sleep: merciful powers,
> Restrain in me the cursed thoughts that nature
> Gives way to in repose!

On Macbeth's entrance we know what Banquo means: he says to Macbeth – and it is the first time he refers to the subject unprovoked,

> I dreamt last night of the three weird sisters.

His will is still untouched: he would repel the 'cursed thoughts'; and they are mere thoughts, not intentions. But still they are 'thoughts', something more, probably, than mere recollections; and they bring with them an undefined sense of guilt. The poison has begun to work.

The passage that follows Banquo's words to Macbeth is difficult to interpret:

> I dreamt last night of the three weird sisters:
> To you they have show'd some truth.
> *Macb.* I think not of them;
> Yet, when we can entreat an hour to serve,
> We would spend it in some words upon that business,
> If you would grant the time.
> *Ban.* At your kind'st leisure.

> *Macb.* If you shall cleave to my consent, when 'tis,
> It shall make honour for you.
>   *Ban.*   So I lose none
> In seeking to augment it, but still keep
> My bosom franchised and allegiance clear,
> I shall be counselled.
>   *Macb.*   Good repose the while!
>   *Ban.* Thanks, sir: the like to you!

Macbeth's first idea is, apparently, simply to free himself from any suspicion which the discovery of the murder might suggest, by showing himself, just before it, quite indifferent to the predictions, and merely looking forward to a conversation about them at some future time. But why does he go on, 'If you shall cleave', etc.? Perhaps he foresees that, on the discovery, Banquo cannot fail to suspect him, and thinks it safest to prepare the way at once for an understanding with him (in the original story he makes Banquo his accomplice *before* the murder). Banquo's answer shows three things, – that he fears a treasonable proposal, that he has no idea of accepting it, and that he has no fear of Macbeth to restrain him from showing what is in his mind.

Duncan is murdered. In the scene of discovery Banquo of course appears, and his behaviour is significant. When he enters, and Macduff cries out to him,

> O Banquo, Banquo,
> Our royal master's murdered,

and Lady Macbeth, who has entered a moment before, exclaims,

> Woe, alas!
> What, in our house?

his answer,

> Too cruel anywhere,

shows, as I have pointed out, repulsion, and we may be pretty sure that he suspects the truth at once. After a few words to Macduff he remains absolutely silent while the scene is continued for nearly forty lines. He is watching Macbeth and listening as he tells how he put the chamberlains to death in a frenzy of loyal rage. At last Banquo appears to have made up his mind. On Lady Macbeth's fainting he proposes that they shall all retire, and that they shall afterwards meet,

And question this most bloody piece of work
To know it further. Fears and scruples[9] shake us:
In the great hand of God I stand, and thence
Against the undivulged pretence[10] I fight
Of treasonous malice.

His solemn language here reminds us of his grave words about 'the instruments of darkness', and of his later prayer to the 'merciful powers'. He is profoundly shocked, full of indignation, and determined to play the part of a brave and honest man.

But he plays no such part. When next we see him, on the last day of his life, we find that he has yielded to evil. The Witches and his own ambition have conquered him. He alone of the lords knew of the prophecies, but he has said nothing of them. He has acquiesced in Macbeth's accession, and in the official theory that Duncan's sons had suborned the chamberlains to murder him. Doubtless, unlike Macduff, he was present at Scone to see the new king invested. He has, not formally but in effect, 'cloven to' Macbeth's 'consent'; he is knit to him by 'a most indissoluble tie'; his advice in council has been 'most grave and prosperous'; he is to be the 'chief guest' at that night's supper. And his soliloquy tells us why:

Thou hast it now: king, Cawdor, Glamis, all,
As the weird women promised, and, I fear,
Thou play'dst most foully for't: yet it was said
It should not stand in thy posterity,
But that myself should be the root and father
Of many kings. If there come truth from them –
As upon thee, Macbeth, their speeches shine –
Why, by the verities on thee made good,
May they not be my oracles as well,
And set me up in hope? But hush! no more.

This 'hush! no more' is not the dismissal of 'cursed thoughts': it only means that he hears the trumpets announcing the entrance of the King and Queen.

His punishment comes swiftly, much more swiftly than Macbeth's, and saves him from any further fall. He is a very fearless man, and still so far honourable that he has no thought of *acting* to bring about the

---

[9] = doubts.
[10] = design.

fulfilment of the prophecy which has beguiled him. And therefore he
has no fear of Macbeth. But he little understands him. To Macbeth's
tormented mind Banquo's conduct appears highly suspicious. *Why*
has this bold and circumspect[11] man kept his secret and become his
chief adviser? In order to make good *his part* of the predictions after
Macbeth's own precedent. Banquo, he is sure, will suddenly and
secretly attack him. It is not the far-off accession of Banquo's descendants that he fears; it is (so he tells himself) swift murder; not that the
'barren sceptre' will some day droop from his dying hand, but that it
will be wrenched away now (III.i.62).[12] So he kills Banquo. But the
Banquo he kills is not the innocent soldier who met the Witches and
daffed their prophecies aside, nor the man who prayed to be delivered
from the temptation of his dreams.

Macbeth leaves on most readers a profound impression of the
misery of a guilty conscience and the retribution of crime. And the
strength of this impression is one of the reasons why the tragedy is
admired by readers who shrink from *Othello* and are made unhappy
by *Lear.* But what Shakespeare perhaps felt even more deeply, when
he wrote this play, was the *incalculability* of evil, – that in meddling
with it human beings do they know not what. The soul, he seems to
feel, is a thing of such inconceivable depth, complexity, and delicacy,
that when you introduce into it, or suffer to develop in it, any change,
and particularly the change called evil, you can form only the vaguest
idea of the reaction you will provoke. All you can be sure of is that it
will not be what you expected, and that you cannot possibly escape it.
Banquo's story, if truly apprehended, produces this impression quite
as strongly as the more terrific stories of the chief characters, and
perhaps even more clearly, inasmuch as he is nearer to average human
nature, has obviously at first a quiet conscience, and uses with evident
sincerity the language of religion.

---

[11]   'tis much he dares,
    And, to that dauntless temper of his mind,
    He hath a wisdom that doth guide his valour
    To act in safety.
[12]   So when he hears that Fleance has escaped he is not much troubled (III.iv.29):

        The worm that's fled
    Hath nature that in time will venom breed,
    No teeth for the present.

I have repeated above what I have said before, because the meaning of Macbeth's soliloquy is
frequently misconceived.

3

Apart from his story Banquo's character is not very interesting, nor is it, I think, perfectly individual. And this holds good of the rest of the minor characters. They are sketched lightly, and are seldom developed further than the strict purposes of the action required. From this point of view they are inferior to several of the less important figures in each of the other three tragedies. The scene in which Lady Macduff and her child appear, and the passage where their slaughter is reported to Macduff, have much dramatic value, but in neither case is the effect due to any great extent to the special characters of the persons concerned. Neither they, nor Duncan, nor Malcolm, nor even Banquo himself, have been imagined intensely, and therefore they do not produce that sense of unique personality which Shakespeare could convey in a much smaller number of lines than he gives to most of them.[13] And this is of course even more the case with persons like Ross, Angus, and Lennox, though each of these has distinguishable features. I doubt if any other great play of Shakespeare's contains so many speeches which a student of the play, if they were quoted to him, would be puzzled to assign to the speakers. Let the reader turn, for instance, to the second scene of the Fifth Act, and ask himself why the names of the persons should not be interchanged in all the ways mathematically possible. Can he find, again, any signs of character by which to distinguish the speeches of Ross and Angus in Act I. scenes ii. and iii., or to determine that Malcolm must have spoken I.iv.2–11? Most of this writing, we may almost say, is simply Shakespeare's writing, not that of Shakespeare become another person. And can anything like the same proportion of such writing be found in *Hamlet*, *Othello* or *King Lear?*

Is it possible to guess the reason of this characteristic of *Macbeth?* I cannot believe it is due to the presence of a second hand. The writing, mangled by the printer and perhaps by 'the players', seems to be sometimes obviously Shakespeare's, sometimes sufficiently Shakespearean to repel any attack not based on external evidence. It may be, as the shortness of the play has suggested to some, that Shakespeare was hurried, and, throwing all his weight on the principal characters, did not exert himself in dealing with the rest. But there is another possi-

---

[13] Virgilia in *Coriolanus* is a famous example. She speaks about thirty-five lines.

bility which may be worth considering. *Macbeth* is distinguished by
its simplicity – by grandeur in simplicity, no doubt, but still by
simplicity. The two great figures indeed can hardly be called simple,
except in comparison with such characters as Hamlet and Iago; but in
almost every other respect the tragedy has this quality. Its plot is quite
plain. It has very little intermixture of humour. It has little pathos
except of the sternest kind. The style, for Shakespeare, has not much
variety, being generally kept at a higher pitch than in the other three
tragedies; and there is much less than usual of the interchange of verse
and prose.[14] All this makes for simplicity of effect. And, this being so,
is it not possible that Shakespeare instinctively felt, or consciously
feared, that to give much individuality or attraction to the subordinate figures would diminish this effect, and so, like a good artist,
sacrificed a part to the whole? And was he wrong? He has certainly
avoided the overloading which distresses us in *King Lear*, and has
produced a tragedy utterly unlike it, not much less great as a dramatic
poem, and as a drama superior.

I would add, though without much confidence, another suggestion. The simplicity of *Macbeth* is one of the reasons why many readers feel that, in spite of its being intensely 'romantic', it is less unlike
a classical tragedy than *Hamlet* or *Othello* or *King Lear*. And it is possible that this effect is, in a sense, the result of design. I do not mean
that Shakespeare intended to imitate a classical tragedy; I mean only
that he may have seen in the bloody story of Macbeth a subject suitable for treatment in a manner somewhat nearer to that of Seneca, or
of the English Senecan plays familiar to him in his youth, than was
the manner of his own mature tragedies. The Witches doubtless are
'romantic', but so is the witchcraft in Seneca's* *Medea* and *Hercules
Oetaeus*; indeed it is difficult to read the account of Medea's preparations (670–739) without being reminded of the incantation in
Macbeth. Banquo's Ghost again is 'romantic', but so are Seneca's
ghosts. For the swelling of the style in some of the great passages –
however immeasurably superior these may be to anything in Seneca –
and certainly for the turgid bombast which occasionally appears in
Macbeth, and which seems to have horrified Jonson, Shakespeare
might easily have found a model in Seneca. Did he not think that this

---

[14] The percentage of prose is, roughly, in *Hamlet* $30^2/3$, in *Othello* $16^1/3$, in *King Lear* $27^1/3$,
in *Macbeth* $8^1/2$.

was the high Roman manner? Does not the Sergeant's speech, as Coleridge observed, recall the style of the 'passionate speech' of the Player in *Hamlet* – a speech, be it observed, on a Roman subject?[15] And is it entirely an accident that parallels between Seneca and Shakespeare seem to be more frequent in *Macbeth* than in any other of his undoubtedly genuine works except perhaps *Richard III*, a tragedy unquestionably influenced either by Seneca or by English Senecan plays?[16] If there is anything in these suggestions, and if we suppose that Shakespeare meant to give to his play a certain classical tinge, he might naturally carry out this idea in respect to the characters, as well as in other respects, by concentrating almost the whole interest on the important figures and leaving the others comparatively shadowy.

---

[15] Cf. Note F. There are also *in Macbeth* several shorter passages which recall the Player's speech. Cf. 'Fortune . . . showed like a rebel's whore' (I.ii.14). 'Out! out! thou strumpet Fortune!'

The form 'eterne' occurs in Shakespeare only in *Macbeth*, III.ii.38, and in the 'proof eterne' of the Player's speech. Cf. 'So, as a painted tyrant, Pyrrhus stood,' with *Macbeth*, V.viii.26; 'the rugged Pyrrhus, like the Hyrcanian beast', with 'the rugged Russian bear . . . or the Hyrcan tiger' (*Macbeth*, III.iv.100); 'like a neutral to his will and matter' with *Macbeth*, I.v.47. The words 'Till he unseam'd him from the nave to the chaps', in the Sergeant's speech, recall the words 'Then from the navel to the throat at once He ript old Priam', in *Dido Queen of Carthage*,* where these words follow those others, about Priam falling with the mere wind of Pyrrhus' sword, which seem to have suggested 'the whiff and wind of his fell sword' in the Player's speech.

[16] See Cunliffe,* *The Influence of Seneca on Elizabethan Tragedy*. The most famous of these parallels is that between 'Will all great Neptune's Ocean', etc., and the following passages:

> Quis eluet me Tanais? aut quae barbaris
> Maeotis undis Pontico incumbens mari?
> Non ipse toto magnus Oceano pater
> Tantum expiarit sceleris.* (*Hipp.* 715.)
> Quis Tanais, aut quis Nilus, aut quis Persica
> Violentus unda Tigris, aut Rhenus ferox,
> Tagusve Ibera turbidus gaza fluens,
> Abluere dextram poterit? Arctoum licet
> Maeotis in me gelida transfundat mare,
> Et tota Tethys per meas currat manus,
> Haerebit altum facinus. (*Herc. Furens*, 1323.)*

(The reader will remember Othello's 'Pontic sea' with its 'violent pace'.) Medea's incantation in Ovid's* *Metamorphoses*, vii.197 ff., which certainly suggested Prospero's speech, *Tempest*, V.i.33 ff., should be compared with Seneca, *Herc. Oet.*, 452 ff., 'Artibus magicis,' etc. It is of course highly probable that Shakespeare read some Seneca at school. I may add that in the *Hippolytus*, besides the passage quoted above, there are others which might have furnished him with suggestions. Cf. for instance *Hipp.* 30 ff., with the lines about the Spartan hounds in *Mids. Night's Dream*, IV.i.117 ff., and Hippolytus' speech, beginning 483, with the Duke's speech in *As You Like It*, II.i.

4

Macbeth being more simple than the other tragedies, and broader and more massive in effect, three passages in it are of great importance as securing variety in tone, and also as affording relief from the feelings excited by the Witch-scenes and the principal characters. They are the passage where the Porter appears, the conversation between Lady Macduff and her little boy, and the passage where Macduff receives the news of the slaughter of his wife and babes. Yet the first of these, we are told even by Coleridge, is unworthy of Shakespeare and is not his; and the second, with the rest of the scene which contains it, appears to be usually omitted in stage representations of *Macbeth*.

I question if either this scene or the exhibition of Macduff's grief is required to heighten our abhorrence of Macbeth's cruelty. They have a technical value in helping to give the last stage of the action the form of a conflict between Macbeth and Macduff. But their chief function is of another kind. It is to touch the heart with a sense of beauty and pathos, to open the springs of love and of tears. Shakespeare is loved for the sweetness of his humanity, and because he makes this kind of appeal with such irresistible persuasion; and the reason why *Macbeth*, though admired as much as any work of his, is scarcely loved, is that the characters who predominate cannot make this kind of appeal, and at no point are able to inspire unmingled sympathy. The two passages in question supply this want in such measure as Shakespeare thought advisable in *Macbeth*, and the play would suffer greatly from their excision. The second, on the stage, is extremely moving, and Macbeth's reception of the news of his wife's death may be intended to recall it by way of contrast. The first brings a relief even greater, because here the element of beauty is more marked, and because humour is mingled with pathos. In both we escape from the oppression of huge sins and sufferings into the presence of the wholesome affections of unambitious hearts; and, though both scenes are painful and one dreadful, our sympathies can flow unchecked.[17]

Lady Macduff is a simple wife and mother, who has no thought for anything beyond her home. Her love for her children shows her at once that her husband's flight exposes them to terrible danger. She is in an agony of fear for them, and full of indignation against him. It

---

[17] Cf. Coleridge's note on the Lady Macduff scene.

does not even occur to her that he has acted from public spirit, or that there is such a thing.

What had he done to make him fly the land?

He must have been mad to do it. He fled for fear. He does not love his wife and children. He is a traitor. The poor soul is almost beside herself – and with too good reason. But when the murderer bursts in with the question 'Where is your husband?' she becomes in a moment the wife, and the great noble's wife:

> I hope, in no place so unsanctified
> Where such as thou may'st find him.

What did Shakespeare mean us to think of Macduff s flight, for which Macduff has been much blamed by others beside his wife? Certainly not that fear for himself, or want of love for his family, had anything to do with it. His love for his country, so strongly marked in the scene with Malcolm, is evidently his one motive.

> He is noble, wise, judicious, and best knows
> The fits o' the season,

says Ross. That his flight was 'noble' is beyond doubt. That it was not wise or judicious in the interest of his family is no less clear. But that does not show that it was wrong; and, even if it were, to represent its consequences as a judgment on him for his want of due consideration is equally monstrous and ludicrous.[18] The further question whether he did fail in due consideration, or whether for his country's sake he deliberately risked a danger which he fully realized, would in

---

[18] It is nothing to the purpose that Macduff himself says,

> Sinful Macduff,
> They were all struck for thee! naught that I am,
> Not for their own demerits, but for mine,
> Fell slaughter on their souls.

There is no reason to suppose that the sin and demerit he speaks of is that of leaving his home. And even if it were, it is Macduff that speaks, not Shakespeare, any more than Shakespeare speaks in the preceding sentence,

> Did heaven look on,
> And would not take their part?

And yet Brandes (ii.104) hears in these words 'the voice of revolt ... that sounds later through the despairing philosophy of *King Lear*'. It sounds a good deal earlier too; *e.g.* in *Tit. And.*, IV.i.81, and *2 Henry VI*, II.i.154. The idea is a commonplace of Elizabethan tragedy.

Shakespeare's theatre have been answered at once by Macduff's expression and demeanour on hearing Malcolm's words,

> Why in the rawness left you wife and child,
> Those precious motives, those strong knots of love,
> Without leave-taking?

It cannot be decided with certainty from the mere text; but, without going into the considerations on each side, I may express the opinion that Macduff knew well what he was doing and that he fled without leave-taking for fear his purpose should give way. Perhaps he said to himself, with Coriolanus,

> Not of a woman's tenderness to be,
> Requires nor child nor woman's face to see.

Little Macduff suggests a few words on Shakespeare's boys (there are scarcely any little girls). It is somewhat curious that nearly all of them appear in tragic or semi-tragic dramas. I remember but two exceptions: little William Page, who said his *Hic, haec, hoc* to Sir Hugh Evans; and the page before whom Falstaff walked like a sow that hath overwhelmed all her litter but one; and it is to be feared that even this page, if he is the Boy of *Henry V*, came to an ill end, being killed with the luggage.

> So wise so young, they say, do ne'er live long,

as Richard observed of the little Prince of Wales. Of too many of these children (some of the 'boys', *e.g.* those in *Cymbeline*, are lads, not children) the saying comes true. They are pathetic figures, the more so because they so often appear in company with their unhappy mothers, and can never be thought of apart from them. Perhaps Arthur is even the first creation in which Shakespeare's power of pathos showed itself mature;[19] and the last of his children, Mamillius, assuredly proves that it never decayed. They are almost all of them noble figures, too, – affectionate, frank, brave, high-spirited, 'of an open and free nature' like Shakespeare's best men. And almost all of them, again, are amusing and charming as well as pathetic; comical in their mingled acuteness and *naïveté*, charming in their confidence in them-

---

[19] And the idea that it was the death of his son Hamnet, aged eleven, that brought this power to maturity is one of the more plausible attempts to find in his dramas a reflection of his private history. It implies however as late a date as 1596 for *King John*.

selves and the world, and in the seriousness with which they receive the jocosity of their elders, who commonly address them as strong men, great warriors, or profound politicians.

Little Macduff exemplifies most of these remarks. There is nothing in the scene of a transcendent kind, like the passage about Mamillius' never-finished 'Winter's Tale' of the man who dwelt by a churchyard, or the passage about his death, or that about little Marcius and the butterfly, or the audacity which introduces him, at the supreme moment of the tragedy, outdoing the appeals of Volumnia and Virgilia by the statement,

> 'A shall not tread on me:
> I'll run away till I'm bigger, but then I'll fight.

Still one does not easily forget little Macduff s delightful and well justified confidence in his ability to defeat his mother in argument; or the deep impression she made on him when she spoke of his father as a 'traitor'; or his immediate response when he heard the murderer call his father by the same name, –

> Thou liest, thou shag-haired villain.

Nor am I sure that, if the son of Coriolanus had been murdered, his last words to his mother would have been, 'Run away, I pray you.'

I may add two remarks. The presence of this child is one of the things in which *Macbeth* reminds us of *Richard III*. And he is perhaps the only person in the tragedy who provokes a smile. I say 'perhaps', for though the anxiety of the Doctor to escape from the company of his patient's husband makes one smile, I am not sure that it was meant to.

5

The Porter does not make me smile: the moment is too terrific. He is grotesque; no doubt the contrast he affords is humorous as well as ghastly; I dare say the groundlings roared with laughter at his coarsest remarks. But they are not comic enough to allow one to forget for a moment what has preceded and what must follow. And I am far from complaining of this. I believe that it is what Shakespeare intended, and that he despised the groundlings if they laughed. Of course he could have written without the least difficulty speeches five times as humorous; but he knew better. The Gravediggers make us laugh; the old Countryman who brings the asps to Cleopatra makes us smile at least. But the Gravedigger scene does not come at a moment of extreme tension; and it is long. Our distress for Ophelia is not so absorbing that we refuse to be interested in the man who digs her grave, or even continue throughout the long conversation to remember always with pain that the grave is hers. It is fitting, therefore, that he should be made decidedly humorous. The passage in *Antony and Cleopatra* is much nearer to the passage in *Macbeth*, and seems to have been forgotten by those who say that there is nothing in Shakespeare resembling that passage.[20] The old Countryman comes at a moment of tragic exaltation, and the dialogue is appropriately brief. But the moment, though tragic, is emphatically one of exaltation. We have not been feeling horror, nor are we feeling a dreadful suspense. We are going to see Cleopatra die, but she is to die gloriously and to triumph over Octavius. And therefore our amusement at the old Countryman and the contrast he affords to these high passions, is untroubled, and it was right to make him really comic. But the Porter's case is quite different. We cannot forget how the knocking that makes him grumble sounded to Macbeth, or that within a few minutes of his opening the gate Duncan will be discovered in his blood; nor can we help feeling that in pretending to be porter of hell-gate he is terribly near the truth. To give him language so humorous that it would ask us almost to lose the sense of these things would have been a fatal mistake – the kind of mistake that means want of dramatic imagination. And that was not the sort of error into which Shakespeare fell.

To doubt the genuineness of the passage, then, on the ground that it is not humorous enough for Shakespeare, seems to me to show this want. It is to judge the passage as though it were a separate composition, instead of conceiving it in the fullness of its relations to its surroundings in a stage-play. Taken by itself, I admit, it would bear no indubitable mark of Shakespeare's authorship, not even in the phrase 'the primrose way to the everlasting bonfire', which Coleridge thought Shakespeare might have added to an interpolation of 'the players'. And if there were reason (as in my judgment there is not) to suppose that Shakespeare thus permitted an interpolation or that he collabo-

---

[20] Even if this were true, the retort is obvious that neither is there anything resembling the murder-scene in *Macbeth*.

rated with another author, I could believe that he left 'the players' or his collaborator to write the *words* of the passage. But that anyone except the author of the scene of Duncan's murder *conceived* the passage is incredible.[21]

The speeches of the Porter, a low comic character, are in prose. So is the letter of Macbeth to his wife. In both these cases Shakespeare follows his general rule or custom. The only other prose-speeches occur in the sleep-walking scene, and here the use of prose may seem strange. For in great tragic scenes we expect the more poetic medium of expression and this is one of the most famous of such scenes. Besides, unless I mistake, Lady Macbeth is the only one of Shakespeare's great tragic characters who on a last appearance is denied the dignity of verse.

Yet in this scene also he adheres to his custom. Somnambulism is an abnormal condition, and it is his general rule to assign prose to persons whose state of mind is abnormal. Thus, to illustrate from these four plays, Hamlet when playing the madman speaks prose, but in soliloquy, in talking with Horatio, and in pleading with his mother, he speaks verse.[22] Ophelia in her madness either sings snatches of

---

[21] I have confined myself to the single aspect of this question on which I had what seemed something new to say. Professor Hales's* defence of the passage on fuller grounds, in the admirable paper reprinted in his *Notes and Essays on Shakespeare*, seems to me quite conclusive. I may add two notes. (1) The references in the Porter's speeches to 'equivocation', which have naturally, and probably rightly, been taken as allusions to the Jesuit Garnet's* appeal to the doctrine of equivocation in defence of his perjury when on trial for participation in the Gunpowder Plot, do not stand alone in *Macbeth*. The later prophecies of the Witches Macbeth calls 'the equivocation of the fiend That lies like truth' (V.v.43); and the Porter's remarks about the equivocator who 'could swear in both the scales against either scale, who committed treason enough for God's sake, yet could not equivocate to heaven', may be compared with the following dialogue (IV.ii.45):

> *Son.* What is a traitor?
> *Lady Macduff.* Why, one that swears and lies.
> *Son.* And be all traitors that do so?
> *Lady Macduff.* Everyone that does so is a traitor, and must be hanged.

Garnet, as a matter of fact, *was* hanged in May, 1606; and it is to be feared that the audience applauded this passage.

(2) The Porter's soliloquy on the different applicants for admittance has, in idea and manner, a marked resemblance to Pompey's soliloquy on the inhabitants of the prison, in *Measure for Measure*, VI.iii.1 ff.; and the dialogue between him and Abhorson on the 'mystery' of hanging (IV.ii.22 ff.) is of just the same kind as the Porter's dialogue with Macduff about drink.

[22] In the last Act, however, he speaks in verse even in the quarrel with Laertes at Ophelia's grave. It would be plausible to explain this either from his imitating what he thinks the rant of Laertes, or by supposing that his 'towering passion' made him forget to act the madman. But in the final scene also he speaks in verse in the presence of all. This again might be accounted for

songs or speaks prose. Almost all Lear's speeches, after he has become definitely insane, are in prose: where he wakes from sleep recovered, the verse returns. The prose enters with that speech which closes with his trying to tear off his clothes; but he speaks in verse – some of it very irregular – in the Timon-like speeches where his intellect suddenly in his madness seems to regain the force of his best days (IV.vi.). Othello, in IV.i., speaks in verse till the moment when Iago tells him that Cassio has confessed. There follow ten lines of prose – exclamations and mutterings of bewildered horror – and he falls to the ground unconscious.

The idea underlying this custom of Shakespeare's evidently is that the regular rhythm of verse would be inappropriate where the mind is supposed to have lost its balance and to be at the mercy of chance impressions coming from without (as sometimes with Lear), or of ideas emerging from its unconscious depths and pursuing one another across its passive surface. The somnambulism of Lady Macbeth is such a condition. There is no rational connection in the sequence of images and ideas. The sight of blood on her hand, the sound of the clock striking the hour for Duncan's murder, the hesitation of her husband before that hour came, the vision of the old man in his blood, the idea of the murdered wife of Macduff, the sight of the hand again, Macbeth's 'flaws and starts' at the sight of Banquo's ghost, the smell on her hand, the washing of hands after Duncan's murder again, her husband's fear of the buried Banquo, the sound of the knocking at the gate – these possess her, one after another, in this chance order. It is not much less accidental than the order of Ophelia's ideas; the great difference is that with Ophelia total insanity has effaced or greatly weakened the emotional force of the ideas, whereas to Lady Macbeth each new image or perception comes laden with anguish. There is, again, scarcely a sign of the exaltation of disordered imagination; we are conscious rather of an intense suffering which forces its way into light against resistance, and speaks a language for the most part strikingly bare in its diction and simple in its construction. This language stands in strong contrast with that of Macbeth in the surrounding

---

by saying that he is supposed to be in a lucid interval, as indeed his own language at 239 ff. implies. But the probability is that Shakespeare's real reason for breaking his rule here was simply that he did not choose to deprive Hamlet of verse on his last appearance. I wonder the disuse of prose in these two scenes has not been observed, and used as an argument, by those who think that Hamlet, with the commission in his pocket, is now resolute.

scenes, full of a feverish and almost furious excitement, and seems to express a far more desolating misery.

The effect is extraordinarily impressive. The soaring pride and power of Lady Macbeth's first speeches return on our memory, and the change is felt with a breathless awe. Any attempt, even by Shakespeare, to draw out the moral enfolded in this awe, would but weaken it. For the moment, too, all the language of poetry – even of Macbeth's poetry – seems to be touched with unreality, and these brief toneless sentences seem the only voice of truth.[23]

---

[23] The verse-speech of the Doctor, which closes this scene, lowers the tension towards that of the next scene. His introductory conversation with the Gentlewoman is written in prose (sometimes very near verse), partly, perhaps, from its familiar character, but chiefly because Lady Macbeth is to speak in prose.

NOTE A

EVENTS BEFORE THE OPENING OF THE ACTION IN *HAMLET*

In Hamlet's first soliloquy he speaks of his father as being 'but two months dead, – nay, not so much, not two'. He goes on to refer to the love between his father and mother, and then says (I.ii.145)

> And yet, within a month –
> Let me not think on't – Frailty, thy name is woman! –
> A little month, or ere those shoes were old
> With which she follow'd my poor father's body,
> Like Niobe, all tears, why she, even she –
> O God! a beast, that wants discourse of reason,
> Would have mourn'd longer – married with my uncle.

It seems hence to be usually assumed that at this time – the time when the action begins – Hamlet's mother has been married a little less than a month.

On this assumption difficulties, however, arise, though I have not found them referred to. Why has the Ghost waited nearly a month since the marriage before showing itself? Why has the King waited nearly a month before appearing in public for the first time, as he evidently does in this scene? And why has Laertes waited nearly a month since the coronation before asking leave to return to France (I.i.53)?

To this it might be replied that the marriage and the coronation were separated by some weeks; that, while the former occurred nearly a month before the time of this scene, the latter has only just taken place; and that what the Ghost cannot bear is, not the mere marriage, but the accession of an incestuous murderer to the throne. But anyone who will read the King's speech at the opening of the scene will certainly conclude that the marriage has only just been celebrated, and also that it is conceived as involving the accession of Claudius to the throne. Gertrude is described as the 'imperial jointress' of the State, and the King says that the lords consented to the marriage, but makes no separate mention of his election.

The solution of the difficulty is to be found in the lines quoted above. The marriage followed, within a month, not the *death of*

Hamlet's father, but the *funeral*. And this makes all clear. The death happened nearly two months ago. The funeral did not succeed it immediately, but (say) in a fortnight or three weeks. And the marriage and coronation, coming rather less than a month after the funeral, have just taken place. So that the Ghost has not waited at all; nor has the King, nor Laertes.

On this hypothesis it follows that Hamlet's agonized soliloquy is not uttered nearly a month after the marriage which has so horrified him, but quite soon after it (though presumably he would know rather earlier what was coming). And from this hypothesis we get also a partial explanation of two other difficulties. (*a*) When Horatio, at the end of the soliloquy, enters and greets Hamlet, it is evident that he and Hamlet have not recently met at Elsinore. Yet Horatio came to Elsinore for the funeral (I.ii.176). Now even if the funeral took place some three weeks ago, it seems rather strange that Hamlet, however absorbed in grief and however withdrawn from the Court, has not met Horatio; but if the funeral took place some seven weeks ago, the difficulty is considerably greater. (*b*) We are twice told that Hamlet has '*of late*' been seeking the society of Ophelia and protesting his love for her (I.iii.91, 99). It always seemed to me, on the usual view of the chronology, rather difficult (though not, of course, impossible) to understand this, considering the state of feeling produced in him by his mother's marriage, and in particular the shock it appears to have given to his faith in woman. But if the marriage has only just been celebrated the words 'of late' would naturally refer to a time before it. This time presumably would be subsequent to the death of Hamlet's father, but it is not so hard to fancy that Hamlet may have sought relief from mere *grief* in his love for Ophelia.

But here another question arises: May not the words 'of late' include, or even wholly refer to,[1] a time prior to the death of Hamlet's father? And this question would be answered universally, I suppose, in the negative, on the ground that Hamlet was not at Court but at Wittenberg when his father died. I will deal with this idea in a separate note, and will only add here that, though it is quite possible that

---

1 This is intrinsically not probable, and is the more improbable because in Q 1 Hamlet's letter to Ophelia (which must have been written before the action of the play begins) is signed 'Thine ever the most unhappy Prince *Hamlet*'. 'Unhappy' *might* be meant to describe an unsuccessful lover, but it probably shows that the letter was written after his father's death.

Shakespeare never imagined any of these matters clearly, and so produced these unimportant difficulties, we ought not to assume this without examination.

NOTE B

WHERE WAS HAMLET AT THE TIME OF HIS FATHER'S DEATH?

The answer will at once be given: 'At the University of Wittenberg. For the King says to him (I.ii.112):

> For your intent
> In going back to school in Wittenberg,
> It is most retrograde to our desire.

The Queen also prays him not to go to Wittenberg: and he consents to remain.'

Now I quite agree that the obvious interpretation of this passage is that universally accepted, that Hamlet, like Horatio, was at Wittenberg when his father died; and I do not say that it is wrong. But it involves difficulties, and ought not to be regarded as certain.

(1) One of these difficulties has long been recognized. Hamlet, according to the evidence of Act V., Scene i., is thirty years of age; and that is a very late age for a university student. One solution is found (by those who admit that Hamlet *was* thirty) in a passage in Nash's* *Pierce Penniless:* 'For fashion sake some [Danes] will put their children to schoole, but they set them not to it till they are fourteene years old, so that you shall see a great boy with a beard learne his A.B.C. and sit weeping under the rod when he is thirty years old.' Another solution, as we saw (p. 84), is found in Hamlet's character. He is a philosopher who lingers on at the University from love of his studies there.

(2) But there is a more formidable difficulty, which seems to have escaped notice. Horatio certainly came from Wittenberg to the funeral. And observe how he and Hamlet meet (I.ii.160).

Hor.   Hail to your lordship!
Ham.   I am glad to see you well:
        Horatio, – or I do forget myself.

Hor.	The same, my lord, and your poor servant ever.
Ham.	Sir, my good friend; I'll change that name with you: And what make you from Wittenberg, Horatio? Marcellus?
Mar.	My good lord –
Ham.	I am very glad to see you. Good even, sir.[1]
	But what, in faith, make you from Wittenberg?
Hor.	A truant disposition, good my lord.
Ham.	I would not hear your enemy say so,
	Nor shall you do my ear that violence,
	To make it truster of your own report
	Against yourself: I know you are no truant.
	But what is your affair in Elsinore?
	We'll teach you to drink deep ere you depart.
Hor.	My lord, I came to see your father's funeral.
Ham.	I pray thee, do not mock me, fellow-student;
	I think it was to see my mother's wedding.

Is not this passing strange? Hamlet and Horatio are supposed to be fellow students at Wittenberg, and to have left it for Elsinore less than two months ago. Yet Hamlet hardly recognizes Horatio at first, and speaks as if he himself lived at Elsinore (I refer to his bitter jest, 'We'll teach you to drink deep ere you depart'). Who would dream that Hamlet had himself just come from Wittenberg, if it were not for the previous words about his going back there?

How can this be explained on the usual view? Only, I presume, by supposing that Hamlet is so sunk in melancholy that he really does almost 'forget himself'[2] and forget everything else, so that he actually is in doubt who Horatio is. And this, though not impossible, is hard to believe.

'Oh no,' it may be answered, 'for he is doubtful about Marcellus too; and yet, if he were living at Elsinore, he must have seen Marcellus often.' But he is *not* doubtful about Marcellus. That note of interrogation after 'Marcellus' is Capell's conjecture: it is not in any Quarto or any Folio. The fact is that he knows perfectly well the man who lives at Elsinore, but is confused by the appearance of the friend who comes from Wittenberg.

---

[1] These three words are evidently addressed to Bernardo.

[2] Cf. Antonio in his melancholy (*Merchant of Venice*, I.i.6),

And such a want-wit sadness makes of me
That I have much ado to know myself.

(3) Rosencrantz and Guildenstern are sent for, to wean Hamlet from his melancholy and to worm his secret out of him, because he has known them from his youth, and is fond of them (II.ii.I ff.). They come *to* Denmark (II.ii.247 ff.): they come therefore *from* some other country. Where do they come from? They are, we hear, Hamlet's 'school-fellows' (III.iv.202). And in the first Quarto we are directly told that they were with him at Wittenberg:

> *Ham.*   What, Gilderstone, and Rossencraft,
>   Welcome, kind school-fellows, to Elsanore.
> *Gil.*   We thank your grace, and would be very glad
>   You were as when we were at Wittenberg.

Now let the reader look at Hamlet's first greeting of them in the received text, and let him ask himself whether it is the greeting of a man to fellow students whom he left two months ago: whether it is not rather, like his greeting of Horatio, the welcome of an old fellow student, who has not seen his visitors for a considerable time (II.ii.226 f.).

(4) Rosencrantz and Guildenstern tell Hamlet of the players who are coming. He asks what players they are, and is told, 'Even those you were wont to take such delight in, the tragedians of the city.' He asks, 'Do they hold the same estimation they did when I was in the city?' Evidently he has not been in the city for some time. And this is still more evident when the players come in, and he talks of one having grown a beard, and another having perhaps cracked his voice, since they last met. What then is this city, where he has not been for some time, but where (it would appear) Rosencrantz and Guildenstern live? It is not in Denmark ('Comest thou to beard me in Denmark?'). It would seem to be Wittenberg.[3]

All these passages, it should be observed, are consistent with one another. And the conclusion they point to is that Hamlet has left the University for some years and has been living at Court. This again is consistent with his being thirty years of age, and with his being mentioned as a soldier and a courtier as well as a scholar (III.i.159). And it is inconsistent, I believe, with nothing in the play, unless with the mention of his 'going back to school in Wittenberg'. But it is not

---

[3] In *Der Bestrafte Brudermord** it is Wittenberg. Hamlet says to the actors: 'Were you not, a few years ago, at the University of Wittenberg? I think I saw you act there': Furness's *Variorum*, ii.129. But it is very doubtful whether this play is anything but an adaptation and enlargement of *Hamlet* as it existed in the stage represented by Q 1.

really inconsistent with that. The idea may quite well be that Hamlet, feeling it impossible to continue at Court, after his mother's marriage and Claudius' accession, thinks of the University where, years ago, he was so happy, and contemplates a return to it. If this were Shakespeare's meaning he might easily fail to notice that the expression 'going back to school in Wittenberg' would naturally suggest that Hamlet had only just left 'school'.

I do not see how to account for these passages except on this hypothesis. But it in its turn involves a certain difficulty. Horatio, Rosencrantz and Guildenstern seem to be of about the same age as Hamlet. How then do *they* come to be at Wittenberg? I had thought that this question might be answered in the following way. If 'the city' is Wittenberg, Shakespeare would regard it as a place like London, and we might suppose that Horatio, Rosencrantz and Guildenstern were living there, though they had ceased to be students. But this can hardly be true of Horatio, who, when he (to spare Hamlet's feelings) talks of being 'a truant', must mean a truant from his University. The only solution I can suggest is that, in the story or play which Shakespeare used, Hamlet and the others were all at the time of the murder young students at Wittenberg, and that when he determined to make them older men (or to make Hamlet, at any rate, older) he did not take trouble enough to carry this idea through all the necessary detail, and so left some inconsistencies. But in any case the difficulty in the view which I suggest seems to me not nearly so great as those which the usual view has to meet.[4]

NOTE C

HAMLET'S AGE

The chief arguments on this question may be found in Furness's *Variorum Hamlet*, vol. I., pp. 391 ff. I will merely explain my position briefly.

Even if the general impression I received from the play were that Hamlet was a youth of eighteen or twenty, I should feel quite unable

---

[4] It is perhaps worth while to note that in *Der Bestrafte Brudermord* Hamlet is said to have been 'in Germany' at the time of his father's murder.

to set it against the evidence of the statements in v.i. which show him to be exactly thirty, unless these statements seemed to be casual. But they have to my mind, on the contrary, the appearance of being expressly inserted in order to fix Hamlet's age; and the fact that they differ decidedly from the statements in Q 1 confirms that idea. So does the fact that the Player-King speaks of having been married thirty years (III.ii.165), where again the number differs from that in Q 1.

If V.i. did not contain those decisive statements, I believe my impression as to Hamlet's age would be uncertain. His being several times called 'young' would not influence me much (nor at all when he is called 'young' simply to distinguish him from his father, *as he is in the very passage which shows him to be thirty*). But I think we naturally take him to be about as old as Laertes, Rosencrantz and Guildenstern, and take them to be less than thirty. Further, the language used by Laertes and Polonius to Ophelia in I.iii. would certainly, by itself, lead one to imagine Hamlet as a good deal less than thirty; and the impression it makes is not, to me, altogether effaced by the fact that Henry V at his accession is said to be in 'the very May-morn of his youth' – an expression which corresponds closely with those used by Laertes to Ophelia. In some passages, again, there is an air of boyish petulance. On the other side, however, we should have to set (1) the maturity of Hamlet's thought; (2) his manner, on the whole, to other men and to his mother, which, I think, is far from suggesting the idea of a mere youth; (3) such a passage as his words to Horatio at III.ii.59 ff., which imply that both he and Horatio have seen a good deal of life (this passage has in Q 1 nothing corresponding to the most significant lines). I have shown in Note B that it is very unsafe to argue to Hamlet's youth from the words about his going back to Wittenberg.

On the whole I agree with Professor Dowden that, apart from the statements in V.i., one would naturally take Hamlet to be a man of about five and twenty.

It has been suggested that in the old play Hamlet was a mere lad; that Shakespeare, when he began to work on it,[1] had not determined to make Hamlet older; that, as he went on, he did so determine; and that this is the reason why the earlier part of the play makes (if it does so) a different impression from the later. I see nothing very improba-

---

[1] Of course we do not know that he did work on it.

ble in this idea, but I must point out that it is a mistake to appeal in support of it to the passage in V.i. as found in Q 1; for that passage does not in the least show that the author (if correctly reported) imagined Hamlet as a lad. I set out the statements in Q 2 and Q 1.

Q 2 says:

(1) The grave-digger came to his business on the day when old Hamlet defeated Fortinbras:

(2) On that day young Hamlet was born:

(3) The grave-digger has, at the time of speaking, been sexton for thirty years:

(4) Yorick's skull has been in the earth twenty-three years:

(5) Yorick used to carry young Hamlet on his back.

This is all explicit and connected, and yields the result that Hamlet is now thirty.

Q 1 says:

(1) Yorick's skull has been in the ground a dozen years:

(2) It has been in the ground ever since old Hamlet overcame Fortinbras

(3) Yorick used to carry young Hamlet on his back.

From this nothing whatever follows as to Hamlet's age, except that he is more than twelve![2] Evidently the writer (if correctly reported) has no intention of telling us how old Hamlet is. That he did not imagine him as very young appears from his making him say that he has noted 'this seven year' (in Q 2 'three years') that the toe of the peasant comes near the heel of the courtier. The fact that the Player-King in Q 1 speaks of having been married forty years shows that here too the writer has not any reference to Hamlet's age in his mind.[3]

---

[2] I find that I have been anticipated in this remark by H. Türck* (*Jahrbuch* for 1990, p. 267 ff.).

[3] I do not know if it has been observed that in the opening of the Player-King's speech, as given in Q 2 and the Folio (it is quite different in Q 1), there seems to be a reminiscence of Greene's *Alphonsus King of Arragon*,* Act IV., lines 33 ff. (Dyce's *Greene and Peele*, p. 239):

Thrice ten times Phoebus with his golden beams
Hath compassed the circle of the sky,
Thrice ten times Ceres hath her workmen hir'd,
And fill'd her barns with fruitful crops of corn,
Since first in priesthood I did lead my life.

NOTE D

'MY TABLES – MEET IT IS I SET IT DOWN'

This passage has occasioned much difficulty, and to many readers seems even absurd. And it has been suggested that it, with much that immediately follows it, was adopted by Shakespeare, with very little change, from the old play.

It is surely in the highest degree improbable that, at such a critical point, when he had to show the first effect on Hamlet of the disclosures made by the Ghost, Shakespeare would write slackly or be content with anything that did not satisfy his own imagination. But it is not surprising that we should find some difficulty in following his imagination at such a point.

Let us look at the whole speech. The Ghost leaves Hamlet with the words, 'Adieu, adieu! Hamlet, remember me'; and he breaks out:

> O all you host of heaven! O earth! what else?
> And shall I couple hell? O, fie! Hold, hold, my heart;
> And you, my sinews, grow not instant old,
> But bear me stiffly up. Remember thee!
> Ay, thou poor ghost, while memory holds a seat
> In this distracted globe. Remember thee!
> Yea, from the table of my memory
> I'll wipe away all trivial fond records,
> All saws of books, all forms, all pressures past,
> That youth and observation copied there;
> And thy commandment all alone shall live
> Within the book and volume of my brain,
> Unmix'd with baser matter: yes, by heaven!
> O most pernicious woman!
> O villain, villain, smiling, damned villain!
> My tables – meet it is I set it down,
> That one may smile, and smile, and be a villain;
> At least I'm sure it may be so in Denmark: [Writing
> So, uncle, there you are. Now to my word;
> It is 'Adieu, adieu! remember me.'
> I have sworn 't.

The man who speaks thus was, we must remember, already well-nigh overwhelmed with sorrow and disgust when the Ghost appeared to him. He has now suffered a tremendous shock. He has learned that his mother was not merely what he supposed but an adulteress, and that his father was murdered by her paramour. This knowledge too has come to him in such a way as, quite apart from the *matter* of the communication, might make any human reason totter. And, finally, a terrible charge has been laid upon him. Is it strange, then, that he should say what is strange? Why, there would be nothing to wonder at if his mind collapsed on the spot.

Now it is just this that he himself fears. In the midst of the first tremendous outburst, he checks himself suddenly with the exclamation 'O, fie!' (cf. the precisely similar use of this interjection, II.ii.17). He must not let himself feel: he has to live. He must not let his heart break in pieces ('hold' means 'hold together'), his muscles turn into those of a trembling old man, his brain dissolve – as they threaten in an instant to do. For, if they do, how can he – *remember*? He goes on reiterating this 'remember' (the 'word' of the Ghost). He is, literally, afraid that he will *forget* – that his mind will lose the message entrusted to it. Instinctively, then, he feels that, if he is to remember, he must wipe from his memory everything it already contains; and the image of his past life rises before him, of all his joy in thought and observation and the stores they have accumulated in his memory. All that is done with for ever: nothing is to remain for him on the 'table' but the command, 'remember me'. He swears it; 'yes, by heaven!' That done, suddenly the repressed passion breaks out, and, most characteristically, he thinks *first* of his mother; then of his uncle, the smooth-spoken scoundrel who has just been smiling on him and calling him 'son'. And in bitter desperate irony he snatches his tables from his breast (they are suggested to him by the phrases he has just used, 'table of my memory', 'book and volume'). After all, he *will* use them once again; and, perhaps with a wild laugh, he writes with trembling fingers his last observation: 'One may smile, and smile, and be a villain.'

But that, I believe, is not merely a desperate jest. It springs from that *fear of forgetting*. A time will come, he feels, when all this appalling experience of the last half-hour will be incredible to him, will seem a mere nightmare, will even, conceivably, quite vanish from his mind. Let him have something in black and white that will bring it back and *force* him to remember and believe. What is there so unnatural in this, if you substitute a note-book or diary for the 'tables'?[1]

But why should he write that particular note, and not rather his 'word', 'Adieu, adieu! remember me'? I should answer, first, that a grotesque jest at such a moment is thoroughly characteristic of Hamlet (see p. 127), and that the jocose 'So, uncle, there you are!' shows his state of mind; and, secondly, that loathing of his uncle is vehement in his thoughts at this moment. Possibly, too, he might remember that 'tables' are stealable, and that if the appearance of the Ghost should be reported, a mere observation on the smiling of villains could not betray anything of his communication with the Ghost. What follows shows that the instinct of secrecy is strong in him.

It seems likely, I may add, that Shakespeare here was influenced, consciously or unconsciously, by recollection of a place in *Titus Andronicus* (IV.i.). In that horrible play Chiron and Demetrius, after outraging Lavinia, cut out her tongue and cut off her hands, in order that she may be unable to reveal the outrage. She reveals it, however, by taking a staff in her mouth, guiding it with her arms, and writing in the sand, 'Stuprum. Chiron. Demetrius.' Titus soon afterwards says:

> I will go get a leaf of brass,
> And with a gad of steel will write these words,
> And lay it by. The angry northern wind
> Will blow these sands, like Sibyl's leaves, abroad,
> And where's your lesson then?

Perhaps in the old *Hamlet*,* which may have been a play something like *Titus Andronicus*, Hamlet at this point did write something of the Ghost's message in his tables. In any case Shakespeare, whether he wrote *Titus Andronicus* or only revised an older play on the subject, might well recall this incident, as he frequently reproduces other things in that drama.

---

[1] The reader will observe that this suggestion of a further reason for his making the note may be rejected without the rest of the interpretation being affected.

NOTE E

THE GHOST IN THE CELLARAGE

It has been thought that the whole of the last part of I.v., from the entrance of Horatio and Marcellus, follows the old play closely, and that Shakespeare is condescending to the groundlings.

Here again, whether or no he took a suggestion from the old play, I see no reason to think that he wrote down to his public. So far as Hamlet's state of mind is concerned, there is not a trace of this. Anyone who has a difficulty in understanding it should read Coleridge's note. What appears grotesque is the part taken by the Ghost, and Hamlet's consequent removal from one part of the stage to another. But, as to the former, should we feel anything grotesque in the four injunctions 'Swear!' if it were not that they come from under the stage – a fact which to an Elizabethan audience, perfectly indifferent to what is absurdly called stage illusion, was probably not in the least grotesque? And as to the latter, if we knew the Ghost-lore of the time better than we do, perhaps we should see nothing odd in Hamlet's insisting on moving away and proposing the oath afresh when the Ghost intervenes.

But, further, it is to be observed that he does not merely propose the oath afresh. He first makes Horatio and Marcellus swear never to make known what they have *seen*. Then, on shifting his ground, he makes them swear never to speak of what they have *heard*. Then, moving again, he makes them swear that, if he should think fit to play the antic, they will give no sign of knowing aught of him. The oath is now complete; and, when the Ghost commands them to swear the last time, Hamlet suddenly becomes perfectly serious and bids it rest. [In Fletcher's* *Woman's Prize*,* V.iii., a passage pointed out to me by Mr. C. J. Wilkinson, a man taking an oath shifts his ground.]

NOTE F

THE PLAYER'S SPEECH IN *HAMLET*

There are two extreme views about this speech. According to one, Shakespeare quoted it from some play, or composed it for the occasion, simply and solely in order to ridicule, through it, the bombastic style of dramatists contemporary with himself or slightly older; just as he ridicules in *2 Henry IV* Tamburlaine's* rant about the kings who draw his chariot, or puts fragments of similar bombast into the mouth of Pistol. According to Coleridge, on the other hand, this idea is 'below criticism'. No sort of ridicule was intended. 'The lines, as epic narrative, are superb.' It is true that the language is 'too poetical – the language of lyric vehemence and epic pomp, and not of the drama'; but this is due to the fact that Shakespeare had to distinguish the style of the speech from that of his own dramatic dialogue.

In essentials I think that what Coleridge says[1] is true. He goes too far, it seems to me, when he describes the language of the speech as merely 'too poetical'; for with much that is fine there is intermingled a good deal that, in epic as in drama, must be called bombast. But I do not believe Shakespeare meant it for bombast.

I will briefly put the arguments which point to this conclusion. Warburton long ago stated some of them fully and cogently, but he misinterpreted here and there, and some arguments have to be added to his.

1. If the speech was meant to be ridiculous, it follows either that Hamlet in praising it spoke ironically, or that Shakespeare, in making Hamlet praise it sincerely, himself wrote ironically. And both these consequences are almost incredible.

Let us see what Hamlet says. He asks the player to recite 'a passionate speech'; and, being requested to choose one, he refers to a speech he once heard the player declaim. This speech, he says, was never 'acted' or was acted only once; for the play pleased not the million. But he, and others whose opinion was of more importance than this, thought it an excellent play, well constructed, and composed with

---

[1] It is impossible to tell whether Coleridge formed his view independently, or adopted it from Schlegel. For there is no record of his having expressed his opinion prior to the time of his reading Schlegel's *Lectures*, and, whatever he said to the contrary, his borrowings from Schlegel are demonstrable.

equal skill and temperance. One of these other judges commended it because it contained neither piquant indecencies nor affectations of phrase, but showed 'an honest method, as wholesome as sweet, and by very much more handsome than fine'.[2] In this play Hamlet 'chiefly loved' one speech; and he asks for a part of it.

Let the reader now refer to the passage I have just summarized; let him consider its tone and manner; and let him ask himself if Hamlet can possibly be speaking ironically. I am sure he will answer No. And then let him observe what follows. The speech is declaimed. Polonius interrupting it with an objection to its length, Hamlet snubs him, bids the player proceed, and adds, 'He's for a jig or a tale of bawdry: or he sleeps.' 'He,' that is, 'shares the taste of the million for sallets in the lines to make the matter savoury, and is wearied by an honest method.'[3] Polonius later interrupts again, for he thinks the emotion of the player too absurd; but Hamlet respects it; and afterwards, when he is alone (and therefore can hardly be ironical), in contrasting this emotion with his own insensibility, he betrays no consciousness that there was anything unfitting in the speech that caused it.

So far I have chiefly followed Warburton, but there is an important point which seems not to have been observed. All Hamlet's praise of the speech is in the closest agreement with his conduct and words elsewhere. His later advice to the player (III.ii.) is on precisely the same lines. He is to play to the judicious, not to the crowd, whose opinion is worthless. He is to observe, like the author of Aeneas' speech, the 'modesty' of nature. He must not tear a 'passion' to tatters, to split the ears of the incompetent, but in the very tempest of passion is to keep a temperance and smoothness. The million, we gather from the first passage, cares nothing for construction; and so, we learn in the second passage, the barren spectators want to laugh at the clown instead of attending to some necessary question of the play. Hamlet's hatred of exaggeration is marked in both passages. And so (as already pointed out, p. 111) in the play-scene, when his own lines are going to be delivered, he impatiently calls out to the actor to leave his damnable faces and begin; and at the grave of Ophelia he is furious

---

[2] Clark and Wright* well compare Polonius' antithesis of 'rich, not gaudy'; though I doubt if 'handsome' implies richness.

[3] Is it not possible that 'mobled queen', to which Hamlet seems to object, and which Polonius praises, is meant for an example of the second fault of affected phraseology, from which the play was said to be free and an instance of which therefore surprises Hamlet?

with what he thinks the exaggeration of Laertes, burlesques his language, and breaks off with the words,

> Nay, an thou'lt mouth,
> I'll rant as well as thou.

Now if Hamlet's praise of the Aeneas and Dido play and speech is ironical, his later advice to the player must surely be ironical too: and who will maintain that? And if in the one passage Hamlet is serious but Shakespeare ironical, then in the other passage all those famous remarks about drama and acting, which have been cherished as Shakespeare's by all the world, express the opposite of Shakespeare's opinion: and who will maintain that? And if Hamlet and Shakespeare are both serious – and nothing else is credible – then, to Hamlet and Shakespeare, the speeches of Laertes and Hamlet at Ophelia's grave are rant, but the speech of Aeneas to Dido is *not* rant. Is it not evident that he meant it for an exalted narrative speech of 'passion', in a style which, though he may not have adopted it, he still approved and despised the million for not approving, – a speech to be delivered with temperance or modesty, but not too tamely neither? Is he not aiming here to do precisely what Marlowe aimed to do when he proposed to lead the audience

> From jigging veins of rhyming mother-wits,
> And such conceits as clownage keeps in pay,*

to 'stately' themes which beget 'high astounding terms'? And is it strange that, like Marlowe in *Tamburlaine*, he adopted a style marred in places by that which *we* think bombast, but which the author meant to be more 'handsome than fine'?

2. If this is so, we can easily understand how it comes about that the speech of Aeneas contains lines which are unquestionably grand and free from any suspicion of bombast, and others which, though not free from that suspicion, are nevertheless highly poetic. To the first class certainly belongs the passage beginning, 'But as we often see.' To the second belongs the description of Pyrrhus, covered with blood that was

> Baked and impasted with the parching streets,
> That lend a tyrannous and damned light
> To their lord's murder;

and again the picture of Pyrrhus standing like a tyrant in a picture, with his uplifted arm arrested in act to strike by the crash of the falling towers of Ilium. It is surely impossible to say that these lines are *merely* absurd and not in the least grand; and with them I should join the passage about Fortune's wheel, and the concluding lines.

But how can the insertion of these passages possibly be explained on the hypothesis that Shakespeare meant the speech to be ridiculous?

3. 'Still,' it maybe answered, 'Shakespeare *must* have been conscious of the bombast in some of these passages. How could he help seeing it? And, if he saw it, he cannot have meant seriously to praise the speech.' But why must he have seen it? Did Marlowe know when he wrote bombastically? Or Marston?* Or Heywood? Does not Shakespeare elsewhere write bombast? The truth is that the two defects of style in the speech are the very defects we do find in his writings. When he wished to make his style exceptionally high and passionate he always ran some risk of bombast. And he was even more prone to the fault which in this speech seems to me the more marked, a use of metaphors which sound to our ears 'conceited' or grotesque. To me at any rate the metaphors in 'now is he total gules' and 'mincing with his sword her husband's limbs' are more disturbing than any of the bombast. But, as regards this second defect, there are many places in Shakespeare worse than the speech of Aeneas; and, as regards the first, though in his undoubtedly genuine works there is no passage so faulty, there is also no passage of quite the same species (for his narrative poems do not aim at epic grandeur), and there are many passages where bombast of the same kind, though not of the same degree, occurs.

Let the reader ask himself, for instance, how the following lines would strike him if he came on them for the first time out of their context:

> Whip me, ye devils,
> From the possession of this heavenly sight!
> Blow me about in winds! Roast me in sulphur!
> Wash me in steep-down gulfs of liquid fire!

Are Pyrrhus's 'total gules' any worse than Duncan's 'silver skin laced with his golden blood', or so bad as the chamberlains' daggers 'unmannerly breech'd with gore'?[4] If 'to bathe in reeking wounds', and 'spongy officers', and even 'alarum'd by his sentinel the wolf, Whose howl's his watch', and other such phrases in *Macbeth*, had occurred in the speech of Aeneas, we should certainly have been told that they were meant for burlesque. I open *Troilus and Cressida* (because, like the speech of Aeneas, it has to do with the story of Troy), and I read, in a perfectly serious context (IV.v.6 f.):

> Thou, trumpet, there's thy purse.
> Now crack thy lungs, and split thy brazen pipe:
> Blow, villain, till thy sphered bias cheek
> Outswell the colic of puff'd Aquilon:
> Come, stretch thy chest, and let thy eyes spout blood;
> Thou blow'st for Hector.

'Splendid!' one cries. Yes, but if you are told it is also bombastic, can you deny it? I read again (V.v.7)

> bastard Margarelon
> Hath Doreus prisoner,
> And stands colossus-wise, waving his beam,
> Upon the pashed corses of the kings.

Or, to turn to earlier but still undoubted works, Shakespeare wrote in *Romeo and Juliet*,

> here will I remain
> With worms that are thy chamber-maids;

and in *King John*,

> And pick strong matter of revolt and wrath
> Out of the bloody finger-ends of John;

and in *Lucrece*,

> And, bubbling from her breast, it doth divide
> In two slow rivers, that the crimson blood
> Circles her body in on every side,
> Who, like a late-sack'd island, vastly stood
> Bare and unpeopled in this fearful flood.
>> Some of her blood still pure and red remain'd,
>> And some look'd black, and that false Tarquin stain'd.

---

[4] The extravagance of these phrases is doubtless intentional (for Macbeth in using them is trying to act a part), but the absurdity of the second can hardly be so.

Is it so very unlikely that the poet who wrote thus might, aiming at a peculiarly heightened and passionate style, write the speech of Aeneas?

4. But, pursuing this line of argument, we must go further. There is really scarcely one idea, and there is but little phraseology, in the speech that cannot be paralleled from Shakespeare's own works. He merely exaggerates a little here what he has done elsewhere. I will conclude this Note by showing that this is so as regards almost all the passages most objected to, as well as some others. (1) 'The Hyrcanian beast' is Macbeth's 'Hyrcan tiger' (III.iv.101), who also occurs in 3 *Hen. VI* I.iv.155. (2) With 'total pules' Steevens compared *Timon* IV.iii.59 (an undoubtedly Shakespearean passage),

> With man's blood paint the ground, gules, gules.

(3) With 'baked and impasted' *cf. John* III.iii.42, 'If that surly spirit melancholy Had baked thy blood.' In the questionable *Tit. And.* V.ii.201 we have, 'in that paste let their vile heads be baked' (a paste made of blood and bones, *ib.* 188), and in the undoubted *Richard II* III.ii.154 (quoted by Caldecott) Richard refers to the ground

> Which serves as paste and cover to our bones.

(4) 'O'er-sized with coagulate gore' finds an exact parallel in the 'blood-siz'd field' of the *Two Noble Kinsmen*, I.i.99, a scene which, whether written by Shakespeare (as I fully believe) or by another poet, was certainly written in all seriousness. (5) 'With eyes like carbuncles' has been much ridiculed, but Milton (*P.L.* ix.500) gives 'carbuncle eyes' to Satan turned into a serpent (Steevens*), and why are they more outrageous than ruby lips and cheeks (*J.C.* III.i.260, *Macb.* III.iv.115, *Cym.* II.ii.17)? (6) Priam falling with the mere wind of Pyrrhus's sword is paralleled, not only in *Dido Queen of Carthage*, but in *Tr. and Cr.* V.iii.40 (Warburton). (7) With Pyrrhus standing like a painted tyrant *cf. Macb.* V.viii.25 (Delius*). (8) The forging of Mars's armour occurs again in *Tr. and Cr.* IV.v.255, where Hector swears by the forge that stithied Mars his helm, just as Hamlet himself alludes to Vulcan's stithy (III.ii.89). (9) The idea of 'strumpet Fortune' is common: *e.g. Macb.* I.ii.15, 'Fortune . . . show'd like a rebel's whore.' (10) With the 'rant' about her wheel Warburton compares *Ant. and Cl.* IV.xv.43, where Cleopatra would

> rail so high
> That the false huswife Fortune break her wheel.

(11) Pyrrhus minces with his sword Priam's limbs, and Timon (IV.iii.122) bids Alcibiades 'mince' the babe 'without remorse'.[5]

NOTE G

HAMLET'S APOLOGY TO LAERTES

Johnson, in commenting on the passage (V.ii.237–55), says: 'I wish Hamlet had made some other defence; it is unsuitable to the character of a good or a brave man to shelter himself in falsehood.' And Seymour* (according to Furness) thought the falsehood so ignoble that he rejected lines 239–50 as an interpolation!

I wish first to remark that we are mistaken when we suppose that Hamlet is here apologizing specially for his behaviour to Laertes at Ophelia's grave. We naturally suppose this because he has told Horatio that he is sorry he 'forgot himself on that occasion, and that he will court Laertes' favours (V.ii.75 ff.). But what he says in that very passage shows that he is thinking chiefly of the greater wrong he has done Laertes by depriving him of his father:

> For, by the image of my cause, I see
> The portraiture of his.

---

[5] Steevens observes that Heywood uses the phrase 'guled with slaughter', and I find in his *Iron Age* various passages indicating that he knew the speech of Aeneas (cf. p. 118 for another sign that he knew *Hamlet*). The two parts of the *Iron Age* were published in 1632, but are said, in the preface to the Second, to have 'been long since writ'. I refer to the pages of vol. 3 of Pearson's *Heywood* (1874). (1) p. 329, Troilus 'lyeth imbak'd In his cold blood'. (2) p. 341, of Achilles' armour:

> *Vulcan* that wrought it out of gadds of Steele
> With his *Ciclopian* hammers, never made
> Such noise upon his Anvile forging it,
> Than these my arm'd fists in *Hisses* wracke.

(3) p. 357, 'till *Hecub's* reverent lockes Be gul'd in slaughter'. (4) p. 357, '*Scamander* plaines Ore-spread with intrailes bak'd in blood and dust'. (5) p. 378, 'We'll rost them at the scorching flames of *Troy*' (6) p. 379, 'tragicke slaughter, clad in gules and sables' (cf. 'sable arms' in the speech in *Hamlet*). (7) p. 384, 'these lockes, now knotted all, As bak't in blood'. Of these, all but (1) and (2) are in Part II. Part I has many passages which recall *Troilus and Cressida*. Mr. Fleay's* speculation as to its date will be found in his *Chronicle History of the English Drama*, i. p. 285.

For the same writer's ingenious theory (which is of course incapable of proof) regarding the relation of the player's speech in *Hamlet* to Marlowe and Nash's *Dido,* see Furness's Variorum *Hamlet.*

And it is also evident in the last words of the apology itself that he is referring in it to the deaths of Polonius and Ophelia:

Sir, in this audience,
Let my disclaiming from a purposed evil
Free me so far in your most generous thoughts,
That I have shot mine arrow o'er the house,
And hurt my brother.

But now, as to the falsehood. The charge is not to be set aside lightly; and, for my part, I confess that, while rejecting of course Johnson's notion that Shakespeare wanted to paint 'a good man', I have momentarily shared Johnson's wish that Hamlet had made 'some other defence' than that of madness. But I think the wish proceeds from failure to imagine the situation.

In the first place, *what* other defence can we wish Hamlet to have made? I can think of none. He cannot tell the truth. He cannot say to Laertes, 'I meant to stab the King, not your father'. He cannot explain why he was unkind to Ophelia. Even on the false supposition that he is referring simply to his behaviour at the grave, he can hardly say, I suppose, 'You ranted so abominably that you put me into a towering passion'. *Whatever* he said, it would have to be more or less untrue.

Next, what moral difference is there between feigning insanity and asserting it? If we are to blame Hamlet for the second, why not equally for the first?

And, finally, even if he were referring simply to his behaviour at the grave, his excuse, besides falling in with his whole plan of feigning insanity, would be as near the truth as any he could devise. For we are not to take the account he gives to Horatio, that he was put in a passion by the bravery of Laertes' grief, as the whole truth. His raving over the grave is not *mere* acting. On the contrary, that passage is the best card that the believers in Hamlet's madness have to play. He is really almost beside himself with grief as well as anger, half-maddened by the impossibility of explaining to Laertes how he has come to do what he has done, full of wild rage and then of sick despair at this wretched world which drives him to such deeds and such misery. It is the same rage and despair that mingle with other feelings in his outbreak to Ophelia in the Nunnery-scene. But of all this, even if he were clearly conscious of it, he cannot speak to Horatio; for his love to Ophelia is a subject on which he has never opened his lips to his friend.

If we realize the situation, then, we shall, I think, repress the wish that Hamlet had 'made some other defence' than that of madness. We shall feel only tragic sympathy.

As I have referred to Hamlet's apology, I will add a remark on it from a different point of view. It forms another refutation of the theory that Hamlet has delayed his vengeance till he could publicly convict the King, and that he has come back to Denmark because now, with the evidence of the commission in his pocket, he can safely accuse him. If that were so, what better opportunity could he possibly find than this occasion, where he has to express his sorrow to Laertes for the grievous wrongs which he has unintentionally inflicted on him?

NOTE H

THE EXCHANGE OF RAPIERS

I am not going to discuss the question. how this exchange ought to be managed. I wish merely to point out that the stage-direction fails to show the sequence of speeches and events. The passage is as follows (Globe text):

> *Ham.* Come, for the third, Laertes: you but dally;
> I pray you, pass with your best violence;
> I am afeared you make a wanton of me.
> *Laer.* Say you so? come on.   [*They play.*
> *Osr.* Nothing, neither way.
> *Laer.* Have at you now!
>   [*Laertes wounds Hamlet; then, in scuffling, they change rapiers, and Hamlet wounds Laertes.*[1]
> *King.* Part them; they are incensed.
> *Ham.* Nay, come, again.   [*The Queen falls.*[2]
> *Osr.*   Look to the Queen there, ho!
> *Hor.* They bleed on both sides. How is it, my lord?
> *Osr.* How is't, Laertes?

---

[1] So Rowe. The direction in Q 1 is negligible, the text being different. Q 2 etc. have nothing, Ff. simply 'In scuffling they change rapiers'.
[2] Capell.* The Quartos and Folios have no directions.

The words 'and Hamlet wounds Laertes' in Rowe's stage-direction destroy the point of the words given to the King in the text. If Laertes is already wounded, why should the King care whether the fencers are parted or not? What makes him cry out is that, while he sees his purpose effected as regards Hamlet, he also sees Laertes in danger through the exchange of foils in the scuffle. Now it is not to be supposed that Laertes is particularly dear to him; but he sees instantaneously that, if Laertes escapes the poisoned foil, he will certainly hold his tongue about the plot against Hamlet, while, if he is wounded, he may confess the truth; for it is no doubt quite evident to the King that Laertes has fenced tamely because his conscience is greatly troubled by the treachery he is about to practise. The King therefore, as soon as he sees the exchange of foils, cries out, 'Part them; they are incensed.' But Hamlet's blood is up. 'Nay, come, again,' he calls to Laertes, who cannot refuse to play, and *now* is wounded by Hamlet. At the very same moment the Queen falls to the ground; and ruin rushes on the King from the right hand and the left.

The passage, therefore, should be printed thus:

Laer.   Have at you now!
                    [Laertes wounds Hamlet; then, in scuffling, they change
                                                                                    rapiers.
King.   Part them; they are incensed.
Ham.   Nay, come, again.
           [They play, and Hamlet wounds Laertes. The Queen falls

NOTE I

THE DURATION OF THE ACTION IN *OTHELLO*

The quite unusual difficulties regarding this subject have led to much discussion, a synopsis of which may be found in Furness's Variorum edition, pp. 358–72. Without detailing the facts I will briefly set out the main difficulty, which is that, according to one set of indications (which I will call A), Desdemona was murdered within a day or two of her arrival in Cyprus, while, according to another set (which I will call B), some time elapsed between her arrival and the catastrophe. Let us take A first, and run through the play.

(A) Act I. opens on the night of Othello's marriage. On that night he is despatched to Cyprus, leaving Desdemona to follow him.

In Act II, Sc. i., there arrive at Cyprus, first, in one ship, Cassio; then, in another, Desdemona, Iago, and Emilia; then, in another, Othello (Othello, Cassio, and Desdemona being in three different ships, it does not matter, for our purpose, how long the voyage lasted). On the night following these arrivals in Cyprus the marriage is consummated (II.iii.9), Cassio is cashiered, and, on Iago's advice, he resolves to ask Desdemona's intercession 'betimes in the morning' (II.iii.335).

In Act III, Sc. iii. (the Temptation scene), he does so: Desdemona does intercede: Iago begins to poison Othello's mind: the handkerchief is lost, found by Emilia, and given to Iago: he determines to leave it in Cassio's room, and, renewing his attack on Othello, asserts that he has seen the handkerchief in Cassio's hand: Othello bids him kill Cassio within three days, and resolves to kill Desdemona himself. All this occurs in one unbroken scene, and evidently on the day after the arrival in Cyprus (see III.i.33).

In the scene (iv.) following the Temptation scene Desdemona sends to bid Cassio come, as she has interceded for him: Othello enters, tests her about the handkerchief, and departs in anger: Cassio, arriving, is told of the change in Othello, and, being left *solus*, is accosted by Bianca, whom he requests to copy the work on the handkerchief which he has just found in his room (II.188 f.). All this is naturally taken to happen in the later part of the day on which the events of III.i–iii. took place, *i.e.* the day after the arrival in Cyprus; but I shall return to this point.

In IV.i. Iago tells Othello that Cassio has confessed, and, placing Othello where he can watch, he proceeds on Cassio's entrance to rally him about Bianca; and Othello, not being near enough to hear what is said, believes that Cassio is laughing at his conquest of Desdemona. Cassio here says that Bianca haunts him and 'was here *even now*'; and Bianca herself, coming in, reproaches him about the handkerchief 'you gave me *even now*'. There is therefore no appreciable time between III.iv. and IV.i. In this same scene Bianca bids Cassio come to supper *to-night*, and Lodovico, arriving, is asked to sup with Othello *to-night*. In IV.ii. Iago persuades Roderigo to kill Cassio *that night* as he comes from Bianca's. In IV.iii. Lodovico, after supper, takes his leave, and Othello bids Desdemona go to bed on the instant and dismiss her attendant.

In Act V., *that night*, the attempted assassination of Cassio, and the murder of Desdemona, take place.

From all this, then, it seems clear that the time between the arrival in Cyprus and the catastrophe is certainly not more than a few days, and most probably only about a day and a half; or, to put it otherwise, that most probably Othello kills his wife about twenty-four hours after the consummation of their marriage!

The only *possible* place, it will be seen, where time can elapse is between III.iii. and III.iv. And here Mr. Fleay would imagine a gap of at least a week. The reader will find that this supposition involves the following results. (*a*) Desdemona has allowed at least a week to elapse without telling Cassio that she has interceded for him. (*b*) Othello, after being convinced of her guilt, after resolving to kill her, and after ordering Iago to kill Cassio within three days, has allowed at least a week to elapse without even questioning her about the handkerchief, and has so behaved during all this time that she is totally unconscious of any change in his feelings. (*c*) Desdemona, who reserves the handkerchief evermore about her to kiss and talk to (III.iii.295), has lost it for at least a week before she is conscious of the loss. (*d*) Iago has waited at least a week to leave the handkerchief in Cassio's chamber; for Cassio has evidently only just found it, and wants the work on it copied before the owner makes inquiries for it. These are all gross absurdities. It is certain that only a short time, most probable that not even a night, elapses between III.iii. and III.iv.

(B) Now this idea that Othello killed his wife, probably within twenty-four hours, certainly within a few days, of the consummation of his marriage, contradicts the impression produced by the play on all uncritical readers and spectators. It is also in flat contradiction with a large number of time-indications in the play itself. It is needless to mention more than a few. (*a*) Bianca complains that Cassio has kept away from her for a week (III.iv.173). Cassio and the rest have therefore been more than a week in Cyprus, and, we should naturally infer, considerably more. (*b*) The ground on which Iago builds throughout is the probability of Desdemona's having got tired of the Moor; she is accused of having repeatedly committed adultery with Cassio (*e.g.* V. i.210); these facts and a great many others, such as Othello's language in III.iii.338 ff., are utterly absurd on the supposition that he murders his wife within a day or two of the night when he consummated his marriage. (*c*) Iago's account of Cassio's dream implies (and indeed states) that he had been sleeping with Cassio 'lately', *i.e.* after arriving at Cyprus: yet, according to A, he had only spent one night in Cyprus, and we are expressly told that Cassio never went to bed on that night. Iago doubtless was a liar, but Othello was not an absolute idiot.

Thus (1) one set of time-indications clearly shows that Othello murdered his wife within a few days, probably a day and a half, of his arrival in Cyprus and the consummation of his marriage; (2) another set of time-indications implies quite as clearly that some little time must have elapsed, probably a few weeks; and this last is certainly the impression of a reader who has not closely examined the play.

It is impossible to escape this result. The suggestion that the imputed intrigue of Cassio and Desdemona took place at Venice before the marriage, not at Cyprus after it, is quite futile. There is no positive evidence whatever for it; if the reader will merely refer to the difficulties mentioned under B above, he will see that it leaves almost all of them absolutely untouched; and Iago's accusation is uniformly one of adultery.

How then is this extraordinary contradiction to be explained? It can hardly be one of the casual inconsistencies, due to forgetfulness, which are found in Shakespeare's other tragedies; for the scheme of time indicated under A seems deliberate and self-consistent, and the scheme indicated under B seems, if less deliberate, equally self-consistent. This does not look as if a single scheme had been so vaguely imagined that inconsistencies arose in working it out; it points to some other source of contradiction.

'Christopher North',* who dealt very fully with the question, elaborated a doctrine of Double Time, Short and Long. To do justice to this theory in a few words is impossible, but its essence is the notion that Shakespeare, consciously or unconsciously, wanted to produce on the spectator (for he did not aim at readers) two impressions. He wanted the spectator to feel a passionate and vehement haste in the action; but he also wanted him to feel that the action was fairly probable. Consciously or unconsciously he used Short Time (the scheme of A) for the first purpose, and Long Time (the scheme of B) for the second. The spectator is affected in the required manner by both, though without distinctly noticing the indications of the two schemes.

The notion underlying this theory is probably true, but the theory itself can hardly stand. Passing minor matters by, I would ask the reader to consider the following remarks. (*a*) If, as seems to be maintained, the spectator does not notice the indications of 'Short Time' at all, how can they possibly affect him? The passion, vehemence and haste of Othello affect him, because he perceives them; but if he does not perceive the hints which show the duration of the action from the arrival in Cyprus to the murder, these hints have simply no existence for him and are perfectly useless. The theory, therefore, does not explain the existence of 'Short Time'. (*b*) It is not the case that 'Short Time' is wanted only to produce an impression of vehemence and haste, and 'Long Time' for probability. The 'Short Time' is equally wanted for probability: for it is grossly improbable that Iago's intrigue should not break down if Othello spends a week or weeks between the successful temptation and his execution of justice. (*c*) And this brings me to the most important point, which appears to have escaped notice. The place where 'Long Time' is wanted is not *within* Iago's intrigue. 'Long Time' is required simply and solely because the intrigue and its circumstances presuppose a marriage consummated, and an adultery possible, for (let us say) some weeks. But, granted that lapse between the marriage and the temptation, there is no reason whatever why more than a few days or even one day should elapse between this temptation and the murder. The whole trouble arises because the temptation begins on the morning after the consummated marriage. Let some three weeks elapse between the first night at Cyprus and the temptation; let the brawl which ends in the disgrace of Cassio occur not on that night but three weeks later; or again let it occur that night, but let three weeks elapse before the intercession of Desdemona and the temptation of Iago begin. All will then be clear. Cassio has time to make acquaintance with Bianca, and to neglect her: the Senate has time to hear of the perdition of the Turkish fleet and to recall Othello: the accusations of Iago cease to be ridiculous; and the headlong speed of the action after the temptation has begun is quite in place. Now, too, there is no reason why we should not be affected by the hints of time ('to-day', 'to-night', 'even now'), which we *do* perceive (though we do not calculate them out). And, lastly, this supposition corresponds with our natural impression, which is that the temptation and what follows it take place some little while after the marriage, but occupy, themselves, a very short time.

Now, of course, the supposition just described is no fact. As the play stands, it is quite certain that there is no space of three weeks, or anything like it, either between the arrival in Cyprus and the brawl, or between the brawl and the temptation. And I draw attention to the supposition chiefly to show that quite a small change would remove the difficulties, and to insist that there is nothing wrong at all in regard to the time from the temptation onward. How to account for the existing contradictions I do not at all profess to know, and I will merely mention two possibilities.

Possibly, as Mr. Daniel* observes, the play has been tampered with. We have no text earlier than 1622, six years after Shakespeare's death. It may be suggested, then, that in the play, as Shakespeare wrote it, there was a gap of some weeks between the arrival in Cyprus and Cassio's brawl, or (less probably) between the brawl and the temptation. Perhaps there was a scene indicating the lapse of time. Perhaps it was dull, or the play was a little too long, or devotees of the unity of time made sport of a second breach of that unity coming just after the breach caused by the voyage. Perhaps accordingly the owners of the play altered, or hired a dramatist to alter, the arrangement at this point, and this was unwittingly done in such a way as to produce the contradictions we are engaged on. There is nothing intrinsically unlikely in this idea; and certainly, I think, the amount of such corruption of Shakespeare's texts by the players is usually rather underrated than otherwise. But I cannot say I see any signs of foreign alteration in the text, though it is somewhat odd that Roderigo, who makes no complaint on the day of the arrival in Cyprus when he is being persuaded to draw Cassio into a quarrel that night, should, directly after the quarrel (II.iii.370), complain that he is making no advance in his pursuit of Desdemona, and should speak as though he had been in Cyprus long enough to have spent nearly all the money he brought from Venice.

Or, possibly, Shakespeare's original plan was to allow some time to elapse after the arrival at Cyprus, but when he reached the point he found it troublesome to indicate this lapse in an interesting way, and convenient to produce Cassio's fall by means of the rejoicings on the night of the arrival, and then almost necessary to let the request for intercession, and the temptation, follow on the next day. And perhaps he said to himself, No one in the theatre will notice that all this makes an impossible position: and I can make all safe by using language that implies that Othello has after all been married for some time. If so, probably he was right. I do not think anyone does notice the impossibilities either in the theatre or in a casual reading of the play.

Either of these suppositions is possible: neither is, to me, probable. The first seems the less unlikely. If the second is true, Shakespeare did in *Othello* what he seems to do in no other play. I can believe that he may have done so; but I find it very hard to believe that he produced this impossible situation without knowing it. It is one thing to read a drama or see it, quite another to construct and compose it, and he appears to have imagined the action in *Othello* with even more than his usual intensity.

NOTE J

THE 'ADDITIONS' TO *OTHELLO* IN THE FIRST FOLIO. THE PONTIC SEA

The first printed *Othello* is the first Quarto (Q 1), 1622; the second is the first Folio (F 1), 1623. These two texts are two distinct versions of the play. Q 1 contains many oaths and expletives where less 'objectionable' expressions occur in F 1. Partly for this reason it is believed to represent the *earlier* text, perhaps the text as it stood before the Act of 1605 against profanity on the stage. Its readings are frequently superior to those of F 1, but it wants many lines that appear in F 1, which probably represents the acting version in 1623. I give a list of the longer passages absent from Q 1:

- (*a*) I.i.122–138. 'If t' . . . 'yourself.'
- (*b*) I.ii.72–77. 'Judge' . . . 'thee'
- (*c*) I.iii.24–30. 'For' . . . 'profitless.'
- (*d*) III.iii.383–390. '*Oth.* By' . . . 'satisfied! *Iago.*'
- (*e*) III.iii.453–460. 'Iago.' . . . 'heaven,'
- (*f*) IV.i.38–44. 'To confess' . . . 'devil!'
- (*g*) IV.ii.73–76, 'Committed!' . . . 'committed!'
- (*h*) IV.ii.151–164. 'Here' . . . 'make me.'
- (*i*) IV.iii.31–53. 'I have' . . . 'not next.' and 55–57. '*Des* [*Singing*]' . . . 'men.'
- (*j*) IV.iii.60–63. 'I have' . . . 'question.'

(*k*)   IV.iii.87–104. 'But I' . . . 'us so.'
(*l*)   V.ii.151–154. 'O mistress' . . . 'Iago.'
(*m*)   V.ii.185–193. 'My mistress' . . . 'villany!'
(*n*)   V.ii.266–272. 'Be not' . . . 'wench!'

Were these passages after-thoughts, composed after the version represented by Q 1 was written? Or were they in the version represented by Q 1, and only omitted in printing, whether accidentally or because they were also omitted in the theatre? Or were some of them after-thoughts, and others in the original version?

I will take them in order. (*a*) can hardly be an afterthought. Up to that point Roderigo had hardly said anything, for Iago had always interposed; and it is very unlikely that Roderigo would now deliver but four lines, and speak at once of 'she' instead of 'your daughter'. Probably this 'omission' represents a 'cut' in stage performance. (*b*) This may also be the case here. In our texts the omission of the passage would make nonsense, but in Q 1 the 'cut' (if a cut) has been mended, awkwardly enough, by the substitution of 'Such' for 'For' in line 78. In any case, the lines cannot be an addition. (*c*) cannot be an after-thought, for the sentence is unfinished without it; and that it was not meant to be interrupted is clear, because in Q 1 line 31 begins 'And', not 'Nay'; the Duke might say 'Nay' if he were cutting the previous speaker short, but not 'And'. (*d*) is surely no addition. If the lines are cut out, not only is the metre spoilt, but the obvious reason for Iago's words, 'I see, Sir, you are eaten up with passion', disappears, and so does the reference of his word 'satisfied' in 393 to Othello's 'satisfied' in 390. (*e*) is the famous passage about the Pontic Sea, and I reserve it for the present. (*f*) As Pope observes, 'no hint of this trash in the first edition', the 'trash' including the words 'Nature would not invest herself in such shadowing passion without some instruction. It is not words that shake me thus'! There is nothing to prove these lines to be original or an after-thought. The omission of (*g*) is clearly a printer's error, due to the fact that lines 72 and 76 both end with the word 'committed'. No conclusion can be formed as to (*h*), nor perhaps (*i*), which includes the whole of Desdemona's song; but if (*j*) is removed the reference in 'such a deed' in 64 is destroyed. (*k*) is Emilia's long speech about husbands. It cannot well be an after-thought, for 105–6 evidently refer to 103–4 (even the word 'uses' in 105 refers to 'use' in 103). (*l*) is no after-thought, for 'if he says so' in

155 must point back to 'my husband say that she was false!' in 152. (*m*) might be an after-thought, but, if so, in the first version the ending 'to speak' occurred twice within three lines, and the reason for Iago's sudden alarm in 193 is much less obvious. If (*n*) is an addition the original collocation was:

> but O vain boast!
> Who can control his fate? 'Tis not so now.
> Pale as thy smock!

which does not sound probable.

Thus, as it seems to me, in the great majority of cases there is more or less reason to think that the passages wanting in Q 1 were nevertheless parts of the original play, and I cannot in any one case see any positive ground for supposing a subsequent addition. I think that most of the gaps in Q 1 were accidents of printing (like many other smaller gaps in Q 1), but that probably one or two were 'cuts' – *e.g.* Emilia's long speech (*k*). The omission of (*i*) might be due to the state of the MS.: the words of the song may have been left out of the dialogue, as appearing on a separate page with the musical notes, or may have been inserted in such an illegible way as to baffle the printer.

I come now to (*e*), the famous passage about the Pontic Sea. Pope supposed that it formed part of the original version, but approved of its omission, as he considered it 'an unnatural excursion in this place'. Mr. Swinburne thinks it an after-thought, but defends it. 'In other lips indeed than Othello's, at the crowning minute of culminant agony, the rush of imaginative reminiscence which brings back upon his eyes and ears the lightning foam and tideless thunder of the Pontic Sea might seem a thing less natural than sublime. But Othello has the passion of a poet closed in as it were and shut up behind the passion of a hero' (*Study of Shakespeare*, p. 184). I quote these words all the more gladly because they will remind the reader of my lectures of my debt to Mr. Swinburne here; and I will only add that the reminiscence here is of *precisely the same character* as the reminiscences of the Arabian trees and the base Indian in Othello's final speech. But I find it almost impossible to believe that Shakespeare *ever* wrote the passage without the words about the Pontic Sea. It seems to me almost an imperative demand and of imagination that Iago's set speech, if I may use the phrase, should be preceded by a speech of somewhat the same dimensions, the contrast of which should heighten the horror of its hypocrisy; it seems to me that Shakespeare must have felt this; and it is difficult to me to think that he ever made the lines,

> In the due reverence of a sacred vow
> I here engage my words,

follow directly on the one word 'Never' (however impressive that word in its isolation might be). And as I can find no *other* 'omission' in Q 1 which appears to point to a subsequent addition, I conclude that this 'omission' *was* an omission, probably accidental, conceivably due to a stupid 'cut'. Indeed it is nothing but Mr. Swinburne's opinion that prevents my feeling certainty on the point.

Finally, I may draw attention to certain facts which may be mere accidents, but may possibly be significant. Passages (*b*) and (*c*) consist respectively of six and seven lines; that is, they are almost of the same length, and in a MS. might well fill exactly the same amount of space. Passage (*d*) is eight lines long; so is passage (*e*). Now, taking at random two editions of Shakespeare, the Globe and that of Delius, I find that (*b*) and (*c*) are $6^1/4$ inches apart in the Globe, 8 in Delius; and that (*d*) and (*e*) are separated by $7^3/4$ inches in the Globe, by $8^3/4$ in Delius. In other words, there is about the same distance in each case between two passages of about equal dimensions.

The idea suggested by these facts is that the MS. from which Q 1 was printed was mutilated in various places; that (*b*) and (*c*) occupied the bottom inches of two successive pages, and that these inches were torn away; and that this was also the case with (*d*) and (*e*).

This speculation has amused me and may amuse some reader. I do not know enough of Elizabethan manuscripts to judge of its plausibility.

NOTE K

OTHELLO'S COURTSHIP

It is curious that in the First Act two impressions are produced which have afterwards to be corrected.

1. We must not suppose that Othello's account of his courtship in his famous speech before the Senate is intended to be exhaustive. He is accused of having used drugs or charms in order to win

Desdemona; and therefore his purpose in his defence is merely to show that his witchcraft was the story of his life. It is no part of his business to trouble the Senators with the details of his courtship, and he so condenses his narrative of it that it almost appears as though there was no courtship at all, and as though Desdemona never imagined that he was in love with her until she had practically confessed her love for him. Hence she has been praised by some for her courage, and blamed by others for her forwardness.

But at III.iii.70 f. matters are presented in quite a new light. There we find the following words of hers:

> What! Michael Cassio,
> That came a-wooing with you, and so many a time,
> When I have spoken of you dispraisingly,
> Hath ta'en your part.

It seems, then, she understood why Othello came so often to her father's house, and was perfectly secure of his love before she gave him that very broad 'hint to speak'. I may add that those who find fault with her forget that it was necessary for her to take the first open step. She was the daughter of a Venetian grandee, and Othello was a black soldier of fortune.

2. We learn from the lines just quoted that Cassio used to accompany Othello in his visits to the house; and from III.iii.93 f. we learn that he knew of Othello's love from first to last and 'went between' the lovers 'very oft'. Yet in Act I. it appears that, while Iago on the night of the marriage knows about it and knows where to find Othello (I.i.158 f.), Cassio, even if he knows where to find Othello (which is doubtful: see I.ii.44), seems to know nothing about the marriage. See I.ii.49:

> *Cas.* Ancient, what makes he here?
> *Iago.* 'Faith, he to-night hath boarded a land carack:
> If it prove lawful prize, he's made for ever.
> *Cas.* I do not understand.
> *Iago.* He's married.
> *Cas.* To who?

It is possible that Cassio does know, and only pretends ignorance because he has not been informed by Othello that Iago also knows. And this idea is consistent with Iago's apparent ignorance of Cassio's part in the courtship (III.iii.93). And of course, if this were so, a word from Shakespeare to the actor who played Cassio would enable him to make all clear to the audience. The alternative, and perhaps more probable, explanation would be that, in writing Act I., Shakespeare had not yet thought of making Cassio Othello's confidant, and that, after writing Act III., he neglected to alter the passage in Act I. In that case the further information which Act III. gives regarding Othello's courtship would probably also be an after-thought.

NOTE L

OTHELLO IN THE TEMPTATION SCENE

One reason why some readers think Othello 'easily jealous' is that they completely misinterpret him in the early part of this scene. They fancy that he is alarmed and suspicious the moment he hears Iago mutter 'Ha! I like not that', as he sees Cassio leaving Desdemona (III.iii.35). But, in fact, it takes a long time for Iago to excite surprise, curiosity, and then grave concern – by no means yet jealousy – even about Cassio; and it is still longer before Othello understands that Iago is suggesting doubts about Desdemona too. ('Wronged' in 143 certainly does not refer to her, as 154 and 162 show.) Nor, even at 171, is the exclamation 'O misery' meant for an expression of Othello's own present feelings; as his next speech clearly shows, it expresses an *imagined* feeling, as also the speech which elicits it professes to do (for Iago would not have dared here to apply the term 'cuckold' to Othello). In fact it is not until Iago hints that Othello, as a foreigner, might easily be deceived, that he is seriously disturbed about Desdemona.

Salvini* played this passage, as might be expected, with entire understanding. Nor have I ever seen it seriously misinterpreted on the stage. I gather from the Furness Variorum that Fechter* and Edwin Booth* took the same view as Salvini. Actors have to ask themselves what was the precise state of mind expressed by the words they have to repeat. But many readers never think of asking such a question.

The lines which probably do most to lead hasty or unimaginative readers astray are those at 90, where, on Desdemona's departure, Othello exclaims to himself:

Excellent wretch! Perdition catch my soul
But I do love thee! and when I love thee not,
 Chaos is come again.

He is supposed to mean by the last words that his love is *now*
suspended by suspicion, whereas, in fact, in his bliss, he has so totally
forgotten Iago's 'Ha! I like not that', that the tempter has to begin all
over again. The meaning is, 'If ever I love thee not, Chaos will have
come again'. The feeling of insecurity is due to the excess of *joy*, as in
the wonderful words after he rejoins Desdemona at Cyprus (II.i.191):

　　　　　If it were now to die,
'Twere now to be most happy: for, I fear
My soul hath her content so absolute
That not another comfort like to this
Succeeds in unknown fate.

If any reader boggles at the use of the present in 'Chaos is come again',
let him observe 'succeeds' in the lines just quoted, or let him look at
the parallel passage in *Venus and Adonis*, 1019:

For, he being dead, with him is beauty slain:
And, beauty dead, black Chaos comes again.

Venus does not know that Adonis is dead when she speaks thus.

NOTE M

QUESTIONS AS TO *OTHELLO*, ACT IV, SCENE i

(1) The first part of the scene is hard to understand, and the commentators give little help. I take the idea to be as follows. Iago sees that he
must renew his attack on Othello; for, on the one hand, Othello, in
spite of the resolution he had arrived at to put Desdemona to death,
has taken the step, without consulting Iago, of testing her in the
matter of Iago's report about the handkerchief; and, on the other
hand, he now seems to have fallen into a dazed lethargic state, and
must be stimulated to action. Iago's plan seems to be to remind
Othello of everything that would madden him again, but to do so by

professing to make light of the whole affair, and by urging Othello to put the best construction on the facts, or at any rate to acquiesce. So he says, in effect: 'After all, if she did kiss Cassio, that might mean little. Nay, she might even go much further without meaning any harm.[1] Of course there is the handkerchief (10); but then why should she *not* give it away?' Then, affecting to renounce this hopeless attempt to disguise his true opinion, he goes on: 'However, I cannot, as your friend, pretend that I really regard her as innocent: the fact is, Cassio boasted to me in so many words of his conquest. [Here he is interrupted by Othello's swoon.] But, after all, why make such a fuss? You share the fate of most married men, and you have the advantage of not being deceived in the matter.' It must have been a great pleasure to Iago to express his real cynicism thus, with the certainty that he would not be taken seriously and would advance his plot by it. At 208–10 he recurs to the same plan of maddening Othello by suggesting that, if he is so fond of Desdemona, he had better let the matter be, for it concerns no one but him. This speech follows Othello's exclamation 'O Iago, the pity of it', and this is perhaps the moment when we most of all long to destroy Iago.

(2) At 216 Othello tells Iago to get him some poison, that he may kill Desdemona that night. Iago objects: 'Do it not with poison: strangle her in her bed, even the bed she hath contaminated.' Why does he object to poison? Because through the sale of the poison he himself would be involved? Possibly. Perhaps his idea was that, Desdemona being killed by Othello, and Cassio killed by Roderigo, he would then admit that he had informed Othello of the adultery, and perhaps even that he had undertaken Cassio's death; but he would declare that he never meant to fulfil his promise as to Cassio, and that he had nothing to do with Desdemona's death (he seems to be preparing for this at 285). His buying poison might wreck this plan. But it may be that his objection to poison springs merely from contempt for Othello's intellect. He can trust him to use violence, but thinks he may bungle anything that requires adroitness.

(3) When the conversation breaks off here (225) Iago has brought Othello back to the position reached at the end of the Temptation scene (III.iii.). Cassio and Desdemona are to be killed; and, in addi-

---

[1] The reader who is puzzled by this passage should refer to the conversation at the end of the thirtieth tale in the *Heptameron*.*

tion, the time is hastened; it is to be 'tonight', not 'within three days'. The constructional idea clearly is that, after the Temptation scene, Othello tends to relapse and wait, which is terribly dangerous to Iago, who therefore in this scene quickens his purpose. Yet Othello relapses again. He has declared that he will not expostulate with her (IV.i.217). But he cannot keep his word, and there follows the scene of accusation. Its *dramatic* purposes are obvious, but Othello seems to have no purpose in it. He asks no questions, or, rather, none that shows the least glimpse of doubt or hope. He is merely torturing himself.

NOTE N

TWO PASSAGES IN THE LAST SCENE OF *OTHELLO*

(1) V.ii.71 f. Desdemona demands that Cassio be sent for to 'confess' the truth that she never gave him the handkerchief. Othello answers that Cassio *has* confessed the truth – has confessed the adultery. The dialogue goes on:

Des. He will not say so.
Oth.   No, his mouth is stopp'd:
      Honest Iago hath ta'en order for 't.
Des. O! my fear interprets: what, is he dead?
Oth. Had all his hairs been lives, my great revenge
      Had stomach for them all.
Des. Alas! he is *betray'd* and I undone.

It is a ghastly idea, but I believe Shakespeare means that, at the mention of Iago's name, Desdemona suddenly sees that *he* is the villain whose existence he had declared to be impossible when, an hour before, Emilia had suggested that someone had poisoned Othello's mind. But her words rouse Othello to such furious indignation ('Out, strumpet! Weep'st thou for him to my face?') that 'it is too late'.

(2) V.ii.286 f.

Oth. I look down towards his feet; but that's a fable.
      If that thou be'st a devil, I cannot kill thee.
                                        [*Wounds Iago*

> *Lod.*   Wrench his sword from him.
> *Iago.*   I bleed, sir, but not killed.

Are Iago's strange words meant to show his absorption of interest in himself amidst so much anguish? I think rather he is meant to be alluding to Othello's words, and saying, with a cold contemptuous smile, 'You see he is right; I *am* a devil'.

NOTE O

OTHELLO ON DESDEMONA'S LAST WORDS

I have said that the last scene of *Othello*, though terribly painful, contains almost nothing to diminish the admiration and love which heighten our pity for the hero (p. 169). I said 'almost' in view of the following passage (V.ii.123 ff.):

> *Emil.*   O, who hath done this deed?
> *Des.*   Nobody; I myself. Farewell:
> Commend me to my kind lord: O, farewell!   [*Dies.*
> *Oth.*   Why, how should she be murder'd?[1]
> *Emil.*   Alas, who knows?
> *Oth.*   You heard her say herself, it was not I.
> *Emil.*   She said so: I must needs report the truth.
> *Oth.*   She's, like a liar, gone to burning hell:
>   'Twas I that kill'd her.
> *Emil.*   O, the more angel she,
>   And you the blacker devil!
> *Oth.*   She turn'd to folly, and she was a whore.

This is a strange passage. What did Shakespeare mean us to feel? One is astonished that Othello should not be startled, nay thunderstruck, when he hears such dying words coming from the lips of an obdurate adulteress. One is shocked by the moral blindness or obliquity which takes them only as a further sign of her worthlessness. Here alone, I think, in the scene sympathy with Othello quite disappears.

---

[1] He alludes to her cry, 'O falsely, falsely murder'd!'

Did Shakespeare mean us to feel thus, and to realize how completely confused and perverted Othello's mind has become? I suppose so: and yet Othello's words continue to strike me as very strange, and also as not *like* Othello, – especially as at this point he was not in anger, much less enraged. It has sometimes occurred to me that there is a touch of personal animus in the passage. One remembers the place in *Hamlet* (written but a little while before) where Hamlet thinks he is unwilling to kill the King at his prayers, for fear they may take him to heaven; and one remembers Shakespeare's irony, how he shows that those prayers do *not* go to heaven, and that the soul of this praying murderer is at that moment as murderous as ever (see p. 145), just as here the soul of the lying Desdemona is angelic *in* its lie. Is it conceivable that in both passages he was intentionally striking at conventional 'religious' ideas; and, in particular, that the belief that a man's everlasting fate is decided by the occupation of his last moment excited in him indignation as well as contempt? I admit that this fancy seems un-Shakespearean, and yet it comes back on me whenever I read this passage. [The words 'I suppose so' (1.9 of this paragraph) gave my conclusion; but I wish to withdraw the whole Note.]

NOTE P

DID EMILIA SUSPECT IAGO?

I have answered No (p. 185), and have no doubt about the matter; but at one time I was puzzled, as perhaps others have been, by a single phrase of Emilia's. It occurs in the conversation between her and Iago and Desdemona (IV.ii.30 f.):

> I will be hang'd if some eternal villain,
> Some busy and insinuating rogue,
> Some cogging, cozening slave, *to get some office*,
> Have not devised this slander; I'll be hang'd else.

Emilia, it may be said, knew that Cassio was the suspected man, so that she must be thinking of *his* office, and must mean that Iago has poisoned Othello's mind in order to prevent his reinstatement and to get the lieutenancy for himself. And, it may be said, she speaks indefinitely so that Iago alone may understand her (for Desdemona does not know that Cassio is the suspected man). Hence, too, it may be said, when, at V.ii.190, she exclaims,

> Villany, villany, villany!
> I think upon't, I think: I smell't: O villany!
> *I thought so then*: – I'll kill myself for grief;

she refers in the words italicized to the occasion of the passage in IV.ii., and is reproaching herself for not having taken steps on her suspicion of Iago.

I have explained in the text why I think it impossible to suppose that Emilia suspected her husband; and I do not think anyone who follows her speeches in V.ii., and who realizes that, if she did suspect him, she must have been simply *pretending* surprise when Othello told her that Iago was his informant, will feel any doubt. Her idea in the lines at IV.ii.130 is, I believe, merely that someone is trying to establish a ground for asking a favour from Othello in return for information which nearly concerns him. It does not follow that, because she knew Cassio was suspected, she must have been referring to Cassio's office. She was a stupid woman, and, even if she had not been, she would not put two and two together so easily as the reader of the play. In the line,

> I thought so then: I'll kill myself for grief,

I think she certainly refers to IV.ii.130 f. and also IV.ii.15 (Steevens' idea* that she is thinking of the time when she let Iago take the handkerchief is absurd). If 'I'll kill myself for grief' is to be taken in close connection with the preceding words (which is not certain), she may mean that she reproaches herself for not having acted on her general suspicion, or (less probably) that she reproaches herself for not having suspected that Iago was the rogue.

With regard to my view that she failed to think of the handkerchief when she saw how angry Othello was, those who believe that she did think of it will of course also believe that she suspected Iago. But in addition to other difficulties, they will have to suppose that her astonishment, when Othello at last mentioned the handkerchief, was mere acting. And anyone who can believe this seems to me beyond argument. [I regret that I cannot now discuss some suggestions made to me in regard to the subjects of Notes O and P.]

NOTE Q

IAGO'S SUSPICION REGARDING CASSIO AND EMILIA

The one expression of this suspicion appears in a very curious manner. Iago, soliloquizing, says (II.i.311)

> Which thing to do,
> If this poor trash of Venice, whom I trash
> For his quick hunting, stand the putting on,
> I'll have our Michael Cassio on the hip,
> Abuse him to the Moor in the rank [F. right] garb –
> For I fear Cassio with my night-cap too –
> Make the Moor thank me, etc.

Why '*For* I fear Cassio', etc.? He can hardly be giving himself an additional reason for involving Cassio; the parenthesis must be explanatory of the preceding line or some part of it. I think it explains 'rank garb' or 'right garb', and the meaning is, 'For Cassio is what I shall accuse him of being, a seducer of wives'. He is returning to the thought with which the soliloquy begins, 'That Cassio loves her, I do well believe it'. In saying this he is unconsciously trying to believe that Cassio would at any rate *like* to be an adulterer, so that it is not so very abominable to say that he *is* one. And the idea 'I suspect him with Emilia' is a second and stronger attempt of the same kind. The idea probably was born and died in one moment. It is a curious example of Iago's secret subjection to morality.

NOTE R

REMINISCENCES OF *OTHELLO* IN *KING LEAR*

The following is a list, made without any special search, and doubtless incomplete, of words and phrases in *King Lear* which recall words and phrases in *Othello*, and many of which occur only in these two plays:

'waterish', I.i.261, appears only here and in *O.* III.iii.15.

'fortune's alms', I.i.281, appears only here and in *O.* III.iv.122.

'decline' seems to be used of the advance of age only in I.ii.78 and *O.* III.iii.265.

'slack' in 'if when they chanced to slack you', II.iv.248, has no exact parallel in Shakespeare, but recalls 'they slack their duties', *O.* IV.iii.88.

'allowance' (= authorization), I.iv.228, is used thus only in *KL.*, *O.* I.i.128, and two places in *Hamlet* and *Hen. VIII.*

'besort', vb., I.iv.272, does not occur elsewhere, but 'besort', sb., occurs in *O.* I.iii.239 and nowhere else.

Edmund's 'Look, sir, I bleed', II.i43, sounds like an echo of Iago's 'I bleed, sir, but not killed', *O.* V.ii.288.

'potential', II.i.78, appears only here, in *O.* I.ii.13, and in the *Lover's Complaint* (which, I think, is certainly not an early poem).

'poise' in 'occasions of some poise', II.i.122, is exactly like 'poise' in 'full of poise and difficult weight', *O.* III.iii.82, and not exactly like 'poise' in the three other places where it occurs.

'conjunct', used only in II.ii.125 (Q), V.i.12, recalls 'conjunctive', used only in *H.* IV.vii. 14, *O.* I.iii.374 (F).

'grime', vb., used only in II. iii. 9, recalls 'begrime', used only in *O.* III.iii.387 and *Lucrece.*

'unbonneted', III.i.14, appears only here and in *O.* I.ii.23.

'delicate', III.iv.12, IV.iii.15, IV.vi.188, is not a rare word with Shakespeare; he uses it about thirty times in his plays. But it is worth notice that it occurs six times in *O.*

'commit', used intr. for 'commit adultery', appears only in III.iv.83, but cf. the famous iteration in *O.* IV.ii.72 f.

'stand in hard cure', III.vi.107, seems to have no parallel except *O.* II.i.51, 'stand in bold cure'.

'secure' = make careless, IV.i.22, appears only here and in *O.* I.iii.10 and (not quite the same sense) *Tim.* II.ii.185.

Albany's 'perforce must wither', IV.ii.35, recalls Othello's 'It must needs wither', V.ii.15.

'deficient', IV.vi.23, occurs only here and in *O.* I.iii.63.

'the safer sense', IV.vi.81, recalls 'my blood begins my safer guides to rule', *O.* II.iii.205.

'fitchew', IV.vi.124, is used only here, in *O.* IV.i.150, and in *T. C.* V.i.67 (where it has not the same significance).

Lear's 'I have seen the day, with my good biting falchion I would have made them skip', V.iii.276, recalls Othello's 'I have seen the day, That with this little arm and this good sword', etc., V.ii.261.

The fact that more than half of the above occur in the first two Acts of *King Lear* may possibly be significant: for the farther removed Shakespeare was from the time of the composition of *Othello*, the less likely would be the recurrence of ideas or words used in that play.

NOTE S

KING LEAR AND *TIMON OF ATHENS*

That these two plays are near akin in character, and probably in date, is recognized by many critics now; and I will merely add here a few references to the points of resemblance mentioned in the text (p. 210), and a few notes on other points.

(1) The likeness between Timon's curses and some of the speeches of Lear in his madness is, in one respect, curious. It is natural that Timon, speaking to Alcibiades and two courtezans, should inveigh in particular against sexual vices and corruption, as he does in the terrific passage IV.iii.82–166; but why should Lear refer at length, and with the same loathing, to this particular subject (IV.vi.112–132)? It almost looks as if Shakespeare were expressing feelings which oppressed him at this period of his life.

The idea may be a mere fancy, but it has seemed to me that this pre-occupation, and sometimes this oppression, are traceable in other plays of the period from about 1602 to 1605 (*Hamlet, Measure for Measure, Troilus and Cressida, All's Well, Othello*); while in earlier plays the subject is handled less, and without disgust, and in later plays (e.g. *Anthony and Cleopatra, The Winter's Tale, Cymbeline*) it is also handled, however freely, without this air of repulsion (I omit *Pericles* because the authorship of the brothel-scenes is doubtful).

(2) For references to the lower animals, similar to those in *King Lear*, see especially *Timon*, I.i.259; II.ii.180; III.vi.103 f.; IV.i.2, 36; IV.iii.49 f., 177 ff., 325 ff. (surely a passage written or, at the least,

rewritten by Shakespeare), 392, 426 f. I ignore the constant abuse of
the dog in the conversations where Apemantus appears.

(3) Further points of resemblance are noted in the text at pp.
210–11, 271, 285, and many likenesses in word, phrase and idea
might be added, of the type of the parallel 'Thine Do comfort and not
burn', *Lear*, II.iv.176, and 'Thou sun, that comfort'st, burn!' *Timon*,
V.i.134.

(4) The likeness in style and versification (so far as the purely
Shakespearean parts of *Timon* are concerned) is surely unmistakable,
but some readers may like to see an example. Lear speaks here
(IV.vi.164 ff.):

> Thou rascal beadle, hold thy bloody hand!
> Why dost thou lash that whore? Strip thine own back;
> Thou hotly lust'st to use her in that kind
> For which thou whipp'st her. The usurer hangs the cozener.
> Through tatter'd clothes small vices do appear;
> Robes and furr'd gowns hide all. Plate sin with gold,
> And the strong lance of justice hurtless breaks;
> Arm it in rags, a pigmy's straw does pierce it.
> None does offend, none, I say, none; I'll able 'em:
> Take that of me, my friend, who have the power
> To seal the accuser's lips. Get thee glass eyes;
> And, like a scurvy politician, seem
> To see the things thou dost not.

And Timon speaks here (IV.iii.1.ff.):

> O blessed breeding sun, draw from the earth
> Rotten humidity; below thy sister's orb
> Infect the air! Twinn'd brothers of one womb,
> Whose procreation, residence, and birth,
> Scarce is dividant, touch them with several fortunes,
> The greater scorns the lesser: not nature,
> To whom all sores lay seige, can bear great fortune,
> But by contempt of nature.
> Raise me this beggar, and deny't that lord:
> The senator shall bear contempt hereditary,
> The beggar native honour.
> It is the pasture lards the rother's sides,
> The want that makes him lean. Who dares, who dares,
> In purity of manhood stand upright

And say 'This man's a flatterer'? if one be,
So are they all: for every grise of fortune
Is smooth'd by that below: the learned pate
Ducks to the golden fool: all is oblique;
There's nothing level in our cursed natures,
But direct villany.

The reader may wish to know whether metrical tests throw any light on the chronological position of *Timon*; and he will find such information as I can give in Note BB. But he will bear in mind that results arrived at by applying these tests to the whole play can have little value, since it is practically certain that Shakespeare did not write the whole play. It seems to consist (1) of parts that are purely Shakespearean (the text, however, being here, as elsewhere, very corrupt); (2) of parts untouched or very slightly touched by him; (3) of parts where a good deal is Shakespeare's but not all (*e.g.*, in my opinion, III.v., which I cannot believe, with Mr. Fleay, to be wholly, or almost wholly, by another writer). The tests ought to be applied not only to the whole play but separately to (1), about which there is little difference of opinion. This has not been done: but Dr. Ingram* has applied one test, and I have applied another, to the parts assigned by Mr. Fleay to Shakespeare* (see Note BB.)[1] The result is to place *Timon* between *King Lear* and *Macbeth* (a result which happens to coincide with that of the application of the main tests to the whole play): and this result corresponds, I believe, with the general impression which we derive from the three dramas in regard to versification.

NOTE T

DID SHAKESPEARE SHORTEN *KING LEAR*?

I have remarked in the text (pp. 219 ff.) on the unusual number of improbabilities, inconsistencies, etc., in *King Lear*. The list of examples

---

[1] These are I.i.; II.i.; II.ii., except 194–204; in III.vi. Timon's verse speech; IV.i.; IV.ii. 1–28; IV. iii., except 292–362, 399–413, 454–543; V.i., except 1–50; V.ii.; V.iv. I am not to be taken as accepting this division throughout.

given might easily be lengthened. Thus (*a*) in IV.iii. Kent refers to a letter which he confided to the Gentleman for Cordelia; but in III.i. he had given to the Gentleman not a letter but a message. (*b*) In III.i. again he says Cordelia will inform the Gentleman who the sender of the message was; but from IV.iii. it is evident that she has done no such thing, nor does the Gentleman show any curiosity on the subject. (*c*) In the same scene (III.i.) Kent and the Gentleman arrange that whichever finds the King first shall halloo to the other; but when Kent finds the King he does not halloo. These are all examples of mere carelessness as to matters which would escape attention in the theatre – matters introduced not because they are essential to the plot, but in order to give an air of verisimilitude to the conversation. And here is perhaps another instance. When Lear determines to leave Goneril and go to Regan he says, 'call my train together' (I.iv.275). When he arrives at Gloster's house Kent asks why he comes with so small a train, and the Fool gives a reply which intimates that the rest have deserted him (II.iv.63 ff.). He and his daughters, however, seem unaware of any diminution; and, when Lear 'calls to horse' and leaves Gloster's house, the doors are shut against him partly on the excuse that he is 'attended with a desperate train' (308). Nevertheless in the storm he has no knights with him, and in III.vii.15 ff. we hear that 'some five or six and thirty of his knights'[1] are 'hot questrists after him', as though the real reason of his leaving Goneril with so small a train was that he had hurried away so quickly that many of his knights were unaware of his departure.

This prevalence of vagueness or inconsistency is probably due to carelessness; but it may possibly be due to another cause. There are, it has sometimes struck me, slight indications that the details of the plot were originally more full and more clearly imagined than one would suppose from the play as we have it; and some of the defects to which I have drawn attention might have arisen if Shakespeare, finding his matter too bulky, had (*a*) omitted to write some things originally intended, and (*b*), after finishing his play, had reduced it by excision, and had not, in these omissions and excisions, taken sufficient pains to remove the obscurities and inconsistencies occasioned by them.

Thus, to take examples of (*b*), Lear's 'What, fifty of my followers at

---

[1] It has been suggested that 'his' means 'Gloster's'; but 'him' all through the speech evidently means Lear.

a clap!' (I.iv.315) is very easily explained if we suppose that in the preceding conversation, as originally written, Goneril had mentioned the number. Again the curious absence of any indication why Burgundy should have the first choice of Cordelia's hand might easily be due to the same cause. So might the ignorance in which we are left as to the fate of the Fool, and several more of the defects noticed in the text.

To illustrate the other point (*a*) that Shakespeare may have omitted to write some things which he had originally intended, the play would obviously gain something if it appeared that, at a time shortly before that of the action, Gloster had encouraged the King in his idea of dividing the kingdom, while Kent had tried to dissuade him. And there are one or two passages which suggest that this is what Shakespeare imagined. If it were so, there would be additional point in the Fool's reference to the lord who counselled Lear to give away his land (I.iv.154), and in Gloster's reflection (III.iv.168),

> His daughters seek his death: ah, that good Kent!
> He said it would be thus:

('said', of course, not to the King but to Gloster and perhaps others of the council). Thus too the plots would be still more closely joined. Then also we should at once understand the opening of the play. To Kent's words, 'I thought the King had more affected the Duke of Albany than Cornwall', Gloster answers, 'It did always seem so to us'. Who are the 'us' from whom Kent is excluded? I do not know, for there is no sign that Kent has been absent. But if Kent, in consequence of his opposition, had fallen out of favour and absented himself from the council, it would be clear. So, besides, would be the strange suddenness with which, after Gloster's answer, Kent changes the subject; he would be avoiding, in presence of Gloster's son, any further reference to a subject on which he and Gloster had differed. That Kent, I may add, had already the strongest opinion about Goneril and Regan is clear from his extremely bold words (I.i.165),

> Kill thy physician, and the fee bestow
> Upon thy foul disease.

Did Lear remember this phrase when he called Goneril 'a disease that's in my flesh' (II.iv.225)?

Again, the observant reader may have noticed that Goneril is not only represented as the fiercer and more determined of the two sisters but also strikes one as the more sensual. And with this may be connected one or two somewhat curious points: Kent's comparison of Goneril to the figure of Vanity in the Morality plays (II.ii.38); the Fool's apparently quite irrelevant remark (though his remarks are scarcely ever so), 'For there was never yet fair woman but she made mouths in a glass' (III.ii.35) ; Kent's reference to Oswald (long before there is any sign of Goneril's intrigue with Edmund) as 'one that would be a bawd in way of good service' (II.ii.20), and Edgar's words to the corpse of Oswald (IV.vi.257), also spoken before he knew anything of the intrigue with Edmund,

> I know thee well: a serviceable villain;
> As duteous to the vices of thy mistress
> As badness would desire.

Perhaps Shakespeare had conceived Goneril as a woman who before her marriage had shown signs of sensual vice; but the distinct indications of this idea were crowded out of his exposition when he came to write it, or, being inserted, were afterwards excised. I will not go on to hint that Edgar had Oswald in his mind when (III.iv.87) he described the serving-man who 'served the list of his mistress' heart, and did the act of darkness with her'; and still less that Lear can have had Goneril in his mind in the declamation against lechery referred to in Note S.

I do not mean to imply, by writing this note, that I believe in the hypotheses suggested in it. On the contrary I think it more probable that the defects referred to arose from carelessness and other causes. But this is not, to me, certain; and the reader who rejects the hypotheses may be glad to have his attention called to the points which suggested them.

NOTE U

MOVEMENTS OF THE *DRAMATIS PERSONÆ* IN ACT II OF *KING LEAR*

I have referred in the text to the obscurity of the play on this subject, and I will set out the movements here.

When Lear is ill-treated by Goneril his first thought is to seek refuge with Regan (I.iv.274 f., 327 f.). Goneril, accordingly, who had foreseen this, and, even before the quarrel, had determined to write to Regan (I.iii.25), now sends Oswald off to her, telling her not to receive Lear and his hundred knights (I.iv.354 f.). In consequence of this letter Regan and Cornwall immediately leave their home and ride by night to Gloster's house, sending word on that they are coming (II.i.1 ff., 81, 120 ff.). Lear, on his part, just before leaving Goneril's house, sends Kent with a letter to Regan, and tells him to be quick, or Lear will be there before him. And we find that Kent reaches Regan and delivers his letter before Oswald, Goneril's messenger. Both the messengers are taken on by Cornwall and Regan to Gloster's house.

In II.iv. Lear arrives at Gloster's house, having, it would seem, failed to find Regan at her own home. And, later, Goneril arrives at Gloster's house, in accordance with an intimation which she had sent in her letter to Regan (II.iv.186 f.).

Thus all the principal persons except Cordelia and Albany are brought together; and the crises of the double action – the expulsion of Lear and the blinding and expulsion of Gloster – are reached in Act III. And this is what was required.

But it needs the closest attention to follow these movements. And, apart from this, difficulties remain.

1. Goneril, in despatching Oswald with the letter to Regan, tells him to hasten his return (I.iv.363). Lear again is surprised to find that *his* messenger has not been sent back (II.iv.1 f., 36 f.). Yet apparently both Goneril and Lear themselves start at once, so that their messengers *could* not return in time. It may be said that they expected to meet them coming back, but there is no indication of this in the text.

2. Lear, in despatching Kent, says (I.v.1):

> Go you before to Gloster with these letters. Acquaint my daughter no further with anything you know than comes from her demand out of the letter.

This would seem to imply that Lear knew that Regan and Cornwall were at Gloster's house, and meant either to go there (so Koppel) or to summon her back to her own home to receive him. Yet this is clearly not so, for Kent goes straight to Regan's house (II.i.124, II.iv.1, 27 ff., 114 ff.).

Hence it is generally supposed that by 'Gloster', in the passage just quoted, Lear means not the Earl but the *place*, that Regan's home was there; and that Gloster's castle was somewhere not very far off. This is to some extent confirmed by the fact that Cornwall is the 'arch' or patron of Gloster (II.i.60 f., 112 ff.). But Gloster's home or house must not be imagined quite close to Cornwall's, for it takes a night to ride from the one to the other, and Gloster's house is in the middle of a solitary heath with scarce a bush for many miles about (II.iv.304).

The plural 'these letters' in the passage quoted need give no trouble, for the plural is often used by Shakespeare for a single letter; and the natural conjecture that Lear sent one letter to Regan and another to Gloster is not confirmed by anything in the text.

The only difficulty is that, as Koppel points out, 'Gloster' is nowhere else used in the play for the place (except in the phrase 'Earl of Gloster' or 'my lord of Gloster'); and – what is more important – that it would unquestionably be taken by the audience to stand in this passage for the Earl, especially as there has been no previous indication that Cornwall lived at Gloster. One can only suppose that Shakespeare forgot that he had given no such indication, and so wrote what was sure to be misunderstood, – unless we suppose that 'Gloster' is a mere slip of the pen, or even a misprint, for 'Regan'. But, apart from other considerations, Lear would hardly have spoken to a servant of 'Regan', and, if he had, the next words would have run 'Acquaint her', not 'Acquaint my daughter'.

NOTE V

SUSPECTED INTERPOLATIONS IN *KING LEAR*

There are three passages in *King Lear* which have been held to be additions made by 'the players'.

The first consists of the two lines of indecent doggerel spoken by the Fool at the end of Act I.; the second, of the Fool's prophecy in rhyme at the end of III.ii.; the third, of Edgar's soliloquy at the end of III.vi.

It is suspicious (1) that all three passages occur at the ends of scenes, the place where an addition is most easily made; and (2) that in each case the speaker remains behind alone to utter the words after the other persons have gone off.

I postpone discussion of the several passages until I have called attention to the fact that, if these passages are genuine, the number of scenes which end with a soliloquy is larger in *King Lear* than in any other undoubted tragedy. Thus, taking the tragedies in their probable chronological order (and ignoring the very short scenes into which a battle is sometimes divided),[1] I find that there are in *Romeo and Juliet* four such scenes, in *Julius Caesar* two, in *Hamlet* six, in *Othello* four,[2] in *King Lear* seven,[3] in *Macbeth* two,[4] in *Antony and Cleopatra* three, in *Coriolanus* one. The difference between *King Lear* and the plays that come nearest to it is really much greater than it appears from this list, for in *Hamlet* four of the six soliloquies, and in *Othello* three of the four, are *long* speeches, while most of those in *King Lear* are quite short.

Of course I do not attach any great importance to the fact just noticed, but it should not be left entirely out of account in forming an opinion as to the genuineness of the three doubted passages.

(*a*) The first of these, I.v.54–5, I decidedly believe to be spurious. (1) The scene ends quite in Shakespeare's manner without it. (2) It does not seem likely that at the *end* of the scene Shakespeare would have introduced anything *violently* incongruous with the immediately preceding words,

---

[1] I ignore them partly because they are not significant for the present purpose, but mainly because it is impossible to accept the division of battle-scenes in our modern texts, while to depart from it is to introduce intolerable inconvenience in reference. The only proper plan in Elizabethan drama is to consider a scene ended as soon as no person is left on the stage, and to pay no regard to the question of locality, – a question theatrically insignificant and undetermined in most scenes of an Elizabethan play, in consequence of the absence of movable scenery. In dealing with battles the modern editors seem to have gone on the principle (which they could not possibly apply generally) that, so long as the place is not changed, you have only one scene. Hence in *Macbeth*, Act V., they have included in their Scene vii. three distinct scenes; yet in *Antony and Cleopatra*, Act III., following the right division for a wrong reason, they have two scenes (viii. and ix.), each less than four lines long.

[2] One of these (V.i.) is not marked as such, but it is evident that the last line and a half form a soliloquy of one remaining character, just as much as some of the soliloquies marked as such in other plays.

[3] According to modern editions, eight, Act II., scene ii., being an instance. But it is quite ridiculous to reckon as three scenes what are marked as scenes ii., iii., iv. Kent is on the lower stage the whole time, Edgar in the so-called scene iii. being on the upper stage or balcony. The editors were misled by their ignorance of the stage arrangements.

[4] Perhaps three, for v. iii. is perhaps an instance, though not so marked.

Oh let me not be mad, not mad, sweet heaven!
Keep me in temper: I would not be mad!

(3) Even if he had done so, it is very unlikely that the incongruous words would have been grossly indecent. (4) Even if they had been, surely they would not have been *irrelevantly* indecent and evidently addressed to the audience, two faults which are not in Shakespeare's way. (5) The lines are doggerel. Doggerel is not uncommon in the earliest plays; there are a few lines even in the *Merchant of Venice*, a line and a half, perhaps, in *As You Like It*; but I do not think it occurs later, not even where, in an early play, it would certainly have been found, *e.g.* in the mouth of the Clown in *All's Well*. The best that can be said for these lines is that they appear in the Quartos, *i.e.* in reports, however vile, of the play as performed within two or three years of its composition.

(*b*) I believe, almost as decidedly, that the second passage, III ii.79 ff., is spurious. (1) The scene ends characteristically without the lines. (2) They are addressed directly to the audience. (3) They destroy the pathetic and beautiful effect of the immediately preceding words of the Fool, and also of Lear's solicitude for him. (4) They involve the absurdity that the shivering timid Fool would allow his master and protector, Lear and Kent, to go away into the storm and darkness, leaving him alone. (5) It is also somewhat against them that they do not appear in the Quartos. At the same time I do not think one would hesitate to accept them if they occurred at any natural place *within* the dialogue.

(*c*) On the other hand I see no sufficient reason for doubting the genuineness of Edgar's soliloquy at the end of III.vi. (1) Those who doubt it appear not to perceive that *some* words of soliloquy are wanted; for it is evidently intended that, when Kent and Gloster bear the King away, they should leave the Bedlam behind. Naturally they do so. He is only accidentally connected with the King; he was taken to shelter with him merely to gratify his whim, and as the King is now asleep there is no occasion to retain the Bedlam; Kent, we know, shrank from him, 'shunn'd [his] abhorr'd society' (V.iii.210). So he is left to return to the hovel where he was first found. When the others depart, then, he must be left behind, and surely would not go off without a word. (2) If his speech is spurious, therefore, it has been substituted for some genuine speech; and surely that is a supposition not to be entertained except under compulsion. (3) There is no such compulsion in the speech. It is not very good, no doubt; but the use of rhymed and somewhat antithetic lines in a gnomic passage is quite in Shakespeare's manner, *more* in his manner than, for example, the rhymed passages in I.i.183–190, 257–269, 281–284, which nobody doubts; quite like many places in *All's Well*, or the concluding lines of *King Lear* itself. (4) The lines are in spirit of one kind with Edgar's fine lines at the beginning of Act IV. (5) Some of them, as Delius observes, emphasize the parallelism between the stories of Lear and Gloster. (6) The fact that the Folio omits the lines is, of course, nothing against them.

NOTE W

THE STAGING OF THE SCENE OF LEAR'S REUNION WITH CORDELIA

As Koppel has shown,* the usual modern stage-directions[1] for this scene (IV.vii.) are utterly wrong and do what they can to defeat the poet's purpose.

It is evident from the text that the scene shows the *first* meeting of Cordelia and Kent and the *first* meeting of Cordelia and Lear, since they parted in I.i. Kent and Cordelia indeed are doubtless supposed to have exchanged a few words before they come on the stage; but Cordelia has not seen her father at all until the moment before she begins (line 26), 'O my dear father!' Hence the tone of the first part of the scene, that between Cordelia and Kent, is kept low in order that the latter part, between Cordelia and Lear, may have its full effect.

The modern stage-direction at the beginning of the scene, as found, for example, in the Cambridge and Globe editions, is as follows:

> 'SCENE vii. – A tent in the French camp. LEAR on a bed asleep, soft music playing; *Gentleman*, and others attending.
> Enter CORDELIA, KENT, and *Doctor*.'

---

[1] There are exceptions: *e.g.*, in the editions of Delius and Mr. W. J. Craig.*

At line 25, where the Doctor says 'Please you, draw near', Cordelia is supposed to approach the bed, which is imagined by some editors visible throughout at the back of the stage, by others as behind a curtain at the back, this curtain being drawn open at line 25.

Now, to pass by the fact that these arrangements are in flat contradiction with the stage-directions of the Quartos and the Folio, consider their effect upon the scene. In the first place, the reader at once assumes that Cordelia has already seen her father; for otherwise it is inconceivable that she would quietly talk with Kent while he was within a few yards of her. The edge of the later passage where she addresses him is therefore blunted. In the second place, through Lear's presence the reader's interest in Lear and his meeting with Cordelia is at once excited so strongly that he hardly attends at all to the conversation of Cordelia and Kent; and so this effect is blunted too. Thirdly, at line 57, where Cordelia says,

> O, look upon me, sir,
> And hold your hands in benediction o'er me!
> No, sir, you must not kneel,

the poor old King must be supposed either to try to get out of bed, or actually to do so, or to kneel, or to try to kneel, on the bed. Fourthly, consider what happens at line 81.

Doctor.   Desire him to *go in*; trouble him no more
             Till further settling.
Cor.   Will't please your highness *walk*?
Lear.   You must bear with me;
             Pray you now, forget and forgive; I am old and foolish.
                      [*Exeunt all but Kent and Gentleman.*

If Lear is in a tent containing his bed, why in the world, when the doctor thinks he can bear no more emotion, is he made to walk out of the tent? A pretty doctor!

But turn now to the original texts. Of course they say nothing about the place. The stage-direction at the beginning runs, in the Quartos, 'Enter Cordelia, Kent, and Doctor'; in the Folio, 'Enter Cordelia, Kent, and Gentleman'. They differ about the Gentleman and the Doctor, and the Folio later wrongly gives to the Gentleman the Doctor's speeches as well as his own. This is a minor matter. But they agree in *making no mention of Lear*. He is not on the stage at all.

Thus Cordelia, and the reader, can give their whole attention to Kent.

Her conversation with Kent finished, she turns (line 12) to the Doctor and asks 'How does the King?[2] The Doctor tells her that Lear is still asleep, and asks leave to wake him. Cordelia assents and asks if he is 'arrayed', which does not mean whether he has a night-gown on, but whether they have taken away his crown of furrow weeds and tended him duly after his mad wanderings in the fields. The Gentleman says that in his sleep 'fresh garments' (not a night-gown) have been put on him. The Doctor then asks Cordelia to be present when her father is waked. She assents, and the Doctor says, 'Please you, draw near. Louder the music there.' The next words are Cordelia's, 'O my dear father!'

What has happened? At the words 'is he arrayed?', according to the Folio, '*Enter Lear in a chair carried by Servants*'. The moment of this entrance, as so often in the original editions, is doubtless too soon. It should probably come at the words 'Please you, draw near', which *may*, as Koppel suggests, be addressed to the bearers. But that the stage-direction is otherwise right there cannot be a doubt (and that the Quartos omit it is no argument against it, seeing that, according to their directions, Lear never enters at all).

This arrangement (1) allows Kent his proper place in the scene, (2) makes it clear that Cordelia has not seen her father before, (3) makes her first sight of him a theatrical crisis in the best sense, (4) makes it quite natural that he should kneel, (5) makes it obvious why he should leave the stage again when he shows signs of exhaustion, and (6) is the only arrangement which has the slightest authority, for 'Lear on a bed asleep' was never heard of till Capell proposed it. The ruinous change of the staging was probably suggested by the version of that unhappy Tate.

Of course the chair arrangement is primitive, but the Elizabethans did not care about such things. What they cared for was dramatic effect.

---

[2] And it is possible that, as Koppel suggests, the Doctor should properly enter at this point; for if Kent, as he says, wishes to remain unknown, it seems strange that he and Cordelia should talk as they do before a third person. This change however is not necessary, for the Doctor might naturally stand out of hearing till he was addressed; and it is better not to go against the stage-direction without necessity.

NOTE X

THE BATTLE IN *KING LEAR*

I found my impression of the extraordinary ineffectiveness of this battle (p. 218) confirmed by a paper of James Spedding (*New Shakespere Society Transactions*, 1877, on Furness's *King Lear*, p. 312 f.); but his opinion that this is the one technical defect in *King Lear* seems certainly incorrect, and his view that this defect is not due to Shakespeare himself will not, I think, bear scrutiny.

To make Spedding's view quite clear I may remind the reader that in the preceding scene the two British armies, that of Edmund and Regan, and that of Albany and Goneril, have entered with drum and colours, and have departed. Scene ii. is as follows (Globe):

SCENE II. – *A field between the two camps.*

Alarum within. Enter, with drum and colours, LEAR, CORDELIA, *and* Soldiers, *over the stage; and exeunt. Enter* EDGAR *and* GLOSTER.

Edg.   Here, father, take the shadow of this tree
        For your good host; pray that the right may thrive:
        If ever I return to you again,
        I'll bring you comfort.
Glo.   Grace go with you, sir!
                                   [*Exit* Edgar.
        Alarum and retreat within. Re-enter EDGAR.
Edg.   Away, old man; give me thy hand; away!
        King Lear hath lost, he and his daughter ta'en:
        Give me thy hand; come on.
Glo.   No farther, sir; a man may rot even here.
Edg.   What, in ill thoughts again? Men must endure
        Their going hence, even as their coming hither:
        Ripeness is all: come on.
Glo.   And that's true too.   [*Exeunt.*

The battle, it will be seen, is represented only by military music within the tiring-house, which formed the back of the stage. 'The scene,' says Spedding, 'does not change; but "alarums" are heard, and afterwards a "retreat", and on the same field over which that great army has this moment passed, fresh and full of hope, re-appears, with tidings that all is lost, the same man who last left the stage to follow and fight in it.[1] That Shakespeare meant the scene to stand thus, no one who has the true faith will believe.'

Spedding's suggestion is that things are here run together which Shakespeare meant to keep apart. Shakespeare, he thinks, continued Act IV. to the '*exit* Edgar' after 1. 4 of the above passage. Thus, just before the close of the Act, the two British armies and the French army had passed across the stage, and the interest of the audience in the battle about to be fought was raised to a high pitch. Then, after a short interval, Act V. opened with the noise of battle in the distance, followed by the entrance of Edgar to announce the defeat of Cordelia's army. The battle, thus, though not fought on the stage, was shown and felt to be an event of the greatest importance.

Apart from the main objection of the entire want of evidence of so great a change having been made, there are other objections to this idea and to the reasoning on which it is based. (1) The pause at the end of the present Fourth Act is far from 'faulty', as Spedding alleges it to be; that Act ends with the most melting scene Shakespeare ever wrote; and a pause after it, and before the business of the battle, was perfectly right. (2) The Fourth Act is already much longer than the Fifth (about fourteen columns of the Globe edition against about eight and a half), and Spedding's change would give the Fourth nearly sixteen columns, and the Fifth less than seven. (3) Spedding's proposal requires a much greater alteration in the existing text than he supposed. It does not simply shift the division of the two Acts, it requires the disappearance and re-entrance of the blind Gloster. Gloster, as the text stands, is alone on the stage while the battle is being fought at a distance, and the reference to the tree shows that he was on the main or lower stage. The main stage had no front curtain; and therefore, if Act IV. is to end where Spedding wished it to end, Gloster must go off unaided at its close, and come on again unaided for Act V. And this means that the *whole* arrangement of the present Act V. Sc. ii. must be changed. If Spedding had been aware of this it is not likely that he would have broached his theory.[2]

---

[1] Where did Spedding find this? I find no trace of it, and surely Edgar would not have risked his life in the battle, when he had, in case of defeat, to appear and fight Edmund. He does not appear 'armed', according to the Folio, till V.iii.117.

[2] Spedding supposed that there was a front curtain, and this idea, coming down from Malone and Collier,* is still found in English works of authority. But it may be stated without hesitation that there is no positive evidence at all for the existence of such a curtain, and abundant evidence against it.

It is curious that he does not allude to the one circumstance which throws some little suspicion on the existing text. I mean the contradiction between Edgar's statement that, if ever he returns to his father again, he will bring him comfort, and the fact that immediately afterwards he returns to bring him discomfort. It is possible to explain this psychologically, of course, but the passage is not one in which we should expect psychological subtlety.

NOTE Y

SOME DIFFICULT PASSAGES IN *KING LEAR*

The following are notes on some passages where I have not been able to accept any of the current interpretations, or on which I wish to express an opinion or represent a little-known view.

1. *Kent's soliloquy at the end of* II.ii.

(*a*) In this speech the application of the words 'Nothing almost sees miracles but misery' seems not to have been understood. The 'misery' is surely not that of Kent but that of Lear, who has come 'out of heaven's benediction to the warm sun', *i.e.* to misery. This, says Kent, is just the situation where something like miraculous help may be looked for; and he finds the sign of it in the fact that a letter from Cordelia has just reached him; for his course since his banishment has been so obscured that it is only by the rarest good fortune (something like a miracle) that Cordelia has got intelligence of it. We may suppose that this intelligence came from one of Albany's or Cornwall's servants, some of whom are, he says (III.i.23),

> to France the spies and speculations
> Intelligent of our state.

(*b*) The words 'and shall find time', etc., have been much discussed. Some have thought that they are detached phrases from the letter which Kent is reading: but Kent has just implied by his address to the sun that he has no light to read the letter by.[1] It has also been

---

[1] The 'beacon' which he bids approach is not the moon, as Pope supposed. The moon was

suggested that the anacoluthon is meant to represent Kent's sleepiness, which prevents him from finishing the sentence, and induces him to dismiss his thoughts and yield to his drowsiness. But I remember nothing like this elsewhere in Shakespeare, and it seems much more probable that the passage is corrupt, perhaps from the loss of a line containing words like 'to rescue us' before 'From this enormous state' (with 'state' cf. 'our state' in the lines quoted above).

When we reach III.i. we find that Kent has now read the letter; he knows that a force is coming from France and indeed has already 'secret feet' in some of the harbours. So he sends the Gentleman to Dover.

2. *The Fool's Song in* II.iv.

At II.iv.62 Kent asks why the King comes with so small a train. The Fool answers, in effect, that most of his followers have deserted him because they see that his fortunes are sinking. He proceeds to advise Kent ironically to follow their example, though he confesses he does not intend to follow it himself. 'Let go thy hold when a great wheel runs down a hill, lest it break thy neck with following it: but the great one that goes up the hill, let him draw thee after. When a wise man gives thee better counsel, give me mine again: I would have none but knaves follow it, since a fool gives it.

> That sir which serves and seeks for gain,
>   And follows but for form,
> Will pack when it begins to rain,
>   And leave thee in the storm.
>
> But I will tarry; the fool will stay,
>   And let the wise man fly:
> The knave turns fool that runs away;
>   The fool no knave, perdy.'

The last two lines have caused difficulty. Johnson wanted to read

> The fool turns knave that runs away,
>   The knave no fool, perdy;

---

up and shining some time ago (II.ii.35), and lines 1 and 141–2 imply that not much of the night is left.

i.e. if I ran away, I should prove myself to be a knave and a wise man, but, being a fool, I stay, as no knave or wise man would. Those who rightly defend the existing reading misunderstand it, I think. Shakespeare is not pointing out, in 'The knave turns fool that runs away', that the wise knave who runs away is really a 'fool with a circumbendibus', 'moral miscalculator as well as moral coward'. The Fool is referring to his own words, 'I would have none but knaves follow [my advice to desert the King], since a fool gives it'; and the last two lines of his song mean, 'The knave who runs away follows the advice given by a fool; but I, the fool shall not follow my own advice by turning knave.'

For the ideas compare the striking passage in *Timon*, I.i.64 ff.

3. '*Decline your head.*'

At IV.ii.18 Goneril, dismissing Edmund in the presence of Oswald, says:

> This trusty servant
> Shall pass between us: ere long you are like to hear,
> If you dare venture in your own behalf,
> A mistress's command. Wear this; spare speech;
> Decline your head: this kiss, if it durst speak,
> Would stretch thy spirits up into the air.

I copy Furness's note* on 'Decline': 'STEEVENS thinks that Goneril bids Edmund decline his head that she might, while giving him a kiss, appear to Oswald merely to be whispering to him. But this, WRIGHT says, is giving Goneril credit for too much delicacy, and Oswald was a "serviceable villain". DELIUS suggests that perhaps she wishes to put a chain around his neck.'

Surely 'Decline your head' is connected, not with 'Wear this' (whatever 'this' maybe), but with 'this kiss', etc. Edmund is a good deal taller than Goneril, and must stoop to be kissed.

4. *Self-cover'd.*

At IV.ii.59 Albany, horrified at the passions of anger, hate, and contempt expressed in his wife's face, breaks out:

> See thyself, devil!
> Proper deformity seems not in the fiend
> So horrid as in woman.

Gon.	O vain fool!
Alb.	Thou changed and self-cover'd thing, for shame,
	Be-monster not thy feature. Were't my fitness
	To let these hands obey my blood,
	They are apt enough to dislocate and tear
	Thy flesh and bones: howe'er thou art a fiend,
	A woman's shape doth shield thee.

The passage has been much discussed, mainly because of the strange expression 'self-cover'd', for which of course emendations have been proposed. The general meaning is clear. Albany tells his wife that she is a devil in a woman's shape, and warns her not to cast off that shape by bemonstering her feature (appearance), since it is this shape alone that protects her from his wrath. Almost all commentators go astray because they imagine that, in the words 'thou changed and self-cover'd thing', Albany is speaking to Goneril as a *woman* who has been changed into a fiend. Really he is addressing her as a fiend which has changed its own shape and assumed that of a woman; and I suggest that 'self-cover'd' means either 'which hast cover'd or concealed thyself', or 'whose self is covered' [so Craig in Arden edition], not (what of course it ought to mean) 'which hast been covered *by* thyself'.

Possibly the last lines of this passage (which does not appear in the Folios) should be arranged thus:

> To let these hands obey my blood, they're apt enough
> To dislocate and tear thy flesh and bones:
> Howe'er thou art a fiend, a woman's shape
> Doth shield thee.

Gon.	Marry, your manhood now –	
Alb.		What news?

5. *The stage-directions at* V.i.37, 39.

In V.i. there first enter Edmund, Regan, and their army or soldiers: then, at line 18, Albany, Goneril, and their army or soldiers. Edmund and Albany speak very stiffly to one another, and Goneril bids them defer their private quarrels and attend to business. Then follows this passage (according to the modern texts):

Alb.	Let's then determine
	With the ancient of war on our proceedings.

Edm. I shall attend you presently at your tent.
Reg. Sister, you'll go with us?
Gon. No.
Reg. 'Tis most convenient: pray you, go with us.
Gon. [*Aside*] O, ho, I know the riddle. – I will go.
         As they are going out, enter EDGAR *disguised.*
Edg. If e'er your grace had speech with man so poor,
         Hear me one word.
Alb.   I'll overtake you. Speak.
                    [*Exeunt all but* ALBANY *and* EDGAR.

It would appear from this that all the leading persons are to go to
a Council of War with the ancient (plural) in Albany's tent; and they
are going out, followed by their armies, when Edgar comes in. Why
in the world, then, should Goneril propose (as she apparently does) to
absent herself from the Council; and why, still more, should Regan
object to her doing so? This is a question which always perplexed me,
and I could not believe in the only answers I ever found suggested,
viz., that Regan wanted to keep Edmund and Goneril together in
order that she might observe them (Moberly, quoted in Furness), or
that she could not bear to lose sight of Goneril, for fear Goneril
should effect a meeting with Edmund after the Council (Delius, if I
understand him).

But I find in Koppel what seems to be the solution
(*Verbesserungsvorschläge*, p. 127 f.). He points out that the modern
stage-directions are wrong. For the modern direction 'As they are
going out, enter Edgar disguised', the Ff. read, 'Exeunt both the
armies. Enter Edgar.' For 'Exeunt all but Albany and Edgar' the Ff.
have nothing, but Q 1 has 'exeunt' after 'word'. For the first direction
Koppel would read, 'Exeunt Regan, Goneril, Gentlemen, and
Soldiers': for the second he would read, after 'overtake you', 'Exit
Edmund'.

This makes all clear. Albany proposes a Council of War. Edmund
assents, and says he will come at once to Albany's tent for that
purpose. The Council will consist of Albany, Edmund, and the
ancient of war. Regan, accordingly, is going away with her soldiers;
but she observes that Goneril shows no sign of moving with *her*
soldiers; and she at once suspects that Goneril means to attend the
Council in order to be with Edmund. Full of jealousy, she invites
Goneril to go with *her*. Goneril refuses, but then, seeing Regan's

motive, contemptuously and ironically consents (I doubt if 'O ho, I know the riddle' should be 'aside', as in modern editions, following Capell). Accordingly the two sisters go out, followed by their soldiers; and Edmund and Albany are just going out, in a different direction, to Albany's tent when Edgar enters. His words cause Albany to stay; Albany says to Edmund, as Edmund leaves, 'I'll overtake you'; and then, turning to Edgar, bids him 'speak'.

6. V.iii.151 ff.

When Edmund falls in combat with the disguised Edgar, Albany produces the letter from Goneril to Edmund, which Edgar had found in Oswald's pocket and had handed over to Albany. This letter suggested to Edmund the murder of Albany. The passage in the Globe edition is as follows:

Gon.   This is practice, Gloucester:
      By the law of arms thou wast not bound to answer
      An unknown opposite: thou art not vanquish'd,
      But cozen'd and beguiled.
Alb.   Shut your mouth, dame,
      Or with this paper shall I stop it: Hold, sir;
      Thou worse than any name, read thy own evil:
      No tearing lady; I perceive you know it.
                              [*Gives the letter to Edmund.*
Gon. Say, if I do, the laws are mine, not thine:
      Who can arraign me for't?
Alb.   Most monstrous! oh!
      Know'st thou this paper?
Gon.   Ask me not what I know.   [*Exit.*
Alb. Go after her: she's desperate: govern her.
Edm. What you have charged me with, that have I done;
      And more, much more; the time will bring it out.
      'Tis past, and so am I. But what art thou
      That hast this fortune on me?

The first of the stage-directions is not in the Qq. or Ff.: it was inserted by Johnson. The second ('Exit') is both in the Qq. and in the Ff., but the latter place it after the words 'arraign me for't'. And they give the words 'Ask me not what I know' to Edmund, not to Goneril, as in the Qq. (followed by the Globe).

I will not go into the various views of these lines, but will simply say what seems to me most probable. It does not matter much where precisely Goneril's 'exit' comes; but I believe the Folios are right in giving the words 'Ask me not what I know' to Edmund. It has been pointed out by Knight that the question 'Know'st thou this paper?' cannot very well be addressed to Goneril, for Albany has already said to her, 'I perceive you know it'. It is possible to get over this difficulty by saying that Albany wants her confession: but there is another fact which seems to have passed unnoticed. When Albany is undoubtedly speaking to his wife, he uses the plural pronoun, 'Shut *your* mouth, dame,' 'No tearing, lady; I perceive *you* know it.' When then he asks 'Know'st *thou* this paper?' he is probably *not* speaking to her.

I should take the passage thus. At 'Hold, sir [omitted in Qq.] Albany holds the letter out towards Edmund for him to see, or possibly gives it to him.[2] The next line, with its 'thou', is addressed to Edmund, whose 'reciprocal vows' are mentioned in the letter. Goneril snatches at it to tear it up: and Albany, who does not know whether Edmund ever saw the letter or not, says to her 'I perceive *you* know it', the 'you' being emphatic (her very wish to tear it showed she knew what was in it). She practically admits her knowledge, defies him, and goes out to kill herself. He exclaims in horror at her, and, turning again to Edmund, asks if *he* knows it. Edmund, who of course does not know it, refuses to answer (like Iago), not (like Iago) out of defiance, but from chivalry towards Goneril; and, having refused to answer *this* charge, he goes on to admit the charges brought against himself previously by Albany (82 f.) and Edgar (130 f.). I should explain the change from 'you' to 'thou' in his speech by supposing that at first he is speaking to Albany and Edgar together.

7. V.iii.278.

> Lear, looking at Kent, asks,
> > Who are you?
> > Mine eyes are not o' the best: I'll tell you straight.
> *Kent.*   If fortune brag of two she loved *and* hated (Qq. *or*),
> > One of them we behold.

Kent is not answering Lear, nor is he speaking of himself. He is speaking of Lear. The best interpretation is probably that of Malone,

---

[2] 'Hold' can mean 'take'; but the word 'this' in line 160 ('Know'st thou this paper?') favours the idea that the paper is still in Albany's hand.

according to which Kent means, 'We see the man most hated by Fortune, whoever may be the man she has loved best'; and perhaps it is supported by the variation of the text in the Qq., though their texts are so bad in this scene that their support is worth little. But it occurs to me as possible that the meaning is rather: 'Did Fortune ever show the extremes *both* of her love *and* of her hatred to any other man as she has shown them to this man?'

8. *The last lines.*

> *Alb.* Bear them from hence. Our present business
> Is general woe. [*To Kent and Edgar*] Friends of my soul, you twain
> Rule in this realm, and the gored state sustain.
> *Kent.* I have a journey, sir, shortly to go;
> My master calls me, I must not say no.
> *Alb.* The weight of this sad time we must obey;
> Speak what we feel, not what we ought to say.
> The oldest hath borne most: we that are young
> Shall never see so much, nor live so long.

So the Globe. The stage-direction (right, of course) is Johnson's. The last four lines are given by the Ff. to Edgar, by the Qq. to Albany. The Qq. read '*have* borne most'.

To whom ought the last four lines to be given, and what do they mean? It is proper that the principal person should speak last, and this is in favour of Albany. But in this scene at any rate the Ff., which give the speech to Edgar, have the better text (though Ff. 2, 3, 4 make Kent die after his two lines!); Kent has answered Albany, but Edgar has not; and the lines seem to be rather more appropriate to Edgar. For the 'gentle reproof of Kent's despondency (if this phrase of Halliwell's is right) is like Edgar; and, although we have no reason to suppose that Albany was not young, there is nothing to prove his youth.

As to the meaning of the last two lines (a poor conclusion to such a play) I should suppose that 'the oldest' is not Lear, but 'the oldest of us', viz., Kent, the one survivor of the old generation: and this is the more probable if there is a reference to him in the preceding lines. The last words seem to mean, 'We that are young shall never see so much *and yet* live so long': *i.e.* if we suffer so much, we shall not bear it as he has. If the Qq. 'have' is right, the reference is to Lear, Gloster and Kent.

NOTE Z

SUSPECTED INTERPOLATIONS IN
MACBETH

I have assumed in the text that almost the whole of *Macbeth* is genuine; and, to avoid the repetition of arguments to be found in other books,[1] I shall leave this opinion unsupported. But among the passages that have been questioned or rejected there are two which seem to me open to serious doubt. They are those in which Hecate appears: viz., the whole of III.v.; and IV.i.39–43.

These passages have been suspected (1) because they contain stage-directions for two songs which have been found in Middleton's *Witch;** (2) because they can be excised without leaving the least trace of their excision; and (3) because they contain lines incongruous with the spirit and atmosphere of the rest of the Witch-scenes: *e.g.* III.v.10 f.:

> all you have done
> Hath been but for a wayward son,
> Spiteful and wrathful, who, as others do,
> Loves for his own ends, not for you;

and IV.i.41, 2:

> And now about the cauldron sing,
> Like elves and fairies in a ring.

The idea of sexual relation in the first passage, and the trivial daintiness of the second (with which cf. III.v.34,

> Hark! I am call'd; my little spirit, see,
> Sits in a foggy cloud, and stays for me)

suit Middleton's Witches quite well, but Shakespeare's not at all; and it is difficult to believe that, if Shakespeare had meant to introduce a personage supreme over the Witches, he would have made her so unimpressive as this Hecate. (It may be added that the original stage-direction at IV.i.39, 'Enter Hecat and the other three Witches', is suspicious.)

---

[1] *E.g.* Mr. Chambers's excellent little edition in the Warwick series.*

I doubt if the second and third of these arguments, taken alone, would justify a very serious suspicion of interpolation; but the fact, mentioned under (1), that the play has here been meddled with, trebles their weight. And it gives some weight to the further fact that these passages resemble one another, and differ from the bulk of the other Witch passages, in being iambic in rhythm. (It must, however, be remembered that, supposing Shakespeare *did* mean to introduce Hecate, he might naturally use a special rhythm for the parts where she appeared.)

The same rhythm appears in a third passage which has been doubted: IV.i.125–132. But this is not *quite* on a level with the other two; for (1), though it is possible to suppose the Witches, as well as the Apparitions, to vanish at 124, and Macbeth's speech to run straight on to 133, the cut is not so clean as in the other cases; (2) it is not at all clear that Hecate (the most suspicious element) is supposed to be present. The original stage-direction at 133 is merely 'The Witches Dance, and vanish'; and even if Hecate had been present before, she might have vanished at 43, as Dyce makes her do.

NOTE AA

HAS *MACBETH* BEEN ABRIDGED?

Macbeth is a very short play, the shortest of all Shakespeare's except the *Comedy of Errors*. It contains only 1993 lines, while *King Lear* contains 3298, *Othello* 3324, and *Hamlet* 3924. The next shortest of the tragedies is *Julius Caesar*, which has 2440 lines. (The figures are Mr. Fleay's.* I may remark that for our present purpose we want the number of the lines in the first Folio, not those in modern composite texts.)

Is there any reason to think that the play has been shortened? I will briefly consider this question, so far as it can be considered apart from the wider one whether Shakespeare's play was rehandled by Middleton or some one else.

That the play, as we have it, is *slightly* shorter than the play Shakespeare wrote seems not improbable. (1) We have no Quarto of *Macbeth*; and, generally, where we have a Quarto or Quartos of a play, we find them longer than the Folio text. (2) There are perhaps a few signs of omission in our text (over and above the plentiful signs of corruption). I will give one example (I.iv.33–43). Macbeth and Banquo, returning from their victories, enter the presence of Duncan (14), who receives them with compliments and thanks, which they acknowledge. He then speaks as follows:

> My plenteous joys,
> Wanton in fulness, seek to hide themselves
> In drops of sorrow. Sons, kinsmen, thanes,
> And you whose places are the nearest, know,
> We will establish our estate upon
> Our eldest Malcolm, whom we name hereafter
> The Prince of Cumberland; which honour must
> Not unaccompanied invest him only,
> But signs of nobleness, like stars, shall shine
> On all deservers. From hence to Inverness,
> And bind us further to you.

Here the transition to the naming of Malcolm, for which there has been no preparation, is extremely sudden; and the matter, considering its importance, is disposed of very briefly. But the abruptness and brevity of the sentence in which Duncan invites himself to Macbeth's castle are still more striking. For not a word has yet been said on the subject; nor is it possible to suppose that Duncan has conveyed his intention by message, for in that case Macbeth would of course have informed his wife of it in his letter (written in the interval between scenes iii. and iv.). It is difficult not to suspect some omission or curtailment here. On the other hand Shakespeare may have determined to sacrifice everything possible to the effect of rapidity in the First Act; and he may also have wished, by the suddenness and brevity of Duncan's self-invitation, to startle both Macbeth and the audience, and to make the latter feel that Fate is hurrying the King and the murderer to their doom.

And that any *extensive* omissions have been made seems not likely. (1) There is no internal evidence of the omission of anything essential to the plot. (2) Forman, who saw the play in 1610, mentions nothing which we do not find in our play; for his statement that Macbeth was made Duke of Northumberland is obviously due to a confused recollection of Malcolm's being made Duke of Cumberland. (3) Whereabouts could such omissions occur? Only in the first part, for the rest is full enough. And surely anyone who wanted to cut the play down would have operated, say, on Macbeth's talk with Banquo's murderers, or on III.vi., or on the very long dialogue of Malcolm and Macduff, instead of reducing the most exciting part of the drama. We might indeed suppose that Shakespeare himself originally wrote the first part more at length, and made the murder of Duncan come in the Third Act, and then *himself* reduced his matter so as to bring the murder back to its present place, perceiving in a flash of genius the extraordinary effect that might thus be produced. But, even if this idea suited those who believe in a rehandling of the play, what probability is there in it?

Thus it seems most likely that the play always was an extremely short one. Can we, then, at all account for its shortness? It is possible, in the first place, that it was not composed originally for the public stage, but for some private, perhaps royal, occasion, when time was limited. And the presence of the passage about touching for the evil (IV.iii.140 ff.) supports this idea. We must remember, secondly, that some of the scenes would take longer to perform than ordinary scenes of mere dialogue and action; *e.g.* the Witch-scenes, and the Battle-scenes in the last Act, for a broad-sword combat was an occasion for an exhibition of skill.[1] And, lastly, Shakespeare may well have felt that a play constructed and written like *Macbeth*, a play in which a kind of fever-heat is felt almost from beginning to end, and which offers very little relief by means of humorous or pathetic scenes, ought to be short, and would be unbearable if it lasted so long as *Hamlet* or even *King Lear*. And in fact I do not think that, in reading, we feel *Macbeth* to be short: certainly we are astonished when we hear that it is about half as long as *Hamlet*. Perhaps in the Shakespearean theatre too it appeared to occupy a longer time than the clock recorded.

---

[1] These two considerations should also be borne in mind in regard to the exceptional shortness of the *Midsummer Night's Dream* and the *Tempest*. Both contain scenes which, even on the Elizabethan stage, would take an unusual time to perform. And it has been supposed of each that it was composed to grace some wedding.

NOTE BB

THE DATE OF *MACBETH*: METRICAL TESTS

Dr. Forman saw *Macbeth* performed at the Globe in 1610. The question is how much earlier its composition or first appearance is to be put.

It is agreed that the date is not earlier than that of the accession of James I in 1603. The style and versification would make an earlier date almost impossible. And we have the allusions to 'two-fold balls and treble sceptres' and to the descent of Scottish kings from Banquo; the undramatic description of touching for the King's Evil (James performed this ceremony); and the dramatic use of witchcraft, a matter on which James considered himself an authority.*

Some of these references would have their fullest effect early in James's reign. And on this ground, and on account both of resemblances in the character of Hamlet and Macbeth, and of the use of the supernatural in the two plays, it has been held that *Macbeth* was the tragedy that came next after *Hamlet*, or, at any rate, next after *Othello*.

These arguments seem to me to have no force when set against those that point to a later date (about 1606) and place *Macbeth* after *King Lear*.[1] And, as I have already observed, the probability is that it also comes after Shakespeare's part of *Timon*, and immediately before *Antony and Cleopatra* and *Coriolanus*.

I will first refer briefly to some of the older arguments in favour of this later date, and then more at length to those based on versification.

(1) In II.iii.4–5, 'Here's a farmer that hang'd himself on the expectation of plenty', Malone found a reference to the exceptionally low price of wheat in 1606.

(2) In the reference in the same speech to the equivocator who could swear in both scales and committed treason enough for God's sake, he found an allusion to the trial of the Jesuit Garnet, in the spring of 1606, for complicity in the Gunpowder Treason and Plot. Garnet protested on his soul and salvation that he had not held a

---

[1] The fact that *King Lear* was performed at Court on December 26, 1606, is of course very far from showing that it had never been performed before.

certain conversation, then was obliged to confess that he had, and thereupon 'fell into a large discourse defending equivocation'. This argument, which I have barely sketched, seems to me much weightier than the first; and its weight is increased by the further references to perjury and treason pointed out on p. 335.

(3) Halliwell* observed what appears to be an allusion to *Macbeth* in the comedy of the *Puritan*,* 4to, 1607: 'we'll ha' the ghost i' th' white sheet sit at upper end o' th' table'; and Malone had referred to a less striking parallel in *Caesar and Pompey*,* also pub. 1607:

Why, think you, lords, that 'tis ambition's spur
That pricketh Caesar to these high attempts?

He also found a significance in the references in *Macbeth* to the genius of Mark Antony being rebuked by Caesar, and to the insane root that takes the reason prisoner, as showing that Shakespeare, while writing *Macbeth*, was reading Plutarch's* *Lives*, with a view to his next play *Antony and Cleopatra* (*S.R.* 1608).

(4) To these last arguments, which by themselves would be of little weight, I may add another, of which the same may be said. Marston's reminiscences of Shakespeare are only too obvious. In his *Dutch Courtezan*,* 1605, I have noticed passages which recall *Othello* and *King Lear*, but nothing that even faintly recalls *Macbeth*. But in reading *Sophonisba*,* 1606, I was several times reminded of *Macbeth* (as well as, more decidedly, of *Othello*). I note the parallels for what they are worth.

With *Sophonisba*, Act. I. Sc. ii.:

Upon whose tops the Roman eagles stretch'd
Their large spread wings, which fann'd the evening aire
To us cold breath,

cf. *Macbeth*, I.ii.49:

Where the Norweyan banners flout the sky
And fan our people cold.

Cf. *Sophonisba*, a page later: 'yet doubtful stood the fight,' with *Macbeth*, I.ii.7, 'Doubtful it stood' ['Doubtful long it stood'?] In the same scene of *Macbeth* the hero in fight is compared to an eagle, and his foes to sparrows; and in *Soph.* III.ii. Massinissa in fight is compared to a falcon, and his foes to fowls and lesser birds. I should not note this were it not that all these reminiscences (if they are such) recall one and the same scene. In *Sophonisba* also there is a tremendous description of the witch Erictho (IV.i.), who says to the person consulting her, 'I know thy thoughts', as the Witch says to Macbeth, of the Armed Head, 'He knows thy thought'.

(5) The resemblances between *Othello* and *King Lear* pointed out on pp. 209–210 and in Note R form, when taken in conjunction with other indications, an argument of some strength in favour of the idea that *King Lear* followed directly on *Othello*.

(6) There remains the evidence of style and especially of metre. I will not add to what has been said in the text concerning the former; but I wish to refer more fully to the latter, in so far as it can be represented by the application of metrical tests. It is impossible to argue here the whole question of these tests. I will only say that, while I am aware, and quite admit the force, of what can be said against the independent, rash, or incompetent use of them, I am fully convinced of their value when they are properly used.

Of these tests, that of rhyme and that of feminine endings, discreetly employed, are of use in broadly distinguishing Shakespeare's plays into two groups, earlier and later, and also in marking out the very latest dramas; and the feminine-ending test is of service in distinguishing Shakespeare's part in *Henry VIII* and the *Two Noble Kinsmen*. But neither of these tests has any power to separate plays composed within a few years of one another. There is significance in the fact that the *Winter's Tale*, the *Tempest, Henry VIII*, contain hardly any rhymed five-foot lines; but none, probably, in the fact that *Macbeth* shows a higher percentage of such lines than *King Lear, Othello,* or *Hamlet*. The percentages of feminine endings, again, in the four tragedies, are almost conclusive against their being early plays, and would tend to show that they were not among the latest; but the differences in their respective percentages, which would place them in the chronological order *Hamlet, Macbeth, Othello, King Lear* (König*), or *Macbeth, Hamlet, Othello, King Lear* (Hertzberg*), are of scarcely any account.[2] Nearly all scholars, I think, would accept these statements.

The really useful tests, in regard to plays which admittedly are not widely separated, are three which concern the endings of speeches and

---

[2] I have not tried to discover the source of the difference between these two reckonings.

lines. It is practically certain that Shakespeare made his verse progressively less formal, by making the speeches end more and more often within a line and not at the close of it; by making the sense overflow more and more often from one line into another; and, at last, by sometimes placing at the end of a line a word on which scarcely any stress can be laid. The corresponding tests may be called Speech-ending test, the Overflow test, and the Light and Weak Ending test.

I. The Speech-ending test has been used by König,[3] and I will first give some of his results. But I regret to say that I am unable to discover certainly the rule he has gone by. He omits speeches which are rhymed throughout, or which end with a rhymed couplet. And he counts only speeches which are 'mehrzeilig'. I suppose this means that he counts any speech consisting of two lines or more, but omits not only one-line speeches, but speeches containing more than one line but less than two; but I am not sure.

In the plays admitted by everyone to be early the percentage of speeches ending with an incomplete line is quite small. In the *Comedy of Errors*, for example, it is only 0·6. It advances to 12·1 in *King John*, 18·3 in *Henry V*, and 21·6 in *As You Like It*. It rises quickly soon after, and in no play written (according to general belief) after about 1600 or 1601 is it less than 30. In the admittedly latest plays it rises much higher, the figures being as follows: *Antony* 77·5, *Cor.* 79, *Temp.* 84·5, *Cym.* 85, *Win. Tale* 87·6, *Henry VIII* (parts assigned to Shakespeare by Spedding) 89. Going back, now, to the four tragedies, we find the following figures: *Othello* 41·4, *Hamlet* 51·6, *Lear* 60·9, *Macbeth* 77·2. These figures place *Macbeth* decidedly last, with a percentage practically equal to that of *Antony*, the first of the final group.

I will now give my own figures for these tragedies, as they differ somewhat from König's, probably because my method differs. (1) I have included speeches rhymed or ending with rhymes, mainly because I find that Shakespeare will sometimes (in later plays) end a speech which is partly rhymed with an incomplete line (e.g. *Ham.* III.ii.187, and the last words of the play: or *Macb.* V.i.87, V.ii.31). And if such speeches are reckoned, as they surely must be (for they may be, and are, highly significant), those speeches which end with

---

[3] *Der Vers in Shakspere's Dramen*, 1888.

complete rhymed lines must also be reckoned. (2) I have counted any speech exceeding a line in length, however little the excess may be; *e.g.*

> I'll fight till from my bones my flesh be hacked.
> Give me my armour:

considering that the incomplete line here may be just as significant as an incomplete line ending a longer speech. If a speech begins within a line and ends brokenly, of course I have not counted it when it is equivalent to a five-foot line; *e.g.*

> Wife, children, servants, all
> That could be found:

but I do count such a speech (they are very rare) as

> My lord, I do not know:
> But truly I do fear it:

for the same reason that I count

> You know not
> Whether it was his wisdom or his fear.

Of the speeches thus counted, those which end somewhere within the line I find to be in *Othello* about 54 per cent.; in *Hamlet* about 57; in *King Lear* about 69; in *Macbeth* about 75.[4] The order is the same as König's, but the figures differ a good deal. I presume in the last three cases this comes from the difference in method; but I think König's figures for *Othello* cannot be right, for I have tried several methods and find that the result is in no case far from the result of my own, and I am almost inclined to conjecture that König's 41·4 is really the percentage of speeches ending with the close of a line, which would give 58·6 for the percentage of the broken-ended speeches.[5]

We shall find that other tests also would put *Othello* before *Hamlet*, though close to it. This may be due to 'accident' – *i.e.* a cause or causes unknown to us; but I have sometimes wondered whether the last revi-

---

[4] In the parts of *Timon* (Globe text) assigned by Mr. Fleay to Shakespeare, I find the percentage to be about 74.5. König gives 62.8 as the percentage in the whole of the play.

[5] I have noted also what must be a mistake in the case of *Pericles*. König gives 17·1 as the percentage of the speeches with broken ends. I was astounded to see the figure, considering the style in the undoubtedly Shakespearean parts; and I find that, on my method, in Acts III., IV., V. the percentage is about 71, in the first two Acts (which show very slight, if any, traces of Shakespeare's hand) about 19. I cannot imagine the origin of the mistake here.

sion of *Hamlet* may not have succeeded the composition of *Othello*. In this connection the following fact may be worth notice. It is well known that the differences of the Second Quarto of *Hamlet* from the First are much greater in the last three Acts than in the first two – so much so that the editors of the Cambridge Shakespeare suggested that Q 1 represents an old play, of which Shakespeare's rehandling had not then proceeded much beyond the Second Act, while Q 2 represents his later completed rehandling. If that were so, the composition of the last three Acts would be a good deal later than that of the first two (though of course the first two would be revised at the time of the composition of the last three). Now I find that the percentage of speeches ending with a broken line is about 50 for the first two Acts, but about 62 for the last three. It is lowest in the First Act, and in the first two scenes of it is less than 32. The percentage for the last two Acts is about 65.

II. The Enjambement or Overflow test is also known as the End-stopped and Run-on line test. A line may be called 'end-stopped' when the sense, as well as the metre, would naturally make one pause at its close; 'run-on' when the mere sense would lead one to pass to the next line without any pause.[6] This distinction is in a great major-ity of cases quite easy to draw: in others it is difficult. The reader cannot judge by rules of grammar, or by marks of punctuation (for there is a distinct pause at the end of many a line where most editors print no stop): he must trust his ear. And readers will differ, one making a distinct pause where another does not. This, however, does not matter greatly, so long as the reader is consistent; for the impor-tant point is not the precise number of run-on lines in a play, but the difference in this matter between one play and another. Thus one may disagree with König in his estimate of many instances, but one can see that he is consistent.

In Shakespeare's early plays, 'overflows' are rare. In the *Comedy of Errors*, for example, their percentage is 12·9 according to König[7] (who excludes rhymed lines and some others). In the generally admitted last plays they are comparatively frequent. Thus, according to König, the

---

[6] I put the matter thus, instead of saying that, with a run-on line, one does pass to the next line without any pause, because, in common with many others, I should not in any case what-ever wholly ignore the fact that one line ends and another begins.

[7] These overflows are what König calls 'schroffe Enjambements', which he considers to correspond with Furnivall's 'run-on lines'.

percentage in the *Winter's Tale* is 37·5, in the *Tempest* 41·5, in *Antony* 43·3, in *Coriolanus* 45·9, in *Cymbeline* 46, in the parts of *Henry VIII* assigned by Spedding to Shakespeare 53·18. König's results for the four tragedies are as follows: *Othello*, 19·5; *Hamlet*, 23·1; *King Lear*, 29·3; *Macbeth*, 36·6; (*Timon*, the whole play, 32·5). *Macbeth* here again, therefore, stands decidedly last: indeed it stands near the first of the latest plays.

And no one who has ever attended to the versification of *Macbeth* will be surprised at these figures. It is almost obvious, I should say, that Shakespeare is passing from one system to another. Some passages show little change, but in others the change is almost complete. If the reader will compare two somewhat similar soliloquies, 'To be or not to be' and 'If it were done when 'tis done', he will recognize this at once. Or let him search the previous plays, even *King Lear*, for twelve consecutive lines like these:

> If it were done when 'tis done, then 'twere well
> It were done quickly: if the assassination
> Could trammel up the consequence, and catch
> With his surcease success; that but this blow
> Might be the be-all and the end-all here,
> But here, upon this bank and shoal of time,
> We 'Id jump the life to come. But in these cases
> We still have judgment here; that we but teach
> Bloody instructions, which, being taught, return
> To plague the inventor: this even-handed justice
> Commends the ingredients of our poison'd chalice
> To our own lips.

Or let him try to parallel the following (III.vi.37 f.):

> and this report
> Hath so exasperate the king that he
> Prepares for some attempt of war.
> *Len.* Sent he to Macduff?
> *Lord.* He did: and with an absolute 'Sir, not I,'
> The cloudy messenger turns me his back
> And hums, as who should say 'You'll rue the time
> That clogs me with this answer.'
> *Len.* And that well might
> Advise him to a caution, to hold what distance
> His wisdom can provide. Some holy angel

> Fly to the court of England, and unfold
> His message ere he come, that a swift blessing
> May soon return to this our suffering country
> Under a hand accurs'd!

or this (IV.iii.118 f.):

> Macduff, this noble passion,
> Child of integrity, hath from my soul
> Wiped the black scruples, reconciled my thoughts
> To thy good truth and honour. Devilish Macbeth
> By many of these trains hath sought to win me
> Into his power, and modest wisdom plucks me
> From over-credulous haste: but God above
> Deal between thee and me! for even now
> I put myself to thy direction, and
> Unspeak mine own detraction, here abjure
> The taints and blames I laid upon myself,
> For strangers to my nature.

I pass to another point. In the last illustration the reader will observe not only that 'overflows' abound, but that they follow one another in an unbroken series of nine lines. So long a series could not, probably, be found outside *Macbeth* and the last plays. A series of two or three is not uncommon; but a series of more than three is rare in the early plays, and far from common in the plays of the second period (König).

I thought it might be useful for our present purpose, to count the series of four and upwards in the four tragedies, in the parts of *Timon* attributed by Mr. Fleay* to Shakespeare, and in *Coriolanus*, a play of the last period. I have not excluded rhymed lines in the two places where they occur, and perhaps I may say that my idea of an 'overflow' is more exacting than König's. The reader will understand the following table at once if I say that, according to it, *Othello* contains three passages where a series of four successive overflowing lines occurs, and two passages where a series of five such lines occurs (see top of page 384):

(The figures for *Macbeth* and *Timon* in the last column must be borne in mind. I observed nothing in the non-Shakespeare part of *Timon* that would come into the table, but I did not make a careful search. I felt some doubt as to two of the four-series in *Othello* and again in *Hamlet*, and also whether the ten-series in *Coriolanus* should not be put in column 7).

	4	5	6	7	8	9	10	No. of Lines. Fleay).
Othello	3	2	–	–	–	–	–	2,758
Hamlet	7	–	–	–	–	–	–	2,571
Lear	6	2	–	–	–	–	–	2,312
Timon	7	2	1	1	–	–	–	1,031(?)
Macbeth	7	5	1	1	–	1	–	1,706
Coriolanus	16	14	7	1	2	–	1	2,563

III. *The light and weak ending test.*

We have just seen that in some cases a doubt is felt whether there is an 'overflow' or not. The fact is that the 'overflow' has many degrees of intensity. If we take, for example, the passage last quoted, and if with König we consider the line

The taints and blames I laid upon myself

to be run-on (as I do not), we shall at least consider the overflow to be much less distinct than those in the lines

                        but God above
Deal between thee and me! for even now
I put myself to thy direction, and
Unspeak my own detraction, here abjure.

And of these four lines the third runs on into its successor at much the greatest speed.

'Above', 'now', 'abjure', are not light or weak endings: 'and' is a weak ending. Prof. Ingram gave the name weak ending to certain words on which it is scarcely possible to dwell at all, and which, therefore, precipitate the line which they close into the following. Light endings are certain words which have the same effect in a slighter degree. For example, *and, from, in, of,* are weak endings; *an, are, I, he,* are light endings.

The test founded on this distinction is, within its limits, the most satisfactory of all, partly because the work of its author can be absolutely trusted. The result of its application is briefly as follows. Until quite a late date light and weak endings occur in Shakespeare's works in such small numbers as hardly to be worth consideration.[8]

---

[8] The number of light endings, however, in *Julius Caesar* (10) and *All's Well* (12) is worth notice.

But in the well-defined group of last plays the numbers both of light and of weak endings increase greatly, and, on the whole, the increase apparently is progressive (I say apparently, because the order in which the last plays are generally placed depends to some extent on the test itself). I give Prof. Ingram's table of these plays, premising that in *Pericles, Two Noble Kinsmen,* and *Henry VIII* he uses only those parts of the plays which are attributed by certain authorities to Shakespeare (*New Shakspere Soc. Trans.,* 1874).

	Light endings	Weak	Percentage of light in verse lines.	Percentage of weak in verse lines.	Percentage of both.
Antony & Cleopatra	71	28	2.53	1.	3.53
Coriolanus	60	44	2.34	1.71	4.05
Pericles	20	10	2.78	1.39	4.17
Tempest	42	25	2.88	1.71	4.59
Cymbeline	78	52	2.90	1.93	4.83
Winter's Tale	57	43	3.12	2.36	5.48
Two Noble Kinsmen	50	34	3.63	2.47	6.10
Henry VIII	45	37	3.93	3.23	7.16

Now, let us turn to our four tragedies (with *Timon*). Here again we have one doubtful play, and I give the figures for the whole of *Timon*, and again for the parts of *Timon* assigned to Shakespeare by Mr. Fleay, both as they appear in his amended text and as they appear in the Globe (perhaps the better text).

	Light	Weak
Hamlet	8	0
Othello	2	0
Lear	5	1
Timon (whole)	16	5
(Sh. in Fleay)	14	7
(Sh. in Globe)	13	2
Macbeth	21	2

Now here the figures for the first three plays tell us practically nothing. The tendency to a freer use of these endings is not visible. As to *Timon*, the number of weak endings, I think, tells us little, for probably only two or three are Shakespeare's; but the rise in the number of light endings is so marked as to be significant. And most significant is this rise in the case of *Macbeth*, which, like Shakespeare's part of *Timon*, is much shorter than the preceding plays. It strongly confirms the impression that in *Macbeth* we have the transition to Shakespeare's last style, and that the play is the latest of the five tragedies.[9]

NOTE CC

WHEN WAS THE MURDER OF DUNCAN FIRST PLOTTED?

A good many readers probably think that, when Macbeth first met the Witches, he was perfectly innocent; but a much larger number would say that he had already harboured a vaguely guilty ambition, though he had not faced the idea of murder. And I think there can be no doubt that this is the obvious and natural interpretation of the scene. Only it is almost necessary to go rather further, and to suppose that his guilty ambition, whatever its precise form, was known to his wife and shared by her. Otherwise, surely, she would not, on reading his letter, so instantaneously assume that the King must be murdered in their castle; nor would Macbeth, as soon as he meets her, be aware (as he evidently is) that this thought is in her mind.

But there is a famous passage in *Macbeth* which, closely considered, seems to require us to go further still, and to suppose that, at some time before the action of the play begins, the husband and wife had explicitly discussed the idea of murdering Duncan at some favourable opportunity, and had agreed to execute this idea. Attention seems to have been first drawn to this passage by Koester in vol. I. of the *Jahrbücher d. deutschen Shakespeare-Gesellschaft*, and on it is based the interpretation of the play in Werder's very able *Vorlesungen über Macbeth.**

---

[9] The Editors of the Cambridge Shakespeare might appeal in support of their view, that parts of Act V. are not Shakespeare's, to the fact that the last of the light endings occurs at IV.iii.165.

The passage occurs in i.vii., where Lady Macbeth is urging her husband to the deed:

Macb.   Prithee, peace:
     I dare do all that may become a man;
     Who dares do more is none.
Lady M.   What beast was't, then,
     That made you break this enterprise to me?
     When you durst do it, then you were a man;
     And, to be more than what you were, you would
     Be so much more the man. Nor time nor place
     Did then adhere, and yet you would make both:
     They have made themselves, and that their fitness now
     Does unmake you. I have given suck, and know
     How tender 'tis to love the babe that milks me:
     I would, while it was smiling in my face,
     Have pluck'd my nipple from his boneless gums,
     And dash'd the brains out, had I so sworn as you
     Have done to this.

Here Lady Macbeth asserts (1) that Macbeth proposed the murder to her: (2) that he did so at a time when there was no opportunity to attack Duncan, no 'adherence' of 'time' and 'place': (3) that he declared he would *make* an opportunity, and swore to carry out the murder.

Now it is possible that Macbeth's 'swearing' might have occurred in an interview off the stage between scenes v. and vi., or scenes vi. and vii.; and, if in that interview Lady Macbeth had with difficulty worked her husband up to a resolution, her irritation at his relapse, in sc. vii., would be very natural. But, as for Macbeth's first proposal of murder, it certainly does not occur in our play, nor could it possibly occur in any interview off the stage; for when Macbeth and his wife first meet, 'time' and 'place' *do* adhere; 'they have made themselves'. The conclusion would seem to be, either that the proposal of the murder, and probably the oath, occurred in a scene at the very beginning of the play, which scene has been lost or cut out; or else that Macbeth proposed, and swore to execute, the murder at some time prior to the action of the play.[1] The first of these hypotheses is most

---

[1] The 'swearing' *might* of course, on this view, occur off the stage within the play; but there is no occasion to suppose this if we are obliged to put the proposal outside the play.

improbable, and we seem driven to adopt the second, unless we consent to burden Shakespeare with a careless mistake in a very critical passage.

And, apart from unwillingness to do this, we can find a good deal to say in favour of the idea of a plan formed at a past time. It would explain Macbeth's start of fear at the prophecy of the kingdom. It would explain why Lady Macbeth, on receiving his letter, immediately resolves on action; and why, on their meeting, each knows that murder is in the mind of the other. And it is in harmony with her remarks on his probable shrinking from the act, to which, *ex hypothesi*, she had already thought it necessary to make him pledge himself by an oath.

Yet I find it very difficult to believe in this interpretation. It is not merely that the interest of Macbeth's struggle with himself and with his wife would be seriously diminished if we felt he had been through all this before. I think this would be so; but there are two more important objections. In the first place the violent agitation described in the words,

> If good, why do I yield to that suggestion
> Whose horrid image doth unfix my hair
> And make my seated heart knock at my ribs,

would surely not be natural, even in Macbeth, if the idea of murder were already quite familiar to him through conversation with his wife, and if he had already done more than 'yield' to it. It is not as if the Witches had told him that Duncan was coming to his house. In that case the perception that the moment had come to execute a merely general design might well appal him. But all that he hears is that he will one day be King – a statement which, supposing this general design, would not point to any immediate action.[2] And, in the second place, it is hard to believe that, if Shakespeare really had imagined the murder planned and sworn to before the action of the play, he would have written the first six scenes in such a manner that practically all readers imagine quite another state of affairs, and *continue to imagine*

---

[2] To this it might be answered that the effect of the prediction was to make him feel, 'Then I shall succeed if I carry out the plan of murder,' and so make him yield to the idea over again. To which I can only reply, anticipating the next argument, 'How is that Shakespeare wrote the speech in such a way that practically everybody supposes the idea of murder to be occurring to Macbeth for the first time?'

it even after they have read in scene vii. the passage which is troubling us. Is it likely, to put it otherwise, that his idea was one which nobody seems to have divined till late in the nineteenth century? And for what possible reason could he refrain from making this idea clear to his audience, as he might so easily have done in the third scene?[3] It seems very much more likely that he himself imagined the matter as nearly all his readers do.

But, in that case, what are we to say of this passage? I will answer first by explaining the way in which I understood it before I was aware that it had caused so much difficulty. I supposed that an interview had taken place after scene v., a scene which shows Macbeth shrinking, and in which his last words were 'we will speak further'. In this interview, I supposed, his wife had so wrought upon him that he had at last yielded and pledged himself by oath to do the murder. As for her statement that he had 'broken the enterprise' to her, I took it to refer to his letter to her, – a letter written when time and place did not adhere, for he did not yet know that Duncan was coming to visit him. In the letter he does not, of course, openly 'break the enterprise' to her, and it is not likely that he would do such a thing in a letter; but if they had had ambitious conversations, in which each felt that some half-formed guilty idea was floating in the mind of the other, she might naturally take the words of the letter as indicating much more than they said; and then in her passionate contempt at his hesitation, and her passionate eagerness to overcome it, she might easily accuse him, doubtless with exaggeration, and probably with conscious exaggeration, of having actually proposed the murder. And Macbeth, knowing that when he wrote the letter he really had been thinking of murder, and indifferent to anything except the question whether murder should be done, would easily let her statement pass unchallenged.

This interpretation still seems to me not unnatural. The alternative (unless we adopt the idea of an agreement prior to the action of the play) is to suppose that Lady Macbeth refers throughout the passage to some interview subsequent to her husband's return, and that, in making her do so, Shakespeare simply forgot her speeches on welcom-

---

[3] It might be answered here again that the actor, instructed by Shakespeare, could act the start of fear so as to convey quite clearly the idea of definite guilt. And this is true; but we ought to do our best to interpret the text before we have recourse to this kind of suggestion.

ing Macbeth home, and also forgot that at any such interview 'time' and 'place' did 'adhere'. It is easy to understand such forgetfulness in a spectator and even in a reader; but it is less easy to imagine it in a poet whose conception of the two characters throughout these scenes was evidently so burningly vivid.

NOTE DD

DID LADY MACBETH REALLY FAINT?

In the scene of confusion where the murder of Duncan is discovered, Macbeth and Lennox return from the royal chamber; Lennox describes the grooms who, as it seemed, had done the deed:

> Their hands and faces were all badged with blood;
> So were their daggers, which unwiped we found
> Upon their pillows:
> They stared, and were distracted; no man's life
> Was to be trusted with them.

Macb.   O, yet I do repent me of my fury
> That I did kill them.

Macd.   Wherefore did you so?

Macb.   Who can be wise, amazed, temperate and furious,
> Loyal and neutral, in a moment? No man:
> The expedition of my violent love
> Outrun the pauser, reason. Here lay Duncan,
> His silver skin laced with his golden blood;
> And his gash'd stabs look'd like a breach in nature
> For ruin's wasteful entrance; there, the murderers,
> Steep'd in the colours of their trade, their daggers
> Unmannerly breech'd with gore: who could refrain,
> That had a heart to love, and in that heart
> Courage to make's love known?

At this point Lady Macbeth exclaims, 'Help me hence, ho!' Her husband takes no notice, but Macduff calls out 'Look to the lady.' This, after a few words 'aside' between Malcolm and Donalbain, is repeated by Banquo, and, very shortly after, all except Duncan's sons *exeunt.* (The stage-direction 'Lady Macbeth is carried out', after Banquo's exclamation 'Look to the lady', is not in the Ff. and was introduced by Rowe. If the Ff. are right, she can hardly have fainted *away.* But the point has no importance here.)

Does Lady Macbeth really turn faint, or does she pretend? The latter seems to have been the general view, and Whately pointed out that Macbeth's indifference betrays his consciousness that the faint was not real. But to this it may be answered that, if he believed it to be real, he would equally show indifference, in order to display his horror at the murder. And Miss Helen Faucit and others have held that there was no pretence.

In favour of the pretence it may be said (1) that Lady Macbeth, who herself took back the daggers, saw the old King in his blood, and smeared the grooms, was not the woman to faint at a mere description; (2) that she saw her husband over-acting his part, and saw the faces of the lords, and wished to end the scene, – which she succeeded in doing.

But to the last argument it may be replied that she would not willingly have run the risk of leaving her husband to act his part alone. And for other reasons (indicated above, p. 330 f.) I decidedly believe that she is meant really to faint. She was no Goneril. She knew that she could not kill the King herself; and she never expected to have to carry back the daggers, see the bloody corpse, and smear the faces and hands of the grooms. But Macbeth's agony greatly alarmed her, and she was driven to the scene of horror to complete his task; and what an impression it made on her we know from that sentence uttered in her sleep, 'Yet who would have thought the old man to have had so much blood in him?' She had now, further, gone through the ordeal of the discovery. Is it not quite natural that the reaction should come, and that it should come just when Macbeth's description recalls the scene which had cost her the greatest effort? Is it not likely, besides, that the expression on the faces of the lords would force her to realize, what before the murder she had refused to consider, the horror and the suspicion it must excite? It is noticeable, also, that she is far from carrying out her intention of bearing a part in making their 'griefs and clamours roar upon his death' (I.vii.78). She has left it all to her husband, and, after uttering but two sentences, the second of which is answered very curtly by Banquo, for some time (an interval of 33 lines) she has said nothing. I believe Shakespeare means this interval to be occupied in desperate efforts on her part to prevent herself from giving way, as she sees for the first time something of the truth to which she was formerly so blind, and which will destroy her in the end.

It should be observed that at the close of the Banquet scene, where she has gone through much less, she is evidently exhausted.

Shakespeare, of course, knew whether he meant the faint to be real: but I am not aware if an actor of the part could show the audience whether it was real or pretended. If he could, he would doubtless receive instructions from the author.

NOTE EE

DURATION OF THE ACTION IN *MACBETH*: MACBETH' S AGE. 'HE HAS NO CHILDREN'

1. The duration of the action cannot well be more than a few months. On the day following the murder of Duncan his sons fly and Macbeth goes to Scone to be invested (II.iv.). Between this scene and Act iii. an interval must be supposed, sufficient for news to arrive of Malcolm being in England and Donalbain in Ireland, and for Banquo to have shown himself a good counsellor. But the interval is evidently not long: e.g. Banquo's first words are 'Thou hast it now' (III.i.1). Ban quo is murdered on the day when he speaks these words. Macbeth's visit to the Witches takes place the next day (III.iv.132). At the end of this visit (IV.i.) he hears of Macduff's flight to England, and deter-mines to have Macduff s wife and children slaughtered without delay; and this is the subject of the next scene (IV.ii). No great interval, then, can be supposed between this scene and the next, where Macduff, arrived at the English court, hears what has happened at his castle. At the end of the scene (IV.iii.237) Malcolm says that 'Macbeth is ripe for shaking, and the powers above put on their instruments': and the events of Act V. evidently follow with little delay, and occupy but a short time. Holinshed's Macbeth appears to have reigned seventeen years: Shakespeare's may perhaps be allowed as many weeks.

But, naturally, Shakespeare creates some difficulties through wish-ing to produce different impressions in different parts of the play. The main effect is that of fiery speed, and it would be impossible to imagine the torment of Macbeth's mind lasting through a number of years, even if Shakespeare had been willing to allow him years of outward success. Hence the brevity of the action. On the other hand time is wanted for the degeneration of his character hinted at in IV. iii. 57f., for the development of his tyranny, for his attempts to entrap Malcolm (*ib.* 117 f.), and perhaps for the deepening of his feeling that his life had passed into the sere and yellow leaf. Shakespeare, as we have seen, scarcely provides time for all this, but at certain points he produces an impression that a longer time has elapsed than he has provided for, and he puts most of the indications of this longer time into a scene (IV. iii.) which by its quietness contrasts strongly with almost all the rest of the play.

2. There is no unmistakable indication of the ages of the two principal characters; but the question, though of no great importance, has an interest. I believe most readers imagine Macbeth as a man between forty and fifty, and his wife as younger but not young. In many cases this impression is doubtless due to the custom of the theatre (which, if it can be shown to go back far, should have much weight), but it is shared by readers who have never seen the play performed, and is then presumably due to a number of slight influences probably incapable of complete analysis. Such readers would say, 'The hero and heroine do not speak like young people, nor like old ones'; but, though I think this is so, it can hardly be demonstrated. Perhaps however the following small indications, mostly of a different kind, tend to the same result.

(1) There is no positive sign of youth. (2) A young man would not be likely to lead the army. (3) Macbeth is 'cousin' to an old man.[1] (4) Macbeth calls Malcolm 'young', and speaks of him scornfully as 'the boy Malcolm'. He is probably therefore considerably his senior. But Malcolm is evidently not really a boy (see I.ii.3 f. as well as the later Acts). (5) One gets the impression (possibly without reason) that Macbeth and Banquo are of about the same age; and Banquo's son, the boy Fleance, is evidently not a mere child. (On the other hand the children of Macduff, who is clearly a good deal older than Malcolm, are all young; and I do not think there is any sign that Macbeth is older than Macduff). (6) When Lady Macbeth, in the banquet scene, says,

---

[1] So in Holinshed, as well as in the play, where however 'cousin' need not have its specific meaning.

> Sit, worthy friends: my lord is often thus,
> And hath been from his youth,

we naturally imagine him some way removed from his youth. (7) Lady Macbeth saw a resemblance to her father in the aged king. (8) Macbeth says,

> I have lived long enough: my way[2] of life
> Is fall'n into the sere, the yellow leaf:
> And that which should accompany old age,
> As honour, love, obedience, troops of friends,
> I may not look to have.

It is, surely, of the old age of the soul that he speaks in the second line, but still the lines would hardly be spoken under any circumstances by a man less than middle-aged.

On the other hand I suppose no one ever imagined Macbeth, or on consideration could imagine him, as *more* than middle-aged when the action begins. And in addition the reader may observe, if he finds it necessary, that Macbeth looks forward to having children (I.vii.72), and that his terms of endearment ('dearest love', 'dearest chuck') and his language in public ('sweet remembrancer') do not suggest that his wife and he are old; they even suggest that she at least is scarcely middle-aged. But this discussion tends to grow ludicrous.

For Shakespeare's audience these mysteries were revealed by a glance at the actors, like the fact that Duncan was an old man, which the text, I think, does not disclose till V.i.44.

3. Whether Macbeth had children or (as seems usually to be supposed) had none, is quite immaterial. But it is material that, if he had none, he looked forward to having one; for otherwise there would be no point in the following words in his soliloquy about Banquo (III.i.58 f.):

>   Then prophet-like
> They hail'd him father to a line of kings:
> Upon my head they placed a fruitless crown,
> And put a barren sceptre in my gripe,
> Thence to be wrench'd with an unlineal hand,
> No son of mine succeeding. If't be so,
> For Banquo's issue have I filed my mind.

---

[2] 'May', Johnson conjectured, without necessity.

And he is determined that it shall not 'be so':

> Rather than so, come, fate, into the list
> And champion me to the utterance!

Obviously he contemplates a son of his succeeding, if only he can get rid of Banquo and Fleance. What he fears is that Banquo will kill him; in which case, supposing he has a son, that son will not be allowed to succeed him, and, supposing he has none, he will be unable to beget one.

I hope this is clear; and nothing else matters. Lady Macbeth's child (I.vii.54) may be alive or may be dead. It may even be, or have been, her child by a former husband; though if Shakespeare had followed history in making Macbeth marry a widow (as some writers gravely assume) he would probably have told us so. It may be that Macbeth had many children or that he had none. We cannot say, and it does not concern the play. But the interpretation of a statement on which some critics build, 'He has no children', has an interest of another kind, and I proceed to consider it.

These words occur at IV.iii.216. Malcolm and Macduff are talking at the English Court, and Ross, arriving from Scotland, brings news to Macduff of Macbeth's revenge on him. It is necessary to quote a good many lines:

> *Ross.* Your castle is surprised; your wife and babes
> Savagely slaughter'd: to relate the manner,
> Were, on the quarry of these murder'd deer,
> To add the death of you.
> *Mal.*   Merciful heaven!
> What, man! ne'er pull your hat upon your brows;
> Give sorrow words: the grief that does not speak
> Whispers the o'er-fraught heart and bids it break.
> *Macd.* My children too?
> *Ross.*   Wife, children, servants, all
> That could be found.
> *Macd.*   And I must be from thence!
> My wife kill'd too?
> *Ross.*   I have said.
> *Mal.*   Be comforted:
> Let's make us medicines of our great revenge,
> To cure this deadly grief.

> *Macd.* He has no children. All my pretty ones?
> Did you say all? O hell-kite! All?
> What, all my pretty chickens and their dam
> At one fell swoop?
> *Mal.* Dispute it like a man.
> *Macd.* I shall do so;
> But I must also feel it as a man:
> I cannot but remember such things were,
> That were most precious to me. –

Three interpretations have been offered of the words 'He has no children.'

(*a*) They refer to Malcolm, who, if he had children of his own, would not at such a moment suggest revenge, or talk of curing such a grief. Cf. *King John*, III. iv. 91, where Pandulph says to Constance,

> You hold too heinous a respect of grief,

and Constance answers,

> He talks to me that never had a son.

(*b*) They refer to Macbeth, who has no children, and on whom therefore Macduff cannot take an adequate revenge.

(*c*) They refer to Macbeth, who, if he himself had children, could never have ordered the slaughter of children. Cf. *3 Henry VI*, V.v.63, where Margaret says to the murderers of Prince Edward,

> You have no children, butchers! if you had,
> The thought of them would have stirred up remorse.

I cannot think interpretation (*b*) the most natural. The whole idea of the passage is that Macduff must feel *grief* first and before he can feel anything else, *e.g.* the desire for vengeance. As he says directly after, he cannot at once 'dispute' it like a man, but must 'feel' it as a man; and it is not till ten lines later that he is able to pass to the thought of revenge. Macduff is not the man to conceive at any time the idea of killing children in retaliation; and that he contemplates it *here*, even as a suggestion, I find it hard to believe.

For the same main reason interpretation (*a*) seems to me far more probable than (*c*). What could be more consonant with the natural course of the thought, as developed in the lines which follow, than that Macduff, being told to think of revenge, not grief, should answer, 'No one who was himself a father would ask that of me in the very first moment of loss'? But the thought supposed by interpretation (*c*) has not this natural connection.

It has been objected to interpretation (*a*) that, according to it, Macduff would naturally say 'You have no children', not 'He has no children'. But what Macduff does is precisely what Constance does in the line quoted from *King John*. And it should be noted that, all through the passage down to this point, and indeed in the fifteen lines which precede our quotation, Macduff listens only to Ross. His questions 'My children too?' 'My wife killed too?' show that he cannot fully realize what he is told. When Malcolm interrupts, therefore, he puts aside his suggestion with four words spoken to himself, or (less probably) to Ross (his relative, who knew his wife and children), and continues his agonized questions and exclamations. Surely it is not likely that at that moment the idea of (*c*), an idea which there is nothing to suggest, would occur to him.

In favour of (*c*) as against (*a*) I see no argument except that the words of Macduff almost repeat those of Margaret; and this fact does not seem to me to have much weight. It shows only that Shakespeare might easily use the words in the sense of (*c*) if that sense were suitable to the occasion. It is not unlikely, again, I think, that the words came to him here because he had used them many years before;[3] but

---

[3] As this point occurs here, I may observe that Shakespeare's later tragedies contain many such reminiscences of the tragic plays of his young days. For instance, cf. *Titus Andronicus*, I.i.150 f.:

In peace and honour rest you here, my sons,
*   *   *

Secure from worldly chances and mishaps!
Here lurks no treason, here no envy swells,
Here grow no damned drugs: here are no storms,
No noise, but silence and eternal sleep,

with *Macbeth*, III.ii.22 f.:

     Duncan is in his grave;
After life's fitful fever he sleeps well;
Treason has done his worst: nor steel, nor poison,
Malice domestic, foreign levy, nothing,
Can touch him further.

In writing IV.i. Shakespeare can hardly have failed to remember the conjuring of the Spirit, and the ambiguous oracles, in 2 *Henry VI* I.iv. The 'Hyrcan tiger' of *Macbeth* III.iv.101, which is also alluded to in *Hamlet*, appears first in 3 *Henry VI* I.iv.155. Cf. *Richard III* II.i.92, 'Nearer in bloody thoughts, but not in blood,' with *Macbeth* II.iii.146, 'the near in blood, the nearer bloody'; *Richard III* IV.ii. 64, 'But I am in So far in blood that sin will pluck on sin,' with *Macbeth* III.iv.136, 'I am in blood stepp'd in so far,' etc. These are but a few instances. (It makes no difference whether Shakespeare was author or reviser of *Titus* and *Henry VI*).

it does not follow that he knew he was repeating them; or that, if he did, he remembered the sense they had previously borne; or that, if he did remember it, he might not use them now in another sense.

NOTE FF

THE GHOST OF BANQUO

I do not think the suggestions that the Ghost on its first appearance is Banquo's, and on its second Duncan's, or *vice versa*, are worth discussion. But the question whether Shakespeare meant the Ghost to be real or a mere hallucination, has some interest, and I have not seen it fully examined.

The following reasons may be given for the hallucination view:

(1) We remember that Macbeth has already seen one hallucination, that of the dagger; and if we failed to remember it Lady Macbeth would remind us of it here:

> This is the very painting of your fear;
> This is the air-drawn dagger which, you said,
> Led you to Duncan.

(2) The Ghost seems to be created by Macbeth's imagination: for his words,

> now they rise again
> With twenty mortal murders on their crowns,

describe it, and they echo what the murderer had said to him a little before,

> Safe in a ditch he bides
> With twenty trenched gashes on his head.

(3) It vanishes the second time on his making a violent effort and asserting its unreality:

> Hence, horrible shadow!
> Unreal mockery, hence!

This is not quite so the first time, but then too its disappearance follows on his defying it:

Why what care I? If thou canst nod, speak too.

So, apparently, the dagger vanishes when he exclaims, 'There's no such thing!'

(4) At the end of the scene Macbeth himself seems to regard it as an illusion:

> My strange and self-abuse
> Is the initiate fear that wants hard use.

(5) It does not speak, like the Ghost in *Hamlet* even on its last appearance, and like the Ghost in *Julius Caesar*.

(6) It is visible only to Macbeth.

I should attach no weight to (6) taken alone (see p. 117). Of (3) it may be remarked that Brutus himself seems to attribute the vanishing of Caesar's Ghost to his taking courage: 'now I have taken heart thou vanishest:' yet he certainly holds it to be real. It may also be remarked on (5) that Caesar's Ghost says nothing that Brutus' own forebodings might not have conjured up. And further it may be asked why, if the Ghost of Banquo was meant for an illusion, it was represented on the stage, as the stage-directions and Forman's account show it to have been.

On the whole, and with some doubt, I think that Shakespeare (1) meant the judicious to take the Ghost for an hallucination, but (2) knew that the bulk of the audience would take it for a reality. And I am more sure of (2) than of (1).

Notes

p. 1: Aristotle   (384–22 BC), Greek philosopher; his *Poetics* (c.350 BC) provides the first extant theory of tragedy.

p. 1: Corneille   Pierre Corneille (1606–84), French dramatist, leading exponent of neoclassical approach to tragedy, author of *Le Cid* (1637).

p. 2: 'Shakespeare the Man'   possibly an allusion to Walter Bagehot's 1901 book of this title. For Bradley, reviewing Bagehot's essay for his own lecture on the same topic, this 'idea of Shakespeare' is that of 'the competent "general reader" more fully developed'; his own view, though advanced with characteristic tentativeness, is that the closest self-portrait that we have is found in the character of Hamlet, which 'may explain to us why Hamlet is the most fascinating character, and the most inexhaustible, in all imaginative literature. What else should he be, if the world's greatest poet, who was able to give almost the reality of nature to creations totally unlike himself, put his own soul straight into this creation, and when he wrote Hamlet's speeches write down his own heart?' (A. C. Bradley, 'Shakespeare the Man', *Oxford Lectures on Poetry* (1909; repr. London: Macmillan, 1965), pp. 315, 357).

p. 3: Dante   Dante Alighieri (1265–1321), Italian poet, author of the *Divine Comedy*, written between 1306 and 1321, which takes its protagonist on a tour of Purgatory, Heaven and Hell.

p. 3: Chaucer   Geoffrey Chaucer (1343–1400), English poet, author of *The Canterbury Tales* (1387–94).

p. 3: 'Anhanged . . . clowde'   quoting *The Monk's Tale*, ll. 2759–66.

p. 4: *Arden of Feversham*   anonymous domestic tragedy published in 1592.

p. 4: *A Yorkshire Tragedy*   domestic tragedy, published in 1608 and included in the 1663 third Folio of Shakespeare's works; now attributed to Thomas Middleton.

p. 4: Symonds   John Addington Symonds (1840–93), English critic; *Shakspere's Predecessors in the English Drama* was published in 1884.

p. 5: Tourgénief   Ivan Turgenev (1818–83), Russian novelist and playwright; the novella *King Lear of the Steppes* was published in 1870.

p. 6: *The Woman in White*   mystery thriller, published in 1860, by the popular Victorian novelist Wilkie Collins (1824–89).

p. 9: Hegel   Georg Wilhelm Friedrich Hegel (1770–1831), leading German idealist philosopher. The proponent of a dialectical approach to ethics, politics, religion and art, Hegel regarded history as progressive and teleological, characterized by patterns of contradiction and negation. Hegel's theory of tragedy, which focuses primarily upon Greek examples, emphasizes its concern with the conflicts between abstract forces and competing ethical principles.

p. 19: Wordsworth's lines   William Wordsworth (1770–1850), English poet; and Bradley's other great passion. The quotation is from *The Excursion* (1814), ll. 556–7.

p. 21: Dr. Johnson   Samuel Johnson (1709–84), essayist and Shakespearean editor, whose *The Plays of William Shakespeare* was published in 1765.

p. 21: Δράσαντι παθεῖν 'the doer must suffer'; refers to Aeschylus, *Choephori*, l. 313.

p. 27: Mr. R. G. Moulton Richard G. Moulton (1849–1924), English critic, author of *Shakespeare as a Dramatic Artist: A Popular Illustration of the Principles of Scientific Criticism* (Oxford, 1885).

p. 27: Gustav Freytag (1816–95), German dramatic theorist and critic, author of *Die Technik des Dramas* (Leipzig, 1863, 1898).

p. 28: Remorse Charles Appleyard's play *Remorse. A Drama in Three Acts* (1871), a crime-does-not-pay melodrama set in a snowbound Alpine village on Christmas Eve. In the climactic third act, during a dream sequence in which the guilt-stricken villain is put on trial for the secret murder of a Polish Jew committed fifteen years before, the intervention of a mesmerist prompts him to re-enact the crime under hypnosis.

p. 28: The Cenci verse tragedy, written in 1819, by English poet and radical political activist Percy Bysshe Shelley (1792–1827); set in Rome in 1599, it dramatizes the downfall of the tyrannical Count Cenci, at the hands of his daughter Beatrice (whom he has raped) and her stepmother.

p. 28: Such a play exists the anonymously authored *Thomas of Woodstock* (c.1592), which depicts the historical events prior to the opening of Shakespeare's play.

p. 48: Jonson Ben Jonson (1572–1637), poet and playwright, whose dramatic works were characterized by their careful assimilation of neoclassical forms and techniques (and who criticized Shakespeare for his failure to observe these); he provided a dedicatory verse to the 1623 Folio in which he declared that its author was 'not of an age, but for all time'.

p. 48: Heminge and Condell John Heminge (1566–1630) and Henry Condell (1576–1627), actors in Shakespeare's company, the Lord Chamberlain's (subsequently the King's) Men, who oversaw the publication of the 1623 Folio.

p. 48: Sidney Sir Philip Sidney (1554–86), courtier, soldier and poet; author of the sonnet sequence *Astrophil and Stella* (1591), the prose romance *Arcadia* (1590), and of *An Apology for Poetry* (1595), which attempted to apply Aristotelian principles to the dramatic works of his contemporaries.

p. 48: Mermaid London tavern during Shakespeare's time.

p. 48: Drummond William Drummond (1585–1649), Scottish poet, who recorded Ben Jonson's views of Shakespeare.

p. 48: Fuller Thomas Fuller (1608–61), writer, whose *The History of the Worthies of England* (1662) offers the first biography of Shakespeare.

p. 49: Decameron sequence of one hundred interlinked stories by the Italian writer Giovanni Boccaccio (1313–75).

p. 51: E. Kilian Eugen Kilian (1862–1925), German scholar; refers to 'Der Shakspearesche Monolog und seine Spielweisse', *Shakespeare Jahrbuch*, 39 (1903), xiv–xlii.

p. 51: Burbage Richard Burbage (1568–1619), leading player of the Lord Chamberlain's (then King's) Men, who took the lead roles in Shakespeare's plays.

p. 53: Michael Angelo Michelangelo Buonarroti (1475–1564), Italian painter and sculptor; best known for his fresco on the ceiling of the Sistine Chapel in the Vatican (completed in 1512), and the sculptures *Pietà* (1499) and *David* (1504).

p. 54: Milton John Milton (1608–74), English poet, essayist and Parliamentarian, author of *Paradise Lost* (1667), *Paradise Regained* and *Samson Agonistes* (1671).

p. 54: Pope Alexander Pope (1688–1744), English poet and editor, author of *The Rape of the Lock* (1712–14) and *The Dunciad* (1728); his *Works of Shakespeare* appeared in 1725.

p. 54: Tennyson Alfred Lord Tennyson (1809–92), English poet, author of *In Memoriam* (1850).

p. 58: Swift Jonathan Swift (1667–1745), Irish novelist, pamphleteer and satirist; author of *Gulliver's Travels* (1726).

p. 65: Hanmer Sir Thomas Hanmer (1677–1746), English politician and editor, whose illustrated edition of Shakespeare was published in 1744. The quotation is from Hanmer's *Some Remarks on the Tragedy of Hamlet, Prince of Denmark* (London, 1736), p. 33; cited in H. H. Furness (ed.), *A New Variorum Edition of Shakespeare: Hamlet*, vol. II (Philadelphia and London: J. B. Lippincott, 1877), p. 144.

p. 65: Henry Mackenzie (1745–1831), Scottish tax inspector, playwright, novelist, journalist and editor of the journal *The Mirror*; the picaresque novel *The Man of Feeling* was published in 1771.

p. 65: Furness Horace Howard Furness (1833–1912), American scholar and editor of the New Variorum edition of Shakespeare's works (1871 onwards), encyclopaedic volumes which collated all variants with extracts of critical commentary, and which formed Bradley's primary source for quotations from his critical predecessors.

p. 67: Werder Karl Friedrich Werder, German scholar.

p. 70: Schmidt Alexander Schmidt (1816–87), German scholar; refers to his *Shakespeare-Lexicon. Vollstänser englischer Sprachschatz mit allen Wörten, Wendungen und Satzbildungen in den Werken des Dichters* (Berlin, 1874–5).

p. 72: Goethe Johann Wolfgang von Goethe (1749–1832), German Romantic novelist, poet, dramatist, scientist and philosopher; author of the two parts of *Faust* (1808, 1832).

p. 73: 'a lovely . . . away' from Goethe's novel *Wilhelm Meister's Apprenticeship* (1795–6); quoted in Furness, *Variorum Hamlet*, vol. II, p. 273.

p. 73: Werther exquisitely melancholy protagonist of Goethe's novel *The Sorrows of Young Werther* (1774), who is driven to suicide as a result of unrequited love.

p. 73: Mr. Tree Sir Herbert Beerbohm Tree (1853–1917), English actor-manager, renowned for his elaborate and spectacular productions at Her (and then His) Majesty's Theatre, London, from 1897 to 1915.

p. 75: Schlegel August Wilhelm Schlegel (1767–1845), German translator, editor and critic. His *Lectures* appeared in English translation in 1815, and his German-language edition, in collaboration with Ludwig Tieck (1773–1853), of Shakespeare's works was published between 1825 and 1833.

p. 75: Coleridge Samuel Taylor Coleridge (1772–1834), English poet and essayist.

p. 76: Professor Dowden Edward Dowden (1843–1914), Irish scholar and critic; author of the influential *Shakspere: A Critical Study of his Mind and Art* (1875). Bradley wrote that 'In everything that I have written on

Shakespeare I am indebted to Professor Dowden' (*Oxford Lectures on Poetry*, p. viii).

p. 79: Burton   Robert Burton (1577–1640), English clergyman and author of the prose work *The Anatomy of Melancholy* (1621), which combined medical investigation, ethical, religious and philosophical speculation, and cultural commentary.

p. 80: *herrlich wie am ersten Tag*   'as wonderful as on the first day'; quoted from the Prologue to Goethe's *Faust: A Tragedy* (1808), l. 250.

p. 102: Heywood   Thomas Heywood (1573–1641), English poet, dramatist and prose writer; *The Second Part of the Iron Age* was written around 1612–13 but not published until 1652.

p. 109: David's . . . Absalom   in the Book of Samuel, Absalom leads a rebellion against his father David, the King of Israel, but is defeated and put to death.

p. 130: Theobald   Lewis Theobald (1688–1744), English editor, whose *The Works of Shakespeare* was published in 1733.

p. 130: Warburton   William Warburton (1698–1779), English bishop, theologian and editor, whose edition of Shakespeare appeared in 1747.

p. 133: *ceteris paribus*   other things being equal.

p. 133: Mr. Swinburne   Algernon Charles Swinburne (1837–1909), English poet and essayist, author of *A Study of Shakespeare* (London, 1880).

p. 135: Ulrici   Hermann Ulrici (1806–84), German scholar; author of *Shakespeares dramatische Kunst* (Lepizig, 1847, trans as *Shakespeare's Dramatic Art*, London, 1876).

p. 135: *Oedipus Tyrannus*   tragedy by Greek dramatist Sophocles (496–406 BC).

p. 135: δυσδαίμονες   'ill-fated', quoting Sophocles, *Antigone*, l. 274.

p. 139: 'Culturgeschichte'   cultural history.

p. 139: Wife of Bath   character in Chaucer's *Canterbury Tales*, renowned for her prodigious appetite for husbands.

p. 148: Toussaint L'Ouverture   (*c*.1743–1803), originally named Toussaint de Breda, L'Ouverture ('the one who finds an opening') was a former slave who led a successful revolt against the French occupiers of Haiti at the turn of the nineteenth century, thereby securing the island's independence. Wordsworth's sonnet 'To Toussaint L'Ouverture' was published in 1802.

p. 149: Sir Thomas Elyot   (*c*.1490–1546), diplomat and political theorist, author of the educational and political treatise *The Book of the Governor* (1531).

p. 149: Hunter   Joseph Hunter (1783–1861), English critic, author of *New Illustrations of the Life, Studies and Writings of Shakespeare* (London, 1845).

p. 149: *Battle of Alcazar*   play by English dramatist George Peele (1556–96), published in 1594.

p. 151: Lamb   Charles Lamb (1775–1834), romantic prose writer and critic, co-author, with Mary Lamb (1764–1847), of *Tales from Shakespeare* (1807), a widely read collection of prose adaptations of Shakespeare's plays for younger readers, and author of the influential essay 'On the Tragedies of Shakspeare, Considered with Reference to their Fitness for Stage Representation' (1845).

p. 152: Mrs. Jameson   Anna Bronwell Jameson (1794–1860), Anglo-Irish critic; her comments on Desdemona are found in *Characteristics of Women*

(1832), reprinted in H. H. Furness (ed.), *A New Variorum Edition of Shakespeare: Othello* (Philadelphia: J. B. Lippincott, 1886), pp. 413–15.

p. 154: Malone   Edmund Malone (1741–1812), Anglo-Irish editor and scholar, whose editions of Shakespeare were published in 1790 and 1821.

p. 155: form . . . obscured   quoting *Paradise Lost*, Book 1, ll. 591–4.

p. 155: felt . . . loss   quoting *Paradise Lost*, Book 4, ll. 847–9.

p. 157: Hazlitt   William Hazlitt (1778–1830), English essayist and critic, author of *A View of the English Stage* (London, 1817) and *Characters of Shakspear's Plays* (London, 1818).

p. 157: Macchiavelli   Niccolò Machiavelli (1469–1527), Italian political theorist, whose influential and notorious views on the exercise of statecraft were set out in *The Prince* (1513).

p. 157: *Jew of Malta*   1589 tragedy by English dramatist Christopher Marlowe (*c.*1564–93), quoting ll. 14–15.

p. 163: Socrates   (469–399 BC), Greek philosopher, progenitor of a dialogic system of argument and analysis.

p. 165: Captain Rook . . . Mr. Pigeon   minor characters in the 1848 novel *Vanity Fair*, by William Makepeace Thackeray (1811–63).

p. 170: Professor Bain . . . F. H. Bradley   Alexander Bain (1818–1900), psychologist; one of the founding figures in modern psychology, he was instrumental in shifting the discipline away from philosophical speculation and towards practical experiment and scientific observation. Francis Herbert Bradley (1846–1924), philosopher, and brother of A. C. Bradley, who sought to develop a practical, psychologically-based approach to ethics.

p. 172: Mr. Carlyle   Thomas Carlyle (1795–1881), Scottish writer, author of *On Heroes, Hero-Worship, and the Heroic in History* (1841), which discusses Shakespeare as an exemplar of the poet as hero.

p. 176: Napoleon   Napoleon Bonaparte (1769–1821), French Revolutionary General, First Consul, then Emperor of France, who conquered most of the European mainland during the first decade of the nineteenth century, but failed in his attempt to invade Russia in 1812 and was finally defeated by the British and Prussian armies at the Battle of Waterloo in 1815.

p. 182: Nahum Tate   (1652–1715), poet and playwright; his 1681 adaptation of *King Lear* excised the Fool, and introduced a romance between Edgar and Cordelia that not only accounted for her silence in the first scene, but also allowed him to come to her and Lear's rescue at the end; the play closed with fathers and children happily reunited, and Lear restored to the throne.

p. 182: Betterton   Thomas Betterton (1635–1710), English actor, who played Lear in Tate's version.

p. 182: Garrick   David Garrick (1717–79), English actor, manager and playwright, who first played Lear in 1742.

p. 182: Kemble   John Philip Kemble (1757–1823), English actor, who first played Lear in 1788 and continued to do so until 1810.

p. 182: Kean   Edmund Kean (*c.*1787–1833), actor; first played Lear in 1820. Although Kean succeeded in persuading the management of Drury Lane theatre to restore Shakespeare's ending in 1823, it only lasted for three performances, as audiences reportedly 'tittered to see the diminutive actor struggling under the weight of Mrs. W. West's Cordelia' (Jay L. Halio, The New Cambridge

Shakespeare *The Tragedy of King Lear* (Cambridge: Cambridge University Press, 1992), p. 41).

p. 182: Macready William Charles Macready (1793–1873), English actor, who played Lear at Covent Garden in 1838 to great acclaim.

p. 183: *Prometheus Vinctus* Greek tragedy of unknown date, usually ascribed to Aeschylus, in which the Titan Prometheus is nailed to a rock and tormented by Zeus.

p. 183: Beethoven Ludwig van Beethoven (1770–1827), German composer.

p. 183: statues . . . Chapel monumental marble statuary carved by Michelangelo between 1520 and 1534; the chapel is located in the Church of San Lorenzo, Florence.

p. 188: 'that . . . succeed' the final lines of Tate's *King Lear.*

p. 191: *Tale of King Lear* in Lamb's *Tales from Shakespeare* (1807).

p. 191: Spedding James Spedding (1808–81), English scholar, editor of the *Works of Francis Bacon* (1857–74).

p. 194: Rowe Nicholas Rowe (1674–1718), English poet, playwright and the first Shakespearean editor; his edition of the works, based on the fourth Folio, was published in 1709.

p. 195: Caucasus the mythological setting of *Prometheus Vinctus.*

p. 195: Farinata. . . dispitto Farinata (d. 1264), Florentine politician condemned in the *Divine Comedy* to the Sixth Circle of Hell; 'Come . . . dispitto' is a misquotation of Canto X, l. 36: 'com'avesse l'inferno a gran dispitto' ('as if regarding Hell with utter scorn').

p. 197: Empedocles (*c.*490–430 BC), Sicilian poet and philosopher, credited with originating the theory of the four elements (earth, air, fire and water), who argued that the world was governed by the conflict between the abstract forces of Love and Strife.

p. 198: 'Platonic' ideas according to the Greek philosopher Plato (427–347 BC), phenomena in the material world are merely imperfect copies of their ideal forms.

p. 198: *Fairy Queen* epic allegorical poem by the English poet Edward Spenser (*c.*1552–99).

p. 198: Mr. Wyndham George Wyndham (1863–1914), English critic, author of *The Poems of Shakespeare* (London, 1898).

p. 204: Job Old Testament patriarch, a wealthy and righteous man whom God subjects to a series of severe afflictions in order to test his faith.

p. 207: Aeschylus (525-456 BC), Greek dramatist, author of the Oresteian trilogy (*Agamemnon, Choephori, Eumenides*), and *The Persians, Seven Against Thebes* and *Prometheus Vinctus.*

p. 208: Orestes the son of Agamemnon and Clytemnestra in Aeschylus's *Oresteia*, who murders his mother, is pursued by the Furies, but is acquitted by an Athenian jury.

p. 208: Eumenides female agents of vengeance in the *Oresteia.*

p. 208: Apollo Greek god of the sun.

p. 208: Athene Greek goddess of wisdom.

p. 212: ὕβρις hubris, or violent, deluded pride: the classic tragic error, according to Aristotle.

p. 220: Globe   a one-volume reworking of the Cambridge Shakespeare, published in 1864, which remained the standard popular edition for nearly a century.

p. 223: Schmidt's idea   refers to his *Zur Textkritik des 'King Lear'* (Königsberg, 1879).

p. 232: Koppel   Richard Koppel, German scholar.

p. 236: Massinger   Philip Massinger (1583–1640), English playwright, best known for the satirical comedy *A New Way to Pay Old Debts* (1633).

p. 238: Mr. Archer   William Archer (1856–1924), Scottish journalist and drama critic.

p. 238: Cowden Clarke   Mary Cowden Clarke (1809–1908), English writer, best known for *The Girlhood of Shakespeare's Heroines* (1850–2).

p. 259: Reginald Scot's *Discovery*   Reginald Scot (*c*.1538–99), aristocrat, politician; *The Discovery of Witchcraft* (1584) aimed to debunk contemporary mythology about witchcraft, alchemy and astrology.

p. 259: Middleton   Thomas Middleton (1580–1627), English playwright, author of *A Mad World my Masters* (1608), *The Revenger's Tragedy* (1607) and *Women Beware Women* (published in 1657); also credited as co-author of *Macbeth, Measure for Measure* and *Timon of Athens*.

p. 260: Parcae . . . Norns   the three goddesses of Fate or Destiny in, respectively, Roman and Norse mythology.

p. 262: Schlegel   Schlegel's account of the witches is reproduced in H. H. Furness (ed.), *A New Variorum Edition of Shakespeare: Macbeth* (Philadelphia: J. B. Lippincott, 1873), p. 430.

p. 264: Dr. Forman   Dr Simon Forman (1552–1611), physician and astrologer, whose records of his attendance at the playhouses provide eye-witness accounts of early performances of *Macbeth, A Winter's Tale* and *Cymbeline*.

p. 265: *Iliad*   epic account of the Trojan Wars by legendary Greek poet Homer, written at some point between the sixth and eighth centuries BC.

p. 266: Holinshed   Raphael Holinshed (d. 1580), historian, whose *Chronicles of England, and Ireland* (1577) provided sources for *Macbeth*, and Shakespeare's English History plays.

p. 284: Mrs. Siddons   Sarah Siddons (1755–1831), pre-eminent tragic actress of the late eighteenth and early nineteenth century, who first played Lady Macbeth in 1779.

p. 290: Mrs. Siddons's fancy   Siddons's impressions of Lady Macbeth's character and appearance, taken from her 'Remarks on the Character of Lady Macbeth' in Thomas Campbell's *Life of Mrs Siddons* (1834), are excerpted in Furness, *Variorum Macbeth*, p. 472.

p. 290: Dr. Bucknill   J. C. Bucknill, English author of *Mad Folk of Shakespeare* (1867), reprinted in Furness, *Variorum Macbeth*, p. 484.

p. 290: Brandes   Georg Brandes (1842–1927), German scholar, author of *William Shakespeare: A Critical Study* (London, 1896).

p. 290: Madame Bernhardt   Sarah Bernhardt (1844–1923), French actress, whose Lady Macbeth was poorly received when it was seen in London in 1888.

p. 298: Seneca   Lucius Annaeus Seneca (4 BC–AD 65), Roman tragic dramatist.

p. 299: *Dido Queen of Carthage*   play by Christopher Marlowe, published in 1594.

p. 299: Cunliffe   John William Cunliffe (1865–1946), English critic; *The Influence of Seneca on Elizabethan Tragedy* was published in 1893.

p. 299: Quis . . . sceleris   quoting *Phaedra*, ll. 715–18: 'What Tanais will wash me clean, what Maeotis, pouring its barbarous waters into the Pontic sea? Not even with the whole of Ocean could the great father himself cleanse so much guilt' (*Seneca, VIII: Tragedies*, ed. and trans. John G. Fitch (Cambridge, MA: Harvard University Press, 2002), pp. 505–7).

p. 299: Quis . . . facinus   quoting *Hercules Furens*, ll. 1323–9: 'What Tanais or what Nile or what Persian Tigris with its violent waters or fierce Rhine or Tagus, turbid with Spanish treasure, can wash my right hand clean? Though chill Maeotis should pour its northern seas over me and all the Ocean stream across my hands, the deed will stay deeply ingrained' (*Seneca, VII*, pp. 157–9).

p. 299: Ovid   Publius Ovidius Naso (43 BC–AD 17), Roman poet, whose collection of tales of magical transformation, *Metamorphoses* (AD 8; translated into English in 1567), were an important source for Shakespeare and his contemporaries.

p. 305: Professor Hales   John Wesley Hales (1836–1914), English critic; his *Notes and Essays on Shakespeare* was published in 1884.

p. 305: Garnet   Father Henry Garnet (1555–1606), Jesuit Superior in England, convicted of treason for his involvement in the 1605 Gunpowder Plot, and executed in 1606.

p. 310: Nash   Thomas Nashe (1567–1601), English playwright and pamphleteer; the quotation is from his pamphlet *Pierce Penniless his Supplication to the Devil* (1592).

p. 312: *Der Berstrafte Brudermord*   translated into English as *Fratricide Punished*, this German adaptation of *Hamlet* was published in 1781 but dates from 1710, and may record a version of the play as performed during the seventeenth century.

p. 315: H. Türck   Hermann Türck (1856–1933), German scholar, author of *Das Psychologische problem in der Hamlet-tragödie* (Leipzig, 1890).

p. 315: Greene's . . . Arragon   Robert Greene (1558–92), English poet, prose writer and playwright; *Alphonsus, King of Arragon* was written in 1587.

p. 318: the old *Hamlet*   a lost play dating from the 1590s, generally thought to have provided a source for Shakespeare's play.

p. 319: Fletcher   John Fletcher (1579–1625), English playwright; collaborator with Francis Beaumont (*c.*1585–1616) on *Philaster* (1620) and *The Maid's Tragedy* (published in 1619), and with Shakespeare on *All is True* (*Henry VIII*) (published 1623) and *The Two Noble Kinsmen* (published 1634).

p. 319: *The Woman's Prize*   written *c.*1611 and published in 1647, also entitled *The Tamer Tamed*, Fletcher's comedy is a sequel to Shakespeare's *The Taming of the Shrew*.

p. 320: Tamburlaine   protagonist of Marlowe's two-part play *Tamburlaine the Great*, published in 1590.

p. 321: Clark and Wright   William George Clark (1821–78) and W. Aldis Wright (1831–1914), English editors, with John Glover, of the Cambridge edition of Shakespeare (1863–6).

p. 322: From . . . pay   quoting *Tamburlaine, Part One*, Prologue, ll.1–2.

p. 323: Marston   John Marston (*c.*1575–1634), English playwright; best known for the tragicomedy *The Malcontent* (1604).

p. 325: Steevens George Steevens (1736–1800), English editor and critic; his original-spelling edition *Twenty Plays of the Plays of Shakespeare* appeared in 1766.

p. 325: Delius Nikolaus Delius (1813–88), German editor and critic, whose English-language edition of Shakespeare was published between 1854 and 1861.

p. 326: Mr. Fleay Frederick Gard Fleay (1831–1909), English scholar and former clergyman, who originally trained as a natural scientist, and who was notorious for his system of versification tests, which purported to settle questions of chronology and authorship mathematically. His *Biographical Chronicle of the English Drama, 1559–1642* was published in 1891.

p. 326: Seymour E. H. Seymour, author of *Remarks, critical, conjectural, and explanatory, upon the plays of Shakespeare* (London, 1805).

p. 328: Capell Edward Capell (1713–81), English editor, whose edition of 1768 pioneered the practice of collating Folio and Quarto variants.

p. 332: 'Christopher North' one of the speakers in a dialogic essay by one Professor Wilson published in *Blackwood's Magazine*, November 1849, April 1850 and May 1950; reprinted in Furness, *Variorum Othello*, pp. 361–2.

p. 334: Mr. Daniel P. A. Daniel, author of 'Time Analysis of the Plots of Shakespeare's Plays', *New Shakspere Society Transactions*, 1877–9; reprinted in Furness, *Variorum Othello*, pp. 362–3

p. 340: Salvini Tommaso Salvini (1829–1915), Italian actor, who first played his acclaimed Othello in Italy in 1856; it was seen in London in 1875.

p. 340: Fechter Charles Albert Fechter (1822–79), English actor, who unsuccessfully played Othello in 1861.

p. 340: Edwin Booth (1833–93), celebrated American actor, who first played Othello in 1864.

p. 342: *Heptameron* collection of tales, published in 1558, by Margaret of Angoulême, Queen of Navarre (1492–1549). The thirtieth tale, a story of inadvertent incest, concludes with a discussion of the practicalities of preserving one's chastity.

p. 346: Steevens' idea quoted in Furness, *Variorum Othello*, pp. 315–16.

p. 351: Dr. Ingram John K. Ingram, English scholar; refers to 'On the weak endings of Shakespeare. With some account of the verse-tests in general', *New Shakspere Society Transactions*, 1874.

p. 351: by Mr. Fleay . . . Shakespeare refers to F. G. Fleay, *Shakespeare Manual* (London: Macmillan, 1876), pp. 187–208.

p. 359: As Koppel has shown refers to Richard Koppel, *Textkritische Studien über Shakespeares Richard III und King Lear* (Dresden, 1877), cited in Furness, *Variorum King Lear*, p. 364.

p. 359: Mr. W. J. Craig William James Craig (1843–1906), English editor of the Arden Shakespeare (First Series) *The Tragedy of King Lear* (London, 1901).

p. 363: Collier John Payne Collier (1789–1883), English scholar, editor and notorious Shakespearean forger; his edition of Shakespeare's works was published from 1842 to 1844.

p. 366: Furness's note *Variorum King Lear*, p. 240.

p. 372: Middleton's *Witch* tragicomedy probably written during the 1600s but not published until 1778.

p. 372: Mr. Chambers's . . . series   Edmund Kerchever Chambers (1866–1954), English editor of the Warwick Shakespeare *The Tragedy of Macbeth* (London, 1893).

p. 373: Mr. Fleay's   refers to Fleay, *Shakespeare Manual*, p. 259.

p. 376: James . . . authority   James I published a sceptical treatise on witch-craft, *Daemonologie*, in 1597.

p. 377: Halliwell   James Orchard Halliwell-Phillipps (1820–89), English scholar and editor, whose edition of Shakespeare's works was published in 1865.

p. 377: *Puritan*   *The Puritan*, satirical drama published anonymously in 1607 and subsequently attributed to Shakespeare; more recently assigned to Thomas Middleton.

p. 377: *Caesar and Pompey*   Roman tragedy by George Chapman (1559–1634), published in 1631.

p. 377: Plutarch   Mestrius Plutarchus (*c*.46–*c*.120), Roman historian, whose biographies of Greek and Roman statesmen, *Parallel Lives* (translated into English by Sir Thomas North in 1579), supplied the sources for the Roman plays of Shakespeare and his contemporaries.

p. 377: *Dutch Courtezan*   sex comedy by Marston dating *c*.1604.

p. 377: *Sophonisba*   Roman tragedy by Marston dating *c*.1606.

p. 378: König   Goswin König, German critic, author of *Der Vers in Shaksperes Dramen* (Strasburg, 1888).

p. 378: Hertzberg   W. Hertzberg, German scholar, author of 'Metrisches, Grammatisches, Chronologisches zu Shakespeares Dramen', *Shakespeare Jahrbuch*, 13 (1878).

p. 383: Mr. Fleay   refers to *Shakespeare Manual*, pp. 135–6.

p. 386: *Vorlesungen über Macbeth*   published Berlin, 1885.

Index

(The index preserves the distinctive character of Bradley's original entries, but is supplemented by references to the Introduction and endnotes to this edition.)

The titles of plays are in *italics*. The page numbers containing the main discussion of a character are presented in bold type.